Zulu Names

Zulu Names

Adrian Koopman

University of Natal Press
Pietermaritzburg
2002

Zulu Names

ISBN 1 86914 003 6

Published by University of Natal Press
Private Bag X01
Scottsville 3209
South Africa
E-mail: books@nu.ac.za

Editor: Andrea Nattrass
Cover designer: Sumayya Essack
Typesetter: Alpha Typesetters cc
Indexer: Colin Muller
Illustrator: Olive Anderson
Photographer: Adrian Koopman
Map artist: Maurise Bauer
Printed and bound by: Interpak Books, Pietermaritzburg

Contents

Chapter 9: Zulu place names: Historico-cultural background

Chapter 10: eThekwini and uMgungundlovu: The Zulu names of Durban and Pietermaritzburg

Chapter 11: Names of schools

Chapter 12: Names of homesteads

Chapter 16: Names of months and days

PART 5: LINGUISTICS

Chapter 17: Linguistic structures

Acknowledgements

First and foremost I would like to thank Professor Emeritus of the Zulu Department at the University of Natal in Pietermaritzburg, Ant Davey, and fellow-onomastician in African names Minna Saarelma-Maunumaa of Vantaa in Finland. These two friends went through each chapter of the manuscript while the book was being written and made many valuable suggestions, criticisms, and corrections. The blame for any faults of style and fact remain mine, however.

I would also like to express my gratitude to Msawakhe Hlengwa ('Mashasha'), Ndela kaBhekifa Ntshangase, Mbali Shabalala-Machaba, Mary Gordon, and Mary Godlonton. These colleagues, past and present, in isiZulu Studies in the School of Language, Culture and Communication at the Pietermaritzburg campus of the University of Natal, have given me invaluable help over the years.

Thanks are also due to students in onomastics courses, both undergraduate and postgraduate, who over the last 12 years have contributed much onomastic material.

To Andrea Nattrass of the University of Natal Press goes my appreciation for the sensitive and creative way in which problems were handled during the editing process.

And finally, to my wife Jewel (uNomvula) and our children Everett (uVusumuzi) and Olivia (also uNomvula), many thanks for your love and support over the years.

Preface

One of my first onomastic projects was undertaken at the age of 16, when I accompanied my parents on a ten-day tour of the southern parts of England. I still have my analysis of the hundreds of names of the various pubs and inns that we passed *en route*. I can look back at my material and see that of the names I collected, 'The King's Head' was the most popular, closely followed by 'The Royal Oak', 'The White Hart' and 'The Red Lion'.

My interest in Zulu names was kindled in 1972 when I was attempting to improve my practical knowledge of Zulu by working as a clerk in the then Municipal Bantu Administration in Durban (now the KwaMuhle Museum). The work involved the registration of Zulu employees, and it was not long before I was trying to translate the dozens of Zulu names that crossed my desk daily. Soon after that I was looking for a topic for an Honours research project in the then Department of Bantu Languages at the University of Natal in Durban. When Professor Trevor Cope told me that nothing had ever been written on Zulu names, it seemed clear that this was my opportunity to discuss the hundreds of Zulu names I had collected.

Of this present book, approximately a third of the material has been previously published, approximately a third is material that I have collected and researched over the last 20 years but which has not been published before, and the remaining third is material that I have specifically researched for this book from 1998 to 2001. There are many gaps in the material covered. Some of these gaps are there because I have never done research in a particular area, for example, in the Zulu names for groups such as sports teams, choirs, cultural and professional organisations, or in the Zulu names for buses and taxis. Other gaps are deliberate: I have purposely left out material on literary onomastics, believing that this topic belongs to a separate book. A large amount of work on Zulu plant names has also been excluded, again, with the intention of publishing this separately.

This book is not aimed at specialist onomasticians or linguists. Part 5 contains the only technical linguistic material: the linguistic structure of various categories of Zulu names, the concept of onomastic shift, and the onomastic–oral literature continuum. These chapters can be easily skipped by the reader who is not interested in grammatical and morphological detail.

I hope that this book stimulates an interest in Zulu names and naming systems, and that it also acts as a challenge to other onomasticians working with names in the other languages of southern Africa.

Adrian Koopman (**uMantindane wakwaKhumalo**)
May 2002

Part 1

Introduction

Chapter 1

General introduction

1.1 RECENT NAME CHANGES

South Africa in the 1990s was a land of great changes. Inner-city boundaries crumbled with the demise of the Group Areas Act. The apartheid government which had dominated the country for half a century was replaced with a democratic government. The first black president was attended by two praise-singers (**izimbongi**) at his inauguration, and the words 'New South Africa' and 'Rainbow Nation' were on everyone's lips. But perhaps not so well noticed among the high-profile free elections, new African National Congress government and other socio-cultural and socio-political changes, were the socio-onomastic changes: the changes in naming patterns.

The various changes were all recorded in the popular press. Not on the front page necessarily, but tucked among the inner pages, where onomasticians keen to record all this onomastic activity taking place were able to cut out and keep this evidence.

One of the earliest 'name changes' took place in 1994. The *Cape Times* reported on 4 May:

> BLOEMFONTEIN – The name of the Free State capital will soon change back to its original Mangaung, or 'place of the cheetah'.
>
> The region's premier-elect, Mr Patrick Lekota, said yesterday other place and street names that evoked painful memories would also change.

This report evoked national interest and newspapers all over the country had headlines such as 'Bloem soon to change its spots'; 'Bloem change of name promised'; and 'Bloem to change to Mangaung'. The furore died down when it was pointed out by onomasticians that this could not possibly be a 're-naming' because the place known as 'Bloemfontein' by non-Sotho speakers (the minority of the population in the area) had always been known as 'Mangaung' by the majority of the population (Sotho speakers).

Next was Benny Alexander, who decided to change his name to Khoisan X. The *Natal Witness* of 16 September 1994 reported:

> Pan African Congress secretary general Benny Alexander said yesterday that he has changed his name to Khoisan X . . .
>
> . . . the name Alexander was given to his great-grandparents by colonialists because their Khoi name was considered heathen and barbaric.
>
> . . . X said he was not adopting a new name, but restoring an old one . . .

X also called on the government to speed up changes to the names of 'racist colonial symbols'. Nelson Mandela followed shortly on his heels in October 1994 with a decision to change the name of the official residence of the State President in Pretoria. The earlier name 'Libertas' was changed to 'Mahlambandlovu', a Tsonga word meaning 'to purify the elephant', a reference to a cleansing ritual traditionally performed when a new head of state (the 'elephant') takes power.

Then South African Airways decided to change their normal pattern of naming aircraft after species of antelope and mountain ranges and came up with a song title instead. A clipping from the *Natal Witness* of 13 July 1995 reads:

> South African Airways christened the latest addition to its fleet 'Shosholoza' at Johannesburg International Airport yesterday in honour of the recent Springbok Rugby World Cup victory . . .
>
> . . . 'Shosholoza' translates roughly as 'to work hard together' and SAA decided on the name for the Boeing to honour the triumphant Springboks as well as SAA's own employees for their teamwork in successfully handling the Rugby World Cup.

Not clear in this report is that 'Shosholoza' is the title and the opening word of an old freedom-fighters' song which told of people leaving South Africa to undergo military training outside the borders. This song has now become associated with South African rugby. Note that the 1995 report talks of 'Johannesburg International Airport', not the earlier 'Jan Smuts Airport', but that the current name for the South African rugby team, the **'amaBokoboko'** has not yet replaced the name 'Springboks'.

In Pietermaritzburg the Maritzburg Technical College changed its name to the Msunduzi College. The *Natal Witness* of 8 September 1995 reported:

> Pietermaritzburg Technical College yesterday announced a change in its name. The College will now be known as the Msunduzi College, deputy principal Gail du Pisane said, adding that the new name reflects the intention of the college to meet the needs of the wider community of this region.

The *Natal Mercury* of 23 December 1995 had a full page article on the name changes of the past few years. These are the opening paragraphs:

> **New Start, New Names**
> It started with the South African flag. Then it was the national anthem. Now people are going all the way down to rural road names in their determination to wipe out the past and start afresh . . .
>
> . . . the residents of Verwoerdburg, who rechristened their town Centurion, felt they could not have successfully adapted to a democratic South Africa in the constant shadow of apartheid's chief architect.
>
> And long before the major airports officially changed their names, South African Airways had been referring to them as Durban International, Johannesburg International, and the like.

Soon it was the turn of the South African Navy. From the *Sunday Tribune* of 16 March 1997 comes:

> Under NP rule the SA Navy had it tough. It was too English and traditionally close to the Royal Navy.
>
> So it was no surprise when a former defence minister, Frans Erasmus, attempted to make it more 'South African' and almost all vessels carried Afrikaans names.
>
> This was especially obvious in the so-called 'Minister class' of strike vessels, which honours NP politicians such as PW Botha, Magnus Malan, Jim Fouche, the Nazi sympathiser Oswald Pirow, Kobie Coetsee and Erasmus.
>
> Now the navy, in honour of its 75th birthday, is creating a new Warrior class and renaming the strike class fleet.
>
> The only vessel which retains its name is the SAS Jan Smuts. New names include Adam Kok, the Griqua leader; Sekhukhuni, the warrior chief; Makhanda, the Xhosa general; and Galeshewe, the Tswana leader.
>
> PW Botha will be mortified to hear that *his* strike craft will soon be known as Shaka. Cheers and down the hatch.

Rivers and dams have also come in for a fair share of renaming. Here is one such change, reported in the *Sunday Tribune* of 15 March 1998:

> Water Affairs Minister Kader Asmal yesterday renamed the Kafferskuil River in the south-western Cape the Goukou River. The former name has for obvious reasons been offensive in the extreme to black South Africans in particular.

> Asmal told the renaming ceremony the name Kafferskuil powerfully reminded South Africans of a painful period of slavery and apartheid. 'Our masters (used) such names to justify their subjugation of our people and the human rights violations against them.' The renaming was yet another triumph against injustice, he said.
>
> The name Goukou had been given to him by the National Place Names Committee. It was that of a Hassequa chief who had hosted an emissary of Cape Governor Simon van der Stel on the banks of the river more than 300 years ago.

The *Mail & Guardian* (23 to 29 June 2000) reported on page six that: 'The Eastern Cape's first megacity – made up of Port Elizabeth, Uitenhage and Despatch municipalities – is in a race with Pretoria to rename itself "Nelson Mandela Metropole". If they don't get the name their list of alternatives is led by "Greater Cacadu". Have a heart, Madiba!'

From the same issue comes: 'Hundreds of people . . . stopped the traffic outside 123 Schoeman Street, Pretoria, to rename the Ministry of Education Building Sol Plaatje House . . .'.

The same week the *Natal Witness* (22 June 2000) reported the following:

> The Pietermaritzburg-Msunduzi TLC announced this week that it is seeking a name for the new council which will be elected in November to serve a much greater area beyond the current municipal boundaries.
>
> 'Members of the public are invited to submit suggestions, bearing in mind, firstly, that we are seeking a name for the new municipality rather than the city,' said Rob Haswell, the TLC's chief executive officer . . .
>
> Twenty local citizens felt that the new name should be either uMgungundlovu or Msunduzi.

These examples are but a few of the hundreds of name changes that have taken place in South Africa since 1994. It is not just place names that have changed, but the names of people, of institutions, and of objects.

Together with these name changes, the icons and symbols of the nation have altered as well. The new national flag adopted shortly after the new government took power in 1994 was received with general enthusiasm. However, the change of the coat-of-arms in May 2000 was received with less enthusiasm, and was still being debated in the press more than a year later.

It is not only political transformations that have brought about such a number of names changes in South Africa in recent years. Linguistic changes – or at least a combination of political and linguistic changes – have brought South Africa to the long-overdue position of having 11 official languages. From being a country where only the European colonial-origin languages English and Afrikaans were official languages, and the Bantu languages of over three-quarters of the population had no official status at all, we are now a country where English and Afrikaans share official status with

Zulu, Xhosa, Swazi and Ndebele, with Tswana, Sotho and Pedi, and with Venda and Tsonga. This does not only mean that these languages are heard in national, provincial and municipal assemblies, or that government gazettes are now multilingual, but also that names in these languages now take their place beside English and Afrikaans names. The following letter, published in the *Natal Mercury* on 17 August 1994 under the headline 'SA is now recognising those other names', is relevant:

> For speakers of Zulu, Sotho and Xhosa, there is no need to change 'Johannesburg' to 'eGoli' or 'Gauteng', or 'Pretoria' to 'ePitoli' or 'Tshwane'; these are the names by which these cities have long been known.
>
> What is changing in South Africa is that the existence of several million inhabitants of this country is now being acknowledged.
>
> From the major step of granting these inhabitants status as voters comes the corollary of acknowledging their languages as official, and then the acknowledgement that these languages have their own names for various towns and cities.
>
> What is likely to happen is that names which have existed side by side for many years will now be acknowledged officially. 'Bloemfontein' is not going to change into 'Mangaung'. Instead, whites are going to acknowledge Mangaung as an alternative for the capital of the Free State.
>
> After all, millions of Sotho speakers have acknowledged the 'foreign' word 'Bloemfontein' for many years now.

Some five years later (May 1999) came the announcement that the previous Place Names Committee, mothballed after the 1994 elections, would be replaced by a new South African Geographical Names Council. This new council, which is now in place, has full representation of the 11 official languages of South Africa. Provincial committees were in 2000 being set up to deal with naming issues in each province, although it took until 12 October 2001 for the first of these provincial committees – that of KwaZulu-Natal – to be launched.

The Bantu languages of South Africa are showing signs of influence in a number of onomastic areas. Neethling has pointed out in his article (2000) the influence of the term **amaBokoboko** for the Springbok rugby team, and the way this name has not only influenced many other sporting teams, but a variety of other names as well.

A report from the *Natal Witness* of 30 September 1996 on the annual Gay and Lesbian Pride Parade in Johannesburg starts with the headline '"**Amamoffomoffo**" demonstrate for rights in style' (in Afrikaans/South African slang 'moffie' refers to a homosexual). Another report, also from the *Natal Witness*, dated 4 September 1999, is headed 'Encouraging reading through the **Ama-Boeke-Boeke** Prize', and explains that Exclusive Books has invented a tongue-in-cheek rival to Britain's Booker Prize for literature. Reports dated May and June 2000 give the name 'Easy-Ntombis' (< Zulu **izintombi**, 'girls') for the South African National Women's Hockey Team. This kind of linguistic influence has spilt over into the commercial world, and names of institutions such as banks and other financial institutions have changed to African names.

All of these name changes are challenges to onomasticians: challenges to document and record these changes; challenges to interpret and explain them; challenges to teach the background behind these changes; and challenges to assist with further name changes. To be able to do these things, the onomastician must first understand the patterns of nomenclature in the various languages of South Africa. Here lies the major challenge: the undertaking of the exploration of the names of languages such as Tswana, Tsonga and Venda: the anthroponyms, the toponyms, the names of birds and plants, and any other names that help to reveal the complex patterns of namings that speak so eloquently of the link between language and culture. Without understanding the naming patterns of the past and of the present, how can we plan for the name changes of the future?

1.2 WHAT IS 'ONOMASTICS'?

The word 'onomastics' is derived from the Greek word *onoma* which means 'name'. Onomastics is the study of names and naming systems. In any language, names are nouns, that is, linguistic units. As names are *linguistic* units which normally operate within a *social* context, onomastics can be considered a branch of *socio-linguistics*. Although 'onomasticians' (names scholars) may also be geographers, historians, cartographers, librarians, archaeologists, genealogists and scientists, generally they work in departments of linguistics or departments of specific language studies.

For a large part of the 1900s, onomastics in South Africa was mainly restricted to toponymy, the study of place names. Onomastics came of age in South Africa with the formation of the Southern African Names Society in 1980, to be followed shortly thereafter with the first biennial conference in 1981. In 1987 the first volume of the Names Society's journal – *Nomina Africana* – appeared. At the time of writing in 2001, 11 biennial conferences have been held, and 12 volumes of *Nomina Africana* have been published.

South Africa lags sadly behind America and Europe in the scope and quality of onomastics training offered. An exception has been in the field of toponymic training where the Africa South Division of the United Nations Group of Experts on Geographical Names, has run a number of Toponymical Training Courses. These intensive two-week courses are designed for cartographers, surveyors, geographers, town planners, and anyone else interested in all possible aspects of place names' study: the recording of place names, their translation, mapping techniques, Geographical Information Systems, gazetteers, national policies, global standardisation, etc. A number of these courses have been held over the last decade, and they have attracted students from all over southern Africa.

Apart from these, formal training in onomastics in South Africa is extremely limited. The University of Natal, Pietermaritzburg campus, has offered a paper in Zulu onomastics at Honours level since 1991, and the University of the Western Cape has offered a similar Honours level paper in Xhosa onomastics since 1992. In 1999 the Zulu Department on the Durban campus of the University of Natal offered an Honours course in Zulu onomastics for the first time.

In May 2000 the Names Research Unit at the Human Sciences Research Council was closed down, as part of a cost-saving restructuring, and the archival material was transferred to the Onomastics Studies Unit housed in the School of Languages, Communication and Culture at the University of Natal in Pietermaritzburg. This unit, which opened in the second half of 2000, plans to extend the present Honours course in Zulu onomastics into general courses in South African onomastics at undergraduate level, and also to offer a course-work Masters in onomastics. The unit has already attracted Masters and Doctoral students from outside the university. Through these undergraduate courses, the Masters programme, and a sustained research programme in onomastic research it is hoped that this unit will play a leading role in onomastic studies in southern Africa.

1.2.1 Linguistic conventions

Certain linguistic conventions are used throughout this book, including the following:

< means 'derived from': as in **uMbali** < **imbali** (here the name **uMbali** is derived from the noun **imbali**);
> means 'gives rise to': as in **isipho** > **uSipho** (here the noun **isipho** gives rise to the name **uSipho**);
* in front of a word, phrase or sentence indicates that what follows is ungrammatical: as in *the boys runs.

1.3 WHAT ARE NAMES?

The problem of what exactly a 'name' is has troubled philosophers and linguists for many years. Traditionally, the terms 'proper nouns' or 'proper names' are used. Although there is general agreement that all names are nouns, it is difficult if not impossible to find consensus on where the difference lies between those nouns which are names, and those which are not. In English, names are those nouns spelt with a capital letter. However, this is not a very useful guideline because the orthographic convention of the capital letter differs from country to country. For example, in German all nouns begin with a capital letter, so proper nouns are visually indistinguishable from common nouns. In French many words which we would capitalise in English are spelt without a capital. The days of the week and the names of the months are capitalised in English, but in languages such as Finnish and French they are not.

There are many purists among linguists and onomasticians who might argue that certain portions of this book do not deal with names in the strictest sense. Chapter 15 on the 'names' of birds may well be singled out here, and speakers of languages such as French and Finnish may also want to see Chapter 16 on the 'names' of months and days excluded.

1.4 WHAT DIFFERENT SORTS OF NAMES DO WE HAVE?

The study of names can be divided into various subcategories as outlined below.

1.4.1 Literary onomastics

Under this subdiscipline of onomastics the use of names in literature is considered. This is undoubtedly one of the fastest-growing subdisciplines of onomastics in South Africa, and the naming of characters (and other names) in novels, poetry and drama is now being researched in a number of South African languages. The very first issue of *Nomina Africana* (1[1], 1987) had an article by C.W. Malan entitled 'Wankelende Walkures en Flankerende Fiskale: Die Kreatiewe Gebruik van Eiename deur Etienne Leroux' ('Stumbling Valkyries and Flirting Fiscals: The Creative Use of Proper Names [in the works of] Etienne LeRoux'), and subsequent issues have a number of articles looking at the role of naming in English and Afrikaans literature. Less work has been done on the literature of the 'indigenous' languages, but we could mention S.J. Neethling's 1991 'Proper names in some Nguni idioms and proverbs' (5[1]), and L.F. Mathenjwa's 1996 'Naming and Identification in *Maskandi* Poetry' (10[1&2]). Although this book deliberately excludes the topic of literary onomastics – for it essentially requires its own book – a discussion of Zulu names cannot be *totally* divorced from this discipline.

1.4.2 Anthroponyms

This term is derived from the Greek word *anthrōpos* ('man' or 'human', cf. anthropology). There are a number of different types of names given to human beings, the most common being the personal name, the nickname, and the surname.

a. Personal names

These are also known as 'Christian' names, 'first' names, and 'given' names. To illustrate, we can consider the following invented names for an English speaker, an Afrikaans speaker, and a Zulu speaker:

John Peter Smith
Johannes Stephanus Van der Merwe
Bonginkosi Aaron Dlamini

In each case the first two names have been described as 'personal names', 'first names' (or 'forenames'), 'Christian names' and 'given names'. The term 'personal name' implies that these are the names of an individual member of a family (where the surname normally belongs to all members). The terms 'first name' and 'forename' refer to the custom of placing these names before the surname. Consequently, the Japanese and Chinese custom of placing the surname first causes much confusion in countries where the opposite is the norm. The term 'Christian name' is often misleading, and even offensive, as when persons of the Jewish or Muslim faiths are required to complete a form which asks for their Christian names. The term 'given name' refers to the fact that names such as John, Johannes and Bonginkosi are *given* to the child by the parents, as opposed to the surname, which is 'automatically' inherited. This is not always the case: in some African countries, personal names are automatic and inevitable.

All of the terms above have some problems in their uses. This book will use the term 'personal name' as it is the least problematical in the Zulu context. Personal names are discussed in Chapters 2 to 5 and 17 of this book.

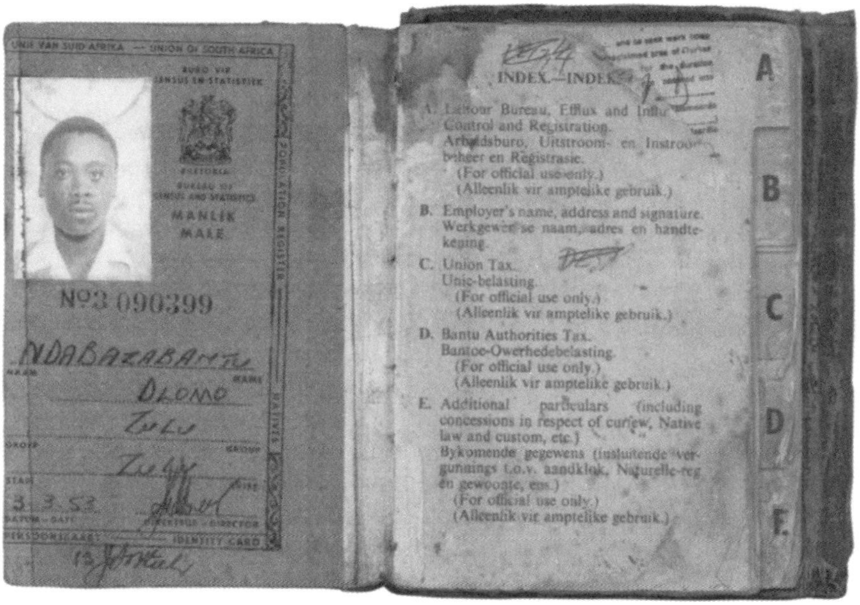

The name in an official identity document: a 'dompas' from the apartheid era.

b. Nicknames

The term 'nickname' is derived from the older English form 'an eke name', where 'eke' means 'additional', 'added'. Nicknames, of course, are not only personal to a particular individual (not to mention individual to a particular person), they are also 'given' names. Nicknames tend to be 'unofficial' and are seldom recorded on an individual's official documents, such as birth certificates, school certificates, drivers' licences, and so on. This is despite the fact that an individual may be known by his or her nickname/s from an early age until death. Zulu nicknames are discussed in Chapter 4.

c. Surnames

The term 'surname' normally applies to the name shared by a nuclear family (mother, father and children). In patrilineal societies the surname is passed from father to sons. Daughters retain the father's surname only until marriage, when they normally adopt the surname of the husband. There are a number of variants of this practice. For reasons which I explain in Chapter 5, I prefer the term 'clan name' to 'surname' when talking about Zulu names such as Cele, Dlamini, Ngcobo, Makhathini, Xulu and Zwane.

1.4.3 Ethnonyms

This term is derived from the Greek *ethnos* ('race', cf. ethnology: the branch of anthropology that deals with races and peoples). Ethnonyms are the names of races, tribes, clans, nations and similar groups. South African ethnonyms – not necessarily politically correct – include San, Khoisan, Khoi-khoi, Bushman, Hottentot, Bantu, Xhosa, Zulu, Venda, Shangaan, Pondo, Hlubi as well as the Euro-origin names Boer, Jew, Greek, Portuguese, etc.

Although not normally considered to be ethnonyms, names may be given to other groups of people: clubs, societies, guilds, organisations such as church groups, service organisations (Rotary, MOTHS, Round Table, Lions), youth organisations, regiments, sporting teams, and so on. The names of regiments are discussed in Chapter 6.

1.4.4 Toponyms

This term is derived from the Greek *topos* ('place', cf. topography: the study or detailed description of the surface features of a region). Toponymy then is the study of place names, sometimes referred to as 'geographical names'. Some onomasticians make a distinction between 'place names' (the names of human habitations, for example, towns and villages), and 'geographical names' (the names of geographical features such as rivers and mountains). Under the general heading of 'toponyms' we could consider then the names of rivers, mountains, lakes, forests, seas, and deserts on the one hand, and countries, provinces, cities, towns, villages, and settlements on the other.

At a more 'micro-level' of human settlement, we could consider street names (a popular research field for onomasticians the world over), and the names of buildings such as flats, hotels, factories – although, strictly speaking, these names lie midway between toponyms and the names of companies and marques (see the introductory paragraph in Chapter 11) – and schools. In rural areas the names of farms and homesteads are worth looking at.

Zulu toponyms are discussed from a number of different angles (for example, historical, orthographic, and semantic angles) in Chapters 7, 8, 9 and 10.

1.4.5 Other names

Ships, cars, trains and aeroplanes may have names. The car marque ISUZU LE has been read by many Zulus as **Isuzu le?** ('Is this an Isuzu?'), which has led a colleague N.N. Ntshangase to paint on the back of his Isuzu bakkie (light pick-up truck) the following:

iSuzu le?
cha . . . cha
uJomb' itshe lo

Is this an Isuzu?
No . . . No
This is Mr Jump-over-the-stone

This innovative onomastic joke has been much admired and imitated among certain members of the Zulu community in Pietermaritzburg.

In South Africa the names of buses have been the subject of some research (see, for example, Voss [1992] and Ntuli [1999]). The names of kombi taxis, however, have not to my knowledge been researched, and this remains an intriguing field of onomastics still to be explored.

There are names for the seasons, months of the year and days of the week. Zulu names for these periods of time are compared to English, Xhosa and other languages in Chapter 16.

Humans name their domestic animals, such as dogs, cats, oxen and horses. The naming of dogs, oxen, and other domestic animals in Zulu is discussed in Chapter 14.

Part 2

Anthroponymy

(Personal names)

Chapter 2

Zulu names and other forms of address

2.1 THE CONCEPT OF THE NAME

To Euro-Western thought generally, a name is not part of a person or a personality. The name is a 'label', a 'tag', something to be used in reference *to* a person, but no more than that. In contrast to this is, for example, the very common Africanist concept of the name illustrated in the following conversation recorded in Berglund's *Zulu Thought-Patterns and Symbolism*, where Berglund is talking to a Zulu **isangoma** ('diviner') about witchcraft practices:

> Our discussion continued in terms of the name of the person who was to be harmed.
> B: . . . 'Everywhere I am told that **umthakathi** mentions the name of the person who is to be killed. Why does **umthakathi** mention the name?'
> 'It is the name of that person.'
> B: . . . 'Is it important that the name should be mentioned?'
> 'It is very important. It is the important thing in **ubuthakathi**. If a man can hide his name from people, then he can hide from much evil. **Umthakathi** can kill a man if he lacks vileness (body-dirt) and hair, but has the name. So the name is very important.'
> B: . . . 'Why is the name so important?'
> 'The name *is* that person. They are the same, the name and the person. It is the word whereby that person is known. That is the name. So the person and the name are one. **Umthakathi** kills a man by combining the words of death with the name. He throws (**ukuphonsa**) these at the man and they kill him' (1975: 287).

The quotation above makes clear the relationship between the name and the individual, and the use of the name in witchcraft. The name in Africa has a different function to the Euro-Western name, for in Africa the name is normally not used either for reference or in direct address. This leads to two distinct socio-linguistic practices: *firstly*, avoidance of names, and common words which are similar to certain names, leads frequently to alternative vocabularies in some societies; and *secondly*, avoidance of personal names leads to a wide variety of alternative forms of address.

> The term 'Euro-Western' is used in two ways in this book: *firstly*, in the South African context, to contrast names of European-language origin (English, Afrikaans-Dutch, Portuguese, etc.) with names of Bantu-language origin (Nguni, Sotho, Venda, etc.), and *secondly*, in a wider context, to contrast names of the 'Western' world (mainly European and North American) with other parts of the world (African, Asian, etc.).

2.2 NAME AVOIDANCE AND ALTERNATIVE VOCABULARIES

There are many societies in the world where the use of names is avoided. In many of these the practice is also to avoid using out loud common words which bear a resemblance to someone's name.

Sir James Frazer's *The Golden Bough* gives a number of examples from different societies. Talking of the Sea Dyaks of Borneo, he states:

> Among the Sea Dyaks a man may not pronounce the name of his father-in-law or mother-in-law without incurring the wrath of the spirits. And since he reckons as his father-in-law and mother-in-law not only the father and mother of his own wife, but also the fathers and mothers of his brothers' wives and sisters' husbands, and likewise the fathers and mothers of all his cousins, the number of tabooed names may be very considerable and the opportunities of error correspondingly numerous. To make confusion worse confounded, the names of persons are often the names of common things, such as moon, bridge, barley, cobra, leopard; so that when any of a man's many fathers-in-law and mothers-in-law are called by such names, these common words may not pass his lips (1949: 244–251).

Such taboos lead to 'avoidance language', that is, the use of regularly recognised alternative forms for certain common words. Respectful avoidance, known in Zulu as **ukuhlonipha**, covers more than just names. A newly married bride, for example, must show respect in her demeanour, in the way she sits and walks, in avoiding certain foodstuffs, as well as in avoiding the names of the senior male members of the lineage she has married into. Krige has the following to say about **hlonipha** behaviour:

> The behaviour towards relatives-in-law is largely bound up with the custom of *hlonipha*. This word literally means to have shame or to shun

> through bashfulness, and affects women to a far greater extent than men . . . [details about dress and eating habits] . . .
>
> Accompanying this *hlonipha* of action is the *hlonipha* of speech. A woman may not use the name . . . of the above-mentioned relatives-in-law nor any word containing the radical of such a name. Another word must be used instead, and so the speech of the women differs considerably from that of the men (1950: 30).

Hlonipha variants are standardised throughout the Zulu-speaking area, and are recorded in Doke and Vilakazi's *Zulu-English Dictionary*, where they are marked with little circles, as follows: '°**khaza** . . . hlonipha term for *thanda*, love' (1958: 385).

Some idea of the range of common words affecting the speech of women can be seen in the following examples:

- °**umnatho** for *umfula* (river);
- °**mqwayi** for *mhlophe* (white);
- °**mncayi** for *mnandi* (tasty);
- °**ummoma** for *isangoma* (diviner);
- °**mvama** for *ningi* (many);
- °**inamana** for *umntwana* (child);
- °**amandambi** for *amanzi* (water).

Some of these **hlonipha** terms are better known than others, and how well a term is known depends on the frequency of occurrence of the word it replaces as an element in Zulu personal names. For example, the **hlonipha** term °**ingcagca** (for *inhlanhla*, 'luck') will be more widely known than the term °**incangu** (for *inhlangu* 'bushbuck') because there are many personal names based on the Zulu word for luck, but names based on the word for bushbuck are few and far between.

An illustration of the way name avoidance works can be seen in the public speeches of Chief Mangosuthu Gatsha Buthelezi, who will never refer to black people as **abantu abamnyama**, but will always use the phrase **abantu abamphisholo**, using the **hlonipha** form °**mphisholo** for the common word **mnyama** (black). This is done in respectful avoidance of the names of his long-deceased great-grandfather **uMnyamana**. In similar fashion, his children, especially the daughters and daughters-in-law, will never refer to a branch of a tree in ordinary speech as *igatsha*, but will always use the **hlonipha** variant °**inaca**.

Hlonipha has, according to local tradition, given us the place name **Amanzimtoti**. The story behind this name is told in Chapter 9 on page 144.

Two points should be made about **hlonipha** behaviour: *firstly*, name avoidance does not apply to older close kin of a name bearer. One's own parents, grandparents, uncles and aunts, and elder siblings may well use one's personal name. In addition, social transformations are bringing about a change in name avoidance patterns. For example, modern, urban, educated couples are starting to use personal names when addressing one another, whereas in the more conservative rural areas, husbands and wives, especially the older ones, still avoid the personal name in daily contact.

Secondly, name avoidance only applies to the personal name which is given to the young child by the parents at birth, the **igama lasekhaya** (literally, 'home name'). Name avoidance does not apply to the European-origin name (**igama lesilungu**), to the clan name or clan praises, or to any nicknames.

As a rule, every Zulu person has three official names. By 'official' I mean the names which are normally found on documents such as birth certificates, school certificates, drivers' licences, bank and pension books, and the like. In any society a person's official names are not necessarily the names by which he or she is known, and this is certainly the case for Zulu. A reasonable starting point, however, for a discussion of terms of address in Zulu society is the official nomenclature. The three names which usually appear on documents are the **igama lasekhaya** (the personal or 'given' name), the **igama lesilungu** (Euro-origin name) and the clan name (usually referred to as 'surname' on official documents). The examples below are invented identities:

Males	*Females*
Sipho Aron Mkhize	**Nonhlanhla Pretty Nxumalo**
Mduduzi Cleopas Dlamini	**Sibongile Abigail Buthelezi**
Vusumuzi Wiseman Xaba	**Lindiwe Gertrude Dlomo**
Nkosinathi David Mchunu	**Thokozile Patience Gumede**
Sibusiso Johannes Sibisi	**Nomazulu Tryphina Khumalo**

2.3 THE *IGAMA LASEKHAYA*: THE HOME NAME

This is the personal name given to each child at or shortly after birth. It is usually given by one of the parents, and occasionally by a grandparent or other close kin. Frequently a child will be given more than one personal name, especially if each parent has a strong reason for choosing a particular name. There is always a reason for choosing the name, and the reason is always linked to the underlying meaning of the name, in contrast to most Euro-Western societies where the reason for giving the name is seldom linked to the underlying meaning. To give an example, a Zulu mother who has had a difficult pregnancy or has lost other children in birth or when very young may decide to name a healthy baby boy **uNkosinomusa** (literally, 'The Lord is merciful') because she believes that God has interceded in her pregnancy to spare her further misfortunes. A Euro-Western mother may name a child **Johannes** (or any of its variants, such as Johan, John, Ian, Sean, etc.) which also has, in its original Hebrew form *io hanas*, the underlying meaning 'The Lord is merciful'. But the reason for choosing such a name in Euro-Western societies is far more likely to be 'That was my father's name' (or the *child's* father, or uncle, or grandfather) or 'we just liked the name'.

The underlying meanings of Zulu personal names and the various reasons why certain names are chosen are discussed in depth in Chapter 3.

The **igama lasekhaya** *may* be used as an address form in Zulu, but its usage is restricted as it is subject to the rules of **ukuhlonipha** or respectful avoidance. Normally this name is only used at home, as implied by **lasekhaya** ('of at home'). Again, normally a child is only addressed by his or her **igama lasekhaya** by close members of the family who are older: mother, father, uncles and aunts, grandparents, and older siblings. Younger siblings address older siblings as 'brother' or 'sister'.

The Zulu personal names, indeed *all* names (Euro-origin, clan name, nicknames) are prefixed with **u-** in the reference form (that is, when talking about someone), thus:

- **USipho usekhaya manje** – Sipho is at home now.
- **Umbonile uMandla**? – Have you seen Mandla?

This noun class prefix is deleted when the name is used in direct address:

- **Sawubona Sipho** – Greetings Sipho!
- **Woza lapha Mandla** – Come here Mandla!

The structure and grammar of personal names is discussed in detail in Chapter 17.

2.4 THE *IGAMA LESILUNGU*: THE EURO-ORIGIN NAME

This name is a name derived from another culture, usually from the colonial language dominant in the area. Thus Euro-origin names are normally from English in Zulu society. The equivalents in other South African languages such as Xhosa, Sotho or Venda may be from Afrikaans. In Angola and Mozambique the equivalent of the **igama lesilungu** is from Portuguese. In other parts of Africa the local inhabitants, in addition to names in their own language, bear names from French or Arabic. In Namibia, particularly among the Ovambo of Northern Namibia, Finnish names such as Matti, Paavo, Taimi and Helvi are widespread (Saarelma-Maunumaa, 1997). It seems to have been a general colonial pattern to insist that local inhabitants of a country take names from the colonial language. As African countries have achieved independence from the colonial powers there has frequently been a reaction against the use of names from colonial languages.

The **igama lesilungu** is also known as **igama lesikole** ('the school name'), **igama lasedolobheni** ('the town name') and **igama lesonto** ('the church name'), giving us clues both as to the social milieu where these names are most frequently used, as well as their origins. Parents are not usually the source of the **igama lesilungu**, and the name may be given by a teacher, a nurse at the hospital, the local priest, or even a (European) employer of the father or mother of the child. This name is usually given when the child is already a few years old, perhaps when being baptised, or when first attending school.

Euro-origin names among the Zulus follow the general English onomastic pattern, with boys being named David, John, James, Edward, and Timothy, while girls carry names such as Mary, Alice, Cynthia, Helen and Barbara. These may sometimes seem old-fashioned to modern English speakers, who no longer name their children Egbert, Cuthbert, Percy, Humphrey and Wilberforce. The Victorian 'morality' names, so popular for girls towards the end of the nineteenth century, are still popular for Zulu girls, and names such as Faith, Hope, Charity, Constance and Prudence can be found all over KwaZulu-Natal.

Certain names, such as 'Pretty' and 'Wiseman' are seldom if ever found among the English-speaking community, but are common among Zulus. Girls may be called Gladness, Beauty, Happiness, Prettygirl and Dolly, while boys can be named Lucky, Goodboy, Wiseman, Braveman and Blessing. At times namegivers can be quite creative, as in the girl's name Pinkypearl and the boy's name Godshero. Very often these names are translations of the **igama lasekhaya** and one may find a Prettygirl whose Zulu name is **uNtombenhle** ('pretty girl'), and a Precious whose other name is **Gugulethu** ('our treasure'). Boys who are named Lucky and Blessing are likely to have been named **uNhlanhla** (< **inhlanhla**, 'luck') and **uSibusiso** (< **isibusiso**, 'blessing') earlier in their lives.

Not so common at the end of the twentieth century but relatively common earlier in the century were names taken randomly from European culture: Insurance, Sixpence, Vitalis, Pepsicola and Superose. The *Natal Witness* of 11 January 1983 reported that Paraffin Gumede had been eaten by a crocodile.

Surnames made famous in European history have also been adopted as personal names: Washington, Lincoln, Churchill, Wordsworth, Hamilton and others.

When the church is involved in the naming, which is frequently the case, the names are biblical in origin. Large proportions of Zulu males bear names such as Aaron, Ephraim, Almon, Caiphas, Ezekial, Moses, Jotham, Meshack and the like. Where the church or mission station is Catholic, the names of saints and popes predominate, and names such as Boniface, Sextus, Pius, and Sebastian abound.

The **igama lesilungu** is used as a form of address in a wide variety of social situations. It is the norm at schools, may be used in the family circle, and is frequently used by non-Zulu speakers (for example, in the work situation). It has a higher frequency of use in the urban context than in the rural.

With the ending of apartheid in the early 1990s, and the birth of the 'new South Africa', these names have increasingly been seen as badges of colonial domination, and have even been referred to by some writers as 'slave names'. It is clear that use of these names will become less and less common. In an *ad hoc* survey I conducted with a group of Zulu-speaking students in May 2001, less than half said that they had an **igama lesilungu**, and those students who did have such a name, said that hardly anyone ever used it.

2.5 THE *ISIBONGO*: THE CLAN NAME

The word **isibongo** is derived from the verb **bonga** ('to thank', 'to praise'). The plural form **izibongo** can cause confusion, as the same word is used for oral praise poetry. One talks of the **izibongo zikaShaka** ('the praises of Shaka'), for example, and this phrase does not mean 'Shaka's surnames', but refers to the lengthy oral poem recited by an **imbongi** ('professional bard', 'praise-singer') on ceremonial occasions.

The **isibongo** is a family name rather than the name of an individual. As with the surname in most Euro-Western cultures, the **isibongo** is shared by all members of a nuclear family, that is, father, mother, sons, and unmarried daughters. For this reason the **isibongo** functions as a surname in the Western context, and the term is very often translated as 'surname'. For various reasons, which I explain in detail in Chapter 5, I prefer the term 'clan name' to 'surname' in reference to the Zulu **isibongo**.

On marriage, a woman may exchange her maiden clan name for that of her husband on official documents, but for all practical social intercourse she retains her maiden clan name, prefixed with **ma-**. Thus a woman born to the Ngcobo clan will be commonly addressed as **MaNgcobo** after marriage, and a woman with the maiden clan name Mkhize will be known to all her new in-laws as **MaMkhize**. This is a form of address with a wide social usage.

In the mid-1990s a new pattern of clan-name usage emerged, particularly among women of a high social profile. This new usage mirrored a form which has been common in certain European countries for many generations: the 'double-barrelled' surname which joins the maiden surname to that of the husband with a hyphen. I suspect that in South Africa it was Winnie Mandela who started the trend when she prefixed Madikizela to Mandela and became Winnie Madikizela-Mandela. Thereafter a number of women prominent in political circles or in television adopted this trend, among them Felicia Mabuza-Suttle, Khanyi Dlomo-Mkhize and Nkosazana Dlamini-Zuma.

The clan name is a common form of address for males, used by younger, older and peers, by either sex, and often used by wives when talking to husbands. It is usually used without a preliminary title. In other words, it is not necessary to prefix the clan name with Mister or its Zulu equivalent **uMnumzane**. This can cause confusion and dismay among English-speaking people who regard it as impolite to address someone by surname only, that is, without a preliminary title.

Each and every clan name in Zulu has its own clan praises (**izithakazelo**).

2.6 THE *ISITHAKAZELO*: THE CLAN PRAISE

From the verb **thakazela** comes the noun **isithakazelo** ('clan praise'), with the plural **izithakazelo**. The clan praise is indeed used as an address form, but its far wider function in Zulu society can be deduced from the several meanings of the verb **thakazela**: 'be genial towards, show courtesy to, welcome, greet on arrival, adulate, praise flatteringly, congratulate'.

Each Zulu **isibongo** has a 'main', or 'primary' **isithakazelo** which is used as a common address form. These may be used by acquaintances meeting in the street, by students of their teachers and professors, and by wives talking to their husbands. Public figures may be referred to by clan praise, as when Chief Mangosuthu Buthelezi is referred to as **Shenge**, or when Nelson Mandela becomes **Madiba**.

In addition to the 'main' clan praise, each Zulu clan name has a number of 'secondary' praise names, which when added to a string of praise phrases, becomes a clan praise poem. **Izithakazelo** in their full form, as when recited at ceremonial occasions, such as when a goat is slaughtered in honour of the ancestors, show marked similarities to the oral praises of kings and chiefs. They have decidedly poetic features, and can be considered to be a bridging form between naming and poetry. It is surprising that clan praises have received so little attention either from onomasticians, or by scholars of oral poetry. As I have pointed out elsewhere:

> Nguni clan praises have long been a neglected area of Southern African oral poetry. It has been the praises of kings and chiefs which have occupied the interests of most scholars during most of the past century, ever since Grant's ground-breaking work on the **izibongo** of Zulu chiefs in 1927.
>
> Why clan praises should have been thus neglected is not clear. They are rich in imagery, and filled with historical narrative, even if much of this is obscure. They are often pungent in their humour, and as with their close literary neighbours – the praises of chiefs – may be bitingly critical. They serve a number of different social functions, and play a significant role in important ceremonial occasions (1999b: 298).

The full uses of **izithakazelo** and their complex interrelationships with clan names will be discussed in Chapter 5, where a list of some common Zulu clan names and their praises will be given.

2.7 NICKNAMES

Nicknames are basically of three types: the 'baby name' or 'pet name' which a mother gives to a very young child, the nickname which is given by peers to an older child or an adult, and the abbreviated form of the **igama lasekhaya**. Several Zulu words exist for the first two forms, but no word seems to be a standard form accepted by all Zulu speakers.

2.7.1 Baby name

Any of the following words may be used to refer to the 'baby name' or 'pet name':

- **isifenqo**, derived from the verb **fenqa** ('talk in sport', 'say in fun');
- **isidlaliso**, from **dlalisa** ('amuse', 'play with');
- **isangelo**, from **anga** ('kiss');
- **isifekethiso**, from **fekethisa** ('amuse', 'play with', 'make a joke', 'say in fun').

As can be seen from the meanings of the base verbs above, these names are 'hugging, kissing and tickling names', used when bouncing a small baby on the knee. These names are usually given by the mother and are generally only used by her and then only in intimate moments. It can happen that such a pet name becomes used by the whole family (both parents, grandparents, siblings), but such a name never goes outside the family. These names are only used until the child reaches puberty.

2.7.2 Peer nickname

Later, when a child leaves the protection of its mother and starts to mix with other children of his or her own age set, peer-group nicknames are given. Bryant states: 'When now at length the babe . . . had grown into a brave and handsome youth, he was wont to flatter him, or more commonly, be flattered by his companions, with some brand new "fancy-name" (**isitopo**), usually one of adulation, by which name, among his set, he henceforth was generally called, instead of by his birth-name' (1949: 434).

Bryant gives as examples of these 'fancy-names' the following: '**uNojiyelwa-kuLala** (He-who-is-hindered-from-lying-down-comfortably – owing to the wound he received in honourable combat), or **uNovandzi** (Agile-legs – owing to his skill in kicking his legs about when performing the **ukuGiya** dance).'

> The **ukuGiya** involves dancing by an individual, usually simulating fighting, in order to demonstrate that individual's speed and agility to a group of peers.

I have not met a mother-tongue Zulu person who is familiar with Bryant's term **isithopho**. It appears to be unknown today. However, the 'fancy-names' themselves (preferably: 'nicknames' or 'personal praises') are common, and they will be discussed in detail in Chapter 4.

2.7.3 Abbreviated forms

It is sometimes difficult to distinguish between a true nickname and an abbreviated form of a personal name. If, for example, a child named Frederick was called 'Shooter' by his school friends (because of his skill in shooting marbles? shooting goals?) we would call this a nickname. If his parents called him 'Freddy', we would say that this was his personal name, in a recognisable abbreviated form. If he was from an Afrikaans-speaking family, Frederick may well have been abbreviated to 'Frikkie' (see Koopman, 1999a). If his friends and family, however, abbreviated Frederick to 'Fricks' or 'Fretto', that is, to a 'non-standard' abbreviated form, we might well call this a nickname. This would be justifiable on onomastic grounds as 'nickname' – as previously discussed – is derived from 'an eke-name' where 'eke' means 'individual'. 'Fricks' and 'Fretto' would indeed be individual or unique in this case.

The same grey area applies to abbreviated forms of Zulu personal names. Most names have recognisable standard forms. **Sibusiso** ('blessing') becomes **Sbu**, while **Vusumuzi** ('awake the family') becomes **Vusi** and sometimes **Vu**.

The following examples show just a few of the common abbreviated forms of Zulu personal names:

Boys

- **Mandla** from **Mandlenkosi** ('strength of the Lord'), **Nkosinamandla** ('the Lord is strong') and any other compound noun with **amandla** ('strength');
- **Musa** from **Msawenkosi** ('the grace of the Lord'), **Nkosinomusa** ('the Lord is gracious') and any other compound noun with **umusa** ('grace');
- **Bheki** from **Bhekinkosi** ('look to the Lord'), **Bhekuyise** ('look to your father') and any other compound noun with **bheka** ('look [up] to');
- **Sbo** from **Sibonelo** ('example'), **Siboniso** ('sign', 'revelation') and similar words.

> As mentioned previously, the Hebrew form of 'the Lord is gracious' – *io hanas* – has given rise to the name Johannes, from which are derived all the Euro-Western names John, Jan, Ivan, Ian, Jean, Juan, Giovanni, etc.

Girls

- **Thoko** from **Thokozile** ('being happy');
- **Ntombi** from **Ntombizethu** ('our girls'), **Ntombenhle** ('beautiful girl'), **Ntombiziningi** ('the girls are many'), and any other compound noun with **intombi** ('girl');
- **Dudu** from **Duduzile** ('having comforted');
- **Jabu** from **Jabulisiwe** ('having made happy') or from any other name with the verb **jabula** ('be happy').

In abbreviating names, Zulu, like English and Afrikaans, may remove the first or the last part of a name. The English girl's name Margareta may possibly be shortened to Marge and Greta, while Elizabeth may become Eliza (Lizzie) and Beth (Betty). The Afrikaans boy's name Stefanus may become Stef and Fanie, while Jacobus may become Jaap and Kobus. In the same way, a Zulu girl's name such as **Ntombizethu** may become **Ntombi** and **Zethu**, while the boy's name **Muziwenhlanhla** ('house of luck') may be abbreviated to both **Muzi** and **Nhlanhla**.

Abbreviated forms of personal names are used as forms of address by family members generally, and this use may last the lifetime of the person so named. But there is a special form of these abbreviations used only in intimate parent–child situations, such as when a baby is being dandled on the knee, and this is only used in the formative years of the child. Let us take a girl called **Jabulisiwe** ('having made happy'). The abbreviated form of this name is **Jabu**, and when an elder sister or brother uses this abbreviation it will have the typical high-low tonal pattern with the length on the penultimate syllable: /**Já:bû**/. When her mother is hugging and kissing little Jabu, though, the tonal pattern will reverse, becoming low-high-falling, and the *final* syllable will be lengthened: /**Jàbû:**/. Frequently this intonational pattern is accompanied by a change of the final vowel to /o/. Thus **Jabulisiwe** > **Jabu** > **Jàbô:** and **Ntombizonke** > **Ntombi** > **Ntòmbô:**.

Although the use of this specialised endearment form of the personal name is usually restricted to the parent–child context, I am informed that it is not uncommon for a teacher of very young children, say at a pre-school, to address a child, irrespective of the child's actual personal name, as /**Mfànô:**/ if a boy (< **umfana**, 'boy') and /**Ntòmbô:**/ if a girl (< **intombi**, 'girl'). I am also informed that this particular intonation pattern may be applied to words such as 'Hello' and **Yebo** ('yes'), thus, when chucking a little baby under the chin, one may say /**Hèllô:**/.

2.8 PATRONYMS

Patronymic address forms use the name of the father of the person being addressed (Greek *patronymikos*, 'name of the father'). Bryant describes the practice in Zulu society:

> . . . after marriage, a woman was referred to, conversationally, by the *father and mother* of her husband simply by her father's name (not her own); thus: 'U-pi uNdwandwe?' – where is Ndwandwe? (i.e. the daughter of Ndwandwe). By her *husband*, and his *married brothers*, and their *wives*, and by the public in general of an equally adult age, she was referred to with the prefix **o-ka** (she-of), placed before her father's name; thus: 'u-pi o-ka-Ndwandwe?' – where is she-of Ndwandwe? (1949: 209).

This is not the case for women only. In Ngubane's novel *Uvalo Lwezinhlonzi*, a book which examines the breakdown of rural traditions in favour of newer urban practices, the main character is continually referred to by the name of his father, thus **Wena kaNomadinane** ('you, son-of-Nomadinane'). We never find out his wife's personal name, for the author and the other characters in the book only ever refer to her as **intombi kaMemunce** ('girl, that is, daughter of Memunce'). The character Zulumacansi introduces himself to his prospective father-in-law with personal name, patronymic and home-area affiliations: **nginguZulumacansi kaBhekokwakhe waseButhunqe bukaMagayi** ('I am Zulumacansi, son of Bhekokwakhe, from Buthunqe under chief Magayi'). Thereafter his father-in-law addresses him as **Wena kaBhekokwakhe** ('you, son of Bhekokwakhe').

The use of patronymics is still common in Zulu rural areas today, but it is a tradition which has nearly died out in urban areas.

2.9 TEKNONYMS

One of the most common forms of address in Africa is that where a married man or woman is addressed as 'father of so-and-so' or 'mother of so-and-so'. I first came across this term in Evans-Pritchard's study of modes of address among the Nuer people of Northern Kenya:

> The teknonymous usage, the naming of the man after his eldest child – **gwan** ('father of so-and-so') . . . [is parallelled by the] . . . usage **man** ('mother of so-and-so') . . . the normal way of addressing and speaking about a married woman. The eldest child's name is generally used, whether a boy or a girl, but occasionally a second child's name is used if the second is a boy and the first is a girl (1948: 170).

The use of teknonyms is extremely common in Zulu society. As with the Nuer, and indeed many other societies in Africa, the name of the eldest child is used, but the name of the second child may also be used if the first is a girl and the second a boy. In many such cases (that is, when the eldest is a girl and the second child a boy) the father will address his wife as **mama ka** . . . ('mother of . . . [girl's name]'), while she will address him as **baba ka** . . . ('father of . . . [boy's name]').

In my study of urban Zulu families in the greater Pietermaritzburg area in the early 1980s I found 54,5 per cent of mothers using teknonyms when addressing their husbands, with another 15 per cent simply using the word **baba** ('father') without the use of the child's name (see Koopman, 1986). Thirty-six per cent of fathers addressed their wives as 'mother of . . .'.

The table on page 29 shows the different types of address forms used by Zulu husbands and wives when talking to each other. The data were collected in the greater Pietermaritzburg area in the early 1980s.

The different types of address forms used by Zulu husbands and wives

Wives addressing husbands		**Husbands addressing wives**	
Baba ka . . . [name of eldest child]	54,5%	Ma- + maiden clan name	38%
Baba	15%	Mama ka . . . [name of eldest child]	36%
Igama lesilungu	8,5%	Mama	10%
Isibongo	8,5%	Igama lasekhaya	6%
Isithakazelo	8,5%	Igama lesilungu	6%
Igama lasekhaya	5%	Other (**nkosikazi**, endearments)	4%

The following two sections – 'Kinship terms' and 'Descriptives' – do not concern *names*, but as kinship terms and descriptive words are commonly used as forms of address they are included in this chapter.

2.10 KINSHIP TERMS

It is not my intention here to give a detailed description of Zulu kinship terminology. Krige has done this in her much-used and much-loved *The Social System of the Zulus*, and it is to her Appendix 1 that you should be directed should you wish to know the appropriate term for 'father's mother's brother's son' (**ubabomncane**), or even 'son's wife's father's father' (**ukoko ka'malokazana wami**).

Rather, I am interested here in the common everyday kinship terms which constitute a common mode of address in the family context.

2.10.1 Addressing one's parents

In my research I have never found anything other than **baba** and **mama** (usually abbreviated to **maa**) used by children when addressing their parents. In the English-speaking world, just to take fathers, one may come across variations such as Dad, Daddy, Pa, Pop, Pops, and Poppa (and rarely: 'Father'). Such variations are extremely rare in Zulu society, and I only know one young lady who regularly addresses her father as 'Babayi'. The use of personal names as a form of address for one's parents is absolutely unheard of, and when I have told Zulu students that this is sometimes (if seldom) done in Euro-Western families, they have reacted with disbelief and horror.

2.10.2 Addressing one's children

Parents are amongst the select group who may address someone by their personal **igama lasekhaya**. They may also use the Euro-origin name, and also frequently use the kinship terms **mntanami** ('my child'), **mfana wami** ('my boy'), **ntombi yakithi** ('girl of our family'), and so on.

2.10.3 Addressing one's siblings

Older children may use the personal names of their younger siblings, but younger children, when addressing older siblings, are more likely to use **mfowethu** ('brother'), **dadewethu** ('sister') and variations of these.

Bryant (1949: 412–456) in his chapter 'The family and the clan' gives further detailed information on forms of address within families.

2.11 DESCRIPTIVES

'Descriptives' are those forms of address which *describe* the person being addressed, usually in terms of age and sex. In the greeting **Sanibona madoda!** ('Greetings, men!'), the noun **amadoda** (with its first vowel deleted, as it is being used in direct address) indicates males of a mature age. In **Ngiyabonga salukazi** ('Thank you, old woman'), the noun **isalukazi** describes a female of an older age; and in **Woza mntanami** ('Come here, my child'), the noun **umntanami** refers to a young child of either sex.

> While not exactly insulting, the term **salukazi** is starting to be regarded with disfavour. The same can be said for the word **ikhehla** ('old man'). However, note that the Zulu word **umfazi** ('woman') is rude in direct address, and even in indirect reference its use should be avoided.

Descriptives include the following:

- **umfana** ('boy');
- **insizwa** ('youth', 'young man');
- **indoda** ('man');
- **ikhehla** ('older man');
- **intombazana** ('younger girl');
- **intombi** ('older girl');
- **isalukazi** ('older woman').

Descriptives also include kinship terms where no kinship exists or is implied. It is common, and polite, to refer to a man of mature age as **baba** ('father'). It is equally common and polite to refer to a woman of a certain age as **mama** ('mother'), and to an older woman as **gogo** ('grandmother'). To one's peers, the terms **umfowethu** ('brother') and **udadewethu** ('sister') can be used, always remembering to drop the first vowel in direct address: **Xolo mfowethu** ('Sorry, my brother'). Modern equivalents of these, especially in urban areas, are **bhuti** ('brother' < Afrikaans *boetie*) and **sisi** ('sister').

Under the heading 'descriptives' come titles of all sorts, from the more general **uMnumzane** ('Mister', 'Sir') and **uNkosikazi** ('Mrs', 'Madam') to more specific terms such as:

- **uPhulofesa** and (modern) **uSolwazi** ('Professor');

- **uDokotela** ('Doctor');
- **uNgqongqoshe** ('Excellency' – in government context);
- **uMhlonishwa** ('Respected one', 'Excellency' – in general context);
- **uMfundisi** ('Reverend');
- **uSayitsheni** ('Sergeant');
- **uKaputeni** ('Captain');
- **uMhloli** ('Inspector');
- **uThisha** ('Teacher');
- **iNkosi yenkantolo** ('Judge').

Also included under the heading 'descriptives' should be the word **intshebe** ('beard'). Greeting a stranger in Western society with 'Hi there, Beard!' would certainly be unusual, if not offensive, but (having had a full beard for the last 25 years) I am perfectly accustomed to strangers greeting me in the streets with **Sawubona Ntshebe!** or just simply **Ntshebe!**

Chapter 3

Reasons for giving names

3.1 INTRODUCTION

In Chapter 2 we looked at a major difference between the Euro-Western and the African concept of the name. Evidence from African societies shows a far greater link between name and person, almost as if the name were a part of the body, leading to potential misuse of the name in witchcraft.

Another major difference between Euro-Western societies and African societies lies in the link between the reason for giving a name and the underlying meaning of the name. To give two hypothetical examples:

Example 1
Family A: English-speaking white South Africans have a son. They are devout Christians and believe that God had a hand in the birth of their child. Consequently, when they put their birth notice in the newspaper, they add the phrase 'Praise the Lord'. The child is named **Robert**, the reason being that the paternal grandfather of the child was named Robert. The parents are unaware that Robert is an old Germanic name meaning 'bright spear'.

Family B: Zulu speakers have a son. They are devout Christians and believe that God had a hand in the birth of their child. As it is considered dangerous to attract the attention of strangers to the existence of a newly born child, they do not put a notice in the newspaper. However, in order to show the world their belief about God's role in the birth of their child, they make another kind of public statement: they name the child **Bonginkosi** ('praise the Lord'). Or perhaps they name the child **Sandlasenkosi** ('hand of the Lord').

Example 2
Family A: Zulu speakers have a daughter after three sons have already been born. Overjoyed that a daughter has finally arrived, they tell the world by naming their daughter **Ntombifikile** ('a girl has arrived').

Family B: Afrikaans-speaking white South Africans have a daughter after three sons have already been born. Overjoyed that a daughter has finally arrived, they name her **Marita**, because that is the name of the child's maternal grandmother. The parents are unaware that Marita is also an abbreviation of Margarita, a name of Greek origin meaning 'pearl'.

I don't want to give the impression that Euro-Western parents only give their children names that belonged to their own parents or other relatives. One might also find parents saying 'We found the name "Marita" in a book, and decided that we liked it.'

Research with my students over the last 15 or so years – both mother-tongue Zulu speakers and mother-tongue English speakers – has shown me that in the vast majority of cases, in Zulu society the reason for giving the name is directly linked to the underlying meaning of the name, and the name-bearer is well aware of the meaning of his or her name. Among students of a Euro-Western background, the reason for giving the name is hardly ever linked to the underlying meaning of the name, and most name-bearers are not aware of this underlying meaning.

3.2 REASONS FOR GIVING NAMES IN ZULU SOCIETY

The categories that follow are based on data that I collected in the early and mid-1980s from approximately 300 families in the greater Pietermaritzburg area (see Koopman, 1986). These categories are:

1. Names referring to the *structure of the family*, where we find reference to the sex of the child, the number and spacing of the children, and twins. This category accounts for 31,2 per cent of the names collected.
2. Names referring to the *perceived role of God in the birth*. These names make up 21,2 per cent of the data.
3. Names referring to the *'state of mind' of the parents*, including feelings of love, pride and happiness, and injunctions to the child. These names account for 18,5 per cent of the total.
4. Names referring to the *circumstances of the birth*, including the birth itself, wider circumstances, and friction in the family. Here we find 14,4 per cent of the names in the data.
5. Names referring to the *wider clan*, including reference to the ancestral spirits, clan membership, and to the custom of **ilobolo**. This category contains 8,1 per cent of the names.
6. *Other* or *miscellaneous*: Those names which do not fit into any of the categories above (6,6 per cent).

3.2.1 Names referring to the structure of the family

In certain societies in Africa, children are simply given names which refer to birth order and sex, such as the following boys' names from Akan speakers of Ghana, given by Chuks-Orji: **Manu** ('second-born'), **Anane** ('fourth-born'), **Msrah** ('sixth-born') and **Nsoah** ('seventh-born'). Chuks-Orji's examples take us right up to **Adusah** ('thirteenth-born') and **Agyeman** ('fourteenth-born')! We even have names which refer to the ordering of husbands and wives. **Afafa** (girl's name) and **Adika** (boy's name) both mean 'first child of second husband' while apparently there are similar boys' and girls' names which mean 'first child of second wife'. Presumably, although Chuks-Orji does not say so, this system can be extended, and children can be given names which mean 'seventh son of third wife' or 'eleventh daughter of second husband'.

In Zulu society birth-order names usually refer to the comparative balance (or imbalance) of boys and girls in a family. To understand the importance of a balanced family, we need to look at both the role played by the ancestors in Zulu society as well as the social custom of **ilobolo**. Ancestral spirits (the **abaphansi**, or 'ones below') enjoy a mutual relationship with the **abaphilayo** ('those still living'). The ancestors look after and protect the living from harm and guide them through the traps and pitfalls of life. In return, the living are obliged to make regular offerings to the ancestors, setting aside a special pot of beer whenever beer is brewed and making sure that goats and/or cattle, depending on the wealth of the family, are offered at regular intervals at rituals known as **imisebenzi**.

> The relationship between the living and the spirit world is still very much in existence. Recognition of the **amadlozi** ('ancestors') is not just a matter for the rural, the elderly, or the illiterate: it is still a feature of the Zulu nation as a whole in the twenty-first century.

The spirits depend on those who follow to keep up these duties. For this reason, a man knows that his eventual existence as an **idlozi** ('ancestor') depends on him having sons who will fulfil their obligations at **imisebenzi**. Without sons, not only does the family line die, but the ancestors die with it. The family with the greatest number of sons is the one which will never die, and indeed we may find a fourth or a fifth son with the name **uMuzikawupheli** ('the family line will never end'). However, a man with a large number of sons, and few or no daughters, is very soon going to become extremely impoverished, because of the custom of **ilobolo**.

It is often believed that **ilobolo** (wrongly translated as 'bride-price') is paid by a husband-to-be to his prospective father-in-law. The transfer of cattle which still constitutes the major proportion of **ilobolo** is a lot more complicated than that. The standard number of cattle used to be eleven for commoners. Of this number, the young man about to wed would normally only be obliged to provide three or four, the balance being made up by his father, his father's brothers, and his own elder brothers. Of the eleven cows going to the clan of the bride, only three or four would go to the bride's father, the remainder would go to *his* brothers, uncles, and other male kin, in order to pay *them* back for similar assistance. This transfer of cattle is one from the male members of one clan collectively to the collective male members of another clan. No father minds contributing four or five cattle to the **ilobolo** of any of his sons, because he expects to get a similar number of cattle back when any of his daughters marry. What is important, of course, is that the number of sons and daughters balance. On the one hand, if there are too many sons, and few daughters, the family line will undoubtedly be safe, but the father's **isibaya** ('cattle kraal') will be empty. On the other hand, if a man has many daughters, and few or no sons, he will eventually become extremely rich in cattle, but there will be nobody to accord him status as an **idlozi** after his death.

Clearly, then, the ideal is a balance between sons and daughters in a family, and it is when this balance is upset that attention is drawn to the imbalance in the naming of the children.

a. Boys in the majority

Let us look first at a family where the majority of children are *boys*.

The name for a first son is often **uVusumuzi** ('wake up the family'), referring to the fact that this boy is the start of a new generation. The next son may be called **uMfanafuthi** ('another boy'), and the one after that perhaps **uMakhosonke** ('all chiefs'). Fourth and fifth boys have names such as **uMzwandile** ('the family has grown') and **uMzikawupheli** ('the family line will never end'). All these names are positive references to a family abundant with male offspring. However, as we noted above, a father is responsible for assisting his sons with their **ilobolo**, and it may be possible for the fifth or sixth boy in a row to receive a name such as **uNkomokazikho** ('there are no cattle'). I have collected a number of examples of this name over the years, and approximately one-third have referred to the number of boys in a family with few girls (the balance has referred to conditions of severe drought). I have also recorded the single name **uBhodlani** ('what is bellowing?'), a name whereby the father has asked the question 'what is bellowing in my cattle-kraal?', knowing full well that the answer is 'Nothing!', because all his cattle have gone to his sons for **ilobolo**.

b. Girls in the majority

Let us now look at the names in a family where *girls* predominate.

The name of the first girl will have no relevance here, but a second daughter in a row commonly receives the name **uNtombifuthi** ('another girl'). Third and fourth girls may receive names such as **uZandile** ('they [girls] have increased') or **uZiningi** ('they [girls] are many'). When the stage of five girls in a row has been reached, we may find names such as **uNtombizonke** ('they are all girls'), **uNtombizodwa** ('only girls'), or even the emphatic **uZanele** ('they are enough'). Occasionally we find the numerals 'three' and 'four' in girls' names: **uNtombizintathu** ('there are three girls') and **uNtombizine** ('there are four girls'). I have only ever found these two numerals, and only in girls' names.

A boy born after many girls may receive the name **uMfanufikile** ('a boy has arrived [at last!]'), or perhaps **uMuzikawukho** ('there is no family'), implying that the family line is in jeopardy. A girl born after many boys may likewise receive the name **uNtombifikile** ('a girl has arrived'), with, again, the implication of 'at last!', or she may receive the name **uZibuyile** ('they [cattle] have returned').

In families which believe that children are born as a result of the active interest of the family's ancestral spirits, the name **Thulani** ('be quiet') suggests 'Stop your activity – we have enough children now!'

c. Twins

The birth of twins is widely regarded in Africa as something special. In some societies twins used to be killed at birth; in others only one twin was killed; in others yet again twins are revered, and grow up with all the privileges of the priestly caste. To the best of my knowledge, the special position of twins is always reflected in the naming system of African societies. In many societies, the names of twins are 'standard' or 'inevitable' or 'automatic'.

Nsimbi (1950: 210) tells us that among the baGanda twins are automatically named **Wasma** (male) and **Babirye** (female) if the first-born twin, and **Kato** (male) and **Nakato** (female) if the second-born twin.

Twins' names in Zulu do not have a specific underlying meaning of 'twin' as is the case in other African societies, but nonetheless twins' names are marked. This is done by pairing them morphologically and semantically, that is to say they will have similar meanings and similar structures. The following pairs of twins are examples.

With **uNhlanhla** (boy: 'luck') and **uNonhlanhla** (girl: 'Miss luck'), both the names are based on the word for 'luck' and the girl's name has the female prefix **no-** in front. Often, when the twins are a boy and a girl, the girl's name will be based on a verb, and the boy's name on the noun that comes from that verb. This is the case for the following three pairs of twins:

- **uMthobisi** (boy: 'one who makes humble') and **uThobile** (girl: 'being humble');
- **Thabó** (boy: 'delight') and **uThabile** (girl: 'delighted');
- **uMduduzi** (boy: 'one who comforts'), with his sister **uDuduzile** ('being comforted').

In the next pair, the names are based on the word **umusa** ('mercy, grace'), the girl having the female prefix **no-**, while the boy's name adds 'His' in reference to God: **uNomusa** (girl: 'Miss grace') and **uMsawakhe** (boy: 'His grace').

The names of the twin brothers **uBongumusa** ('praise the grace [of God]') and **uBongisisa** ('praise [Him] greatly') are both based on the verb **bonga** ('give thanks, praise'), as are the names of the twin sisters **uBongiwe** ('being grateful') and **uSibongile** ('we are grateful'). The final example is also of twin sisters, and here the names are based on the noun **ilanga** ('day'): **uLang-elihle** (girl: 'beautiful day') and **uLangalenjabulo** (girl: 'day of joy').

In Zulu society, children born after twins do not receive special names, as is the case in many other African societies. For example, Nsimbi (1950: 210) tells us that among the baGanda children who follow twins are automatically named (in the following order): **Kiza**, **Kamya**, **Kagwa**, **Kityo**, and **Kotike** (or **Kiterera**). Even children who *precede* twins get a new name – **Kigongo** – which is added to or replaces the previous name.

Chuks-Orji (1972) gives names from the Yoruba, Ganda, Ga, Zaramo, Fante, Ewe and Twi peoples which mean, *inter alia*, 'the elder of twins', 'the younger of twins', 'a twin', 'one who produces twins', 'first child after twins', 'second child after twins', and '(any) child after twins'. Most of these have male and female forms.

Noting that among Chuks-Orji's examples are names which mean 'one who produces twins', we see that *parents* of twins, like the children who precede twins, may be re-named. Schapera (1926: 121) tells us that among the Herero people of Namibia, parents of twins discard their given names, and 'the father receives the new name of **Omupandje** and the mother that of **Onjambari**, i.e. "one who suckles two children".' Within Zulu society, the parents do not receive new names.

3.2.2 Names referring to the perceived role of God

Where some parents see the birth of children as activity by the family's ancestral spirits, others, more commonly, see the hand of God in the birth of a child. Indeed, a common boy's name is **uSandlasenkosi** ('the hand of God'). Girls' names do not use the word 'God' in the name, but refer obliquely to Him, as in: **uSibongile** ('we are grateful [to God]'), **uThandazile** ('having prayed [to God]'), and **uNomusa** ('the grace [of God]'). Boys' names may also refer obliquely to God as in **uMsawakhe** ('His grace'), **uSipho** ('gift [of God]') and **uSibusiso** ('[His] blessing'), but normally boys' names contain the lex-eme **inkosi** ('God'). The following are examples:

- **uNkosinomusa** ('the Lord has mercy');
- **uNkosinathi** ('the Lord is with us');
- **uNkosingiphile** ('God has given me');
- **uBhekinkosi** ('look to the Lord');
- **uBonginkosi** ('praise the Lord');
- **uThembinkosi** ('put your trust in God');
- **uNkosinamandla** ('the Lord has strength');
- **uMandlenkosi** ('strength of the Lord').

> The many English boys' names which begin with Jo- from the Hebrew *Jahveh* (God) – Joseph, Jonah, Joshua, Jonathan and Johannes – are all analogous to Zulu names containing the word **inkosi**. In the same way, **uNkosinomusa** ('the Lord has mercy') is analogous to the English Johannes (and, indeed, John, Jan, Sean, Ian, Jean, Giovanni, Juan, Evan, Ivan, etc.) from the Hebrew *io hanas*, 'Jah is gracious'. And, **uNkosingiphile** ('God has given me') relates to the English Jonathan from the Hebrew for 'Jah has given'.

It may be of interest to look at some of the explanations from parents as to why they chose God-related names. The explanations were taken directly from the parents in field interviews.

Of the name, **uNkosinathi** ('the Lord is with us'), the parents explained: 'We thought that we would never get another son, but after the birth of this boy we saw that the Lord was with us.' The mother of **uBhekinkosi** ('look to the Lord') said of this name, 'Three of my previous children were stillborn, so we looked to the Lord to see that this one would survive, and he did.' There is a similar explanation of the name **uNkosinamandla** ('the Lord has strength'): 'This child survived after two stillbirths. We said to ourselves "clearly the Lord has strength in giving us a child that survives".'

Stillbirths and difficult pregnancies clearly underlie a lot of God-based names, as the next two examples show. The father of **uCelukuphila** ('ask for health') explained the name with 'My wife was very ill during her pregnancy and so I asked the Lord to give her health', while the mother of **uThandazile** ('having prayed') said, 'I was so ill during my pregnancy that I prayed to God for recovery.'

The explanation of **uSithembiso** ('promise') was given as 'The Bible tells us that the Lord would promise anything asked in His name, and here is this son of ours.'

These names can be seen as both messages to God himself, as well as messages to the community, showing the community that their faith and belief in God has resulted in happy and healthy children.

3.2.3 Names referring to the 'state of mind' of the parents

Names referring to the 'state of mind' of the parents in the central reaches of Africa are frequently negative. Such names refer to the constant imminence of sorrow, death, poverty or misfortune. In societies which see frequent stillbirth, or loss of a child in its early years, as the jealousy of neighbours, co-wives, or ancestral spirits, it is not uncommon for the child to be given a name which means 'Who wants him?', 'Turn your back on him' or 'Cast him out'. Such names are meant to mislead the 'jealous powers' into thinking that it will be no harm to the parents to take the child away, as it is unwanted anyway. A variation of this thinking is seen when a far greater proportion of boy children are lost in birth or in their early days. In this case surviving male children will be given a girl's name, also in an attempt to mislead the jealous powers. Similarly, when many girl children have been lost, those that do survive may be given boys' names.

Mönnig explains the concept of spirit deception among the Pedi:

> Families who have had misfortune with previous children will treat a new child in a peculiar manner. Parents who have lost a few children will name a new-born daughter **Mosa** – son – while a son will be called **Ngwanenyana** – small daughter. They will also be clothed and treated as if they belong to the opposite sex. Mothers who have had a number of still-born children will give a child an unpleasant name. These children are treated as if they are unwanted. Their hair is dressed differently from other children, and they are mostly avoided. This is done to confuse the ancestral spirts into thinking that the parents do not care for them, and that taking them away will not further punish the parents (1967: 103).

Chuks-Orji talks of African names generally when he says (1972: 76): 'The first name given may be quite uncomplimentary, for instance "I am dead" or "I am ugly"; in this way it is hoped to avoid the jealousy of the ancestors who might wish to take back to themselves a child who is born especially healthy or goodlooking.' He makes it quite clear that this practice is not done because the parents hate or dislike the children. In fact, giving 'ugly' names is quite the opposite:

> And this love of children is universally to be observed in the names the children bear. Thus even the most uncomplimentary name **Chotsani** 'take it away' (Yao, Malawi) is not in fact an expression of rejection but rather an attempt by the family to conceal or disguise its joy so that the divinities or the ancestors will not take back the precious infant (Ibid.).

Such negative-state-of-mind names are extremely rare in Zulu society, although it is difficult to say whether or not these names were more common in previous times. In over 25 years of collecting Zulu names I have only come across three:

- **uMazaleni** ('on the rubbish heaps');
- **uThandwawubani** ('loved by who?');
- **uMzondeni** ('hate him').

Most parents give names which reflect their joy and happiness in children. Two very common names are **Jabulani** (boy: 'be happy') and **Thokozile** (girl: 'being happy'). Other examples are:

- **Mthandeni** (boy: 'love him');
- **Thandiwe** (girl: 'loved one');
- **Jabulisiwe** (girl: 'having been made happy');
- **Thabisile** (girl: 'having caused joy);
- **Ntokozo** (boy: 'joy');
- **Gugulethu** (girl: 'our treasure').

Parents also feel lucky that a child has been born successfully, and two very common names for boys and girls – **uNhlanhla** and **uNonhlanhla** respectively – are based on the noun **inhlanhla** ('luck'). A variation of this, for a boy, is **uMuziwenhlanhla** ('house of luck').

Parents may express the pride they feel in their beautiful children by giving a name such as **Gabisile** (girl: 'having expressed pride'). The verb **gabisa** is derived from the interjection **gabi**, usually repeated as **gabigabi**, meaning 'look what *I've* got!' Feelings of pride can be seen in the reasons fathers have given to explain their choice of name, rather than in the names themselves. For example, a father explained that he had chosen the name **Muzikayise** ('house of his father') for his fifth son, because 'this is truly a father's house – a *man*'s house – with five sons'. The father who named his third daughter **Nondumiso** (**no** + **indumiso**, 'fame') and another father who named *his* third daughter **Badumile** ('they are famous') both had the same reason, that they would become renowned for the beauty of their daughters.

Fathers (and mothers) can express their pride in beautiful daughters with names such as:

- **uNtombenhle** ('beautiful girl');
- **uMbalenhle** ('beautiful flower');
- **uMbali** ('flower');
- **uNobuhle** (**no** + **ubuhle**, 'beauty').

Most such 'descriptive' names are positive ones referring to beauty, but now and then one comes across names such as **uSalukazi** ('old woman', that is, born with many wrinkles) and the metaphorical **uBhotshwana** ('little cooking pot', in the mother's own words: 'fat, round and black').

Names for boys that I have collected include:

- **uMakhehlana** ('little old men', cf. **uSalukazi** above);
- **uMfanomkhulu** ('big boy', cf. **uNtombenkulu**, 'big girl');
- **uFanyana** ('little boy');
- **uMbuyiseni** ('bring him back'): the mother thought the child looked like his grandfather, and she had therefore 'brought him back' to life with this new baby.

Sometimes the parents are thinking to the future when they name a child. This is especially the case with 'injunction' names, where the name provides some kind of moral direction for the child. These are usually names given to boys, and a large proportion of them remind boys of their duties when they are grown. Many of these names are based on the verb **bheka** ('to have regard for', 'look to' , 'look after'), thus:

- **uBhekinkosi** ('look to the Lord');
- **uBhekuyise** ('look to the father' – either the father of the child, or the Father above);
- **uBhekabafowabo** ('look after the brothers');
- **uBhekamandlovu** ('have regard for the Ndlovu clan').

The following examples of injunction names are given with the parents' explanations:

- **uMlamuli** ('the mediator'): The mother said that in a family with so much friction, at least one person should grow up as a peace-maker.
- **uLindokuhle** ('wait for the good things'): The mother said that when this child had grown up they would expect good things from him.
- **uMuzikayise** ('house of his father'): The father wanted this first-born son to remember that he had to look after the family when he was grown.
- **uSibonelo** ('example'): The mother wanted this boy to be an example to others when he grew older.
- **uMkhumbuleni** ('remember him'): The child was asked to remember his grandfather when he grew up.

Sometimes these injunctions can be very practical, as in **uFunimali** ('seek money'), and both practical and highly individual, as in **uThengithilomu** ('buy a tea-room'), an injunction which has, of course, the same thinking as **uFunimali**.

I finish this section on the 'state of mind' of the parents with an example of a wonderfully relaxed and philosophical state of mind, reflected in the girl's name **uNomvelo** (**no** + **imvelo**, 'nature'). The father explained this name to me as follows: 'You take a girl from another clan, you marry her, a child is born, that's nature!'

3.2.4 Names referring to the circumstances of the birth

In a number of African societies, names refer to the circumstances under which the child was born. Such circumstances might refer to the physical birth itself: a breech presentation, a difficult labour, a caesarean birth, or something else unusual. The name may refer to problems that the mother had during pregnancy. Family circumstances may be referred to: problems in the marriage, unpaid 'bride-price', illegitimate birth, status of the child (especially in the family of a chief or king). The name may refer to something that happened at the time the child was born: the father was drunk, the neighbours were fighting, or even simply that it was raining when the child was born. Sometimes the circumstances belong to a wider arena than the immediate family or homestead. Names may refer to events of national importance: political elections or political coups, festivals, battles and wars, natural disasters such as floods and earthquakes. If the country is finally freed from an oppressor, whether a colonial power or a long-standing dictator, the children of the country will bear names that reflect this.

When South Africa held its first full and free elections in 1994, hundreds of children born at that time were named with the Zulu, Xhosa, Sotho and Venda words for 'freedom', 'election', 'power', and so on. Molema, writing as far back as 1920 about Southern Sotho personal names, states: 'Names of children were taken from events that were taking place about the time of their birth. Thus children born, say, during the South African War might be called Leburu (Boer), Nto (War), Maksone (Maxim), Kganelo (Siege), and so forth' (128).

Even space travel may be reflected in the names of children. Mönnig gives the example of a Pedi child named 'Sputnik', and one of my own examples from Zulu is of a child born in July 1969 named 'Armstrong', after Neil Armstrong. As my informant said: '**Le ngane yaqanjwa ngoArmstrong owaya enyangeni**' ('This child was named after Armstrong who went to the moon').

We can start here by looking at those names which refer to the actual birth itself. These references cannot be elucidated from the names, and we need to look at the reasons given by the mothers in explaining the choice of names:

- **uNomusa** (< **inkosi inomusa**, 'the Lord is merciful'): The mother explained that she was referring to God's help in a successful birth after she had been extremely ill during the last stage of pregnancy.
- **uBongekile** ('being grateful'): Again, the mother was grateful to God, having nearly died while giving birth. (Similar reasons have been found for the names **uBongani** ['be grateful'], **uSibongile** ['we are grateful'] and **uBonginkosi** ['thank the Lord'].)
- **uNomthandazo** (**no** + **umthandazo**, 'prayer'): The mother had been very ill just before the birth and had prayed to God to get better.
- **uSidumo** ('commotion'): The mother said that she had given birth prematurely on her way to Johannesburg because she had been involved in a fight.
- **uPhakamani** ('get up and go'): While the child was being born, some drunks in the road outside heard that a child was being born and loitered around. The mother shouted at them to go.

Sometimes the birth follows a long period of childlessness. Such long periods cause great distress to Zulu mothers for the charge of barrenness is an extremely serious one in Zulu society. In fact, in African society generally, with the need for future generations to look after the ancestors, barrenness is greatly dreaded. As Mönnig (1967: 98) says of the Pedi of the Northern Province: 'Barrenness is, perhaps, the most feared condition in the life of a woman, and affects not only herself, but also her family group which, against the protestations of her husband and his group, gave her to bear children for the husband's group.'

Madubuike (1976: 39) gives an example of a name given to a child after the mother had been accused of barrenness. The name is from the Igbo of Nigeria: '**Nwaiwu** (m) "born out of threats" – other women in the family taunted the woman with her inability to give birth to a . . . child, thereby reminding her that her married life was insecure.'

Ennis gives an example of a 'proverb-name' from the Mbundu people of Angola:

> **Esenje** – from the proverb '*Esenje liwa li mõlĩ ofule; onyima yiwa ka yi mõlĩ omõlã*' (A stone good not it sees a pounding of maize; a back good not it sees a child.). Here is a ledge of rock that would make an excellent place to pound meal and it has never been used! Here is a back just right for carrying a baby and it has none! This is the lament of a childless woman, and a general comment on the way affairs turn out (1945: 3).

The following are examples from Zulu, with the parents' comments explaining the names:

- **uSindisiwe** (girl: 'having been saved'): The father and the mother have been saved from the prospect of eternal childlessness after eight years of it.
- **uThembelihle** (girl: 'lovely hope'): The mother had hoped for a child even though everybody had said that she was barren.
- **uSiphamandla** (boy: 'give us strength'): After having waited for six years for a child, the parents eventually asked the Lord to give them strength.
- **uMduduzi** (boy: 'the comforter'): 'What a comfort to finally have a child after everybody has been telling me that I am barren!'
- **uPhumzile** (girl: < **ungiphumuzile**, 'she has made me rest'): The mother explained that this child had given her rest from her anxieties about barrenness.

Even second children may be given names that refer to barrenness, as in the case I recorded of a second daughter named **uThulile** ('being quiet'): people had previously said of the mother that she was barren, but they were quiet now that she had produced this second child.

The circumstances of the birth may also relate to the father of the child, and the following are examples, again with the parents' explanations of why the name was chosen:

- **uTshani** (boy: 'grass'): The father explained that at the time of the birth he had got lost in some long grass. I am as intrigued by this explanation today as I write this, as I was 15 years ago when I collected the name and its explanation.
- **uMboneni** (boy: 'see him'): This name, given by the mother, refers to her suspicion that the father would probably never be seen again.

- **uMdingi** (boy: 'the needy one'): The father had need of money at the time of the child's birth.
- **uBonisiwe** (girl: 'having been revealed'): The father said that his daughter had been revealed to him in a dream shortly before the birth.
- **uMthetho** (boy: 'law'): The father had been working for a magistrate at the time of the child's birth.
- **Khethani** (boy: 'choose'): At the time of the child's birth, the father had been **induna** ('headman', 'foreman') at a farm when a sheep was lost. He was accused and the magistrate had found him guilty and had told him to *choose* between jail or a fine. The incident was clearly still fresh in his mind.

Often the parents see the birth of the child as marking some sort of progress in their lives, and this may be reflected in the name, as the following examples show:

- **uQhubekile** (girl: 'having progressed'): The father thought he and his wife had progressed in life by having a child.
- **uZwelibanzi** (boy: 'the country is wide'): The mother gave the name when the child was born after they had moved from Matatiele to Pietermaritzburg, a move which the mother thought of as progress in life.
- **uGamelihle** (girl: 'nice name'): The father thought that because of the birth of this child, he had advanced in honour and status in life; in other words, he had a 'nice name' in society.
- **uZakhele** (boy: 'having built for yourself'): The father had just built a house, and the child's birth marked this stage of the family's progress.
- **Badumile** (girl: 'they are well-known'): Both parents were proud of the progress they had made in life: although they had only been married for a very short time, they already had many friends and were well known in the area where they lived.
- **Sakhile** (boy: 'we have built'): The mother explained that they have now indeed 'built on a firm foundation', and that with three children they would never get divorced.
- **uMkhanyiselwa** (boy: 'the one for whom things shine'): When the child was born, the parents were granted a long-awaited building site, and 'it shone in the mother's mind' that this child brought its own luck.

a. Rain names

In Africa, rain is not predictable, and in many parts of Africa, months will go by without any rain. When rain finally does come, there is great joy, for rain is life. Personal names in Africa reflect social values and issues of importance to society, and so we find the importance of rain reflected in personal names.

'Rain names' from Africa include the following: from the Abaluhya of Uganda, the girl's name **Nafula** and the boy's name **Wafula**, both meaning 'born during rainy season'; from Somalia the boy's name **Roble** and the girl's name **Roblai**, both meaning 'the one who brings rain'; from Swahili comes the girl's name **Masika** ('born during rainy season') and from the Waputsi of Uganda comes **Mirumbi**, a boy's name meaning 'born when it was raining'. The name **Mamvura**, a Zezuru name from Zimbabwe, simply means 'rain', as does **Mvula**, which is both an Ngoni name from Malawi and a Luba name from South-East Zaire.

Xhosa and Zulu prefix the feminine marker **-no-** to **imvula** ('rain') to make the common girl's name **Nomvula**. Much less common is the boy's name **Mvuleni** ('in the rain').

Both the 'girls' in my family are 'children of the rain': because of an unseasonable downpour on our wedding day, my wife was immediately given the name **Nomvula** by the Zulu guests present, and as my daughter was born in the middle of six consecutive days of rain, she also received the name **Nomvula**.

Rain can be found in Zulu clan-names and clan-praises as well. An obvious example is the clan name Mkhize ('drizzle'). Bryant states of the Mzolo clan: 'They acquired considerable fame as rain-doctors; but this renown was largely due to the pluvial miracles wrought by a member of the tribe named Gasa' (1929: 358).

Even today the clan praises of the Mzolo people include the line **Wena kaGasa! Mnisi wemvula!** ('Son of Gasa! Bringer of rain!').

b. Days-of-the-week or market-day names

In certain African societies, but especially in West African countries such as Nigeria and Ghana, if the child is born on a certain market-day or day of the week, it may be given a name which reflects this. In the Cameroons, certain days are designated market days for whatever fruit or other product is in season. Thus at certain times of the year there will be regular market days for yams, palm-nut oil and dried fish, and at other times of the year for bananas and groundnuts. If a child is born on one of these regular market days, he or she may well be named 'Groundnut' or 'Dried Fish'.

In Ghana, the day-of-the week name is pre-eminent. In a personal communication on 11 June 1999 Bediako explained that the **kra din** (the 'soul') is the name the child is born with, and the name depends on which day of the week the child was born. This is not a 'given' name, but the name with which you come into the world, hence 'soul' name. Bediako pointed out that the **kra din** or 'soul name' may be used by anyone in society and is therefore the name by which that person is best known, whereas the **ofie din** ('family name') is only for use in the immediate family, and not for 'outside'.

'Day-of-the-week' names are not common in the more southern parts of Africa, and only occasionally does one come across names such as the Xhosa girl's name **Nogcawe** and the Zulu girl's name **Nomasonto**, both of which mean 'born on a Sunday'.

3.2.5 Names referring to the wider clan

a. Boys' names

The name **uVusumuzi** ('wake up the family') has already been mentioned on page 36 above. This name refers to the potential of the first-born son to 'revive the family line' or 'to start a new generation'. Names may include the elements **izwe** or **isizwe** with the meaning 'clan' (although normally the meaning would be 'country' or 'nation'), as in the following two examples: **uPhasizwe** ('support the clan'), where the father had said '**Sesiliphasile izwe, MaXimba**' ('We have supported the clan, Ximba people'), a reference to the adding of a male child to the small AmaXimba clan. In **uZwelibuyile** ('the clan has returned'), again mention is made of a boy to swell the clan numbers. With a small clan, a father might be worried that even though he is adding male children to the clan numbers, they are still few. This is the case with the name **uSikhosiphi** which was explained by the father as being derived from '**Sikhona silaphi?**' ('We are here [but] being where?'), in other words 'even though we now have this second son, we of the Sosibo clan are not many'.

References to the ancestral spirits (**amadlozi**) are frequently found in boys' names, and the following are examples, with the parents' explanations being given:

- **uPhumlani** ('you should all rest now'): In this name, the mother addresses the ancestors, telling them to rest after all their activity in creating this child.
- **uThulani** ('all be quiet'): Again, the ancestors are seen as the creators of children, and in this name the father asks them to quieten their activities, as this is now the fifth child. In another **uThulani**, the father is saying to his own family 'Be quiet now! You have been complaining that I took a girl from far away, but now we have given you and the clan a son.'
- **uMbongeni** ('be grateful to him'): Here the father expressed thanks to his own father (now deceased and therefore an ancestor) for giving him children so quickly.
- **uMkhumbuleni** ('remember him'): The father said that they should all remember the child's grandfather because this boy looked so like him. In similar vein is: **uMbuyiseni** ('bring him back'): the father said the child looked so much like his (recently deceased) grandfather that they immediately held an **ukubuyisa** ceremony to bring back the grandfather's spirit.
- **uMxolisi** ('the apologiser'): The parents had had some difficulty in getting a child. In this name the father apologises to his own (deceased) father for the delay.

Details of the **ukubuyisa** ('to bring back') ceremony are provided in Chapter 5 on pages 84 to 85.

b. Girls' names

Girls' names refer to marriage between clans and commonly to **ilobolo**, the exchange of cattle between clans which cements a marriage. As has been explained above, a father is responsible for some of his own sons' **ilobolo**, and therefore he sees cattle which come to him as part of his daughters' **ilobolo** as *returning* (even if they are not the same cattle). For this reason, many girls' names under this heading are based on the verb **buya** ('to return') and the commonest name is **uZibuyile** ('they have returned') where **zi-** refers to **izinkomo** ('cattle'). Variations that I have found include **uBuyiswa** ('being returned') and **Mabuyi** ('Miss returner').

Fathers who name their daughters in terms of their 'cattle-value' express delight and happiness. We find the father who gave his daughter the two names **uGugu** ('little treasure') and **uZandile** ('they [cattle] have increased'), saying that his daughter was his 'little treasure' because she would bring him many cattle. The father who named his daughter **uThokozani** ('be happy') said that he was very happy, because as this was his second daughter, the cattle he had given as part of his wife's **ilobolo** would now be coming back two-fold. The names **uNonhlanhla** ('luck') and **uSibongile** ('we are grateful') were in two instances recorded from fathers who wanted to express their feelings of luck and gratitude for 'cattle-bearing daughters'.

By contrast, mothers who refer to **ilobolo** when naming their children usually do *not* express their happiness at the thought of all the cattle that are going to flood the **isibaya**, but rather are making a reference to the husband's **ilobolo** payments. The following three are all based on the verb **themba** ('trust', 'hope') and all refer to the husband having fulfilled his promise of completing the **ilobolo** payments before the birth of the child:

- **uSithembiso** ('promise');
- **uThembisile** ('having promised');
- **uThembekile** ('being trustworthy').

I found one particularly interesting name which referred to a daughter's potential for **ilobolo** – the name **uVuthelwaphi**, which literally means 'where will she become ripe?'. The father explained that the child had been born before marriage, and that in such cases, unless the father subsequently pays **ilobolo** and then marries the mother, the child is considered as belonging to the mother's family, and any cattle which may accrue from the child's eventual marriage would go to them. At the time of the child's birth he had not yet made up his mind whether or not he wished to marry the child's mother, and so he was not sure 'where she would ripen', that is, where she would bear fruit in the shape of **ilobolo**.

Clans may be mentioned by name in the personal names of boys, usually after the verb **bheka** ('have regard for', 'look after'), for example:

- **uBhekamandlovu** ('look up to the **Ndlovus**');
- **uBhekamantungwa** ('look to the **Mntungwas**', that is, the **Khumalos**);
- **uBhekabasembo** ('look to those from eMboland', that is, the **Mkhize** clan).

I have not personally recorded any girls' names which specifically mention a clan, but the poet B.W. Vilakazi, in a poem entitled '**Sengiyakholwa**' ('Now I do believe') mentions the name **uNomasomi** (**no** + **AmaSomi**, the plural form of the clan name **Msomi**).

3.2.6 Other or miscellaneous

Some of the names I include under this category have 'explanations' which are confusing or unclear. Others are clear enough, but do not seem to fit into any of the categories already discussed.

Confusing names and explanations include the following:

- **uNomonde** (girl: < Xhosa, 'perseverance'): The grandmother said that this was a suitable name for her illegitimate grandchild.
- **uThulasizwe** (boy: 'be quiet so that we can hear'): The mother explained that the father had given this name to mean 'be quiet you Ximba people so that we can hear what Charlie is saying'. However, I do not know who Charlie was, and why what he had to say was so important.
- **uSigomfana** (boy: 'strong, illicit alcohol'): The father explained that it was time to go and drink some **isigomfana**.
- **uNhlayenza** (boy: meaning obscure): The father said that 'sometimes something just happens'.
- **uKhethani** (boy: 'choose'): The father said that as the mother of the child was his first wife, she could choose where she wanted to go and live.

Reasonably clear explanations that do not fit into other categories include:

- **uMlungisi** (boy: 'arranger'): The mother had arranged the wedding all by herself.
- **uNomkhosi** (girl: **no** + **umkhosi**, 'celebration'): The mother held a grand celebration when the child was born.
- **uThobile** (girl: 'being humble'): The father said he felt humbled by his daughter's birth.
- **uDumazile** (girl: 'being disappointed): In naming this girl, the grandmother indicated her disappointment in the illegitimate birth.

I end this chapter on the reasons why parents name their children with two rather unusual names. The first name is **uMantoza**, a name for which I can find no meaning, and indeed the mother explained that she had chosen a meaningless name simply because she liked the sound of the word. This was the only single case I came across where a parent said that a name had no meaning, and that it had only been chosen for the sound.

The second name comes from a father who had had only male children, and named his seventh and last son **uMbizeni** ('[what shall I] call him?'). He explained that after naming six previous sons, he had 'now run out of names'.

Chapter 4

Nicknames and personal praises

4.1 INTRODUCTION

We have already noted that the term 'nickname' is derived from the earlier form 'an eke name' where 'eke' is the archaic form of 'also', 'moreover'. In terms of its etymology, then, a nickname is an 'also name' or 'extra name', a name additional to a person's formal given name (although we did note that nicknames are also 'given' names). As we saw earlier, nicknames tend to be 'unofficial' and are seldom recorded on an individual's official documents, such as birth certificates, school certificates, drivers' licences, and so on. This is despite the fact that an individual may be known by his or her nick-name/s from an early age until death.

Chambers English Dictionary includes in its meaning of 'nickname', 'a shortened or familiar form of a person's name', giving the example of *Joe* < *Joseph*, but I see this as inconsistent with the etymology of the word: if a person's name is 'Joseph', 'Joe' is not an *extra* name, but a *variation.*

The term 'nickname' overlaps to a great degree with the term 'praise name' which is very much an element of African panegyric, or 'praise poetry'. Opland has stated:

> Among the Xhosa (as amongst the Zulu), names constitute the structural core of *izibongo* . . . These names enjoy an independent currency in society, operating as modes of address or reference, or as honorific salutations. To form an *izibongo*, a sequence of names may be strung together to refer to one individual; a genealogical series of names comprises the poem of a lineage; and clan poems consist collectively of the names of distant ancestors of the clan. Each of these names may be extended by a brief explanation or qualification, so that they become lines or verses, and these verses in turn may be expanded by means of a limited set of traditional devices into a succession of lines that constitute units that may be called stanzas (1990: 242).

A collection of the personal praises of men, women and children can be found in Gunner and Gwala (1994).

When praise names are single words, it is easy to regard the terms 'nickname' and 'praise name' as synonymous. When a young man whose given names are Vusumuzi Aaron is referred to by his peers as **uHushamoya** ('Mr Rustle-of-the-Wind') because of his light, airy grace when dancing, then most onomastics scholars would be happy to call this a 'nickname'. Even if the name is two words, for example **uNsimbi kayigobi** ('Mr Iron-does-not-bend' – a steadfast fighter), or as in the 'boxing names' of various well-known boxers – 'Green Cobra', 'Dancing Shoes', 'Baby Jake', even these would normally be regarded as nicknames. Once the name becomes an extended phrase, for example, the well-known **uNcwincwi ephuza kwezokude iziziba** ('Honey-sucker that drinks at distant pools' – a youth with many girlfriends whom he prudently keeps apart), then some scholars might start wondering about nickname status.

An important difference between the nickname as a Euro-Western onomastic unit and praises as African literary units lies in the usage. In a number of African societies, and certainly in Zulu society, certain social activities are accompanied by the reciting of praises. When a group of men go out hunting the animal to be hunted may be praised as may any of the hunters or even their dogs. When a group of young men compete in the highly athletic **giya** dance, or when they fight with sticks, the dancers and fighters will be encouraged by the enthusiastic recitation of their praises.

So a young man engaged in a stick fight might well be encouraged with '**uNtandukubukwa! Wayebukisa ngezinye izinsizwa izishaye ngenduku zibe ngozi ngozi zibhaleke amakhanda, kwaze kwathiwa ngumabhala ngozipho!**' ('Mr Likes-to-be-looked-at! He who shows off in front of other young men and hits them with a stick [until] they become wounded with scratches on the head, until it is said that he is marked with the scratches of finger-nails.') These praises will not, however, be used in full when the young man is simply being greeted. In such a case, only a key word from the praises, usually the first word, would be used, thus: '**Sawubona Ntandukubukwa!**' ('Greetings, Ntandukubukwa.') Here we could say that the nickname comes from the person's praises.

Molefe, in his very comprehensive study of Zulu nicknames (2000: 84f.), puts such nicknames under the heading 'Nicknames Derived from Praises', and the following two examples are taken from him:

Example 1

Thokozani Nene of Ukhozi radio station is nicknamed **uGxabalembadada uManyathela** ('the old sandal which steps on anything') from his praises:

uGxabalembadada uManyathela
The old sandal which steps on anything.
Untombi zimcel' ukhisi nom' ejahile.
Girls plead for his kiss even when he is in a hurry.

Molefe also tells us that Mr Nene had the additional nickname **uBhukuda-kwesinezingwenya** ('he who swims in crocodile-infested waters'): 'the nickname refers to the tough times he had when he was working for the South African Broadcasting Company during the years 1940 and 1960'.

Example 2
The nickname **uNdukuzephukile** ('the sticks are broken') came from an incident in a famous stick fight, graphically described in the full praises:

Kwakusuk' uthuli lwezinkunzi
The bulls raised dust
Igadla kugadl' enye kunuka
Each attacking the other [until] there came a smell
Uthuvi lwenyoni yegceke
As of poultry dung
Kubamben' inkunzi kaMakhaye
The bull of Makhaye was fighting with
Nenxahi lasemambukeni
A foreign castrated bull
Zaya zephuk' ezikaMakhaye
And then those [sticks] of Makhaye went and broke
Kwavalw' amehlo kuz' imbuka.
Eyes were closed as the foreign one approached.

'As of poultry dung' suggests that this fight between two humans was as fierce as that between two roosters.

We see here that the actual nickname – **uNdukuzephukile** – does not appear as such in the praises of this person. Rather the nickname is a summary of the praises, or the core idea. We will look at further examples from Molefe's collection later in this chapter.

Material collected in the early 1980s in the peri-urban areas around Pietermaritzburg was the basis of a previous study of personal praises or nicknames, published as 'The Praises of Young Zulu Men' (Koopman, 1987b). In that article I divided my examples according to the particular social milieu in which they were coined and used. The following section, a shorter version of the article mentioned above, gives some of the examples of each category.

> Bryant's historical findings have recently come under much criticism. However, there has been no fault found with his anthropological/ethnographic work, which is the nature of the material being utilised in the pages of this book.

4.2 THE PRAISES OF YOUNG ZULU MEN

Bryant says of young Zulu men:

> But not even yet have we reached the end of the Zulu name scheme . . . the Zulu man dearly loved both praise and admiration, and so, to the preceding [birth names], 'praise-names' and other such now became added. When now at length the babe . . . had grown into a brave and handsome youth, he was wont to flatter him[self], or more commonly be flattered by his companions, with some brand-new 'fancy name' (*isitopo*), usually one of adulation, by which name, among his set, he henceforth was generally called, instead of by his birth name (1949: 434).

> The term **isitopo**, with the modern spelling **isithopho**, can be found in Doke and Vilakazi's *Zulu-English Dictionary*, with the meaning 'praise-name', 'pet name', 'term of endearment', but it is not in regular usage today.

Note that Bryant says '*usually* one of adulation', implying that sometimes these 'praise-names' were actually critical. This is correct, as is the case with nicknames generally. Although praise-names generally focus on the more positive attributes of an individual, they may also be biting, sarcastic, and even cruel. Note also that Bryant allows for 'self-praising', and indeed this is common. Finnegan is talking of African youth in general when she writes: 'Self-praises, created and performed by the subject himself, are not uncommon. Among the Sotho, all individuals (or all men) are expected to have some skill in the composition and performance of self-praises . . .' (1970: 116).

I found that my collection of personal praises fell into the following categories, according to the activities they are associated with:

1. Courting praises (**izibongo zokushela**);
2. Dancing praises (**izibongo zokugiya**);
3. Fighting praises (**izibongo zokulwa**);
4. Descriptive praises (for which there is no appropriate Zulu term);

5. Football praises (**izibongo zebhola**);
6. Boxing praises (**izibongo zesibhakela**).

Courting praises and descriptive praises are found in both urban and rural communities; dancing praises and (stick)-fighting praises occur mainly in rural areas; and football and boxing praises feature mainly in urban areas.

4.2.1 Courting praises

> As a result of the AIDS pandemic, it seems likely that the attitude towards sexual responsibility that emerges in some of these courting praises could undergo change over time.

Courting praises refer to one's love of girls (and vice versa), enthusiasm for courting as a social activity, methods used in courting, and so on. Central to the concept of courting is the word **isoka**, with no direct translation into English, but with the rough meaning of 'lover boy', 'Don Juan', and 'Romeo'. The word **isoka** itself is often a base for courting praises as in **uSoka-lezintombi** ('lover of girls'), and **uMasokawoshi**, which, again, is difficult to translate, but could be rendered as 'As for lovers? – Oh my!' or perhaps 'Has he girlfriends? – Say no more!'

An **isoka** has (or believes he has) qualities which attract girls to him, as in the following two praises:

- **Unqwaze lwensizwa, isoka lezintombi, umamalisa ulimi intombi imama-theke** ('tall, robust young man, lover of the girls, he softens his speech – and the girl smiles');
- **iBhunu! Umhlophe wensizwa, ilanga elixhopha abesifazane** ('White man! [< *Boer*] White young man, the sun which dazzles the women-folk' – this is a reference to a light-coloured skin, which is often considered very attractive).

Praises referring to numbers of girlfriends include **uNogwaja ozikhundla-khundla** ('Mr Rabbit who is many holes'), and **uNcwincwi ephuza kwezo-kude iziziba** ('Honey-sucker bird which drinks at distant pools'), with its suggestion that a young man with a number of girlfriends simultaneously is wise to keep them apart. These last two praises belong to a 'common stock', that is to say they can be found again and again all over KwaZulu-Natal and have been in use for many generations. A similar 'stock phrase' is **Izintombi zimcel' ukhis' engafuni** ('girls ask him for a kiss even when he is unwilling'), and we saw this phrase above as part of the praises of Mr Thokozani Nene. Another praise which suggests success in attracting girls is **uGandaganda eMasondosondo abanye** ('Mr Tractor being wheels-wheels the others'), which was explained to me as 'Just as a tractor can ride over anything with its huge wheels, so I can get any girl I want'.

In contrast to the three praises above which suggest 'the more girlfriends the better', the following suggests someone who is very fussy about whom he courts, not just accepting any girl: **uGalela besikiza, ikhekhe elidliwa izinjinga, ngoba izichaka ziyalibalekela** ('Mr Strike-one-blow [where] others [merely] feint; Cake which is eaten by the rich, because the poor run away from it').

A praise which suggests a courting technique is the one-word praise **uMduze** (< **eduze**, 'nearby', 'close by'), given to him by friends in reference to his invariable habit of saying 'Come closer, baby' to any girl he met. And my final example of a courting praise is the single word **uBhasikidi** ('basket'), which is the head-word of the jocular expression **Nongenabhasikidi angaya emakhethe** ('even he without a basket can go to market'), itself a parody of the proverb **Nongenankomo angashela izintombi** ('even he without a cow [for ilobolo purposes] can court girls'). In other words, **uBhasikidi** is the courting praise or nickname of a youth who does not take courting seriously and is certainly not looking for marriage.

4.2.2 Dancing praises

Dancing praises refer to any special mannerisms during the high-kicking individual performance **ukugiya** dance, especially agility of foot movements, and speed of movement. The high-kicking characteristic of **ukugiya** dancing is reflected in the often-used image of a hoe used in agriculture, as in **uGeja likaMamphendu** ('the hoe of Mrs Turn-it-over'), and in **uMagejageja** ('[movement of] many hoes').

Light, delicate movements, as well as speed, are suggested in **uHushumoya** ('rustle of the wind') and frenetic, exuberant dancing is expressed in **uKhuzuhlanya** ('stop the madman'). The praise **uMvemve ongcokazi** ('red-and-white-speckled wagtail') refers to both movement and attire, with 'wagtail' suggesting abrupt, jerky movements, while **ongcokazi** refers to a shield made from the hide of a red-and-white-speckled beast. A very particular mannerism is referred to in **uQhud' elintam'ende ebone ngale kwentaba** ('rooster with very long neck looking way over there at the mountain') which tells of a man who has the habit of dancing with his head well back as if looking up at a mountain.

4.2.3 Fighting praises

These praises refer to skill and ability in formal stick-fighting competitions, and the will to fight or defend oneself. If courting praises are based on the qualities of **ubusoka**, then fighting praises depend on **ubuqhawe** ('manliness, fearlessness, enthusiasm, courage'). Some of the praises included under this heading are clearly not self-conferred, as they refer to the opposite qualities of timidity and cowardice.

Like most other praises, fighting praises range from single words to extended phrases. Examples of single-word praises are:

- **uMpimpiyana** ('little battle-battle');
- **uQathimpi** ('crunch-fight');
- **uMpisikazimudli** ('[even] the hyenas cannot eat him').

Two word praises include:

- **uNgquluzana beyiqhubisa** ('starer-out [until] they carry it [the fight] forward');
- **uSosha elizikhuzayo** ('soldier who commands himself');
- **uNsimbi kayigobi** ('Mr-Iron doesn't bend').

Examples of more extended praises are:

- **uBantu bayazigingqa embuba** ('people roll around in a confined space' – that is, there is no escaping this one when he wants to fight);
- **uBalekani magwala nali iqhawe** ('run away, cowards, here is a hero');
- **uMehlabovu okubheka maqede ushaywe uvalo** (' red [that is, angry] eyes which as soon as you look at them you are struck by fear').

The common use of an initial metaphor can be seen in the following praise, suggesting a large, well-built youth who will only bother with worthy opponents: **uNdlovu! uMagawula umuthi omkhulu ngoba omncane uyaziwela nje** ('Elephant! Mr Chop down a big tree because a small one will simply fall by itself'). One who meets his opponents face to face and thoroughly defeats them is seen in **uManqwamana nenja kwafa ikati** ('He who meets face to face with a dog and there dies a cat'). Stick-*throwing*, rather than stick-*fighting*, is referred to in **uJikijela abhuxeke isigodo esimaholo** ('He [who] throws and sticks into the ground [even] a rough-barked pole').

Praises, as I have said above, are not *always* flattering. They may imply criticism, or even be insulting, as in the following praise, which is clearly not self-conferred: **uGadluthithiza nje, awuliboni yini ikhanda, ufuze ekhaya bonyoko yini? Wagadlela enxenye mfoko MaNene** ('Mr Strike-merely-a-confused-blow, do you not see it, the head, that you should resemble [those] at the home of your mothers? He struck a blow on one side [that is, he missed] this worthless fellow of MaNene').

> **Bonyoko** is an insulting term for 'your mother'.

The same kind of inability to fight can also be expressed in one word: **uNdidiza** ('Mr Act-confusedly'). Cowardice is clearly expressed in **uMaqaba ngejubane ngoba kusinda ezakwaGwala** ('Depender of speed, because those that run away are from the house of Mr Coward').

4.2.4 Descriptive praises

These are praises which either (commonly) describe the appearance of the bearer (for example, height, skin colour, flashing eyes, etc.) or (less commonly) describe his personality. Praises which refer to height include:

- **uMuntumude akaliboni izulu** ('tall person, he doesn't see the sky');
- **Yinde lenyoni ayiboni kaZulu** ('it is tall, this bird, and doesn't see the sky' – here the word for 'sky', **izulu**, has been personified to **kaZulu**);
- **iSukile lendoda** ('he has got up, this man');
- **uJojo** ('long, pointed object');
- **uPhondo lwendod' ende ebamba izulu** ('horn of a tall man that grasps the sky').

Height that is attractive to girls is found in the following praise, which uses the image of a tree: **uMthunzi wokuphumula amatshitshi** ('shade where young maidens rest').

At the other end of the spectrum are praises that refer to shortness of stature, as in **uShort Division isibalo sabantwana** ('Short Division is the arithmetical problem of young children').

References to dark skin are common, such as **uNdod' emnyama** ('dark-skinned man'), and with light and dark contrast: **uNsizwa emnyama ekhanya ngamazinyo** ('dark-skinned youth with shining teeth'). **uZululiyaduma** ('the sky thunders') may suggest a bad temper, but in the words of the respondent: 'When the sky starts to thunder the clouds become black, and they liken him to the clouds.' **uSteelwool** refers to a man with a thick beard covering the face, while **uMkhaba womfazi omitha amawele** ('large stomach of a woman pregnant with twins') refers, of course, to a person with a very large stomach. I was told that whenever this man was drinking with his friends, they would tease him by saying **Mkhabó** ('Paunchy') every time a new round was put on the table.

> This form of the word **Mkhabó**, with its two syllables, and a high tone on a final vowel /o/, is characteristic of endearments to little children. See Chapter 2, page 27.

Descriptive phrases which refer to character are less common, and the following four are the only examples I have:

- **uEnglishman** refers to a man who only spoke English in his classroom and refused to use Zulu when teaching;
- **uCharlie Chaplin** is the nickname of a man who always liked making people laugh;
- **uJuba** ('dove') was given to a man 'because he is merciful';
- **uMpangele ekhala igijima** ('guinea-fowl which sings as it runs') for a man who habitually sang as he went around.

4.2.5 Football praises

Football praises usually (but not always) refer to ability and general performance on the field. With emphasis on speed and agile footwork, such praises are similar to **giya**-praises. The following are examples of performance praises:

- **Shaluza wemfana!** ('keep on the move there, boy!');
- **Shelela** ('slip out of the way');
- **uMshini ozishintshayo** ('machine that changes them [feet] about');
- **uAutomatic! uMshini ozishintshayo! uMadolo enkonyane!** ('Automatic! Machine that changes them about! Knees of the calf!').

Praises often take the form of an extended metaphor and football praises are no exception. The hawk is a successful metaphor for the tackling of another player and taking the ball away from him in **uKhozi olumaphiko olucosha ichwane ngokuphazima kweso** ('wingéd hawk that snatches up a chick in the blink of an eye').

The following two praises belong to one person. The first, given by his grandfather, refers to general ability and agility, and are used in open context. The second, given by his football friends, refers to specific ability on the soccer field, and the praises are only used there:

- **uS'hozi sezulu esethe singabonakala sabangwa ngabakhulu** ('lightning-bolt of the sky, which, as soon as it is seen, draws the attention of the great ones');
- **uMandize ondizele phezu kwezihlwele zahlokoma, ngobuncweti bobu-hlakanipha bakhe** ('flyer who flies above the crowds to their applause, on account of the expertness of his technique').

The image of the bird is similar to the 'wingéd hawk' mentioned above, and ties in well with the image of the lightning bolt. In both praises he is 'above' other people, that is, superior.

The following football praises are in English:

- **uDoctor Moroka**: 'Doctor' here is in the sense of **inyanga**, the Zulu herbalist who has power over others; the term is also used in the sense of 'one who excels'. 'Moroka' refers to the football team 'Moroka Swallows'.
- **uAction Man**, **uDirty Wizard** and **uFour-Man-Power** speak for themselves;
- **uDinga-Baby-put-it-in-the-way**: Here it is not clear whether 'Dinga-Baby' should put his foot in the opponent's way, or the ball in the way of the goal.
- **uAlleluia Amen!** is clearly a praise, but perhaps not in the same sense in which I have been using the word. It suggests an air of triumph and finality as the ball goes into the goal.

4.2.6 Boxing praises

Boxing praises are similar to the football praises **uAction Man** and **uDirty Wizard** mentioned above: they are mostly two-word phrases in English. The following are examples that I have collected:

- **uGoat-in-a-gate** (jumping around the ring?);
- **uGreen Cobra** (obviously a fast striker);
- **uWindmill** (flailing his arms about?);
- **uWalk Tall**;
- **uHappy Boy**;
- **uGolden Boy**;
- **uFive Star Man**;
- **uBaby Lux**;
- **uBaby Jake**;
- **uFighting Prince**;
- **uDancing Shoes**;
- **uThe Hammer**;
- **uBlue Angel**;
- **uYoung Destroyer**;
- **uSkeleton**;
- **uPlayboy**.

The best-known boxer of the 1990s was Dingaan Thobela, nicknamed the 'Rose of Soweto'. Sometimes a boxer may have more than one nickname. A famous boxer in the 1960s was known as **Elijah J. 'One-Hundred-Percent' 'Tap-tap' Makhathini**.

4.3 NICKNAMES FROM MOLEFE'S COLLECTION

Lawrence Molefe has made a solid contribution to the study of Zulu praise names with his 1992 Masters dissertation on the praises of domestic animals, to which was added in 2000 an exhaustive doctoral thesis on Zulu nicknames. The following are some of the more interesting examples from his extensive collection, starting with some nicknames referring to physical characteristics.

uNgangozipho ('as big as a fingernail') is a nickname for a very small person, while **uMbamboziyabalwa** ('ribs are counted') refers to an abnormally thin person. A very thin person whose legs seem to be all knees was given the nickname **uMadolodolo** ('knees-knees'). Three nicknames referring to individuals with large paunchy stomachs are:

- **uSiswanasophuthu** ('little putu-stomach': in fact someone with a very large stomach – **uphuthu** is maize-meal porridge);
- **uMguzuwesisu** ('beer-pot of a stomach');
- **uSisusesele** ('frog-stomach').

uKhandambili ('two-head') and **uMakhandakhanda** ('heads-heads') were both nicknames coined for people with very large heads.

uBhavelimboqo ('bent washbasin') refers to a veteran who has taken many knocks in life.

One of Molefe's examples of football praises is **Yabhal' icomputer** ('the computer wrote'): 'he controls the ball with the speed usually associated with computers printing'.

A Maskandi musician – one who accompanies his own singing of praises on the guitar or another instrument – was given the nickname **uNami-Nawe-Dali** ('you and I, darling') because of his car licence plate NND (from the Nongoma district). I collected a similar nickname in the early 1970s: a man nicknamed **uNawe-futhi** ('and you too'), from the licence plate of his car: NU2.

Two nicknames referring to character types are **uSinqekasikho** ('has no buttocks'), for a person who never sits down and – undoubtedly my favourite from the whole 'Molefe Collection' – **uFishonamasondo** ('fish with wheels'), a nickname for a person who can do all sorts of things which other people cannot do.

4.4 NICKNAMES AND PRAISE NAMES FROM DOKE AND VILAKAZI

The following section is devoted to nicknames collected from Doke and Vilakazi (1958) which has been abbreviated to 'D&V' in this section. I have divided their material into a number of subcategories.

4.4.1 The various names of God

There are a number of alternative names – praise names rather than nicknames – for God in D&V, and they follow in no particular order.

uSimakade is a name which could be translated as 'The Ancient of Days', and it comes from the noun **isimakade** (literally, 'what stood long ago') which means 'very ancient person, animal or thing'. A similar idea is seen in **uMvelingqangi** which literally means 'He who appeared first'.

The equivalent of the English names 'The Almighty' and 'The Allrighteous' can be seen in **uSomandla** and **uSokulunga**. Both these names use the prefix **so-** ('father of'), the former with the noun **amandla** ('strength'), the latter with the noun **ukulunga** ('rightness').

uThixo is a common Zulu name for God. The name has been adopted from Xhosa, which in turn has taken this word from the Nama word for 'God, Supreme Being'.

D&V give the following two names for God, but do not explain their etymology: **uSonganiso** and **uNyanya**. I have never heard nor seen these words used.

4.4.2 Character types

The following are not names for specific individuals, but may be applied to any person of a particular type. For example, the word **uMahlekehlathini**, which literally means 'he who laughs in the bush', may be applied to anyone with a relatively heavy beard.

The following examples refer to persons of a particular physical shape. Someone with thin legs might find himself being referred to as **uMcondo**

kaZimelela, a name which literally means 'Mr Thin-legs son of Mr Walk-with-Sticks'. Such a person might also hear the expression **Suka Mconjwana, kuhlale uDandalibanzi** : 'Get away Mr Thin-leg, let Mr Wide-hips sits down', where **udandalibanzi** means 'someone with wide, strong hips'. A very short person, by contrast, could find himself being addressed as **iNtshonakweneni**, a nickname which literally means 'that which disappears in an overgrown place'.

The following examples all have to do with character types. **uPhoshozwayo** ('talkative person') is a common nickname for a loquacious individual, while **uSimukanandwendwe** ('what is carried away by the wedding procession') is a weak-charactered person who 'goes with the stream'. Similarly gentle gibes can be seen in **iSwelandlebe** ('Mr Lack-Ears'), a nickname for one who takes no advice, and **iNtathabulembu** ('what takes the cobweb') a name which refers to a person lacking initiative or energy. And let us not forget **uSompecempece** ('Mr What's-his-name'). D&V say this is derived from the noun **impecempece** ('pliant, bendable object'), perhaps because a forgotten name has no rigid, recognisable shape.

Rather stronger characters are **uXamukavinjelwa** ('the monitor lizard is not stopped'), a name for a strong-headed person, and **uThulasizwe** ('Mr Be-Quiet-and-let-us-hear'), which can be used for any person in authority. Courageous warriors could be addressed as **uSoyaka** ('the father of flowing plumes') or **uMlamulankunzi** ('separator of contending bulls').

While some of these nicknames are gentle gibes, others are distinctly insulting. A name for a robber or assassin is **uZigibanyongwana** which literally means 'he who discards dignity', while insulting names for cowards are **uGwazisabahle** ('killer of beautiful ones' – that is, defenseless women and children) and **uGwazisabathi-yo** ('killer of those who wail *yo*'). Intriguingly, **uGwazisabantondo** ('stabber of bundles') is an ambivalent nickname, for it can be used insultingly for a coward, as in the two previous examples, or it can be used of a great hero, who kills in piles.

uNkabi(ya)malanga ('ox of days') is a pet name for a friend, and **uMuhle** ('he is good') is, curiously, a name once given to the Native [*sic*] Commissioner of any district.

> The Department of Bantu Administration Headquarters in Durban was known as **KwaMuhle** ('Muhle's Place'). Part of the original buildings now house the KwaMuhle Museum, which has a collection devoted to life under the system of Influx Control and various other aspects of the 'apartheid era'.

The following three are nicknames for members of specific ethnic groups:

- **umNanayi** (aba-): An Indian. **abakwamnanayi**: Indians. 'This word origin-

ates in the Zulu conception of Indian nasal speech where *na, nahi, nayi,* etc. occur.' I would think it equally likely that this comes from the common Indian surname Naidoo.
- **iPhumalimi:** ('what comes out standing'): European, white person. This is a reference to the fact that colonial-type houses had full-length doors, while the doors of the original Zulu beehive huts were so low that people emerged in a kneeling or crouching posture.
- **iSiyendane** is a nickname applied to any member of the Hlubi and Mfengu people who fled southwards from Shaka in the early nineteenth century, and the name is derived from a word meaning 'hairstyle with tasseled fringe'.

Certain nicknames for character-types have given rise to proverbs and other sayings (or possibly the nicknames are taken from the proverbs) such as the following:
- **uGubudele (o-)** (< **gubudela**, 'deceive', 'trick', 'hoodwink'): Proper name applied particularly to a certain character in folklore, that is, Trickster. **UGubudele kaNomantshali, umthungi wezimbenge ezibanzi, angathunga ezincane ziya zibekelana** ('Mr Trickster son of Nomantshali, weaver of open-mouthed baskets, should he weave small ones they would fit one in the other').
- The word **isifumbu** means 'hump, curvature of spine' or 'hunchback', and from this comes the proverb **USifumbu ubona uQhaqhazela** ('Mr Hunchback notices Mr Totterer' – that is, the pot calls the kettle black).
- From the word **cishe** ('almost', 'nearly') comes the nickname **uCishu** ('Mr All-but, Mr Nearly') and thence the saying **UCishu kadliwa** ('Mr Nearly is not eaten' – that is, 'a miss is as good as a mile').

4.4.3 Fingers
D&V give the following names for fingers, describing these as 'children's fanciful names'. Starting with the little finger on the left hand, we have **uCikicane** or **uCiki**, then **owakoCiki** for the ring-finger, **owakoZigwe** for the middle finger, and for the index finger: **uZigwemagwegwe** or **unonkombabantu**, a word which literally means 'that which points to people'. The thumb is known as **uGwegwelunqume**, with the variants **ugwegwe, ugwegwewonqunta,** and **ugwegwe-onqumu**.

> It is curious that the index finger is named **uZigwemagwegwe** or **unonkombabantu**, a word which literally means 'that which points to people', since in Zulu culture it is considered rude to point to people, especially with the index finger. If pointing out is absolutely necessary, the little finger or a closed hand should be used.

On the right hand, we start with the thumb, named **uMwane**, followed by the index finger, with its two names **uNtamusomagidi** and **unonkombabantu**. The middle finger has the delightful name **usogidamasi** meaning 'what dances in the sour milk'. The fourth finger is known as **uMaqathulela**, as well as **umwowane** and **ungweje** (**ungweje** can also be used for the equivalent finger of the left hand). Finally, the little finger on the right hand is **uSozidinjana**, **usodinjana** or **uzidunjana**. This last name comes from **izidumbu** 'corpses': *uZidunjana-ngaphesheya-zilishumi* ('little corpses that are ten across': that is, all ten fingers have been counted to reach this little one).

Together with these nicknames or praise names for the fingers, goes a praise for one's feet: **Uyahamba Badule kaLunyawo!** ('Thou goest well, Tramper, Son of Foot!' – addressed to one's feet), a praise derived from the words **ubadule** ('tramper, one who tramps' – a jocular term) and **unyawo** ('foot').

4.4.4 Fabulous monsters

The following are all names for fabulous monsters found in Zulu **izinganekwane** ('children's stories', 'folktales', 'fables'). These monsters are characteristically found in deep pools and are known to be able to swallow whole villages at one gulp. Fortunately, in these stories, a hero with a sharp blade usually also gets swallowed, and he is able to slice open the monster's stomach from the inside, and so free all the village's inhabitants and cattle.

uSondonzima ('Mr Heavy-foot') is a word for a monster that echoes the 'Big-foot' of the Canadian mountains. This word is also the Zulu for 'heavyweight' in boxing ranking. Another fabulous water-monster is named **iNzawu**, a word which can also mean a sharp-tongued person. Zulu king Dingane used this name for one of his regiments of girls. History does not tell us whether he saw these girls as sharp-tongued, or as large water-monsters.

A frequently occurring monster in Zulu folktales takes the shape of an immense frog. There are a variety of names for this monstrous frog, all combining nonsense syllables with the meaningless stem **-nana**: **inanabahule, unanabahule, unanabosele, inanabuke,** and **unananana**.

In other stories the monster might be named **inqamundolo**, a name which means 'biting off a large multitude of people', or have the delightful name **isiququmadevu**, which literally means 'smelly whiskers'.

Finally, **umnyama** refers to a fabulous animal, said to resemble a sheep, believed to inhabit ponds where the rainbow terminates, and whose fat is said to have the various colours of the rainbow.

4.4.5 Animals

D&V record a few nicknames for animals and birds. The word **umalukobo**, a name 'commonly given to a cow', is adopted from the Afrikaans *malkop* ('mad head'), while the word **ugelegele** ('whirlwind') is the basis of the praise name for the Yellow-billed Kite: **uNhloyile kaGelegele** ('kite, son of the whirlwind').

D&V's nicknames for the domestic cat and the baboon reflect the unerring instinct for the telling characteristic that is so often a feature of Zulu nicknames: the cat is nicknamed **iDlalesula** (literally, 'what eats and wipes away'), and the deep-set eyes of the baboon are reflected in the name **unkophezinganethimvula** ('eyelashes which are not wetted by the rain').

4.4.6 Miscellaneous

The following are miscellaneous nicknames and praise names culled from the pages of D&V. The word **isangqwatha** ('frost') may be expanded into the praise **UMazinyo-mhlophe ofana nesangqwatha** ('White-teeth who resembles frost'), while **umkhaphalanga** ('what drives away the sun') is a nickname for the cool wind following the afternoon sun. The Arum Lily *Stylochiton natalense* is known by the name **umFana kaHlanjana** ('Hlanjana's boy'), variously **umfana-kaNozihlanjana**, and **umfana-kaSihlanjana**.

Two important historical occasions have been remembered through the years by recorded nicknames. The earliest happening, a great famine which occurred in the days of Dingiswayo (that is, towards the end of the eighteenth century), is still remembered by the name **uMadlantule** ('what eats and still wants'). A comparatively more recent event (although still more than 130 years ago), was Sir Theophilus Shepstone's lobolo proclamation of 1869, when there was an unprecedented rush to register marriages. This occasion is still known as **umbhidli kaSomtsewu** ('Somtsewu's attraction' – Shepstone's Zulu name was **uSomtsewu**), from the word **umbhidli** ('attraction, something that draws a large crowd').

To finish this section on nicknames and praise-names taken from D&V's dictionary, here is an undeniable onomastic curiosity. D&V tell us that the Royal Air Force was known by the name **Imbokodwe kamagayisa** ('Grinding-stone, son of Mrs Grinder'). Why the Royal Air Force should have a Zulu praise name, I am at a loss to explain. An intriguing clue, however, can be found in Lugg's *Life Under a Zulu Shield* (1975: 86), where he records a 25-line Zulu praise poem in honour of the Royal Air Force, introduced by the words 'This [that is, the RAF] was given the name of IMBOGODO KA MAGAYISA, the cobble grindstone of the pulveriser'. The poem itself contains the line '**Asethundulwe iMbogodo ka Magayisa**' ('they have been gouged out by the grinding cobble of Magayisa'). Lugg says of these praises that 'During the last war the following poems were composed by NONGEJENI ZUMA, my office induna at the Chief Native Commissioner's Office, Pietermaritzburg' (1975: 80).

The question remains: was the name **Imbokodwe kamagayisa** generally known by the time of the Second World War, leading induna Zuma to use it as the basis of his praise poem, or was he the person who coined the name in the praises that he composed, making the name so well-known that it was able to enter D&V's dictionary by 1948, the date of first publication?

4.5 ZULU NAMES OF NON-ZULUS, ESPECIALLY WHITES

It is well-known that non-Zulu people who have extended contact with Zulu speakers receive Zulu names. Some of these are complimentary, others less so, even insulting, and many display a sharp-edged wit. In this section I would like to look *firstly* at the names of unidentified individuals from contemporary times, drawing mainly from the 1997 collection of Noleen Turner, and then *secondly* at the Zulu names of some well-known historical personalities from early Natal and Zululand.

4.5.1 Unidentified contemporary figures

Turner, in an article tellingly entitled 'Onomastic caricatures', states: 'Nicknames given to employers or co-workers by Black employees, are very often colourful metaphorical descriptions which are succinct allusions to the person's character, physical appearance, behaviour or even idiosyncrasies' (1997: 50).

Such nicknames, says Turner, are 'often clear images of the name bearer in one way or another' (53). They may be descriptive of a physical feature which is unusual or odd, for example, **uZikhalozembuzi** ('nostrils of a goat'); may refer to idiosyncratic behaviour, as in **uMacoshamaphepha** ('picker-up of paper'); or to character traits, as in **uPelepele** ('Mr Chillies', that is, 'hot-tempered'). Turner goes on to provide some of the reasons why such nicknames are given: 'These nicknames are often used to label an individual or express one's dislikes towards another person's attitude or behaviour, or they may simply be used to provide a form of ridicule and repressed antagonism' (54).

Turner shows how some nicknames are in fact Zulu clan names which are phonetically very close to the surname of the person being nicknamed. Thus 'Campbell' becomes **Khambule**, 'McKay' becomes **Makhaye**, 'Bang' becomes **Bhengu**, and 'Lambert' becomes **Lembethe**.

The majority of Turner's examples, however, are 'true' Zulu names, as opposed to phonological equivalents. The examples that follow are taken from the appendix to her article, and follow her categorisation.

a. Reference to physical features

- **uNyonende** ('tall bird'): A very tall person;
- **uNgulubencane** ('little pig'): A short and stout person;
- **uMadolo kaTsotsi** ('Tsotsi's knees' – a 'tsotsi' is a street gangster, a 'skiv'): A person with ugly knees;
- **uNomvukuzane** ('Mr Mole'): Tiny slit-eyes;
- **uMadevaphulinkomishi** ('whiskers that break a cup'): A person with a very long moustache;
- **uFriesland** ('Friesland milk cow' – this is not, of course, a 'true' Zulu name): A woman with very large breasts.

b. Names referring to behavioural traits

- **uMahlafuna** ('Mr Constant Chewer');
- **uKhombanathingi** ('pointing at nothing'): Said of a manager who insisted on showing his workers every insignificant detail of any job given to them;
- **uDinwayini** ('why are you troubled?'): A person with a constant scowl on his face;
- **uBhejane** ('black rhinoceros'): A very aggressive person;
- **uMacimeza** ('closing the eyes'): Someone with the habit of continually blinking;
- **uMashayinqawe** ('Mr Hit-the-pipe'): Heavy pipe-smoker;
- **uNkalankala** ('Mr Crab'): He never walked in a straight line;
- **uMcathama** ('stealthy walker'): An employer constantly turning up unexpectedly to check on his staff;
- **uGundane** ('rat'): A fast-mover found everywhere;
- **uLwembu** ('Miss Spider'): From her habit of continually wrapping her arms around people.

c. Names referring to character traits

- **uNtabakayikhonjwa** ('the mountain is not pointed at'): A person not easily confronted;
- **uMuntukaziwa** ('the person is not known'): An unpredictable person;
- **uDlayedwa** ('he eats on his own'): An unpopular person;
- **uNkunzikayihlehli** ('the bull does not withdraw'): A fighter.

Of interest in these nicknames is the strong reliance on metaphors from the animal world. In the brief list above we find reference to birds, pigs, moles, cows, rhinos, crabs, rats, spiders and bulls.

4.5.2 Well-known historical personalities

Ever since the days whites first arrived at Port Natal, Zulu names have been given to those who have interacted with the Zulu people. Some of these individuals – and their Zulu names – are well-known, such as Bishop Colenso, known as **uSobantu** ('father of the people') both for his championing of Zulu rights as well as for his love for the Zulu language. Another is Sir Theophilus Shepstone, who was known as **uSomtsewu** (also spelt as **uSomseu**). Other historical characters are less well-known, and so, consequently, are their Zulu names. Perhaps only the specialist Natal historian is familiar with Colenso's son, Dr Francis E. Colenso, known as **uMnyaiza** [*sic*] (Webb & Wright, I: 259; meaning obscure); Colenso's daughter, Harriette Colenso, known as **Udlwedlwe** ('a staff' – that is, her father's support); or with Shepstone's children: his sons, William Edward (**uNsokonsokwana** – 'tall, graceful, slender person') and Arthur Jesse (**uMmango** – 'incline, slope'), and his daughter Alice, known as **uNtombazi** (from **intombi**, 'girl' + the feminine sufix **-azi**), which is the same name as Queen

Ntombazi of the Ndwandwe, mother of Zwide, she who was famous for her collection of skulls.

uSomtsewu or **uSomseu** is a particularly curious name. The **-so-** prefix is instantly recognisable as the Zulu name-forming prefix with the rough meaning 'father of', as in **uSobantu** above. The stem **-tsewu**, however, is not a Zulu stem at all, but the Sotho word for 'white'. Could **uSomtsewu** be a combination of Zulu prefix and Sotho stem meaning something like 'Great White Father'? The meaning would certainly fit the larger-than-life paternal role Shepstone played, but the Zulu-Sotho combination would be linguistically and onomastically unique.

A search of historical records reveals Zulu names for whites falling into similar patterns as Turner showed for contemporary nicknames: those names which are a Zuluisation of the surname (less commonly the first name) of the person concerned, and those which are a 'true' Zulu name reflecting the physical appearance or character of the person named.

Some examples of the first group are:

- **uFebana** (Lt. F.G. *Farewell*);
- **uGihuti** (*Gert* Maritz);
- **uGiluti** (Reverend *Grout*);
- **uJubhele** (General *Joubert*);
- **uMalimade** (Sir *Melmoth* Osborne);
- **uPiti** (*Piet* Retief).

Sometimes these adopted forms are prefixed by **uMzi-, uMsi-** or **uMis-** ('Mister'), as in:

- **uMzidoni** (John *Dunn*);
- **uMisbozi** (Alfred *Boast*, Assistant Commissioner, Eshowe, 1906);
- **uMismense** (Col. G. *Mansel*, O.C. Zululand Police, 1906).

The incorporation of the title 'Mister' into a few Zulu names is evidence of the lack of distinction between title and name in the minds of the Zulu namers. An interesting variation of this can be seen in the Zulu 'name' given to the Revd James Allison, known as **uMuneli** (Webb & Wright, I: 150), which is almost certainly a corruption of the Dutch 'Meneer', a title given to 'predikants' and applied to many missionaries, whether Dutch-speaking or not.

Historical figures who have been given 'true' Zulu names include:

- **uGwembetshe** ('the bow-legged one') for William Bazley (pioneer, Natal South Coast, mid-1880s);
- **uPhobana** ('penis') for Frank Fynn (brother of early Port Natal arrival Henry Francis Fynn);

- **uKhamungana** ('the insatiable one') for Captain Allen Gardiner, the first missionary in Natal in the 1820s;
- **uMashiqela** ('dictator', 'one who uses force in government') for C.R. Saunders (Chief Magistrate and Civil Commissioner for Zululand, 1906);
- **uManqanda** (meaning obscure) for B. Colenbrander (Magistrate at Nkandla in 1906);
- **uMakhanda** ('heads') for Col. Sighurt Bourquin, Head of Bantu Administration, Durban, 1970, who was admired for always 'using his head'.

Henry Francis Fynn Junior was known as **uGwalagwala** ('loerie bird') because of his habit of wearing a loerie feather in his hat. Henry Ogle (1824 pioneer in Durban) had the name **uWohlo**, and Byrne Settler John Bazley was known as **uMahalavu** ('Mr Spades'). R.C.A. Samuelson, author of the *King Cetshwayo Zulu Dictionary* and a 1925 Zulu Grammar, was known as **uLubhembhedu**, a name which could mean either 'person of resolute determination' or 'person who walks with stiff rigid gait'.

Harry Lugg, who has given us a number of the Zulu names of white personalities, gives his father's name as **uGwazamazulu** ('Stabber of Zulus'). The senior Lugg took an active part in the Anglo-Zulu War of 1879 and Lugg jnr says, 'After the war my father was always known as Gwazamazulu, the Zulu slayer' (1970: 16). However, nowhere in Lugg's writing can I find his own Zulu name. Faye (1923: 24) gives the Zulu names of H.C. Lugg as **uMagwaza** ('the stabber') and **uMagwaz' iZulu** ('the stabber of the Zulu'), making us wonder whether 'H.C. Lugg' is Henry Lugg (the older Lugg) or Harry Lugg (the younger, and the writer of the books). If Faye's reference is to the younger Lugg, did he inherit the Zulu names from his father? – for Faye's versions are essentially the same as the one which Lugg gives for his own father.

There are also historical figures who have been given both types of names, that is, a 'true' Zulu name, as well as a name which is a Zuluised form of their original name. We find, for example, that Bishop Hans Schreuder (founder of a number of mission stations in Zululand in the mid-1800s, and a Zulu scholar) was known both as **uHanisi** (< *Hans*), as well as **uMankankana**, a name apparently given to him by King Mpande in imitation of the way in which he tried to speak Zulu (Lugg, 1949: 90).

The Boer leader Andries Pretorius was known as **uPotolozi** (< *Pretorius*) as well as **uNgalonkulu** ('brawny-armed'), while the Durban pioneer Henry Francis Fynn was known both as **uMbuyazi** (the 'thefula'ed version of **uMbulazi** 'one who kills' – in **thefula** or **thefuya** speech, /l/ becomes **/y/**, thus: **uMalandela** > **uMayandeya)** as well as **uSifile**, an abbreviation of **uMsifile** (< *Mr Fynn*). And Lugg tells us that '[Dick] King was generally known to the Natives as UDiki, but also by the complimentary name of Mlamulankunzi, acquired probably after his ride to Grahamstown. Literally it means the separating of fighting bulls, i.e. a mediator or peacemaker' (1970: 45).

An unusual way of coining a Zulu name for a white person is the method which in linguistic theory is known as a 'calque' or 'loan translation'. For example, Sir Evelyn *Wood* was known as **uLukhuni** which could be translated as 'The Tough One', but could equally well be from **ulukhuni** ('[piece of] fire*wood*'). John *Bird* (resident magistrate, Pietermaritzburg from 1859 to 1976) was given the Zulu name **uNyoniyentaba** ('*bird* of the mountain'). Turner also gives a few examples of this phenomenon from her data (1997: 58): **uMashimane** ('someone unsuccessful in love') for *Bachelor* and **uMpungose** (< **-mpunga**, 'grey') for *Grey*. Both **Mpungose** and **Mashimane** are, in fact, also common Zulu clan names.

For those looking for further examples, Faye's 1923 *Zulu References* (21–25) gives the Zulu names of 46 white magistrates, with meaning and derivation, with a one page introduction to the topic. His examples follow the pattern shown above, with many of the Zulu names being 'Zulu-isations' of the original, as in **uGiba** for a Mr Gebers, most of these prefixed with **uM'si**, as in **uM'sikilaga** for a Mr Clark. Other names are 'true' Zulu names, as in **uMbhabhama** (which Faye translates as 'he who pounces, is quick to detect') for a Mr Essery.

A number of people have asked me about nicknames for *women*. The astute reader will have noticed that only three names in this whole chapter were nicknames for women. I can only say that in all the years I have been researching Zulu names I have searched for and asked for examples of women's nicknames. I have never been given any, and finding examples has been almost impossible. This extract from the *Sunday Tribune* – dated 21 January 2001 – is the first example of a woman's nickname that I have seen in print:

> She roars around the streets of the township south-west of Durban on her big Honda motorbike. Three years ago, at the age of 16, she caused a scandal in the community by announcing that she was gay. Minenhle Zondi, 19, has been nicknamed 'Sga', short for *S'gangi*, meaning naughty.
>
> 'I have long passed the stage where I think of myself as a teenager experimenting with new ideas. This is as I am,' she says matter of factly.

I do not believe the suggestion put forward by an academic colleague that nicknames, like praise names, reflect the spirit of competition that is usually only found among men. And so I remain convinced that 'somewhere out there' is a wealth of data on women's nicknames waiting for discovery.

Chapter 5

Surnames, clan names and clan praises

5.1 WHAT IS A 'SUR-NAME'?

For reasons that will become apparent in the discussion below, I prefer the use of the term 'clan name' to 'surname' to describe the Zulu **isibongo** – although it is commonly known as, used as, and assumed to be the same as the Euro-Western surname.

The prefix 'sur-' in *surname* is derived, via Old French, from the Latin *super*, meaning 'above', 'beyond', as in *surplus* and *surcharge*. 'Surname', then, implies an 'extra name', a name over and above the personal name. The modern French word *surnom* means 'nickname', again implying an 'extra' name (Janes, 1995: 293).

In the Euro-Western world, these extra names were required when too many people in a village or town had the same personal name. Effective communication was cut short when a simple question such as 'have you seen Eric today?' could refer to five or six or seven different people with the personal name Eric. In such cases it became necessary to further identify the person sought, as in 'Eric with the red hair', 'Eric, John's son', 'Eric the baker', or perhaps 'Eric who lives down by the river'. Over a passage of several decades or centuries, these extra or additional identifying features became names and, moreover, names which would be passed from father to son over the generations.

There are four basic categories of identifying features which underlie modern Euro-Western surnames: physical features, place of origin, trade, and patronymics. I would like to discuss each of these in turn, using as examples Euro-origin surnames of South Africans, such as can be found in any South African telephone directory. Many of these will be English in origin, many others – which we call Afrikaans surnames – of Dutch and French origin, while some will be of Portuguese or German origin.

5.1.1 Physical features as a basis for surnames

Colour of hair, or possibly of skin, can be an identifying factor, as suggested by **Black**, **White**, **Brown**, and their Dutch equivalents (**De**) **Swart**, **De Wit**, and **De Bruin**. Hair colour is the more likely feature in **Van Rooyen** and the French-origin Huguenot equivalent **Le Roux**.

Size (or lack thereof!) is suggested in **De Groot**, **De Lange, Long** and **De Kort**, while strength can be found in **Armstrong**.

5.1.2 Place of origin

An urban origin is clear in the names **Van Staden**, **Stadler**, **De Villiers** and, of course, **D'Urban**, while **Ackerman** suggests a rural origin ('acker' means 'field', cf. English 'acre'). **Du Plessis** is a name which means 'from the enclosed field', while **Duvenage** refers to a person from the vineyard. From the forests and wooded areas come **Van den Bosch**, **Van der Walt** (cf. the once-great forest in southern England known as The Weald), **Da Silva** (a Portuguese surname derived from the Latin word *silva* 'wood', cf. English 'sylvan glade'), and **Du Bois** (French, meaning 'from the forest'), while **Van den Berg** is 'from the mountain'. Manmade structures are referred to in **Du Toit** ('from the roof'), **Van Dyk** ('from the dyke'), **Van der Westhuizen** ('from the houses in the west'), and **Van Oosthuizen** ('from the houses in the east'). One wonders how far to the east was the origin of the first **Eastman**?

The church is the basis of both **Kirkland** and **Kirkwood**, while **Van Niekerk** means 'from the new church'.

Specific towns and cities are referred to in **Van Breda**, **Van Zuydam**, and **Van Amsterdam**; **Van der Merwe** refers to the Merwede River (a river in South Holland which joins the Rhine near Rotterdam), **Van Aardenne** to a specific forest, and **Van Rensburg** to a castle on the Rhine River.

5.1.3 Trade or occupation

This is the source of a great many English surnames. In the days when horses were the main method of land transport, one of the most common occupations was that of the blacksmith and **Smith** remains to this day one of the most common English surnames, with Germanic equivalents **Smit** and **Schmidt**. The Portuguese equivalent is **Ferreira** (literally 'iron-worker' from the Latin *ferrus*, 'iron'). The word 'wright' is a past participial of the verb *wring*, originally meaning simply 'work with the hands'/'make something by hand'. **Wright** is a common enough surname on its own, and it is often compounded with *cart* and *wain* ('wagon') to form **Cartwright** and **Wainwright**.

From the woods come **Timmermann**, **Wood**, **Bosman** and **Forrester**. Other occupations are seen in **Fletcher** ('one who makes arrows'), **Archer** and **Bowman** (who both shoot the arrows that the fletcher makes), **Thatcher**, **Cook**, **Baker**, **Mason**, **Bouwer** ('builder'), **Porter**, **Potter**, **Proctor**, **Shepherd**, **Sheriff**, **Cooper** ('maker of barrels'), **Fisher** (and Afrikaans **Visser**), **Carpenter**, **Harper**, **Farmer**, **Hunter**, **Carter**, **Dyer**, and **Hayward** ('one who has charge of the hay').

Is the Afrikaans **Snyman** the equivalent of the English **Butcher** or **Doctor** or, more likely, **Tailor**?

Gardiner, **Gardener** and **Gardner** have an equivalent in the French-origin **Jardine**. **Coleman** and **Clark** are probably more recognisable in their modern spellings of 'coalman' and 'clerk'. The surname **Marshall** has an interesting history: the word 'marshal' although nowadays referring to a man of the highest rank in an army, originally derives from the words *maar* ('mare') and *schalk* ('knave'), and a marshal was the lowest rank of the grooms in a stable, the one who only looked after the mares.

The English surname **Miller** is semantically linked to both **Havemann** and **Vermeulen**, while **Koopman** has the same meaning as **Chapman** ('vendor', 'street merchant').

5.1.4 Patronymics

Identifying a man as the son of his father is a practice which is found world-wide, although the examples I give below are only taken from the Celtic and the Germanic branches of the Indo-European language family.

The following examples are obvious, and the names of the fathers are still used today as personal names: **Ericson**, **Grahamson**, **Donaldson**, **Harrison**, **Jackson**, **Johnson**, **Jacobson**, **Nicolson** (son of Nicholas, which is also found as **Nixon**), **Richardson**, **Robertson**, **Robinson**, **Thom(p)son**, and **Wilson** ('William's son'). **Anderson** and **Sanderson** are both abbreviations of 'Alexander's son'. Less obvious are **Watson**, **Gibson** (< Gilbert's son), **Ferguson**, **Atkinson** and **Claasen** (Claas's son).

Clarkson may refer to the son of a man named Clark, but could also refer to the son of a clerk.

Sometimes the possessive suffix is used on its own, and 'son' is implied as in: **Andrews**, **Clements**, **Edwards** and **Phillips**. **Pieterse** and **Peters** both mean 'son of Peter', while **Mathews** and **Mattison** both mean 'son of Mathew'.

Irish surnames use **O'** as an abbreviation of 'of' in patronymic surnames (as in the English 'twelve o'clock'), thus **O'Neill** means 'son of Neill'. Other examples are **O'Connell**, **O'Halloran**, **O'Flattery**, **O'Gorman**, **O'Leary** and **O'Reilly**.

The Scottish Gaelic prefix **Mac** also means 'son of', so the following are all patronymics: **Maclean**, **MacGregor**, **MacRorie**, **MacDonald**, **MacLachlan**, **Macleod**, **MacMillan** and **McCormack**. The Scottish personal name Alistair is derived from Alexander, so **Macallister** has the same meaning and origin as **Anderson** and **Sanderson**.

The Welsh **ab** also means 'of' and is used in patronymic surnames. The surname **Bevan** is a shortened form of *ab Evan* ('son of Evan'). As 'Evan' is itself a Welsh form of 'John', **Bevan** has the same origin and meaning as **Johnson**.

5.2 THE MEANINGS OF SOME ZULU CLAN NAMES

In order to see whether Zulu surnames, or preferably 'clan names', have similar origins to the Euro-Western surnames described above, I have taken 50 of the most common Zulu clan names and attempted to provide a meaning for them. These clan names are:

Biyela	Hlatshwayo	Mbatha	Sikhakhane
Buthelezi	Hlengwa	Mchunu	Shangase
Bulose	Hlongwa	Mdlalose	Vilakazi
Cele	Hlubi	Mthethwa	Xaba
Chiliza	Khoza	Ndlovu	Xulu
Dladla	Khumalo	Ngobese	Zondi
Dlamini	Khuzwayo	Ngwenya	Zondo
Dlomo	Khwela	Ntuli	Zulu
Dludla	Luthuli	Nyathi	Zuma
Dube	Mabaso	Nyawose	Zungu
Gumede	Magwaza	Qwabe	Zwane
Gwala	Maphumulo	Sibisi	
Hadebe	Mbhele	Sibiya	

When these clan names are analysed, they fall roughly into three categories: those whose meaning is reasonably certain; those which can be guessed through relationship to an item in the Zulu lexicon; and those which are completely obscure and cannot be related to any existing Zulu word.

> The sources used for the confirmation of the meanings of clan names are too numerous and varied to give here, but they include published sources such as Bryant's 1929 *Olden Times in Zululand and Natal*, a number of articles over the years in the *Echo* supplement to the Pietermaritzburg newspaper the *Natal Witness*, and over 20 years of students' assignments, essays, dissertations and theses.

5.2.1 Reasonably certain meanings

Under this heading I have grouped those clan names where the linguistic structure is perfectly clear and where the meaning has been 'confirmed' by members of the clan in one way or another.

A number of these refer to species of animals. It should be noted that these animals are not 'totemic' for the clans so-named. That is to say, the animal concerned plays no special role in the life of that clan: it is not a sacred animal, nor is it subject to taboos of any kind. The clans which take their names from various animals are the **Dube** ('zebra'), the **Ndlovu** ('elephant'), the **Ngwenya** ('crocodile'), and the **Nyathi** '(buffalo').

The clan name **Zulu** comes from the word meaning 'sky' or 'weather', and the two related clan names **Luthuli** and **Ntuli** both come from the same word meaning 'dust', **Luthuli** from the singular form, and **Ntuli** from the plural form meaning 'dust storms'.

From notable incidents or practices in the remote history of the clan come **Biyela** ('to enclose', 'hedge in'), **Dlamini** ('eat at noon'), and **Mabaso** ('the fire-makers').

Clan names which suggest the character or actions of an individual, perhaps the founder of the clan, are:

- **Gwala** ('coward');
- **Hlatshwayo** ('the stabbed one');
- **Magwaza** ('the stabber');
- **Mthethwa** ('the scolded one');
- **Vilakazi** ('the very lazy one');
- **Shangase** ('the wanderer').

This last clan name is interesting in that it uses the very old name-forming suffix **-se**, here attached to the word **shanga** ('of wandering about'). Other clan names with this suffix are **Mdlalose** and **Nyawose**, where the **-se** has been attached to **umdlalo** ('game') and **unyawo** ('foot') respectively.

5.2.2 Guessed meanings

These are clan names which can be related to existing Zulu words, but these possible etymologies have not been confirmed in any sources that I have been able to find.

We can guess that the following refer to the character or actions of some notable individual in the history of the clan:

- **Dladla** ('one with shaggy hair');
- **Dludla** ('inconsiderate heedless person' or 'one who runs ways and roams about');
- **Hlengwa** ('the redeemed one', 'the assisted one');
- **Hlubi** ('one who throws off skin', that is, changes his appearance)
- **Khoza** ('one who opens up trade' or 'one with fame and great reputation');
- **Khuzwayo** ('one approved of' or 'one sympathised with');
- **Xaba** ('one who causes quarrelling');
- **Zondi** ('one who hates');
- **Zondo** ('hatred').

Clan names which have some sort of botanical relationship include:

- **Hlongwa** ('type of long grass used for thatching');
- **Khumalo** ('species of thorny tree', perhaps *Cassinopsis sapensis*);
- **Ngobese** ('species of bogwood plant');
- **Sikhakhane** ('species of thistle').

Some sort of problem or difficulty is suggested in:

- **Maphumulo** ('resting places from dangers or difficulties');
- **Zuma** ('take by surprise');
- **Zungu** ('conspiracy, plot, treachery').

Even guesswork becomes difficult in relating the following clan names to similar existing words. Does **Cele** come from the noun **icele** ('side', 'edge') and is **Chiliza** from the verb **chiliza** ('push away', 'elbow aside')? Is **Khwela** from the verb meaning 'to mount, climb up', and does **Mbatha** come from the **hlonipha** word for 'homestead'? Did the original **Mbhele** wear an **ibhele** ('square of skin worn in front')? Was the first **Qwabe** renowned for his or her music on the large musical bow known as an **uqwabe**? And does the clan name **Buthelezi** have anything to do with the noun **ubuthelezi** which means 'smoothness', 'slipperiness', as well as 'sensations of having the teeth put on edge'?

5.2.3 Obscure clan names

We can only guess at the answers to the questions above. For nine of the top fifty common clan names, even guesswork is impossible, as the names relate to no known word in the Zulu lexicon: **Bulose**, **Dlomo**, **Gumede**, **Hadebe**, **Mchunu**, **Sibisi**, **Sibiya**, **Xulu** and **Zwane**.

5.3 RELATIONSHIP BETWEEN ETYMOLOGIES OF EURO-WESTERN AND ZULU SURNAMES/CLAN NAMES

From the meanings of the Zulu clan names given or guessed at above, it would seem that the only overlap occurs in the semantic area 'identifying features of individual' (clan founder?). There are no Zulu clan names which indicate profession, geographical origin, or name of father. On the balance of evidence, it is fair to say that the origins of Euro-Western surnames and the origins of Zulu clan names belong to decidedly different cultural patterns. This is surely not surprising.

5.3.1 Scottish and Zulu clans

The reason why I suggested above that the term 'clan name' is preferable to the term 'surname' for the Zulu **isibongo** is that Zulu **izibongo** refer to groups of people very similar to the Scottish clans. In this section I would like to examine some of the similarities.

First, we must understand the concept of the clan. In reference to the Zulu clan, Mzolo (1978: 207) cites Bryant's definition (1949: 421) of a clan as being 'but a magnified family, consisting of an offspring of a single father, the clan's founder'. Mzolo goes on to say:

> This view implies a continuous process of expansion by which a traditional, patrilocal, polygynous, extended family has given rise over the generations to a whole series of such families linked by the

> patrilineal ties between their male heads. However, it is not now the case that all the numerous members of one clan can trace their connections to each other by patrilineal descent from a common ancestor. Nor is the clan as a whole a localised group; its members can be found widely scattered throughout the province of Natal and elsewhere in South Africa (1978: 207).

In the modern context the clan name functions as a surname, and it is found in this role on birth certificates, identity documents, passports, bank-books, drivers' licenses and the various other documents which characterise and define the existence of the modern individual. But the clan is more than simply the sum total of all individuals bearing the same clan name. It is the fact that they share far more than the same name that binds them together into a unified group.

> In a private communication Saarelma raises the question of why some African societies use their clan names as surnames in the Euro-Western context, and others do not. She points out that the Ovambo people have clan names, but they do not use them as surnames, using patronyms instead. The use of patronyms as surnames instead of clan names is common throughout Africa. It is even true of the Xhosa people: their surnames are based on the personal name of a grandfather or great-grandfather, and the surname accordingly changes every two or three generations.

a. Clan members share a sense of a common genealogy

Among the Zulus at least, this sense is expressed in the various forms in which the clan name manifests itself. The forms of the Zulu clan names that I have given above, for example, **Mbatha** and **Mbhele**, are all abbreviated forms. In normal discourse these would take plural forms: **amaMbatha** and **amaBhele**. Frequently these plural forms are themselves given as locatives – **emaMbatheni** and **emaBheleni**, especially with those clans which still have a 'locational identity' (that is, those clans who still form high concentrations in a particular area). One of the most common forms of the Zulu clan name is the **abakwa-** form, literally 'Those of the House of . . .'. Thus: **abakwaDlamini**, **abakwaNdlovu**, with the emphasis on the fact that all clan members are related to the dynastic house ruling this clan.

One could liken this to British royalty, whose names are not associated with 'surnames', but rather with the name of a dynasty: Queen Elizabeth II of the House of Windsor, Queen Victoria of the House of Saxe-Coburg and Gotha, Henry the Eighth of the House of Tudor.

This emphasis on the genealogical relationship can also be seen in the common way in which one Zulu might ask another his clan name: '**Ungowakwabani**?', which literally translates as 'You are of the house of who?', to which the reply is, for example, '**ngingowakwaKhumalo**' ('I am of the House of Khumalo').

Many of the main 'houses' in both the Zulu and the Scottish clan system, have sub-branches, or 'septs'. Both Maclean in his 1990 *The Clan Almanac* and Bryant in his 1929 *Olden Times in Zululand and Natal*, have appendices showing these links. From Maclean we can find that among the many sub-clans of MacDonald are MacCulloch, Shannon, Rorison ('Rory's son'), Purcell, Train, Whannell, Wilkinson, and Sporran. The Buchanan clan numbers among its septs MacCalman, MacCammond, MacCormack, MacGibbon, MacGilbert, MacWhirter, Murchison, Ruskin, and Watson.

Bryant (1929: 681–697) gives similar sub-clan relationships among the Zulu. Almost all the clan names in his list are given in the locative form of the plural. For example, where today we would use the clan name **Mthembu**, Bryant pluralises this as **abaThembu** and then puts it into the locative form **ebaThenjini**. Bryant gives the form **emaHlutshini** where today we would use **Hlubi**, and **emaTolweni** where today we would say **Mzolo**.

In the examples which follow, I have turned all Bryant's forms into modern forms of clan names and, for the parents' clans only, I have put his locative plural form in parentheses afterwards.

- From the parent clan **Mthembu** (**ebaThenjini**) come the sub-clans **Ngxongo**, **Njokwe**, **Nyanzi**, **Sokhela**, **Conci**, **Mkhulisa**, **Mvelase**, and **Ncadi**.
- The **Khumalo** clan (**KwaKhumalo**) is the origin of **Dlodlo**, **Fakazi**, **Gule**, **Nkosi**, and **Sokhulu**.
- The **Mchunu** clan (**emaChunwini**) has given rise to: **Mbhentse**, **Conco**, **Goba**, **Khanyile**, **Majola**, **Mcumane**, **Mhlanzi**, **Myeki**, **Ndawonde**, **Ndlovu**, **Nene**, and **Ximba**.
- From the **Mtshali** people (**emaNtshalini**) come **Madide**, **Jiyane**, **Mashazi**, and **Madonsela**.
- The **Ngwane** clan (**emaNgwaneni**) is the source of a number of sub-clans: **Zigode**, **Zikhali**, **Zitha**, **Bomvu**, **Gozi**, **Made**, **Mbanjwa**, **Mbuthu**, **Mhlungu**, **Mphembeni**, **Ndamane**, and **Sangweni**.

By far the most prolific clan, in terms of numbers of sub-clans, is the **Hlubi** clan (**emaHlutshini**). According to Bryant, all of the following are related to the **Hlubi**:

Khasibe	**Hawule**	**Mkhwane**	**Nqayi**
Kheswa	**Maphela**	**Mlanda**	**Ntete**
Khushwayo	**Masoka**	**Mthambo**	**Phakathi**
Kunene	**Matodlana**	**Mthimkhulu**	**Sidinane**
Langa	**Mavundla**	**Mvemve**	**Vezi**
Lembede	**Maya**	**Mvubu**	**Vundla**

Lubelo	**Mbongwe**	**Mzimba**	**Xaba**
Mabi	**Mdala**	**Ncwana**	**Zidumbu**
Maboko	**Mgidlana**	**Ndlazi**	
Maduna	**Mhila**	**Nkala**	
Mahawu	**Mkuzangwe**	**Nkomonde**	

b. Members of a clan share a common chief

In another comparison with the Scottish clan name here, we may note that although Mackenzies and Macleans may be scattered around the globe, while Duncans can be found in Hong Kong, and Buchanans in New York, their clan chief normally (although not always) inhabits the traditional clan castle 'back home' in Ross-shire, Aberdeenshire or the Isle of Skye. Maclean gives, for example, the following clan chiefs as at 1990:

Farquharson: Capt. A.A.C. Farquharson of Invercauld
MacLaren: Donald MacLaren of MacLaren and Achleskine
Cameron: Col. Sir Donald Cameron of Lochiel, K.T., C.V.O., T.D.
Campbell: The Duke of Argyll
Anstruther: Sir Ralph Anstruther of that Ilk, Bt. K.C.V.O., M.C.
Bruce: The Earl of Elgin and Kincardine, K.T.
Kincaid: Mrs Heather V. Kincaid of Kincaid

In the same way, each clan among the Nguni-speaking peoples has its chief, a known individual who lives in a known place. As Mzolo has pointed out, in today's South Africa, members of a clan may be scattered far and wide, but there is still a 'clan home' where the current clan chief lives. And unless there have been major social or political upheavals (not uncommon in South Africa), it will be a location where generations of the clan's chiefly lineage have lived.

This hereditary position has become blurred in the modern South Africa with new administrative structures. With open elections, it may be possible for a Member of Parliament to be elected who is, for example, a Dlamini by clan, and who becomes 'chief' over an area dominated by members of the Xulu clan. But even so, the position of 'clan chief' still exists within the context of family respect, and a visiting clan member from far away would still be expected to pay his respects to the clan chief if he was passing through the area. Moreover, the visiting clan member would be entitled to hospitality once he had recited his clan praises to establish his identity as a genuine member of the clan.

In a private communication Professor Maphumulo points out that there may be 'minor' clan chiefs in a particular area. For example, there are a number of Maphumulo clan members living at Swayimani near Pietermaritzburg whose 'local' chief is Mhlabunzima Maphumulo of Maqongo. The Maphumulos who live at Eshowe and at Maphumulo (near Kranskop) itself also have local chiefs. But all Maphumulo clan members regard the branch of the clan living near Amanzimtoti as the senior branch, as it was from this group that Mashimane, whose name has become the primary Maphumulo **isithakazelo**, had his home. The Maphumulo chief from this branch is regarded as the 'major' clan chief.

c. Members of a clan share a sense of identity

Members of a Zulu clan share more than simply a common sense of identity: they regard all other members of the clan as brothers and sisters, so much so that there is no inter-marriage between members of the same clan. Even today, a Zulu youth meeting a girl will ask her her clan name at the first opportunity. If she is from the same or a closely-related clan, then any relationship other than a purely platonic one is out. This point will be discussed further below when the function of clan praises is considered.

d. Members of a clan share identifying marks or characteristics

Many Zulu clans have distinct facial or other body marking, usually by scarification. Members of the Ngubane clan traditionally remove the end joint of the little finger on the left hand. Other clans have distinct ways of dressing their hair, or distinct forms of the women's **isicholo** headdress. Others again may have a distinctive way of speaking, or of dancing. Usually the clan name is used with the **isi-** prefix when referring to such a clan characteristic, for example, one might say '**Basina isiMbatha**' ('They dance Mbatha-style') (see Koopman, 1991). This could be linked with the Scottish clan system's distinctive range of clan tartans.

e. Members of a clan share clan praises

All members of a clan share the same clan praises. These are known as **izithakazelo** in Zulu, **iziduko** in Xhosa, and **tinanatelo** in Swazi. Maclean, in giving the praises of various Scottish clans, uses the terms 'slogan' and 'motto' to describe these, but it is probable that there is a specific Gaelic term to describe them.

Scottish clan praises can be found in Gaelic, English, French and Latin. The following are examples:

- For the **Colquhoun** clan: *Si je puis* (French: 'If I can') and *Cnoc Ealachain* (Gaelic: 'the clan's rallying place');
- For the **Chisholm** clan: *Feros ferio* (Latin: 'I am fierce with the fierce');
- For the **Douglas** clan: *Jamais arriere* (French: 'Never behind') and *A Douglas! A Douglas!*;
- For the **Drummond** clan: *Gang warily* (Scottish English: 'Go carefully');
- For the **Duncan** clan: *Disce parti* (Latin: 'Learn to suffer');
- For the **MacLaren** clan: *Creag an Tuirc* (Gaelic: 'The boar's rock');

- For the **MacLean** clan: *Bas no Beatha* (Gaelic: 'Death or life') and *Fear eile airson Eachairn* (Gaelic: 'Another for Hector');
- For the **MacNaughton** clan: *I hope in God* and *Fraoch Eilean* (Gaelic: 'Heathery Island');
- For the **MacNeil** clan: *Vincere vel mari* (Latin: 'To conquer or die') and *Buaidh no bas* (Gaelic: 'Victory or death').

5.4 *IZITHAKAZELO*: CLAN PRAISES

While some of the examples of **izithakazelo** in this section are from my own collection, most have been taken from Sithole's 1982 *Izithakazelo Nezibongo ZakwaZulu.*

5.4.1 The structure of clan praises

In their most basic form clan praises consist of a list of names linked with the genealogy of that clan: usually the name of the founding father, together with the names of the heroes and chiefs from the clan history.

Frequently such names are linked with the possessive prefix **ka-** ('of', or in this context 'son of'). For example, Sithole starts his praises for the Mbatha clan with **Shandu kaNdaba** ('Shandu, son of Ndaba'), and his Mkhize clan praises with **Gubhela! Gcwabe! kaKhabazela kaMavovo!** ('Gubhela! Gcwabe! Son of Khabazela son of Mavovo!').

Such genealogical links may be preceded by **wena** ('you'), as in the example **Wena kaGubhela! Wena kaGcwabe! Wena kaKhabazela kaMavovo** for the **Mkhize** clan praises. **Wena** can also be used in the following way: instead of simply using a single name clan praise, such as **Bomvu** for the **Ngubane** clan or **Mntungwa** for the **Khumalo** clan, an **Ngubane** may be greeted with **Wena osemaBomvini** ('you from amongst the Bomvus') and a **Khumalo** as **Wena osemaNtungweni** ('you of the Mntungwas').

Famous names from the history of the clan – either chiefs or notable heroes and warriors – are interspersed with 'praise phrases': short descriptive or narrative additions to various names. For example, one may praise a member of the **Mhlongo** clan with the praise name **Njomane**. The patronymic can be added: **Njomane kaMgabhi** ('Njomane, son of Mgabhi'). Or one can say **Njomane owaduka iminyakanyaka ngowesine watholakala** ('Njomane who was lost for many years but found on the fourth year'). A member of the **Cele** clan can be praised with the single name **Ndosi**, or this can be expanded to **Ndosi owabuya nensila emfuleni** ('Ndosi who came back dirty from the river'). The single clan name which acts as a peg for the praise phrase may be replaced with **wena**, thus resulting in: **Wena owaduka iminyakanyaka . . .** ('You who were lost for many years . . .') for an **Mhlongo**, and **Wena owabuya nensila . . .** ('You who came back dirty . . .') for a Cele.

The following are further examples of praise phrases attached to various clans:

- **Hadebe** clan: **Izindlubu zamila emthondweni** ('Bean-plants that grew in a place of urination');

- **Ndlovu** clan: **Wena kaNkomo ezidl' ekhaya ngokweswela umelusi** ('You of the Cattle that grazed at home through the lack of a herdsman');
- **Zuma** clan: **Umaphumephethe owaphuma ephethe umcaba ngala nangala, washaya inja ngekhanda** ('Mr Come-out-carrying who came out carrying porridge in this [hand] and that, he warded off the dog with his head');
- **Shangase** clan: **Mashiyamahle sengathi azoshumayela** ('Expressive eyebrows as if they are going to preach');
- **Zungu** clan: **Nyama kayishi, isha ngabaphephezela** ('The meat doesn't burn [by itself], it burns when people blow [on the fire]').

Many of the praise phrases are shared by more than one clan. For example, the phrase **Wena owakhula thina silibele** ('You who grew while we remained behind') and the phrase **Wena owadl' umuntu wamnyenga ngendaba** ('You who conquered the person by deceiving him about the matter') are common to a number of clans.

It should be noted that clan praises, in common with all forms of oral poetry, have no 'fixed' form. That is to say, the various praise phrases and praise names which constitute the praises of a clan may occur in any order. Normally they will begin with what are often referred to as the 'primary praise names' (two or three names which are generally regarded as being the most important of the various praise names found in clan praises). Thereafter both the ordering and the length of the praises will depend on the individual who is reciting them, as well as the occasion on which they are being recited. A more formal occasion, such as a wedding or an **ukubuyisa** ceremony, will require fuller praises than a simple greeting, for example.

As to the number of praises actually known or remembered by individuals, it is safe to say that older clan members, particularly those living in rural areas, have a far greater knowledge of their clan praises than do younger members, especially those living in towns and cities. I well recall my surprise, after a number of years of working in KwaMashu Township outside Durban, where many Zulu youths know only one or two praise names from their clan **izithakazelo** (and many know *none at all*), accompanying the late Douglas Mzolo on a trip to the rural areas around Eshowe when he was doing fieldwork for his Masters thesis on Zulu clan praises. The strings of praises which the older members of the community were able to recite showed that this cultural tradition was very much alive, even if in grave danger of dying in the modern urban environment.

5.4.2 The use of clan praises

Clan praises have a number of functions in society, including: the establishment of identity, address forms, thanking, flattering and congratulating, and maintaining contact with the ancestors in various rites.

a. Clan praises establish identity
I have already mentioned above that clan praises are used to establish clan identity. In fact, they go further than simply establishing *clan* identity: they may be used to establish *related clan* identity. Many clans, both in the Zulu and Swazi societies, are 'sub-clans' of some original 'founder' clan, and although the resultant 'sub-clans' have different clan names, they will share many clan praises. For example, the (Zulu) **Gumede** and **Khuzwayo** clans, share the praise names **Mnguni** and **Qwabe**, while **Gumede** and **Makhanya** share **Khondlo** and **Phakathwayo.** The clans **Ngema** and **Mngadi** share the clan praise **Madlokovu**, while **Khumalo** and **Mabaso** share the praise name **Mnguni**.

b. Praises are used as address forms
Clan praises are frequently used as an address form, particularly for males. My research into common forms of address between Zulu husbands and wives showed that a single clan praise was one of the most common ways in which a wife addresses her husband (Koopman, 1986). Men greeting each other in casual circumstances: at work or on the road, for example, will commonly use the clan praise. Visitors to a homestead are traditionally required to stand outside the fence and recite the praises of the homestead **umnumzane** ('kraal head'), until invited to enter.

c. Praises are used to thank, flatter and congratulate
When thanking someone for a gift or a favour, clan praises are used. As Mzolo describes it: 'If . . . a service [is rendered] which merits appreciation, it is not enough simply to say *Ngiyabonga*, "I thank you". The one who expresses thanks goes further and recites some, if not all, the clan praises' (1978: 212).

Mzolo goes further: 'For some achievement, such as when a mother gives birth to a first born son or even just an ordinary baby, some words of appreciation are expressed and in addition clan praises are recited; saying, "you have done well you of so-and-so", etc.'

From personal experience I can say that the use of clan praises to congratulate someone on an outstanding achievement has added greatly to the flavour of the graduation ceremonies of the University of Natal over the last decade or so.

When a favour is sought from someone, or it is appropriate to flatter someone, again, clan praises are used. They are also used when greeting a friend whom one has not seen for a long time. They are recited to soothe a fretting child, when they function somewhat as lullabies. In short, clan praises are used in a number of ordinary, everyday situations.

d. Clan names may be used to encourage
I would like to illustrate this function of clan praises with a personal story, that of Phineas Dlamini at the end of the Comrades Marathon.

Approximately 15 years ago, Phineas Dlamini was a young man of some 17 years. During the time he had worked for me, he had run back and forth between my house in Lincolnmeade, Pietermaritzburg, and his home near Natal's Table Mountain, a distance of approximately 17 kilometres, making a total of 34 kilometres for the return journey. As a result, young Dlamini had become extremely fit, and had taken all the cross-country and long-distance running trophies first for his school, and then the district. Consequently, he decided he was going to run the Comrades Marathon and, moreover, so he informed me, he was going to win a silver medal at this first attempt – which meant that he would have to complete the 85 kilometre race in under seven-and-a-half-hours. I tried to dissuade him from this ambitious goal, suggesting that at the first attempt, he should be content with a bronze medal simply for finishing in under eleven hours. But he was adamant, and so I arranged to be at the finish of the race to see him win his silver.

We went to the finish, and when seven hours and twenty-nine minutes had passed and there had been no sign of Phineas, I turned to my wife and said, 'It looks like Phineas is not going to get his silver.' At that moment we saw him in the distance entering the stadium, limping, staggering, and clearly totally exhausted. Sixty seconds to go, and he still had to run all the way around the perimeter of the stadium. It was obvious that he was not going to make it without a little assistance. So at the top of my voice I bellowed out the clan praises for his branch of the Dlaminis: **Sibalukhulu! Makaduzela owabonela empuntini!** ('Sibalukhulu! Makaduzela who is faster than any buck!'). Phineas heard me. He was suddenly galvanised into action and absolutely galloped around the field, indeed, 'faster than any buck'. And he made his silver medal, with two seconds to spare!

e. Praises are used in various rites and ceremonies

In addition to the ordinary, everyday situations, clan praises are an important feature of ceremonial occasions. Whenever a beast or a goat is slaughtered for ceremonial purposes, a Zulu **umnumzane** will **thetha amadlozi** ('speak formally to the ancestral spirits'). In a dignified and measured tone, he will greet the spirits, explain what the occasion is about, and then give thanks to the spirits for their assistance, or ask formally for their help, according to requirement. Interspersed with these formal words are the clan praises, appropriately so, for many of the clan praise names and clan praises are the names and the praises of those who have gone before, the **amadlozi**.

At weddings the bride must be introduced to the ancestors of the groom's clan, and the groom to the ancestors of the bride's clan. Again, these formal introductions are accompanied by full recitations of the clan praises.

Approximately a year after the death of a clansman, particularly if he was an **umnumzane**, a ceremony called the **ukubuyisa** ('the bringing back') is held. It is believed that the spirit of the deceased spends a year or so simply 'wandering about', and that the spirit needs to be called back to the clan home, so that it can take up its duties of protecting the interests of the clan members still living. The calling back combines the personal praises of the deceased with the praises of the clan, and the ritual is aided with branches of the **umphafa** tree (*Zizyphus mucronata*, or Buffalo Thorn). In some families branches of this tree are trailed behind individuals as they walk around the homestead, while other families beat the ground with **umphafa** branches as they recite the praises.

According to Mdunyelwa, clan praises are used when fetching the body of the deceased from the mortuary prior to taking it for burial: 'The deceased is fetched from the mortuary a day before the funeral . . . Clan praises are recited when they leave the mortuary. He [the deceased] will be called firstly by his traditional personal name and then by the clan name and clan praises. This is to let him [be] aware that they are leaving with him to his home' (1999: 76).

5.4.3 The relationship between clan names and clan praises

There is a complex relationship between clan name (Zulu **isibongo**) and clan praises (**izithakazelo, tinanatelo**) which manifests on a number of levels. We have already noted above that clans which have split off from one another remain related, and that this relationship is indicated by the sharing of certain praise names and praise phrases. We should further note that inter-related clans may use each other's clan name as a clan praise. Let me try to clarify these potentially confusing statements with some examples.

Two well-known Zulu clans are the **Ngema** and the **Mngadi**. The **Mngadi** clan uses **Ngema** as a clan praise, and the **Ngema** clan uses **Mngadi** as a clan praise. Both clans use **Madlokovu** as an additional clan praise, and thereafter the praises diverge. A similar set-up exists for the **Xulu** and the **Makhathini** clan, **Xulu** using **Makhathini** as an **isithakazelo**, and **Makhathini** using **Xulu**, while both clans add **Gxabashe** as a further clan praise.

To some members of clans involved in such pairing, the two clan names may become interchangeable. It happens frequently that a man may have an identity document which states that his clan name (his 'surname' to a person of Euro-Western background) is **Ngema**, while his driver's license may well provide his 'surname' as **Mngadi**. Confronted with what appears to be a fraudulent situation, a person unfamiliar with the link between clan names and clan praises, may say 'But you can't possibly have two different surnames!'

Substitute Khumalo and Mabaso, or Gumede and Khuzwayo, or any other such linked clan names, and this confusion could arise in any bank, office, or bureau, where someone with a Euro-Western background, steeped in the certain knowledge that a person can only have one surname, comes face to face with the fact that this is not true of Zulu society.

Chapter 6

Regimental names

> The uDloko *ibutho* came straight at the front of the British square. The encircling left horn consisted of the uThulwana, iNdluyengwe, iSangqu, iMbube and uMbonambi. The Zulu right horn was made up of the uMxhapho, iNsukamngeni, uDududu, iQwa, uNokhenke and iNdlondlo *amabutho*. The iNgobamakhosi and uVe attacked the right rear of the square, and the uMcijo the left rear (Laband, 1995: 314).

6.1 INTRODUCTION

The names in this chapter are those of the regiments which were such a feature of Zulu military history over the whole of the nineteenth century. The names recorded here start with the regiments conscripted by Shaka's father Senzangakhona in 1816 and end with those conscripted by Senzangakhona's great-grandson Dinuzulu in 1912. These regimental names differ from all the other names in this book in that they are the only names which are no longer part of a living onomastic tradition in Zulu society today: Dinuzulu was the last of the Zulu kings to form regiments of young men for military purposes. It would therefore be correct to say that these names now have historical value only. I have included them in this book for a number of reasons. *Firstly*, although there are a number of scholars who have listed the regiments of the Zulu kings, only two (Faye and Samuelson) have attempted any explanations of meanings, and this in a very limited way, and no scholars have attempted a comparative analysis of these names. *Secondly*, these names show a number of similarities with other types of Zulu names, such as clan names and clan **izithakazelo** on the one hand, and names of homesteads on the other, while at the same time keeping an onomastic profile all of their own. *Thirdly*, these regimental names are onomastically rich – how could I omit names which translate as 'Khundlase's blanket', 'loin-skin of crocodile hide', 'mountain without a grave', and 'wake up and catch them'?

It must be emphasised that the treatment of the regimental names in this chapter is purely an onomastic one. The reader should not expect a detailed historical treatment of the regiments. Bryant's *Olden Times in Zululand and*

Natal, besides giving one of the most complete lists of regimental names available, together with their dates of formation, also gives some idea of the background to the establishment of regiments. Of the early days of conscription, Bryant states:

> The Zulu regimental system is often erroneously supposed to have been an invention of Shaka; by others, of Dingiswayo. In reality, military regiments were the universal custom before either of them was king. The Nguni habit of banding together youth of a like age started with the old circumcision parties or guilds (Z. *amaButo*, sing. *iButo*, from *buta*, collect together). When, towards the end of the eighteenth century, circumcision fell into disuse, the practice of classifying the youth of the clan in separate groups according to age still continued, but now, not for circumcision, but for general state purposes (1929: 41).

Bryant goes on to point out that as these bands of age-groups grew in size, and started to become used for military purposes, it became appropriate to refer to them as 'regiments'.

Girls of a certain age-group were also given a name, although they were not necessarily conscripted into regiments which served at a military barracks. Doke and Vilakazi, however, refer to such named age-groups as 'regiments', and in the *Zulu-English Dictionary* we find entries such as '**iNtshukumadango**: regiment of girls enrolled by Shaka' and '**iBheje**: a member of one of Dingane's regiments of girls'.

For the regimental names in this chapter I have used Bryant's 1929 *Olden Times*, as did Krige for the Appendix on Zulu regimental names in *The Social System of the Zulus*, which first appeared in 1936. I have also combed Doke and Vilakazi's *Zulu-English Dictionary* for any extra regimental names, apart from consulting the dictionary for meanings. Carl Faye's list of regiments in his 1923 *Zulu References* contains much material about meanings and derivations and includes the praise names of many of the regiments, but for some curious reason Faye's list only begins with the regiments conscripted by Dingane. Samuelson's 1929 *Long, Long Ago* gives an extensive list of the Zulu royal regiments, and includes interpretations. Finally, the four volumes of the James Stuart Archives have been very rich in regimental information, and are the only works which seek to go outside the Zulu royal clan, giving the names of the regiments of various other chiefs such as the Mkhize chiefs.

6.2 VARIATIONS OF NAMES WITHIN THE REGIMENTAL SYSTEM

Standardising the names of the regiments from the different sources is not an easy task, as can be seen by comparing the regiments of Dingane as given by Bryant, Faye, Doke and Vilakazi, and two Stuart sources, in the table below. X indicates that a particular source has identified the name on the left as a regiment of Dingane. It will be noted that of 23 regiments named by the various sources, *only one regiment* is named by all five sources: the **uDlambedlu** regiment.

Regiments of Dingane from five different sources

Name	Bryant	Faye	D&V	JSA (I)	JSA (II)
iziBawu	X				
uDlambedlu	X	X	X	X	X
isiGulutshane	X				
um/imHaye	X		X		
iHlaba	X			X	X
uHlomendlini	X				
umKhandlu			X		
um/imKhulutshane	X		X	X	X
uKokoti	X	X		X	
uKuwela			X		
uMdlenevu		X			
iMpangiso			X		
uNdabakadengizibone				X	
iNdabakawombe		X			X
iNgwegwe		X			
uNqobolondo			X		
iN(t)sewane		X		X	
uNtshamatshe			X		
iziNyosi				X	X
uShoyisa			X		
imVokwe/imVoko	X		X		
iWombe			X		
isiYendane			X		

There are a number of reasons for these variations, apart from the actual accuracy of the oral sources in each case. *Firstly*, a significant number of regiments were housed in military homesteads (**amakhanda**) specifically built for the purpose, and often the regiment took the name of the establishment, and vice versa. But this was not always the case, and occasionally a name purporting to be a regiment name is only the name of the place where that regiment was normally housed, and not the name of the regiment itself.

Secondly, regiments were split into smaller groups, sometimes only into two groups which then served in different localities; but always into battalions (**izigaba**) and companies (**amaviyo**) which each had their own name. Many of these battalion and company names have been irretrievably lost, some have survived intact (together with the name of the headman [**induna**] in charge), and some battalion and company names have become confused over time with regiment names. *Thirdly*, regiments did not die when the king who had formed them died: they were inherited by the next king in line, who may have combined them into larger groups, split them into smaller groups, or simply renamed them. *Fourthly*, most regiments had one or more nicknames or praise names by which they were popularly known.

I would like to expand on each of these four reasons for variations of regimental names, in the following four subsections.

6.2.1 Confusion of regiment name with name of military establishment

Bryant tells us that: 'The first private kraal or national capital built by Shaka after his accession was that of *kwaBulawayo* . . . but it does not appear that there was ever a specific regiment called by that name, though the palace garrison was collectively sometimes referred to as such' (1929: 643).

And indeed, the list of Shaka's regiments in Volume I of the *James Stuart Archives* gives 'Bulawayo' as the name of a regiment (20).

Bryant goes on to say, 'The *umKhandlu* was the name, not of a regiment, but of a military kraal (loc. *emKhandlwini*) . . . and as such was often applied to the particular section of the army quartered there' (1929: 644).

And yet Doke and Vilakazi, under the entry **umkhandlu**, make no mention of a military kraal, but give this as 'one of Dingane's regiments'.

The following are given as names of Shaka's military kraals (**amakhanda**) by various sources in the four volumes of the *James Stuart Archives*: **Bulawayo**, **Mbelebele**, **Khangela**, **umKhandlu**, **uMgumanqa**, **Siphezi** and **uMlambongwenya**. And every one of these is also given as the name of a regiment by one source or another. In the same way, the following are given as among Dingane's military kraals in the Stuart Archives: **Gibabanye**, **eMkhulutshaneni**, **Gibabanye** and **Fasimba**. And again, all of these are also given by one source or another as regimental names.

Sometimes there is a distinction, with some writers using the locative form of a noun for a kraal name, and the non-locative form for the regiment. Doke and Vilakazi, for example, say that **uMbelebele** (non-locative form) is 'one of Shaka's regiments housed at the **eMbelebeleni** [locative form] military kraal'.

To compound the confusion, it could happen that more than one regiment was housed at one military barracks, as for example, when the **uDubinhlangu** regiment was quartered at Senzangakhona's old **eSiklebeni** kraal. Also barracked there was the younger **umGamule** (also known as **uDlambedlu**) regiment. The whole garrison together became known as the **izimPohlo** (the Bachelors Brigade) (Bryant, 1929: 642).

And then again, the converse might happen: a regiment may be split up to serve simultaneously at a number of different barracks. As one of Stuart's sources tells us, 'The Imikulutshane and the Izigulutshane were all buta'd together . . . The Izigulutshane were not an independent and distinct regiment. They were merely distributed among the kraals Nobamba, Siklebe, Mbelebele and Mgungundlovu' (Webb & Wright, II: 93).

And yet **isiGulutshane** is identified as a regimental name by various other sources.

It is not the intention of this book to attempt to sort out which names are regimental names and which the names of military barracks, or, in the many cases where the name does indeed refer to both barracks and the inhabitants, to work out which usage came first. Even assuming that it would be possible to find this out, such a study would need to be a considerable length. Rather, I am trying to illustrate one of the reasons why records of Zulu regimental history do not always tally.

6.2.2 Hierarchy of Zulu military structures

Bryant states:

> Inasmuch as, in the process of continuous warfare, the original Senzangakhona-ites ever more fell out on the field, bodies of younger men were periodically drafted in to maintain the regimental strength. Thus to the Wombes were added, one after the other, the *uNomdayana* (*izinTenjane ezakal' oNgoye*), the *amaPela*, the *iziKwembu*, the *amaKwenkwe*, the *iziZimazane* – all collectively forming the *umBelebele* army division (1929: 643).

Note that Bryant uses the word 'division' to suggest something bigger than a regiment. He goes on to say, 'In a similar manner and for a like reason, with the *izimPohlo* were subsequently embodied the *uGibabanye*, the *uFojisa*, the *imFolozi*, the *inDabankulu*, the *uBekenya* and others, all collectively forming the *isiKlebe* division' (643).

In the two quotes above, Bryant is talking of named units that are *larger* than regiments, which he has called a 'division' or 'army division'. In another work, his 1949 *The Zulu People as they were before the white man came*, he also talks about smaller divisions, as well as about the process of naming a regiment and assigning it identifying accoutrements:

> Whenever it appeared to the authorities that the bigger *Kleza* boys (i.e. those of about 18 years of age) were, collectively in all the military kraals, sufficient in number to form a new *iButo* (or regiment), orders went forth from the king (generally at the time of the annual *umKosi* or royal festival), that they be gathered together. He then conferred on them some new fancy name of their own, gave directions as to what distinguishing dress or body ornament they should wear and what colour their shields should be, and finally nominated some competent notable to be their *inDuna* (or colonel), who, in turn, would appoint from amongst the youths themselves divers 'captains' (*iPini*), one over each *isiGaba* (battalion), there being three or four such battalions to each regiment, each battalion comprising 5 or more *amaViyo* (companies), and each company containing some 50 or more warriors. . . .
>
> . . . [the military barracks] were divided up (like the regiment itself)

first, into two *izinTlangoti* (or sides), and then each side [divided] into *iziGaba* . . . (497)

The verb **kleza** literally means 'drink milk directly from the cow'. Bryant uses the term to describe the boys aged between 13 and 18 who were assigned to a military kraal to function there as herdboys and luggage carriers (**odibi**).

With this description, we now have five possibilities for groups of warriors, each one of which may be named: the largest, the army division (for which there seems to be no specific Zulu term), consisting of a number of regiments; the regiment (**ibutho**); the two halves of the regiment (**izinhla-ngothi**) depending on which side of the military barracks they lived; the battalion (**isigaba**); and the company (**iviyo**). Some of the names of these smaller units have come down to us intact with the names of the man in charge. For example, a Stuart source (Webb & Wright, III: 165) gives us the following names of the **izigaba** (battalions) and **amaviyo** (companies) of Mpande's **isAngqu** (also known as **amaTshitshi**) regiment:

First battalion: **amaJindi**
Companies: 1. amaJindi, 2. amaLandandhlovu, 3. Musiwegudu, 4. oMpo-ndo, 5. amaKabaludaka, 6. iMpanjane

Second battalion: **Ndlaphu**
Companies: 7. iziNgwananda, 8. iziNhlendhla, 9. iziKwili, 10. iziNgwe, 11. amaBuzanganduku, 12. iziRula [Xibakulu – Stuart uses *R* for the voiceless velar fricative]

Third battalion: **Mizimpisi**
Companies: 13. iMpopoma, 14. Msizi, 15. iziMvubu, 16. iziNkolombela, 17. iziNyoni, 18. oQamuqamu, 19. Mtshinane, 20. Mizimpisi (Xibakulu)

Here we see a regiment composed of three battalions, with the following number of companies: First battalion: six companies, Second battalion: six companies, Third battalion: eight companies. The First battalion shares a name with the first company in the battalion: 'amaJindi'; the Second and Third battalions have their own name. Stuart's informant in this case, Mkhando ka Dhlova – of whom Stuart says, 'Mkando . . . a man aged I should think about 74, for he belongs to the Isangqu regiment and was a year or so old when Tshaka was killed. I hope to get a good deal of information from him' (Webb & Wright, III: 145) – not only gives the names of each company but the personal name and clan name of each captain (**induna**) of each company. I have not included these here.

In Bryant's list of regiments in *Olden Times* (1929: 645–646), he indicates military hierarchies through indentation, but does not tell us whether these are divisions divided into regiments, or regiments divided into battalions. Take, for example, the following:

umXapo (umPunga, uHlwayi)
    umLambongwenya
    isiPikili
    inTsukamngeni

From this we assume that **umXapo** (with its alternative names **umPunga** and **uHlwayi**) is the name of a group which comprises the **umLambongwenya**, the **isiPikili** and the **inTsukamngeni**. But is 'umXapo' the name of an army division comprising the three regiments umLambongwenya, isiPikili and inTsukamngeni, or is umXapo the name of a regiment, comprising the three battalions umLambongwenya, etc.?

The same question can be asked about the following indented layout, copied exactly from the same page as the one above:

Indluyengwe (incorp. with uTulwana)	
	IKwentu
inDlu-	imVu-emnyama (to umLambongwenya)
yengwe-	uKandempemvu (umCijo, uNqakamatshe)
encane	umTwisazwe (to uKandempemvu)

There are a number of puzzles here:

- If the **Indluyengwe** were 'incorp[orated]' with the **uTulwana**, what was the name of the combination of these two?
- '**inDluyengwe-encane**' means 'the little **Indluyengwe**'. So was it part of, or partner to, the **Indluyengwe**?
- What does '*to* **umLambongwenya**' and '*to* **uKandempemvu**' mean?
- Clearly, '**IKwentu**', '**imVu-emnyama**', '**uKandempemvu**' and '**umTwisazwe**' are parts of the wider '**inDluyengwe-encane**'. But is **inDluyengwe-encane** an army division, and the other four names of regiments? Surely not, because if '**inDluyengwe-encane**' ('the *little* **inDluyengwe**') is an army division, then what sort of unit is the 'bigger' **Indluyengwe**? So, we ask again: is **inDluyengwe-encane** the name of a regiment, and the other four names of battalions within that regiment? Perhaps, but certainly these four names are regularly given as the names of full regiments by various authorities.

Again, all I can do here is draw attention to the problems caused in regimental identity by the names given to all parts of the military hierarchy, from the largest division to the smallest company. As Bryant himself says of his list:

> Here below we present a general list, as accurate and complete as we have been able to make it, of all Zulu regiments from the accession of Shaka . . . at this distance of time it has not been always possible to disentangle with any certainty, from amidst the mass of names that have come down to us, precisely which were those of regiments (*iButo*), which were those of mere regimental companies (*isiGaba*), which those of military-kraals (*iKanda*) or army-division thereto attached – all three having had their separate distinguishing names (1929: 645–646).

6.2.3 Inherited regiments

The formation of a regiment was the prerogative of a king or chief. But when that chief or king died, the regiment did not just automatically disband, but it was inherited by the king's successor. Such a regiment might then have continued under the new king intact in its membership and under its old identity, or it might have been split up, or compounded with other units, or simply have been re-named. Stuart provides evidence of this happening, '"Amakwentu (went to Kwa Gqikazi) and Indluyengwe (went to Ulundi): both same regiment". In other words, one regiment, split into two and sent to different locations, each half then getting its own name' (Webb & Wright, III: 328). Shaka's first two regiments, we learn from Bryant (1929: 642) were inherited from his father Senzangakhona. Bryant does not tell us what Senzakhona named these regiments but we are told that the first group Shaka re-named the **amaWombe**, and the second group he re-named the **uDubinhlangu**.

One of Stuart's sources (Webb & Wright, II: 92) tells us that Dingane's regiment the **inSewane** was re-named the **Dlambedu** by Mpande. This is confusing, for as we noted above in the table of Dingane's regiments as cited by five different sources, the **uDlambedlu** regiment was the only single regiment that each source identified as being a Dingane regiment. In other words, in the name **Dlambedlu** is enshrined the archetypal Dingane regiment, and yet here is someone claiming that Dingane's successor Mpande renamed a Dingane regiment as 'Dlambedlu'. This kind of information is distinctly puzzling. The same informant (Webb & Wright, II: 95) tells us that Shaka's regiments the **uFojisa** and the **inGcobinga** became the **izimPohlo** and the **izinYosi** respectively, when inherited by Dingane.

Another Stuart source tells us of Shaka's regiment named the **Gibanaye**, that, '. . . Gibabanye – formerly uPoko. This regiment, the Gibabanye, was cut in two and incorporated into the Ntonteleni and the Mkandlweni. One division was called uDhlangubo, the other retained the name Gibabanye' (Webb & Wright, II: 249).

Another story about name changing is also from the Stuart Archives (Webb & Wright, III: 328). It would appear that one of Dinuzulu's regiments went by the name of **inGubokakhundlase** ('Khundlase's blanket'), Khundlase being the name of the mother of Zibebu, Dinuzulu's political rival. It is not clear whether Dinuzulu himself had given this name, but we are told that on his return from exile on the Island of St. Helena, Dinuzulu directed that in order not to offend Zibebu, the regiment's name be changed to **uFelaphakathi** ('die within').

6.2.4 Nicknames and praise names

Perhaps the cause of the most confusion in the identification of regiments stems from their 'extra' names – their praise names or nicknames. Almost all the sources of regimental names continually give a name with another name in parentheses, as in 'Tulwana (amaMboza)', 'Amatshitshi (Isangqu)' and 'Hayelwengwenya (Dakwa-ukusutha)'. In each case, the alternative name for the regiment is being given. Sometimes this parenthesised name is accompanied by another 'extra' name, as in Bryant, 'These shorn warriors he labelled the *uDubintlangu* (alias *inTontela*), but popularly they became referred to as the *uJubingqwanga* (They of the Head-ring Ukase [**ukase** is given as a rare word for 'edict' in the *Collins English Dictionary*])' (1929: 642).

Many indeed, are the references to these extra names. Bryant tells us (644) that when the **umGumanqa** regiment was sent down to the flats near Port Natal to keep an eye on the newly arrived whites, they became known by the nickname **uKhangela-amaNkengane** ('keep an eye on the vagabonds'), which not only gave this regiment another name, but also gave the name **Congella** to that area of Durban.

Stuart (Webb & Wright, II: 92) tells us that such an 'extra' name is known as an **umenanelo**, a word which Doke and Vilakazi define simply as 'a rejoicing'. On the one hand, clearly this word is derived from the verb **enanela** ('to show delight over, to rejoice, to cheer'), and presumably such an extra name was given to a regiment when it had achieved some specific battle honour. On the other hand, on the same page which gives us the word **umenanelo**, Stuart uses the word **isithakazelo** ('clan praise') to refer to these extra regimental names:

> Dingana's regiments:
> Izinyosi – formerly Ingcobinga under Tshaka; or Izingobondo (its *isitakazelo)*
> Dhlambedlu – alias Imgamule (its *isitakazelo)* . . .
> Ihlaba – alias uNomaraye (its *isitakazelo*)
> Kokoti –'to whose bite there is no antidote' (its *isitakazelo*) Mpande called this uNdabakawombe . . .
> Insewane – under Mpande it became the Dhlambedu, Ingwegwe and Imdhlenevu being its *izitakazelo* (Webb & Wright, II: 92).

Here we see a regiment of Shaka named the **inGcobinga**, re-named by Dingane the **izinYosi**, and then being generally known as the **izinGobondo**. Dingane's regiment **Insewane** is re-named **Dhlambedlu** by Mpande, and has two praise names: **Ingwegwe** and **Imdlenevu**.

On another page (Webb & Wright, II: 249) Stuart has recorded the names of various regiments of Shaka, not with their alternative or extra names, but with their praise phrases, which have been translated by editors Webb and Wright ('official' regimental name given in bold):

Isiphezi – The wall of Madilika, also uDonqabatwa.
Mgumanqa – Which stands threateningly in the patch of burnt grass, the Nomande which is at Mateko.
Fasimba – uNomyali, the rough tongue of a beast.
Mbonambi – uMbonambi whose fighting sticks are red (with blood) (**Ndukuzibomvu** – that is, 'red sticks').
Dhlangezwa – The stand of last season's grass.
Ndabenkulu (Velabakuze) – The dun-coloured beasts that bellowed at the Ngoye.

The overlap between the 'official' name given by a king to a regiment, the jocular nickname which the soldiers themselves used, and praise names and praise phrases awarded in honour of military achievements, is similar to the overlap that we have already noted in Chapter 5 between clan names, clan praise names, and the longer clan praises. In Chapter 5 I noted that certain **izibongo** (clan names) and **izithakazelo** (clan praise names) had become virtually interchangeable, and I gave examples of such pairs as **Xulu** and **Makhathini**, **Hadebe** and **Mthimkhulu**, **Ngema** and **Mngadi**, and **Mthembu** and **Mvelase**. Even a quick glance at the lists of regiments in Bryant, Krige, Faye and other sources will show entries such as '**iSangqu** (**amaTshitshi**)' being contrasted with '**amaTshitshi** (**iSangqu**)' and '**uThulwana** (**amaMboza**)' being contrasted with '**amaMboza** (**uThulwana**'), showing that the regiment's name and its praise name or nickname have become completely interchangeable.

Space precludes me from giving a complete list of regiments with their interchangeable forms, but in order to illustrate the point, here are some of the alternative forms (taken this time from Krige, 1950: 406–407):

Regiments of Dingane
umSikaba or **umZinyathi**
inDlondlo or **uShisizwe**
isAngqu or **amaShishi**
umXhapho or **uMpunga** or **uHlwayi**
inDwali or **inKonyan'ebomvu**
uKhandempemvu or **umCijo** or **uNqakamatshe**

Regiments of Cetshwayo
inGobamakhosi or **uNobongowezulu**
uluVe or **uLandandlovu**
uFalaza or **umSizi** or **inZekema**

Regiments of Dinuzulu
imBokod'ebomvu or **inHlansi**
uFelaphakathi or **inGubo-kaKhundlase**
uDakw'ukusuthwa or **uHawulwengwenya**
uMavalana or **uCijimpi** or **inTab'engenaliba**

6.3 UNDERLYING MEANINGS OF ZULU REGIMENT NAMES

Faye is one of the two recorders of Zulu regiments who has tried to give both translation and explanation for the names. Most of his interpretations are useful and insightful, although there are one or two which are rather curious. Two examples will suffice:

1. Faye interprets the name of Mpande's regiment **inDluyengwe** (which to me is clearly **indlu**, 'dwelling', + **ya**, 'of', + **ingwe**, 'leopard) as 'The Leopard's Fine Reddish-Brown Markings' or 'the Leopard's Beauty-Spots' and adds 'Not the Leopard's Lair, as supposed by some.' There is no justification that I can see for assigning the meaning 'red-brown markings' or 'beauty spot' to the Zulu word **indlu**.
2. The other curious interpretation concerns the regimental name **uFalaza**, which Doke and Vilakazi state is derived from the ideophone **falaza** ('be chatty, garrulous'). Faye interprets this name as 'Clouds of the Heavens', suggesting that the name is a contraction of – the ungrammatical phrase – **amaFu-la-ezulu** ('clouds of the sky'). How **amafu** becomes 'fa', where the 'la' comes from, and how **ezulu** becomes 'za', Faye does not explain.

The other interpreter of regimental names is R.C.A. Samuelson, who devoted six pages of his 1929 *Long, Long Ago* to the meanings of these names. Samuelson's interpretations are basically sound, and here and there he contributes something original, such as suggesting that the name of Shaka's **izimPohlo** did not refer to 'bachelors' (Zulu **izimpohlo**), but that the name was derived from the verb **phohloza** ('to smash or crush'). This does make some sense when we realise that the verb **phohloza** is itself derived from the ideophone **phohlo** ('of smashing, crushing').

Some of Samuelson's explanations are a little garbled, as in: 'uDib-inhlangu. – This regiment might be called the Confusers, as it is composed of Diba, "to throw together indiscriminately," and Inhlangu, "a reit buck," which must be a contraction of Izinhlangu , "Reit Bucks" – the whole word meaning, literally, "the throwing indiscriminately together of Reit Bucks," which Reit Bucks might mean the enemy' (1929: 240).

In another example, Samuelson suggests that Mpande's regiment the **isAngqu** (the Zulu name for the Orange River) was given to them 'because this regiment got as far as the Orange River during its operations'. Even assuming that this is true, this suggestion does not explain what the regiment was called *before* that point in their military career when they reached the Orange River. Perhaps 'amaTshitshi', which most authorities give as the nickname of the isAngqu regiment, was their 'real' name, and 'isAngqu' was a praise name conferred on them to mark their arrival at this particular river.

Despite my comments on the interpretations of both Faye and Samuelson, they throw interesting light on the origins of regimental names, and I have balanced their suggestions with my own dictionary-based translations in giving the meanings which form the second half of this chapter.

Many, indeed most, of the regimental names reflect on the character or behaviour of the regiment, whether real or fancied. There is also a surprising number of names which link the regiment to the natural environment. I have made these my two major categories.

6.3.1 Behaviour or character of the regiment

Regimental names under this sub-heading give some idea of the supposed behaviour or character of the regiment, and usually portray the regiment as fierce and aggressive. Many of these names might today be regarded as strongly critical, even libellous, as in **iziHula** (< **isihula**, 'person or animal of greedy, voracious and destructive nature') or **inGcugce** (< **gcugca**, 'rob, pillage, plunder'). Some, while aggressive, are less so, as in the amusing **amaKhabaludaka** ('Kickers of Mud'). Metaphors may be brought into use, as in **inHlansi** ('spark of fire').

a. Aggressive, attacking behaviour

Behaviour that is aggressive and/or attacking is expressed in names such as:

- **uCijimpi** ('press on with the battle' or 'egg on the army');
- **iWombe** (< **isiwombe**, 'onslaught');
- **inZanayo** ('what comes with a fight');
- **uVukayibambe** ('wake up and grab them' or 'up and at 'em');
- **amaBuzangenduku** ('ask by means of a stick').

I include the **uMbonambi** (literally, 'see the bad things') here because of Stuart's suggestion (Webb & Wright, III: 328) that this is a corruption of **bona** + **impi** ('army, battle, fight'), which will allow the not unreasonable interpretation of 'looking for a fight'. Faye (1923: 48) suggests 'The Beholders . . . of Sorrow'.

The regiment can be likened to a person of aggressive behaviour, as in:

- **uBhekenya** ('person with angry, noisy tongue');
- **uBhewula** ('fierce, savage man');
- **uGqikazi** ('very strong personality or authority');
- **umHulugwane** ('voracious, greedy person or animal').

Similar names are **uDlambedlu** ('swallowing impatience'), **uDloko** ('savage, uncontrolled nature'), and **inTshamathe** ('spurt out saliva'), which suggests impatient rage. Less aggressive, perhaps, are:

- **uFojisa** ('humble, humiliate');
- **inGagu** ('conceited boldness');
- **uFalaza** ('gossip, be garrulous'). In *Long, Long Ago* Samuelson (1929: 244) gives the meaning of the **uFalaza** as 'the rubbish talkers', and says that it was 'so named by Cetywayo after his return from captivity, because the Zulus had lost the habit of talking commonsense as they used to before he was taken captive'.

Decidedly out of place in this assorted collection of fierce, savage and voracious people is **uNkisimane** ('person of gentlemanly manner' < English *Englishman*).

Metaphors of hunting can be used, as seen in:

- **uDliki** ('shaking, worrying, like a dog with its prey');
- **inGedle** (< **gedla**, 'grind with teeth', 'bring down in hunt', 'kill off');
- **amaShishi** (< interjection **shishi**!, 'Go it!', 'At him!').

Stinging attacks are seen in the metaphors **imBabazane** ('stinging nettle') and **isiBawu** ('gadfly', 'tsetse-fly'), and destruction in the metaphors **umLilo** ('fire') and **uHlontane** ('torch').

The regiment may be named after a specific aggressive action or intention. This is the case with:

- **uGibabanye** ('take out the others');
- **inGobamakhosi** ('bend the chiefs');
- **isiPhezi** ('bringer to a finish');
- **imPumangingene** ('go out while I come in');
- **amaShayizindlu** ('strikers of huts');
- **uShisizwe** ('burn the country');
- **umThulisazwe**, also given as **umThwisazwe** ('what quietens the country').

I put Mpande's regiment **uKhandempemvu** here, as I translate it as 'hammer the white-faces', in other words, 'target the whites for destruction'. I am not supported here, however, by either Faye or Samuelson, for Faye gives this regiment as meaning 'The Ruddy Sharp Stake', and Samuelson renders the name as 'the head with white and black colouring'.

Swift movement of the regiment is expressed in:

- **uNokhenke** (< **khenka**, 'run, trot, pace along');
- **imPangiso** ('a hurrying, a hastening');
- **uVelabakhuze** ('appear to their surprise');
- **uDududu** ('a rushing of footsteps'). Stuart notes of this last name (Webb & Wright, III: 328) that it was the name of Shaka's favourite bull.

Miscellaneous names that convey something of the character of the regiment include:

- **uDlangezwa** ('eat, that is, "conquer", without feeling');
- **uMagazini** ('in the bloods', perhaps 'in full blood'?);
- **uNdindindi** ('reverberations, dizziness, giddiness');
- **uNsinya** ('tighten, draw taut, as noose around neck');
- **isiXwazi** ('internal injury, bruise, contusion');
- **iziZimane** (< **zimaza**, 'be impressive, imposing');
- **umSonganyathi** ('threaten the buffalo' – this is also the name of the upper portion of the uMngeni River).

b. Men of the regiment

There are a few regimental names which indicate that the regiment was made up of older men, or 'left-overs':

- **uMpunga** ('The Greyheads');
- **uPhefeni** ('bearded man');
- **amaPhela** ('last remnants' – Samuelson translates this as 'The Cockroaches', and says that they were so named because they were expected to swarm all over the country 'eating up' everything in sight);
- **iziYendane** ('Hlubi and Mfengu refugees');
- **umKhandlu** ('assembly of men');
- **umGumanqa** ('assembly of representative men').

We have already heard the story, from Bryant, of how Shaka ordered an already-head-ringed age-group of **Senzangakhona** to take off their head-rings and remain unmarried, naming them **uJubinqwanga** ('order the first ones'), which group then became part of a larger division of unmarried men known as the **izimPohlo** ('bachelors').

c. Weapons

Strongly related to regimental names that refer to warlike behaviour are the names which refer to the weapons used: spears, fighting sticks, shields, and so on. Included here are:

- **umCijo** ('something pointed');
- **inDukukaqwabalanda** ('Qwabalanda's stick' – Doke and Vilakazi tell us that Qwabalanda was one of Dinuzulu's captains);
- **inGwegwe** ('crook', 'stick with hook');
- **izinHlendla** ('barbed assegais');
- **iziKhwili** ('short, thick, knobless fighting sticks');
- **inZawu** ('sharp cutting instrument', 'battle-axe').

That at least some regiments were familiar with guns of some sort can be seen in the names:

- **uHlwayi** ('buck-shot', 'pellets');

- **uMsizi** ('gunpowder');
- **uNqobolondo** ('shell of bullet', 'cartridge case').

The name **uHawulengwenya** ('shield of crocodile skin') is given by some writers as **uHayelwengwenya**, of which Stuart writes: 'Hayelwengwenya . . . The uhaye is a man's buttock-cover of different kinds of bucks, that has been qopa'd (slitted at edges). No-one can wear a buttock-cover of crocodile hide' (Webb & Wright, III: 328).

I certainly prefer the form which translates as 'shield of crocodile skin' as this gives an image of invincibility.

No specific weapons are mentioned in **uHlomendlini** ('armed at home').

6.3.2 The regiment and the natural environment

There are a number of regimental names which link the regiment to various aspects of the natural environment, such as animal and plant life, rivers and other geographical features, and the weather.

a. Animal life

Surprisingly enough, I have not found a single regiment which refers to the lion, despite its martial symbolism and its link to Zulu royalty. The other big cat of Zululand, the leopard, makes an appearance, as does the elephant and other big mammals. Interspersed among these are smaller mammals, domestic mammals, birds, snakes and other reptiles, and insects.

Names which refer to various animals are:

- **isiBhejane** ('black rhinoceros');
- **izinDlovu** ('the elephants');
- **inDluyengwe** ('house of the leopard');
- **uDubinhlangu** ('ignore the bushbuck');
- **izinGulube** ('wild pigs');
- **izinGwe** ('leopards');
- **amaHhashi** ('horses');
- **inKonkoni** ('wildebeest');
- **inKonyanebomvu** ('red calf');
- **iNjanduna** ('male dog');
- **iziMpisi** ('hyenas');
- **imVemnyama** ('black sheep');
- **izimVubu** ('hippos');
- **imVukuzane** ('mole');
- **imiZimpisi** ('kraals of the hyenas');
- **umZwangwenya** ('what perceives a crocodile').

The name **umNgwempisi** presents a problem in interpretation. It could be from **ingwe** ('leopard') + **impisi** ('hyena'), that is, 'leopard-hyena', or from

umunga + **impisi**, which would give us 'acacia of the hyenas', or from **umungu** + **impisi**, that is, 'fine dust of the hyenas'. One way or the other, the hyenas get a mention here.

Snakes are well represented in Zulu regimental names, with:

- **inDlondlo** ('horned mamba', 'horned viper');
- **uDlondlwane** (diminutive of **indlondlo**);
- **uKhokhothi** ('species of non-poisonous spitting snake');
- **iMamba** ('mamba');
- **iNyandezulu** ('species of green snake').

Examples of birds forming the base of regimental names include the following:

- **izinKonjane** ('swallows');
- **inSewane** ('small bird resembling **intiyane** [the waxbill]');
- **izinTaka** ('finches');
- **uluVe** ('Paradise Flycatcher');
- **iziNyoni** ('The Birds').

The regiment **oNobhongoza** ('Egyptian Vultures') provides us with interesting symbolism. Doke and Vilakazi's entry for '**unobhongoza**' tells us that this word refers to both the Egyptian Vulture as well as a regiment of Dingane, and then directs us to the entry **uphalane**, where we read:

> 1. Egyptian vulture . . . (generally seen in pairs). [cf. *unobongoza*]
> 2. Term applied to lovers, and to certain regiments of Dingane which usually accompanied each other (1958: 644).

This makes some sense of the statement by one of Stuart's sources (Webb & Wright, I: 214), made in reference to Dingane's regiments, namely that 'the Izinnyosi [*sic*] and Dlambedhlu were "palane" regiments'. Stuart's source goes on to say that ' "palane" means a great or extra-sized regiment like the Ngobamakhosi', and clearly this means that such an extra-sized regiment consisted of two regiments that 'hunted together'. The symbolism in the name **uNobhongoza** is thus rich and multi-layered: a combination with this 'fidelity in pairing', of 'brother regiments', together with the symbolic strength of a large raptor, again linked with the image of vultures circling above scenes of death and destruction.

When we look at regimental names based on insects, we note that these are all insects that annoy human beings in some way, by stinging, biting, or by being troublesome:

- **isiBawu** ('gadfly', tsetse fly');
- **imBungulu** ('bug');
- **iziNyosi** ('bees');
- **inGobolwane** (**hlonipha** for **impukane**, 'fly').

b. Plant life

Plant references can be found in the following names of regiments, and we see that the first three, like the insect references, are to stinging or stabbing plants:

- **imBabazane** ('stinging nettle');
- **iHlaba** ('species of aloe');
- **iHlabane** ('species of aloe');
- **iKhwani** ('species of tall sedge');
- **uTshani** ('grass');
- **umVuthwamini** (literally, 'what matures at midday': species of maize);
- **uDonqabathwa** (literally, 'the Bushmen's oilplant': a field weed).

The regimental name **umKhuze** could refer to the uMkhuze River or to the species of aromatic tree known as an **umkhuze**.

c. Weather and topography

Certain aspects of the weather can be seen in:

- **uFasimbe** ('haze, haziness');
- the closely-related **inKwenkwezi** ('light bluish haze on distant hills', 'certain conspicuous star');
- **uMungu** ('fine dust');
- **uMoya** ('air', 'wind');
- **iNingizimu** ('South', 'South wind');
- **iNyakatho** ('North', 'North wind');
- **iQhwa** ('snow').

InTabayezwe ('mountain of the country') suggests a certain strength and invincibility, while the curious **amaTshezulu** ('rocks of the sky') makes one think of the possibility of the destructiveness of a heavy shower of meteorites.

The names of a number of rivers coincide with the names of regiments. Whether the regiment was named after the river, or the river after the regiment, or both river and regiment were independently named the same way, is not clear. The **umKhuze** River and regiment were mentioned above, and I have also discussed the **isAngqu** regiment (Zulu name for Orange River). Other river-regiment combinations are:

- the **imFolozi** ('the zig-zagger');
- the **umLambongwenya** ('crocodile river');
- the **umZinyathi** ('house of the buffalo').

6.3.3 Miscellaneous

Certain regimental names suggest that they refer to particular events. For some of these, the events are reasonably well-attested in the historical sources. For example, Shaka's regiment **uBulawayo** ('the one killed') takes its name from the homestead he built and named in reference to his ill-treatment when a child; Mpande's regiment (and homestead) **ukuWela** ('the crossing over') refers to his decision to split with his brother Dingane and cross the Tugela river into Natal, while the story of **iJubingqwanga** ('order the first ones') has already been given in this chapter.

I have not been able to identify the stories which are (possibly) contained in the following names:

- **umBelebele** ('worrisome, never-ending affair');
- **inDaba-kaNdondondo** ('Ndondondo's affair');
- **inDabakawombe** ('the affair of the Wombes');
- **uLandandlovu** ('fetch the elephant');
- **Undabakadengizibona** ('the matters which I have just seen');
- **uNdabankulu** ('the big affair').

References to weapons are not surprising in regimental names, and I have included these above under the heading 'Behaviour or character of the regiment'. Much less obvious is reference to foodstuffs, even if some of these are the food taken by soldiers on journeys:

- **imDlenevu** ('slight burning on mealie grains');
- **uPhoko** ('small sp. of millet roasted by soldiers on journeys');
- **uThwele** ('roasted dried mealies');
- **iNyakeni** ('spoon bag' < **inyaka**, 'pancreas', 'sweetbread').

The remainder of the regimental names in this chapter are distinctly intriguing.

The four names which follow refer to possessions of royalty: one basket, one hat, and two blankets. In **imBenge-ka-kwini** ('the queen's shallow basket') and **isiGqoko-sika-kwini** ('the queen's hat') we encounter the problem of 'kwini' or 'khwini'. I have assumed here that this is an adoptive from English *queen*, but this does seem unlikely for a regimental name. Somehow I would expect something like **imbenge-yenkosikazi** ('the blanket of the high-born lady') or **ingubo-yendlovukazi** ('the blanket of the Great She-Elephant'). Or is '**uK(h)wini**' a personal name derived from **ikhwini** ('meat of a buck mixed with his blood and boiled')? If so, who was uKhwini?

With **inGubo-kaKhundlase** ('Khundlase's blanket') we find ourselves on safer ground, as we already have the story that Khundlase was the mother of Dinuzulu's political rival Zibebu. And with **inGuboyenkosi** ('the king's blanket'), even if the king is not identified, at least **inkosi** is a well-known Zulu word.

There is another mystery in the regimental name **uSiba-lukaMtshelekwana** ('the plume/feather of Mtshelekwana'). Who was Mtshelekwana? What happened to his plume? And why should a regiment have been named after Mtshelekwana's plume?

The name **isiQamelo** ('wooden head-rest') provides a different type of question. Most regimental names, as we have seen, emphasise fighting, turbulence, discord, uproar, and anything disturbing. And here is a name using a symbol of rest and peace: the wooden head-rest.

The name **iNqabayokucasha** ('fortress for hiding') seems at first glance fairly straightforward: it must be, one immediately thinks, a regimental name taken from the name of military barracks built in an impregnable position. And then we find from Faye (1923: 51), that this regiment of King Solomon Nkayishana kaDinuzulu, was originally named **iNqabakucetshwa**, which Faye translates as 'The Will-Not-be-Betrayed-by-Foreigners', a name that suggests a moral standpoint on the part of the young king. There clearly is a story behind this name change.

Faye tells us (1923: 50) that Dinuzulu's regiment **inTabingenaliba** ('hill without a grave') took its name from the proverb **'Kakukh' intab' engenaliba'** ('there is no hill but has its grave'), signifying, says Faye, that 'Where'er you may go, be it far or near, ne'er will you find a Mountain where there's no death.' Whether or not this philosophy is related to that expressed by the same king (Dinuzulu) in naming his earlier regiment **uFelaphakathi** ('die inside'), I cannot say.

There could well be a simple metaphor in **amaTshayadlula** ('the rocks are passing by'). We have noticed that a number of regiments have used the image of stones, whether grinding-stones red with blood (**imBokow'ebomvu**) or rocks falling from the sky (**amaTshezulu**). So why should this regiment not simply refer to itself as 'the rocks which are passing by'?

We end this chapter with three more regimental names and simply leave their origins shrouded in mystery:

- **uGudludonga** ('skirt along the wall');
- **iTshelemali** ('rock of money');
- **uMusiwegudu** ('smoke from the hemp-pipe').

Part 3

Toponymy
(Place names)

Chapter 7

Zulu place names: General introduction and standardisation of spelling

7.1 INTRODUCTION

The term 'place name' is synonymous with 'toponym' and I will use these terms interchangeably in this section although some writers prefer to use the term 'geographical name'. Place names include the names of cities, towns and villages (that is, man-made inhabited areas) as well as the names of geographical features such as mountains (oronyms), and rivers and other water features (hydronyms).

The major function of place names – in whatever country, and in whatever language – is to identify, and thus to provide locational guidance. If someone asks you where you live, and you can say 'In Villa Sans Souci, on Blackmore Avenue, in the town Estcourt', then it is easier to find you than if you say 'in a little hut on top of the ridge a short distance inland from the sea close to the mouth of the big river with lots of crocodiles'. Of course, if you add names to the last statement, and make it 'in a little hut on top of Eagle Ridge, one kilometre inland from the mouth of the Crocodile River', there is also much more chance of finding your home.

In KwaZulu-Natal, among the earlier settlers, as well as the later settled white population, Zulu names have held a fascination over and above their referential function.

Stayt, in the introduction to his *Where on Earth? Place Names of Natal and Zululand* says:

> [Zulu place names] are picturesque and melodious. They are apt, descriptive, meaningful and rich in folk-lore, legend, history and imagery. When you have the trick of it, the words roll beautifully from the tongue, their sounds music in the air, and in no time at all you find yourself wanting to delve deeper and to discover the significance and symbolism that lies beneath the surface (1971).

Note that Stayt's *Where on Earth?* does not have any page numbers which is why these are not given in relation to quotations from this booklet.

Stayt goes on to write about problems of interpretation, and also about problems with the orthography of Zulu place names:

> [The spelling of Zulu place names] is very tricky territory. I like to spell Umdloti as I spelled it as a boy – Umhloti. Others have their own ideas and right away you are faced with Umhloti, Umdhloti, Umdloti, emDloti and Mdloti. And it doesn't matter how good a case the experts make out for spelling it emDloti or Mdloti, would you dream of looking for Umdloti under 'D' or 'M'?
>
> I know I wouldn't.

What causes variations of spelling, such as Stayt's examples above? Is it important to standardise spellings and to be consistent generally in the spelling of Zulu place names? Does it matter whether they are correctly spelt or not, and if they are misspelt, should we try to correct them? This chapter tries to answer these questions, starting the discussion by addressing the last question.

7.2 ORTHOGRAPHY

The spelling of Zulu place names – for close on 200 years mainly the end product of colonial ignorance and indifference – has over the last ten or so years become a contentious issue. Let us take a look at some irate correspondence about misspellings of place names.

Pietermaritzburg correspondent Cyril Shabalala wrote to the *Natal Witness* in January 2000:

> Robin Seal's interest in the correct pronunciation of African words is laudable but what he proposes as a cure is precisely the reason why African words have been corrupted by arrogant colonialists down the centuries.
>
> . . .
>
> There is a school of thought that African words should be anglicised when incorporated into English. This is nothing less than linguistic colonialism and Africans insist that indigenous words should retain their pronunciation regardless of the language of the speaker.
>
> A huge task still awaits us to correct aberrations like Tugela (uThukela) and Umbogintwini (eziMbokodweni), to name just two examples. The Chinese did it with Beijing (who remembers Peking?);

> the Zimbabweans with Gweru (Gwelo); why can't we do it in South Africa? (21 January 2000).

The writer does not mention whether he thinks that Zulu speakers should purge their vocabulary of place names which are *Zuluised* versions of *colonial* names, such as **uDanawuzi** for 'Dannhauser', **ePitoli** for 'Pretoria', and **iFilidi** for 'Vryheid'.

Correspondent Nhlanhla Ndlovu, also from Pietermaritzburg, puts his complaint as follows, in a letter to the *Natal Witness* dated 19 February 1998:

> It is very embarrassing when one misspells Zulu names more than the names of other languages.
>
> If you travel down to Durban you will find a road sign written Shongweni instead of Entshongweni. People must learn how to write correctly. Although isiZulu is regarded as a secondary language, we are proud of it.

In a *Natal Witness* article dated 14 December 1998, under the headline 'Watered-down Lingo', columnist Mbongeni Zondi makes a similar complaint. Starting with a complaint about 'Umgeni Water', 'who call themselves Umgeni, which is wrong because the name is misspelt' Zondi goes on to say:

> I'm tired of people playing around with isiZulu to a point where it is hard to differentiate from Fanakalo. I've heard there's something called the Dusi Canoe Marathon. What is that? Not only is the name shortened but it is also misspelt, The river is called the Umsunduzi. I can go on with a list of other Zulu names that have been savaged to suit minority pronunciation shortcomings, but that's not necessary.

Four days later, this heartfelt cry became the subject of a *Natal Witness* editorial, which started with: 'The question of cross-cultural language usage was spotlighted on this page this week. Many Africans feel that others are insensitively, and even arrogantly, careless in their use of African words, particularly place names', and ended with:

> Before the colonialists arrived there was an oral tradition. African grammatical structures are very different from those of Europe and early attempts to write down words which sounded very strange to European ears resulted in many errors. Still today, as the letters to this newspaper illustrate, there are differences of opinion as to certain correct usages and spellings even among African people.

Professor Phyllis Zungu refers to these incorrect usages and misspellings as 'toponymic lapses' in her article entitled 'Toponymic lapses in Zulu place names'. While her emphasis is on the 'unambiguous locational function' of place names rather than the savage cultural mistreatment of Zulu, she still sees correct spelling as important:

> Toponymic lapses are faults or mistakes in place names which are found in maps, records, telephone directories, signposts, etc. At face value they appear small, but on closer inspection, one realises that they are vitally important, because names should not fail to perform an unequivocal and unambiguous locational function . . . In KwaZulu-Natal, as in other countries, difficulty arises when place names have been wrongly spelt (23).

Zungu lists some of the reasons why Zulu names could have been misspelt on maps and on signboards in the past: 'ignorance or inadequate knowledge of the grammar or latest orthographic rules of the target language, marginalisation of the inhabitants of a particular area and hypercorrection'. The truth of this statement cannot be denied, and perhaps it could simply be stated that the major reason why for most of the twentieth century the maps and signboards of Natal said 'Tugela' instead of 'uThukela' and 'Umbongintwini' instead of 'eZimbokodweni' was that the maps and signboards were written by people whose language was not Zulu.

To a certain extent it is also true to say that colonial arrogance and a sense of Zulu as a 'second-class' language was responsible for the misspellings *staying for so long* even when access to the correct forms was easy. For example, there really is no justification for Map Studio's 1994 *Road Atlas* to spell the **isiKhwebezi** River, a tributary of the Black iMfolozi, as 'Squebezi'.

However, these two factors do not represent the whole picture. In an earlier article on the Zulu place names of the Drakensberg (Koopman, 1983), I showed that a place name such as **iNjasuthi** could have 12 variant spellings, all of which might be acceptable to a mother-tongue Zulu speaker, and none of which would be the result of lack of knowledge by colonial cartographers, whether arrogant or otherwise. It may be useful to refer to that discussion, because it raises orthographical problems which are still unresolved today.

Variations in the spelling of Zulu place names, as well as incorrect rendering on maps, signposts, etc., arise out of a number of factors, of which we can consider the following:

1. Changes in orthography;
2. Mishearing/misrendering of original Zulu name;
3. Inconsistency in noun prefix usage;
4. Inconsistency in use of locative forms;
5. Differences in compounding patterns in Zulu.

7.2.1 Changes in orthography

In 1949 the Zulu Language Board approved a number of changes in Zulu orthography, of which the main changes were **dhl** > **dl**, and the inclusion of **h** in aspirated stops, so **p** has become **ph**, **t** has become **th**, and **k** has become **kh**. Another change in the mid-1980s was to make **h** in words like **ihashi** ('horse') a double **hh**: **ihhashi**. As a result of these orthographical changes there are place names still spelt in the old orthography and others in the new and, very frequently, in both, depending on which map you read, which guidebook you consult, or which road sign you are passing. Thus one may come across **uMdlothi** *and* **uMdhloti**, **Impendhle** *and* **Impendle**, **Hlatikulu** *and* **Hlathikhulu**. One even comes across place names that *combine* the old and new orthographies: ***Hlatikhulu** and ***Hlathikulu**.

7.2.2 The mishearing or misrendering of original names

In Chapter 10 you will find over 20 different spellings of the Zulu name for Pietermaritzburg: **uMgungundlovu**. Only one variant is the result of orthographical changes, and that is **uMgungun<u>dh</u>lovu**. Most of the variants come from the diaries and journals of early visitors who were totally unused to the Zulu language either orally or in written form, and thus produced variations such as 'Megoonloof', 'Umkungings Sloave' and 'Umgingiloova'. This carefree approach to the spelling of Zulu names can perhaps be excused for early travellers with no access to Zulu grammars or dictionaries. One is surprised, though, to find spellings such as **Umgingginghlovu** in a letter to the editor of the *Natal Witness* dated March 1988.

'Tugela' is another example. The original Zulu (in modern spelling) is **uThukela**. The untrained ear finds it difficult to distinguish between Zulu /**g**/ and the voiced, unaspirated /**k**/. I find, for example, that many of my first-year (white) Zulu students who have grown up on farms speaking Zulu, but have never written it, will write a word like **ukufika** ('to arrive') as ***ugufiga**. Then again, English does not distinguish between aspirated and unaspirated stops, so the initial **th** of the Zulu becomes **t** in English. And finally, because in English **t** before **u** is usually pronounced **tyh**, as in 'tuba' and 'tune', not only is **uThukela** misspelt as 'Tugela', it is mispronounced as 'Tyhugela'.

A pre-1980 map of the Drakensberg showed a ridge with a Zulu name spelt as 'Skopongo Ridge'. When I did field research into Zulu names in the Drakensberg for a combined Natal Parks Board and Forestry Department – now all part of KZN Wildlife – mapping exercise, I found that this name was really **ka-Sikhophoco** ('the place of the face deep-sunk in the middle'). This is a clear example of a non-speaker of Zulu writing down what he thinks he has heard.

Misunderstandings also give rise to tautologies, where the generic becomes confused with the specific. It is easy to see how such confusions can arise: the non-Zulu speaker enquires 'What is the name of that?' – pointing to a hill – to which the Zulu-speaking respondent answers **intaba** ('it is a hill'), whereupon the non-Zulu speaker names the feature *Intaba Hill.* In the Drakensberg area I found the following tautologies:

- **eMpophomeni** Falls (< **impophoma**, 'waterfall');
- **eSiqoqweni** Beacon (< **isiqoqo**, 'beacon');
- **eNtubeni** Pass (< **intuba**, 'pass');
- **eChibini** Pan (< **ichibi**, 'pan');
- **eNkangala** Ridge (< **inkangala**, 'ridge').

7.2.3 Inconsistency in noun-prefix usage

Zulu nouns consist of a prefix and a stem, for example:

- **um-lalazi** ('whetstone') > **uMlalazi** River;
- **umu-nga** ('acacia') > **uMngeni** River;
- **isi-phingo** ('species of thorny shrub') > **iSiphingo** River.

There has never been any consistency among cartographers, signboard painters, and the other writers of Zulu toponyms: in some names the full prefix is retained (**uMlalazi**); in others the initial vowel is dropped (**Mlalazi**); and sometimes the full prefix is dropped (**Lalazi**). Then again, there is the question of where to put the capital letter: should it be **Isiphingo**, **iSiphingo** or **isiPhingo**? Should we write **Umngeni**, **uMngeni**, **umNgeni**, **Mngeni**, **mNgeni** or **Ngeni**? (In fact, the totally incorrect form **Umgeni** is the one most often come across.)

The old 'official' guide in this matter, the 1978 *Official Place Names in the Republic of South Africa and South-West Africa* had the ruling that initial vowels be used in all Zulu and Xhosa place names, and the capital be the first consonant, thus: **uMlazi**, **uMgungundlovu**, **iNjasuthi**. But guides are made to be ignored, and for some time in the early 1980s, suddenly all river names in Natal lost their initial vowels and every signboard read 'Sipingo River' or 'Lovu River'. This curious decision, to remove every initial vowel from every Zulu toponym, must have been taken by someone high up in the Natal Provincial Administration. It is pleasing to note that this cavalier decision has since been rescinded and Zulu toponyms once more have their initial vowels.

7.2.4 Inconsistency in the use of locative forms

Zulu nouns have a locative inflection, typically with the prefix **e-** and one of the following suffixes: **-eni**, **-ini**, **-weni** or **-wini**. A few nouns prefix **o-** instead of **e-**, and a few have no suffix, but the majority fit the pattern of **ilanga** ('sun') becoming **elangeni** ('in the sun') and **umthunzi** ('shade') becoming **emthunzini** ('in the shade'). Some accepted forms of Zulu place names are only ever used in the locative form on maps, signboards, etc., such as **Empangeni** and **Eshowe**, as also the **Entabeni** Hospital and the **Elangeni** Hotel, both in Durban.

In most cases, the locative form depends on how the name is used in a sentence. If the name is used in a 'locative context', the locative form must always be used. Let us take the Zulu name for Pietermaritzburg as an example. Zulu speakers will always use the form eMgungundlovu (with the locative prefix e-) in sentences such as:

- **Ngihlala/ngisebenza eMgungundlovu**: I live/work in Pietermaritzburg.
- **Ngiya eMgungundlovu**: I am going to Pietermaritzburg.

The form **uMgungundlovu** will be used in non-locative contexts, such as:

- **UMgungundlovu yidolobha elikhulu**: Pietermaritzburg is a big town.
- **UMgungundlovu yidolobha engilaziyo**: Pietermaritzburg is a town which I know.

In an earlier article, I wrote:

> If the place name has a locative suffix, there must be a locative prefix: **eThekwini** can never be '**iThekwini**'; **eShongweni** [correctly: **eNtshongweni**] can never be '**iShongweni**' . . .
>
> This is a simple fact of Zulu grammar: a locative prefix does not necessarily require a locative suffix, e.g. **esitolo, ekhaya, ekhanda**, but a locative suffix does require a locative prefix (1983: 299).

However, Linda van Huyssteen puts forward a convincing case for Zulu toponyms having a locative suffix but no locative prefix (1994). Fieldwork with Zulu speakers has shown her that in a non-locative context, many Zulu toponyms with a locative suffix were accepted in forms without a locative prefix, and among her examples are **uMthunzini**, **uMkhambathini**, **iMadadeni**, **iSidumbini**, **uZwathini**, **uMngeni** and, indeed, **iMpangeni**. Van Huyssteen's theory and her examples have been a matter for lively debate in the postgraduate Onomastics Honours class in the Department of Zulu at the University of Natal in Pietermaritzburg since she published her article, and the Zulu-speaking students are in general agreement with her theories, but not with all her examples. While certain place names such as **uMthunzini**, **uMkhambathini** and **uMngeni** were accepted by all my students, there was some disagreement about other examples such as **iMadadeni** and especially **iMpangeni**, and I can conclude that for many place names the 'correct' form is very much a matter of personal tastes and beliefs.

There has been no dissent, however, with another of my earlier 'rules' about locative inflection, and that is that locative suffixes are only possible with nouns with simple stems. The nouns **impange** ('Hard Pear tree') and **itheku** ('bay') may and do take locative suffixes to become the place names **eMpangeni** and **eThekwini** (see the first half of Chapter 10 for the debate surrounding this latter name). But compound nouns will not accept locative suffixes. **UMgungundlovu** will become **eMgungundlovu** in a locative context, and **aManzimtoti** will become **eManzimtoti**, but these two names will never become ***eMgungundlovini** and ***eManzimtotini**.

7.2.5 Differences in compounding patterns in Zulu

There are differences in compounding patterns in Zulu, depending on whether the compound noun is a personal name or not (these differences are explained in detail in Chapter 17). Consider the two words **bheka** (verb: 'to watch, look at, after') and **inkosi** (noun: 'chief, king, Lord God'). If these two words are combined to form a common noun meaning 'royal bodyguard', the initial **i-** of **inkosi** will fall away and we will get **ibhekankosi** (that is, 'he who looks after the chief or king'). If the two words are combined to form a personal name meaning 'Look up to the Lord', then the final **-a** of **bheka** will fall away, and we will get **uBhekinkosi.**

With common nouns it is always the first vowel of the second part of the compound noun that falls away. When **qhopha** ('knock', 'tap') is added to **umuthi** ('tree'), it is the first **u-** in **umuthi** that falls aways to produce **isiqhophamuthi** ('woodpecker'). When **dlula** ('surpass') is added to **imithi** ('trees') we get **indlulamithi** ('that which surpasses the trees', that is, a giraffe). With personal names, the **amagama asekhaya** discussed in Chapters 2 and 5, the opposite is the case: it is always the final vowel of the first part of the compound that falls away. When **themba** ('trust') is added to **uyise** ('the father'), it is the final **-a** of **themba** that falls away to give **uThembuyise** ('trust the Father'). When **amandla** ('strength') is added to **enkosi** ('of the Lord') we get the personal name **uMandlenkosi.**

This certainty about which vowel will fall away is *not* a characteristic of compound place names. On the one hand, place names are proper nouns, so they do not behave with the certainty of common nouns. But, on the other hand, place names are not personal names, so they do not behave with the certainty of personal names either. Compound place names sometimes behave like personal names:

- **uMgungundlovu < gung(a) + uNdlovu**
- **uMsonginyathi < song(a) + inyathi**
- **aManzamnyama < amanz(i) + amnyama**
- **iNtambende < intamb(o) + ende**

And sometimes they behave like common nouns:

- **uBilanhlola < bila + (i)nhlola**
- **iMpambanyoni < phamba + (i)nyoni**
- **iMbizankulu < imbiza + (e)nkulu**
- **aManzimtoti < amanzi + (a)mtoti**

And sometimes they behave both ways: there are a number of 'Black Water' rivers in KwaZulu-Natal and some of them are given as **aManzimnyama** and others as **aManzamnyama**, while the area north-west of Pietermaritzburg is known as both **uGezabuso** and **uGezubuso** (< **geza**, 'wash', + **ubuso**, 'the face'). The Drakensberg river known as 'The Satiated Dog', because it is always full of water, is known as **iNjasuthi** and **iNjesuthi** (< **inja**, 'dog', + **esuthi**, 'being full').

7.3 RECOMMENDATIONS

Now let us come back to the statement made above that a place name such as **iNjasuthi** may have 12 possible spellings, all of which could be considered right. We can combine reasons (1), (3), (4) and (5) above (see page 112) to construct a matrix as follows:

	Following compound *noun* pattern	Following compound *name* pattern	
Old orthography	Njasuti	Njesuti	No initial vowel
	iNjasuti	iNjesuti	Initial vowel
	eNjasuti	eNjesuti	Locative inflection
New orthography	Njasuthi	Njesuthi	No initial vowel
	iNjasuthi	iNjesuthi	Initial vowel
	eNjasuthi	eNjesuthi	Locative inflection

Note that we can increase the number of variant spellings by either moving the capital letter to the first letter: **Injasuti, Enjesuthi, Enjasuti**, etc., or by moving it to the first letter of the stem: **nJasuthi, inJesuti, enJasuthi**, etc. Moving the capital to the first letter would give another eight variations, and moving it to the first letter of the stem another twelve, giving us a total of *thirty-two possible spellings* for this single river name, *none of which are corruptions by ignorant or arrogant colonials.*

To further complicate this issue, we may note that Bryant, in the appendix of proper names to his 1905 *A Zulu-English Dictionary*, gives us the spelling '**e-Njisuthi**'. This would be based on the rare variant of the verb **esutha** as **sutha**, with the predicative subject concord **i-** instead of the relative concord **e-**. Thus **inj[a]** + **i** + **suthi** ('the dog is sated'). This would also be an acceptable form.

Clearly this situation is untenable, and any attempts to achieve consistency and standardisation in Zulu place names means that these choices must be narrowed down as much as possible, preferably to one. Here are some recommendations.

We can start by scrapping the old orthography. Clearly there is no justification for making new maps, printing new tourist brochures, or erecting new road signs with spelling that was outmoded over 50 years ago. Then we can say that there is no justification for the dropping of the initial vowel of the name, and indeed there never has been although the practice still persists: a report by Reginald Khumalo in the *Natal Witness* of 29 September 1999, in reference to a new logo for the city, talks of the 'Msunduzi River'. That leaves us with only four possible spellings of **iNjasuthi** if we discount the question of capitalisation for the moment:

iNjasuthi	**iNjesuthi**
eNjasuthi	**eNjesuthi**

Half of the problem with this particular place name is that it accepts both types of compounding procedures, and that is a problem which we will perhaps only find with about half-a-dozen names in the whole of KwaZulu-Natal. There is no point in making a ruling about this, and indeed it is only the Euro-Western mind that sees **iNjasuthi** and **iNjesuthi** as being different. To the vast majority of Zulu speakers these are the same word – as I discovered after much frustrating research in the iNjasuthi valley itself in the early 1980s. Assuming then that we only take one of the compounding types – say **iNjasuthi**, that only leaves us with the problem of whether the standard form of a place name to go onto maps, into guides, and onto signboards, should be in the locative or the non-locative forms. In addition, there is the question of the capitalisation. Let us look at these issues separately.

7.3.1 Locative or non-locative forms

Clearly one or the other needs to be chosen as the standard form. It would be ludicrous to expect cartographers or anyone else in the business of printing Zulu toponyms to have to write both **uMgungundlovu** *and* **eMgungundlovu** (not to mention 'Pietermaritzburg') next to the little dot that marks the position of this city on a map. There are arguments in favour of both forms.

To argue for the adoption of the locative form as the standard, we could say *firstly* that place names by their very nature are inherently locational and by far the greatest proportion of their use is in the locative context. To choose the most commonly occurring form as a norm always makes sense. *Secondly*, we could say that given the complex set of rules which govern the locative inflection of nouns in Zulu, and the near impossibility of explaining these to non-Zulu speakers, it would make sense to give the locative form. If the non-locative form of Durban's Zulu name is **iTheku** (which it is), only a Zulu speaker or someone competent in Zulu grammar would predict that the locative form is **eThekwini**. So why not simply put **eThekwini** on the maps and in the literature? Bryant, in his 'Introduction to Proper Names of Persons, Rivers, Mountains, etc. Dictionary', states:

> *N.B.* We have preferred to enter all names of places in their *locative* form, as that in which they are practically always used. To have registered them under their nominative form might have been inconvenient and misleading; for instance, people would generally look for the Native name of Durban under *eTekwini*, not under *iTeku*, and they would scarcely expect to find *emTonjaneni* under *umTonjana*. Again,

> had we only shown the nominative form, people might often have been at a loss as to the correct manner of constructing the locative, which, as said, would be the form they would almost always require to use (1906: 753).

And then, to argue in favour of the *non*-locative form as a standard. English and Afrikaans belong to the class of languages which indicate location by separate prepositions: 'I live *in* Durban', 'He goes *to* Durban', 'The aeroplane flies *over* Durban'.

Zulu (and Xhosa) belong to another group of languages that express location by inflecting the noun itself. Given that standardisation is not just a local issue, but is a global objective, it could be useful to look at other languages in the world that are inflectional and see how they handle the locative versus non-locative issue. Finnish has a number of nominal inflections, many of them locational in function. Consider the following, based on the city of Turku:

Turusta: from Turku
Turkuun: to Turku
Turussa: in Turku

Other inflections are also used, as in **Turun kadut** ('the streets of Turku'). And yet all maps and all signboards, all guides and brochures, give the nominative form **Turku**. One must accept here that Finnish is under a much stronger obligation to choose the nominative form because there are a number of different locative inflections, whereas Zulu only has one. But the principle is clear: use the uninflected form as the norm, and non-speakers of the language must learn the appropriate inflections.

Here is another argument in favour of the non-locative as the standard form for Zulu place names. One of the reasons put forward for dropping the initial vowel of place names, thus turning **uMlazi** into **Mlazi** and **eThekwini** into **Thekwini** was that if the initial vowel was kept, almost every place name in an atlas index, a gazetteer, or any other alphabetical list, would either be under I or under U, making it more difficult for someone trying to look up a name to find it. If the locative form of place names is the standard, then even the distinction between I and U will be lost, and 99 per cent of Zulu place names will be entered under E. This is not a particularly convincing argument, but it has been offered as a justification.

A third and final argument in favour of the non-locative as standard is that most Zulu place names already on maps and in the literature are already in the non-locative form. Consequently, there would be less to change if these were to be declared officially the standard forms. From a purely practical and economic point of view, there is *some* sense in this argument, but overall I would favour the use of the locational form as a standard.

7.3.2 Where to put the capital letter?

The question of where to put the capital letter does not only affect place names, but also titles of various kinds (titles of people, of books, of administrative units), days of the week, and anything else that is customarily spelt with a capital letter. This is an important issue, and one which has not yet been officially decided for the Zulu language. In May 1999 the KwaZulu-Natal Branch of the Names Society of Southern Africa, together with the Eastern Region of the African Languages Association of Southern Africa, decided to hold a one-day workshop to discuss simply the question of 'Where should the capital letter go?'. Representatives from departments of Zulu in all of KwaZulu-Natal's universities, technical colleges and teacher's training colleges, as well as cartographers, members of language boards, etc. met to debate the issue. Unfortunately, after an entire day of discussions that went round and round the topic most participants were more confused than they had been before the workshop. If we look again at the three letters of complaint received from Zulu-speaking writers given on pages 110 to 111 above, we will find Cyril Shabalala using **uThukela** and **eziMbokodweni** (capital on first letter of stem), while Nhlanhla Ndlovu uses **Entshongweni** (initial capital), as does Mbongeni Zondi with **Umsunduzi**.

The 'capital issue' still needs to be decided, but in the meantime here are some arguments for and against each of the three possible places for a capital: on the first letter (as in **Umngeni**, **Umlazi**); on the first letter of the noun stem (as in **umNgeni** and **umLazi**); or on the first consonant (as in **uMngeni**, **uMlazi** – although, according to Zungu [1998] this last should be the **uMlaza** River).

a. First letter as capital

The argument in favour of making the first letter the capital is simply that this is the norm for place names all over the world. That does not *necessarily* mean that Zulu has to follow suit, but if we are talking about standardisation, again it makes sense to follow the pattern established by the majority.

b. First letter of stem as capital

The argument in favour of making the capital the first letter of the stem (**umNgeni, isiPhingo**) is that nouns are entered in dictionaries by their stems, as prefixes are subject to variation. Should a non-Zulu speaker wish to look up a place name in a dictionary, this will be possible if the initial letter of the stem has been marked by a capital letter. Entries in the indexes of atlases or in gazetteers will thus follow the pattern of lexicons of the language. There is a lot of sense in this argument, and many writers about Zulu (works of anthropology, ethnography, etc.) make their glossaries in this manner. That is to say, a word such as **isibaya** ('cattle kraal') will be written as 'isiBaya' and entered under B. There is an argument against this method – the clumsy appearance of a word that has a capital on the second letter because that is the standard form, and another capital on the first letter if the word is at the beginning of a sentence. Starting a sentence with 'EThekwini' or 'EMpangeni' is not attractive, and is not favoured by anyone I have spoken to.

c. First consonant as capital

The official recommendation of the 1978 *Official Place Names of South Africa* was to put the capital on the first consonant, as in **uMlazi** and **iSiphingo**. And that is the method which my Zulu-speaking colleagues 'feel most comfortable with'. For reasons which they cannot explain, putting the capital on the first consonant 'somehow feels right'. Certainly I feel most comfortable with this, and all Zulu place names in this book follow this method. Intuition is, of course, not a sound academic or linguistic argument. But from a practical point of view, if a standard form is to be set, and Zulu speakers are to be asked to stick with standard forms, then it is surely sensible to ensure that these forms are the ones that they are the most comfortable with.

In addition, there is a sound linguistic argument for putting the capital on the first consonant, and that is to achieve orthographic standardisation between toponyms and anthroponyms. As we saw in Chapter 2 (pages 20 to 27), *all* Zulu anthroponyms (Zulu-origin personal names, Euro-origin personal names, clan names, nicknames, and clan praises) belong to noun class 1a and have the noun class prefix **u-**:

uVusumuzi	**uDlamini**
uJohannes	**uSibalukhulu**

This class prefix drops away when the name is used in direct address, and when the name is used in Euro-Western discourse.

The important point is that because all anthroponyms belong to the same noun class, which has a single letter prefix **u-** which may fall away in certain environments, *the capital letter is always, without any exceptions, on the first consonant.*

There has never, to my knowledge, been debate about this, and it is a standard and invariable practice in written Zulu. How much simpler the question of toponymic orthography would be if the toponyms would simply fall in line with the anthroponyms.

To end this chapter, some food for thought in the form of a letter to the *Natal Witness* on the issue of the spelling of the place name 'Ixopo', another name 'corrupted by ignorant colonialists' and subject to much debate about the correct spelling. On the suggestion that '**eXhobho**' was the correct spelling for this town, a correspondent wrote: 'Sir – Was "eXhobho" the way in which Zulus spelt Ixopo before the colonial settlers brought writing to the Zulu people?'

Chapter 8

The semantics of Zulu place names

8.1 INTRODUCTION

In Chapter 3 we looked at the reasons why parents give their children certain names, and saw how these names could be divided into various categories such as 'Family structure', 'Circumstances of the birth', 'State of mind of the parents', and so on.

Place names are also given for a reason. They may describe the particular feature being named, as in Table Mountain and **iNtabamhlophe** ('white mountain'). They may be named after people, as in Pietermaritzburg, Durban, and **KwaMashu** (named after Sir *Marshall* Campbell, philanthropist and sugar farmer).

They may even, as with personal names in parts of Africa, be named for the 'state of mind' of the people. There are a number of places with Dutch-Afrikaans names such as Vryheid ('freedom'), Helpmekaar ('help one another'), Vereeniging ('unity'), and Weenen ('weeping'). Zulu place names such as **Phumula** ('rest'), **Thandanani** ('love one another'), **eKuthokozeni** ('place of happiness') and **eKuthuleni** ('place of quiet') can be found.

Zulu place names commonly link location and nature by referring to the plant, animal or bird life that is characteristic of the area, as in the river name **uMzingwenya** ('home of the crocodile').

In this chapter, I have divided Zulu place names into four main categories according to their underlying meanings:

1. Places named after their physical features (by far the most common category);
2. Places named after characteristic plant, animal or bird life;
3. Places named after people;
4. Places named after historical incidents or cultural practices.

Sources of names include a variety of maps, including Map Studio's 1994 *Road Map of Southern Africa*, as well as a number of the Directorate of Survey and Mapping's 1: 250 000 and 1: 50 000 series. Botha's 1977 *Watername in Natal* has been very useful for examples of some of KwaZulu-Natal's minor water-bodies. For place names in the Drakensberg I have relied on my own field research conducted in the 1980s (see Koopman, 1983), and for place names in iThala Game Reserve in northern KwaZulu-Natal I have consulted Mbatha's 1992 study.

8.2 PLACES NAMED AFTER PHYSICAL FEATURES

Certainly the most common type of place name is that with an underlying meaning which is a physical description of the place the name refers to. Some of these are immediately obvious, for example, **iNtabankulu** ('big mountain') for a big mountain. Others are less semantically transparent, for example, **iSandlwana**, which relies on a metaphorical comparison with the second stomach of a cow in order to describe the physical shape of the mountain (or, alternatively, 'something like a small hut' – see pages 153 to 154 of Chapter 9 for a detailed analysis of **iSandlwana**). Physical description can include the visual appearance, as in **iNtabamhlophe** ('white mountain'), the 'behaviour' or 'nature' of a river, as in **uMsuluzi** ('that which shifts its position'), or even taste, as in **aManzimtoti** ('sweet waters'). I have tried to group the following examples according to such physical categories as 'size', 'soil type', 'metaphor' and so on.

8.2.1 Geographical location

A place may be named in reference to its geographical location. **iMpendle** ('a bleak, exposed position') lies on a high, exposed plateau, as does **uLundi** ('high place, heights'). Doke and Vilakazi give the place name **eNgudwini** (< **ingudu**, 'bare country', 'uninhabited place'), and this may be the origin of the name **eMagudu**, although other suggestions are given below. **iMpumalanga** ('the east'), a township midway between Pietermaritzburg and Durban, is not quite so obviously in the east as is the homonymous province **iMpumalanga**, previously called 'Eastern Transvaal'. The village of **aMaphumulo** ('resting places, place where resting places are needed') is so named because it is at the end of a long, steep climb. **eNtabazwe** (< **intaba**, 'mountain', + **izwe**, 'country'), the Zulu name for Harrismith, refers to mountainous country.

8.2.2 Soils and stones

Place names may refer to the soil or stones which dominate in the area. For example, **eMahlabathini** takes its name from **amahlabathi** ('whitish, sandy soils'), while the Zulu name for Tongaat – **oHlawe** – means 'gravelly place' (see page 149).

eNhlazatshe, a mountain beyond the upper White Mfolozi, takes its name from **-hlaza** ('green', 'blue') and **itshe** ('stone'), and **eKhetheni**, the name of a mountain located near Newcastle, is derived from **ukhethe** ('shale', 'slate'). Near Nongoma is **aMatshemhlophe** Peak, the name meaning 'white stones'. The same name occurs in the Umfolozi-Hluhluwe Game Reserve. In the iThala Game Reserve we find **eMachobeni** Hill (< plural of **ichobe**, 'sandstone').

Certain rivers may also be named according to the quality of their stones, and this is particularly true if a river is known for good quality grinding stones. Such a river is the **eZimbokodweni** ('grinding stones') on the South Coast, the river which under the name 'Umbogintwini' has raised the hackles of so many language purists. Another reference to the quality grinding stones present in the river, is found in **uMlalazi** (< **lalaza**, 'whet', 'sharpen'). In the Drakensberg we find the stream **iLolambazo** ('sharpen the axe'), as well as a specific large rock, in the Lotheni area, also in the Drakensberg, called **kaLolambazo**.

8.2.3 Shape and size

Place names that refer to the size and shape of the geographical feature are common, and I have already mentioned **iNtabankulu** and **iSandlwana** above.

In the Drakensberg, as well as in other parts of KwaZulu-Natal, one can find the name **iNdanyana**, a double diminutive form of the adjective **-de** ('tall'), so meaning 'tallish, but not very tall', and in the Northern uMnweni valley of the Drakensberg is a hill called **iNdanyazana**, a name which has the structure (**de**, 'tall', + **-azi-**, 'more so', + **-ana**, 'less so'), giving a meaning roughly equivalent to 'a hill which is neither tall nor short'. The English name for this same hill is 'Pimple Hill'. A particularly interesting name is that of the peak **iNtonjelana**, on the escarpment near Cathedral Peak. This insignificant bump would probably not even have received a name at all had it not marked the location of a pass which is a major trading route between Lesotho and KwaZulu-Natal: the **iNtonjelana** Horse Pass. The name literally means 'it is merely a thing, this one', that is, not a proper hill at all.

Size of mountain may not only refer to height, but also to length, as in **eNtabenende** ('at the place of the mountain which is long'). This name is structurally interesting because it has an internal locative: **entabeni** ('at the mountain') + **ende** ('which is long'). Similar is **kwaNtabande** Mountain in the iThala game reserve. And, of course, when talking of the size of rivers, length is the major issue, although catchment area and water volume are also important. All three combine in the **uMzimkhulu**, which is generally accepted as meaning 'The Great Home (of all the rivers?)' (see page 145).

The place name **uMbumbulu**, is derived from **imbumbulu**, of which Doke and Vilakazi say: 'any hard thing, round and smooth, such as cannon ball . . . knob of knob-kerrie', adding that uMbumbulu was so named because it is a place where there are a number of smooth round knolls (1958: 53). This name is similar to the name **iMbulungana** ('little globe') for a round-topped hill found in the iThala Game Reserve.

Olivier's Hoek Pass in the Drakensberg is named **eSungubala**, from the verb **sungubala** ('creep through a narrow aperture').

8.2.4 Behaviour of rivers

Names for rivers include references to the 'behaviour' of the river, such as winding and meandering patterns, seasonal floodings, and so on. The

uMfolozi River, more correctly the **iMfolozi**, is a river which twists and turns, and this is reflected in the name, derived from the verb **foloza** ('to zig-zag'), although there are various other theories for this name (see page 151). Similar in meaning is the **eMsuluzi** (Blaauwkrantz River), from **suluza** ('walk with swaying motion', or 'move position', 'shift'). The **uMpambanyoni** in southern KwaZulu-Natal is another winding river, so much so that birds flying in a straight line over the river are puzzled at its apparent continual change in direction. The name means literally 'that which puzzles the bird'.

Seasonal flooding can be seen in the name **eHlimbithwa** (a tributary of the uMvoti River: < **ihlimbithwa**, 'muddy storm-water, as of river after heavy rains'), and this is probably the underlying reason for the naming of the **aMatikulu** River (an old dialectic variation of **amanzi** + **khulu**, 'big waters'). Another place name which shows a historical dialect form, is **eMandini**, the paper mill town on the banks of the uThukela River: **emandini** is a Lala form of **emanzini** ('in the water').

River names may also reflect the taste of the waters, and I have already mentioned **aManzimtoti** above. Other examples include **emNambithi** (which refers to both the Klip River as well as Ladysmith), derived from the verb **nambitha**, 'be tasty', and **aManzaduma** ('sour, tasteless water'), the name of a small river in the Maphumulo district.

8.2.5 Colour

Place names may reflect the colour of a particular geographical feature, as in the well-known **iNtabamhlophe** ('white mountain') close to Estcourt, with the popular White Mountain Inn nearby. Similar mountain names are **iNtaba-mnyama** ('black mountain') and **iNtabebomvu** ('red mountain'). Mbatha (1992: 13) gives one of each of these names for the iThala Game Reserve. Near **iNkandla** is the **iNsundukazi** Mountain, with the stem **-nsundu** ('brown') suffixed by the augmentative **-kazi**. **-Kazi** here could either refer to the mountain itself, in which case **iNsundukazi** could be interpreted as 'the tall brown mountain', or it could be applied to **-nsundu**, in which case the name would mean 'the very brown mountain'.

Rivers, too, may be named for the colour of their waters or their sands. The most well-known examples are the **iMfolozi eMhlophe** ('white Mfolozi') and the **iMfolozi eMnyama** ('black Mfolozi'). Botha (1977: 108) gives a total of six rivers in KwaZulu-Natal with the name **aManzamnyama** ('black waters') and two rivers with the name **aManzimhlophe** ('white waters'). He also gives the single example of the **aManzimpofu** River ('pale waters') in the iNkandla district, a name similar to the Zulu name for the Mooi River – **iMpofana** ('the pale-coloured one'). Water-colour via metaphor is seen in the **uMlaza** River – often incorrectly given as the **Umlazi** – a reference to water which is cloudy like whey (**umlaza**).

8.2.6 Metaphorical descriptions

Zulu names are often described in popular literature as being 'full of poetry', and certainly it is true that the poetic device of metaphor underlies many place names.

Mount Gilboa, near Lion's River in the Natal midlands, has the Zulu name **eMpumulonja**, from **impumulo** ('snout of animal') + **inja** ('dog'), that is, 'the mountain shaped like a dog's snout'. The image of a large, round and smooth rock is easily seen in **eMpandleni** (< **impandla**, 'bald head'), a hill in the Nkandla district. From the noun **u(lu)phiso** ('earthen beer-pot with small-rimmed mouth') comes the name **oPhisweni**, which refers to a mountain in the uMvoti district, and in the Lower Mfolozi district we find a range of hills known as the **aMakhowe** (< **amakhowe**, 'mushrooms'). East of Dundee is a rock pinnacle with the name **uMuntuyedwa** ('a person on his own').

The Drakensberg is full of metaphorical names for a variety of cliffs, buttresses, and other mountain features, and we can find:

- **eMnweni** ('place of the finger');
- **uCikicane** ('little finger');
- **oPhondweni** ('place of the horn');
- **iMponjwane** ('little horn');
- **aMabedlana** ('little breasts'), this last referring to a pair of similarly shaped conical hills known in English as Sheba's Breasts.

The Drakensberg also gives us the names **iSalukaz' esigay' amabele** ('old woman grinding corn') and **eMakhehlen' amabili** ('two old men').

8.2.7 Miscellaneous descriptions

The **Ifafa** River which is south of Durban probably takes its name from the noun **u(lu)fafa** 'drizzling rain, driving mist'. This is a likely theory because the river rises at a place named **uFafa** in the Ixopo district. For those that do not like this interpretation, however, here is Lugg's theory (1968: 8): 'the river that flows with the sound of fa fa'.

eMthonjaneni, between Melmoth and Ulundi, is named for the small fountain or spring found there (**umthombo**, 'fountain', 'spring', + **-ana**, 'small').

eMaqongqo is a name given to two adjoining mountains in the Nongoma district, derived from the ideophone **qongqo** ('of reaching the summit').

8.3 PLACES NAMED AFTER CHARACTERISTIC PLANT AND ANIMAL LIFE

There are many place names based on the dominant or obvious life forms found in that particular place. Some of these place names refer to trees or shrubs that are characteristic of the area, while others refer to animals or birds that are associated with that place. We can start with the botanical references.

8.3.1 Plants as a basis of place names

There are place names which simply refer to trees generally, without pointing to a particular species. Such names simply emphasise that such and such a place is rather woody, or heavily forested. A name found in several places in KwaZulu-Natal is **kwaHlathikhulu** or **iHlathikhulu** (which is from **ihlathi**, 'forest', 'wooded area', + **-khulu**, 'large'). The diminutive of **amahlathi** ('forests') is the base for the Zulu name of Kearsney village near Durban: **kwaMahlashana**. And there is a place north of the middle Mhlathuze known as **eMthinemide**: (< **emithini**, 'among the trees', + **emide**, 'which are tall'). In similar fashion, the bilingual name **uMhlanga** Rocks refers to the reed-bed (**umhlanga**) which characterises the estuary of the river, around the mouth of which the resort Umhlanga Rocks is built. The **eNhlangeni** River in the Drakensberg derives its name from the noun **inhlanga** ('thicket of reeds').

Other place names are specific about the species of tree or shrub. For example, the **uMkhuze** River (and thus also the Mkhuze Game Reserve) is named after a particular aromatic tree *(Heteropyxis natalensis)*, which is also known as **inkuzwa** and **umkhuzwa**.The nearby Hluhluwe Game Reserve also takes its name from a river, the **uMhluhluwe**, a reference to the Thorny Monkey-rope *(Dalbergia armata)*.

The anglicised place name Illovo Beach is a corruption of the noun **ilovu**, which is the fruit of the **umlovu** tree, or Septee Tree *Cordia caffra*, while the **eNtolwane** hill between Eshowe and Nkandla takes its name from the **intolwane** plant (Elephant's Root or, in Latin, *Elephantorhiza elephantina*). This plant has other onomastic uses, for it commonly figures in the praises of a red bull: **uJamludi obomvu njengentolwane** ('Jamludi who is red like the **intolwane** shrub'). (Although I have stated that this place name is derived from the **intolwane** shrub, I also find myself wondering if by any chance the name is a corruption of English 'tall one'?)

In the place name **eMagudu**, there are two possible interpretations: **amagudu** could be the plural of (1) **igudu** 'dagga-pipe' or of (2) **igudu** 'a species of veld herb (*Hypoxis latifolia*)', or, as suggested on page 124, it could be derived from **ingudu** ('bare country', 'uninhabited place').

There is also a choice, this time between two botanical items, for **eMkhobeni**, the name of a tributary of the uMkhomazi River. This name could be derived from **umkhoba** 'Yellow-wood Tree' (*Podocarpus latifolius*) or from **umkhobe** 'a species of plant of the bean-family, with edible root like sweet potato'. A tributary of the uThukela River is named **eMvuzane**, this from **umvuzane**, the shrub known to botanists as *Gnidia kraussiana* (Pooley, 1998: 292).

The **iNgwavuma** District around the Lubombo Mountains takes its name from the Transvaal Saffron Tree (*Cassine transvaalensis*).

uGibisila is the name of a ridge in the Drakensberg. It is a contraction of the noun **ugibisisila**, the *Bowiea volubilis* plant, in high demand for medicinal purposes, as well as for protective and love charms. Also in the Drakensberg is the **oQalweni** River, taking its name from the **uqalo** bamboo (*Arundinaria tessalata*) which is found in profusion along this river. Two trees have given their names to Drakensberg features: the Cape Myrtle (*Myrsine africana*, Zulu **isiqalaba**) and the Bushman's Tea (*Catha edulis*, Zulu **umhlwazi**) are reflected in **eSiqalabeni** Hill to the east of Cathkin Peak Hotel (and Mbatha gives the example of **eZiqalabeni** Ridge from the iThala Game Reserve) and in the **eMhlwazini** River in the Cathedral Peak area.

Mbatha gives a number of examples of place names in iThala Game Reserve based on words for trees, including:

- **eMnqumeni** Mountain (< **umnquma**, '*Olea africana*');
- **aMasunjwana** Valley (< diminutive plural of **isundu**, '*Phoenix reclinata* palm');
- **uNondomela** Valley ('Tree Fuchsia', *Halleria lucida*).

Doke and Vilakazi state that the South Coast river known as the **uMthwalume** (literally, 'what it carries must stand upright') refers to a species of tree whose bark is used for dysentery, but I can find no record in Pooley's *Trees of Natal* (1993), or Moll's *Trees of Natal* (1981), or Hutchings's *Zulu Medicinal Plants* (1996).

8.3.2 Animals as a basis of place names

iNsimbakazi is the name of a railway station 25 kilometres east of eMpangeni. The name is derived from **insimba** ('genet') + **-kazi** ('large', 'female'). The **eNseleni** River, flowing into Richards Bay, refers to a ratel or honey badger (Zulu **insele**). The Rietvlei River, a tributary of the Mooi River, has the Zulu name **eNyamvubu**, from **nya** ('to excrete') + **imvubu** ('hippopotamus'), that is, 'where the hippo defecates'. In the Drakensberg, the noun **amankentshane** ('wild dogs') is the basis of the name **eMankentshaneni** Hill in the Giant's Castle area (and there is also an **aMankentshana** Mountain in the iThala Game Reserve). **eMpungusheni**, a name for a river in the Cobham Forest, is derived from **impungushe** ('jackal'). The **iMpofana** River at Giant's Castle might mean 'the pale-ish coloured river', but could equally well be the 'river of the small eland' (**impofu**). The colour term **-mpofu** ('tawny', 'pale brown') is almost certainly taken from **impofu** ('eland') and not the other way around. Another name with two possible interpretations is **eNdlovini** Ridge near Lotheni in the Drakensberg. This could mean 'place of the elephant' (**indlovu**), or could mean 'place of the Ndlovu clan'. Botha (1977: 173) gives two **eNdlovini** rivers in KwaZulu-Natal.

Botha's *Watername in Natal* (1977) gives us the following river names which refer to animals:

- **eZimbabaleni** R (< **izimbabala**, 'bushbuck does');
- **eNkunzini** R (< **inkunzi**, 'bull');
- **eNgweni** R (< **ingwe**, 'leopard');
- **uMziki** R ('reedbuck');
- **eMpunzini** R (< **impunzi**, 'duiker').

Mbatha (1992: 46) gives **eManxaleni** ('place of the rheboks') Spring and **iNkawana** ('little monkey') Valley from iThala.

Added to **umuzi** ('homestead') are **imvubu** ('hippo') and **inyathi** ('buffalo') to give two well-known and major rivers: the **uMzimvubu** ('home of the hippo') and the **uMzinyathi** ('home of the buffalo'). The buffalo is also reflected in **uMsonginyathi** ('threatener of the buffalo'), the name for the upper reaches of the **uMngeni** River. Near Mthunzini is the **uMzingwenya** ('home of the crocodile': **umuzi** + **ingwenya**, 'crocodile'), and flowing into the uMlazi river is the **uMzimpunzi** ('home of the duiker': **umuzi** + **impunzi**, 'duiker').

The **uMkhomazi** River, entering the sea 30 kilometres south of Durban, makes reference to whales (**umkhomo**, 'whale', + **-azi**, 'female'). Bulpin (1969: 68) tells the well-known story of Shaka and his warriors being fascinated by the sight of female whales playing with their calves in the shallow waters of the estuary.

The dog is reflected in **eMlambonja**, a tributary of the uThukela. This river name uses the old Zulu word for river – **umlambo** – to which **inja** ('dog') is added. This river, incidentally, is a close neighbour of the **iNjasuthi** ('the well-fed dog') which was discussed in the previous chapter. Near Babanango is the **iNjanduna** ('male dog') Peak.

Another domestic animal is the **intondolo** ('wether') and in the Drakensberg, near the iNjasuthi River, we can find the **iNtondolo** Flats.

oSungulweni Ridge in the iNkandla area is a reference to the blind worm (Zulu **usungulo**).

8.3.3 Birds as a basis of place names

Fish eagles (**izinkwazi**) can be found on nearly every waterway in KwaZulu-Natal, but only one river has been so-named. The **iZinkwazi** River enters the Indian Ocean ten kilometres south of the **uThukela** River. Another eagle is the Bateleur (Zulu **ingqungqulu**) and this bird is reflected in the name of the **iNgqungqulu** River in the Mahlabathini district. A slightly smaller raptor, for a slightly smaller river, can be seen in **kuNhloyile** ('place of the Yellow-billed Kite'), the name of a minor tributary of the uThukela in the iNkandla area.

To go from hawks to doves, we only need to look at the famous battle site of **aMajuba** Mountain (< **amajuba**, 'doves').

eNkwalini (< **inkwali**, 'quail') is the name of a small village found halfway between Eshowe and Melmoth, and **iNtendele** Camp (< **intendele**, 'partridge') is one of the hutted camps at Royal Natal National Park in the Drakensberg.

From iThala, Mbatha gives us the examples:

- **aMankankazane** River (< **inkankane**, 'Hadedah Ibis');
- **iTshelenkonjane** Mountain (< **itshe**, 'rock,' + **lenkonjane**, 'of the swallow');
- **iKholwane** Hill ('hornbill');
- **iTshelamasomi** Rock (< **itshe**, 'rock', + **lamasomi**, 'of the Red-winged Starlings').

Eighty kilometres west of Melmoth we find the small village of **eQhudeni** (< **iqhude**, 'rooster', 'cockerel') and a railway station a few kilometres north of the uThukela is simply named **iNyoni** ('bird').

8.4 PLACES NAMED AFTER HISTORICAL INCIDENTS OR CULTURAL PRACTICES

In my research into place names in the Drakensberg in the early 1980s I found a number of names relating to particular incidents, such as **uMlahla-ngubo** Peak of which I wrote:

> . . . the name is derived from **lahla** (to lose, or discard) + **ingubo** (a blanket, or item of clothing, usually a dress). No-one seems to know who the person was who lost his blanket on this peak, but clearly the name must relate to one such incident – the name cannot refer to a peak or pass where one habitually or characteristically loses blankets, whereas **iNgqamamadolo** ('hobble on the knees') Pass is a place where one characteristically hobbles on the knees (1983: 305).

Mbatha (1992: 33) gives an example of a one-off incident name from iThala in the granite outcrops named **ZikhwamazikaNgcobo** ('Ngcobo's bags') where 'a new witchdoctor **Ngcobo** was buried with his belongings'.

Places are more likely, however, to be named after customs and practices that endure over a period of time, as in Mbatha's example **iNtabayamasosha** ('mountain of soldiers'), a name which refers to the extended use of this place as a camp for soldiers. She also gives the example of a large flat area named **iSicabasembizo** ('plateau of social gatherings') for a place that was regularly used for this purpose.

Perhaps the most curious of Mbatha's examples of place names in the iThala Game Reserve is the mountain name **uMsunuboshwangosinga** ('the tying of the woman's labia with a cord'), a reference to the practice of infibulation.

Botha refers to six rivers in KwaZulu-Natal with the name **iNhlamba-masoka** ('where the **amasoka** wash' – see the section on courting praises on page 55 for a discussion of **amasoka**) and says:

> Dit is nie toevallig dat verskei spruite dié naam gekry het nie. In die tradisionele hut is daar nie wasgeriewe nie; gevolglik het elke kraal-gemeenskap bepaalde plekke in die omliggende spruite waar die verskillende groepe hulle kan was (1977: 180).
>
> [It is not coincidental that different streams have received this name. In the traditional hut there were no ablution facilities; consequently each community had specific places in the surrounding streams where the various groups could wash.]

The social custom of presenting a beast for slaughter to important visitors is reflected in the name of the **Hlabisa** district, a name which comes from the verb **hlabisa** ('cause to stab', 'present a beast for slaughter').

eNgomankulu, which Bryant tells us is the Zulu name for 'Vaal Kop, near Maritzburg', and which Doke and Vilakazi say is the name of a range of hills in the Valley of a Thousand Hills, means 'great national song', as sung at special festivals. I have not been able to establish the link between place and festival. This reminds me of the place name **kwaNongoma** (in northern KwaZulu-Natal). The use of the **no-** prefix tells us that this was originally the name of a person, and probably one skilled in dance and song (**ingoma**).

KwaLahlabantu refers to a precipitious place at the White Umfolozi where people were executed in Mpande's time (< **lahla**, 'throw away', 'discard', + **abantu**, 'people'). Another famous place of execution, relating to Shaka's time, is the cliff known as **Isiwa Samanqe** ('cliff of the vultures'), which lies halfway between Kranskop and Eshowe.

KwaNtabakayikhonjwa – Blinkwater Mountain – in Mvoti county is 'The Mountain Which is not Pointed At': one of a number of mountains which local custom decrees should not be pointed at, usually because of a belief that bad weather will result.

8.5 PLACES NAMED AFTER PEOPLE: ESPECIALLY KWA- NAMES

The locative prefix **kwa-** ('place of') is typically used with an anthroponym, either a personal name, or a clan name or clan praise. It is usually used in the sense of 'home of', so that **kwaSipho** means 'Sipho's house' or 'Sipho's establishment'. **KwaDokotela** could mean 'the doctor's house', that is, where he lives, or 'the doctor's surgery', that is, where he works. This underlying meaning of **kwa-** thus means that most place names incorporating **kwa-** will refer to human settlements, whether large towns, small villages, or single homesteads. Nonetheless, we can and do find geographical features with the **kwa-** prefix, and Botha (1977: 96) gives a number of river names such as **kwaNomlotha, kwaNomabungu** and **kwaNkomokayidli**.

Any map of KwaZulu-Natal will give a number of examples of settlements with **kwa-** names which refer to individuals or clans living in the particular area. The 1: 250 000 series No. 2830 for Richard's Bay gives, for example, **kwaMagwaza**, **kwaMandlakazi**, **kwaMagidela**, and **kwaMawanda** among many others.

Mbatha (1992: 29) gives two examples of place names from iThala Game Reserve where a clan name is prefixed with **kwa-**: **kwaMthethwa** Valley and **kwaMakhathini** Mountain, and six other place names that are clan names without the **kwa-** prefix: **Dlomo**, **Simelane**, **Nzimane**, **Ngcobo**, **Nsingilana** and **Mayaya**.

Two well-known **kwa-** names are **kwaMashu** and **kwaMbonambi**. **KwaMashu** takes its name from the philanthropist Sir *Marshall* Campbell, who donated land for the building of this township, and **kwaMbonambi**, north of eMpangeni, is 'the place of the Mbonambi clan', of whom Bryant tells us that 'The Mbonambis . . . were great as manufacturers of assegai-heads, either obtaining the iron-ore from inland, or the metal itself from fragments of wreckage along their coast' (1929: 104).

And, of course, the first half of the bilingual name **KwaZulu-Natal** is a **kwa**-name, with the personal name **uZulu** (< **izulu**, 'sky', 'weather'), the name of the founder of the Zulu nation whose dates Bryant (1929: 35) gives as born in 1627 and died in 1709. The word 'uZulu' is also used today for the Zulu people as a whole, as in '**Uthini uZulu?**' ('What do the Zulu people think?'). KwaZulu, then, could mean 'the home of a man named Zulu' or 'the place of the Zulu people' (that is, in the wider sense: not the home of the Zulu clan).

The village of Howick, west of Pietermaritzburg, as well as its famous waterfall, are both known as **KwaNogqaza**, in reference to an early chief of the Dlamini clan, while Pomeroy, the village that lies between Greytown and Dundee, is known as **kwaGwalagwala**. This may mean the place where the lourie is found – the Zulu word **igwalagwala** is used for both the Knysna Lourie (*Tauraco corythaix*) as well as the Purple-crested Lourie (*T. porphyreolophus*) – or may be formed on the personal name of someone. As we saw in Chapter 4 (page 69) above, this was the Zulu name of Henry Francis Fynn (junior).

For the majority of place names in this chapter I have simply given one interpretation since only one interpretation is possible. There are, however, a number of names whose interpretation is open to doubt, and a selection of these is dealt with in Chapter 9.

Chapter 9

Zulu place names: Historico-cultural background

9.1 INTRODUCTION

The meanings of Zulu place names have always had a fascination for non-Zulu visitors, and recently have become a valued part of the Zulu culture offered to tourists. For example, the following paragraph comes from a tourism feature in the *Sunday Tribune Magazine* of 5 March 2000, and it is the first paragraph in a story about Babanango which also includes detailed mention of the historical and conservation significance of the Babanango district:

> Locals are proud of their quaintly named town [Babanango] and if they are to be believed, all roads lead to this small village in the heart of Zululand. How this village got its name is a story in itself. Living in the vicinity of Babanango Hill, a peak of approximately 1 600 m, was a chief who sent his son on an errand. His son became lost and during the search, as mists swirled, a retainer exclaimed, 'Babanango!' (Father, there he is.)

Elsewhere we read:

> Babanango is the name of a hill, a stream and a district in Zululand and there are many versions of how the name came about. Carel Birkby in 'Zulu Journey' said the word meant 'The Infant who Cannot Sit Up'. Elsewhere it is translated as 'Father, Where Are You?'. But the most popular story of all is that many years ago a child was lost on the slopes of the mist-shrouded hill and when at last she was found by an elder brother he shouted. 'Ubaba, nango' – 'Father, There she is' (Stayt, 1971).

Searching for the origins of Zulu place names often brings to light a number of conflicting interpretations. Very often local Zulu-speaking residents do not themselves know the origin of Zulu place names in their own area. In the 1980s I conducted field research into the origins of Zulu place names in the Natal Drakensberg, and often when I asked older residents how it was that such-and-such a place had come to be named, I was answered '**Asazi, safika likhona**' ('We don't know, it [the name] was here when we came here').

The names that have been chosen for this chapter are especially those names about whose interpretation there has been some sort of debate, so as to give not only a historical and cultural background to the naming of places in KwaZulu-Natal, but also a background to the *studying* of place names.

In this chapter I am also interested in who has done what in the collecting and interpreting of Zulu place names. Do the various collectors, scholars and translators agree with each other's interpretations? How reliable are the interpretations? If there is more than one interpretation, which one is correct? Or is the notion of only one correct interpretation a Euro-Western concept? Is it not possible, or even likely, that there is more than one 'correct' interpretation of a Zulu place name?

9.1.1 Sources

Surprisingly little has been published on Zulu place names, and the following are the sources that I have used, in chronological order, starting from the earliest.

In addition to the Revd A.T. Bryant's well-known *Olden Times in Zululand and Natal* (1929) I have used his 1905 *Zulu-English Dictionary*, which has a ten-page appendix entitled 'Proper Names of Persons, Rivers, Mountains, etc.'

Doke and Vilakazi's *Zulu-English Dictionary*, first published in 1948, has the occasional entry for a Zulu place name, although there are no specific lists of place names.

Harry Lugg's earliest work, the 1949 *Historic Natal and Zululand* covers people and places of historical interest from Zulu, English and Afrikaans backgrounds. His 1970 *A Natal Family Looks Back* and his 1975 *Life Under a Zulu Shield* both have appendices with a limited number of Zulu place names. The interpretations of the place names in these works of Lugg are, as one might expect, by and large consistent, but now and then different interpretations tell us that Lugg changed his mind about certain place names, for example, the uMzimkhulu River (see page 145). Lugg 'justifies' his own interpretations of Zulu place names on his familiarity with the Zulu language: 'The Zulu names of places in Natal give rise to much speculation and interpretation. My interpretations of the meanings of place names have been gleaned from my study of the Zulu language and from my contacts with many Zulus learned in the history and customs of their people' (1975: 89).

Lugg's 1968 *Zulu Place Names in Natal* (ed. A.T. Cope), published as a 15-page mini-booklet by the *Daily News* in aid of their Milk Fund, is almost word for word the same material as in the place name appendix of Lugg's *Natal Family*.

'The Wayfarer' was the pen-name of Don Stayt, who wrote a column in the *Daily News* for some years. His 1971 *Where On Earth? Place-Names of Natal and Zululand* relies heavily on Lugg.

T.V. Bulpin's 1969 *Natal and the Zulu Country* gives a translation for every Zulu place name mentioned. Chapter One ('Veil of Lost Years') is particularly rich in Zulu toponyms. Bulpin's Zulu nomenclature is exceptionally accurate. Although Bulpin does not give his sources for the interpretation of Zulu names, the undated predecessor of this work, *To The Shores of Natal*, makes the following comments about Zulu spellings:

> . . . the author is indebted to D. McK. Malcolm of the Natal University for his aid and advice on spellings and interpretations.
>
> An attempt has been made to give an etymology for African place names of historical importance mentioned in this book. In this connection, no interpretation has been given unless a minimum of six Africans resident in the immediate vicinity of the place mentioned have independently concurred on the interpretation.
>
> Essay competitions in Natal African schools also resulted in nearly 4,000 separate studies of local place names, and the author must express his thanks to all those school principals who stimulated their pupils to take an interest in making enquiries from the old and knowledgeable people in their districts (11).

P.E. Raper's 1987 *A Dictionary of Southern African Place Names* contains a number of Zulu place names, and is a useful summary of existing sources.

T.J.R. Botha's 1977 *Watername in Natal* contains a number of useful summaries of interpretations of various Zulu hydronyms.

Let us take a bus tour through KwaZulu-Natal. As we go, we will stop here and there at interesting mountains and rivers, and look at what the various writers named above have to say about their Zulu names. The tour starts in Pietermaritzburg, the capital of KwaZulu-Natal (as at December 2001). The Zulu name of Pietermaritzburg is **uMgungundlovu** and, for reasons of space only, we will look at this name in Chapter 10. But while we are in Pietermaritzburg, let us look at the name of a river running through Pietermaritzburg – the **uMsunduzi** – starting-point for the famous 'Dusi' Canoe Marathon.

9.2 A TOPONYMICAL BUS TOUR

9.2.1 uMsunduzi

Botha (1977: 156) points out that there are seven rivers in KwaZulu-Natal with the name **uMsunduzi** or **uMsunduze**. He is correct when he states that all scholars agree that the name is a personification based on the verb **sunduza** ('to push forcefully'), but that there is disagreement as to whether the name should end in **-i** or **-e**. Lugg gives both spellings in *Natal Family*: '**emSunduze (Umsunduzi)** The pushing river' (1970: 48), but only has one spelling in *Zulu Shield*:

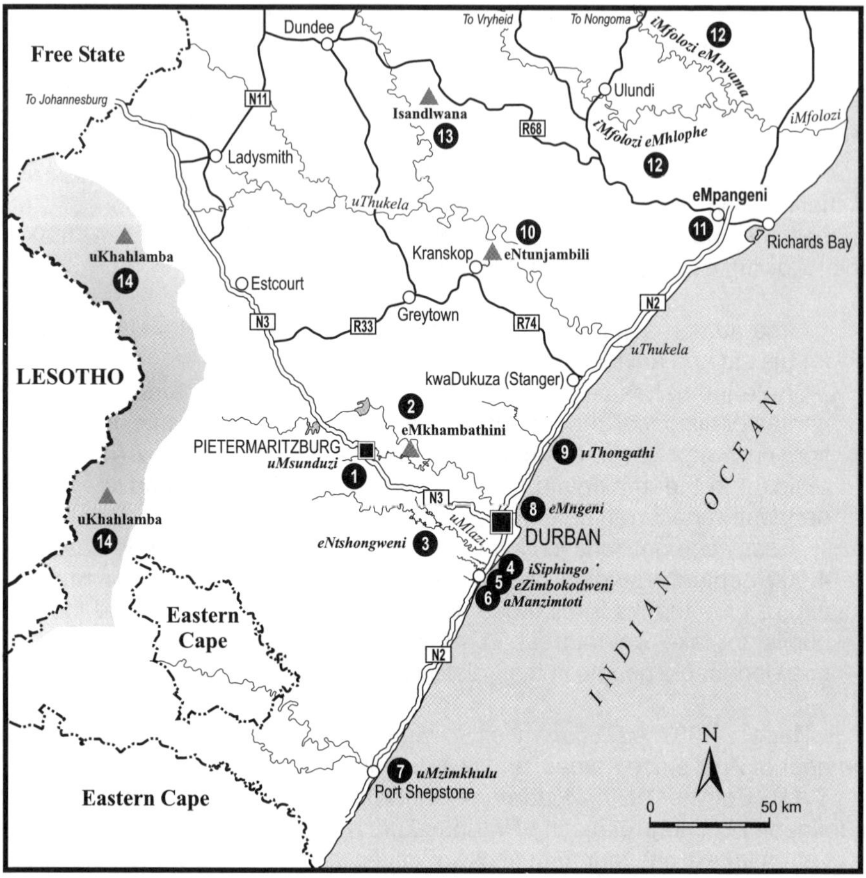

A 'bus tour' through KwaZulu-Natal.

> 'The River that pushes everything before it' of which there are several, the best known being the one that flows through Pietermaritzburg on which annual canoe races to Durban are a great feature.
>
> Another Umsunduze flows into the Umfolozi near its mouth, on the upper sources of which is the site of Dingiswayo's chief kraal, oYengweni. There is a third, a tributary of the Mkuze near the Hluhluwe settlement (1975: 108).

Bulpin is also in favour of the **-e** ending: 'At the head of the valley, where the *Msunduze* (the river that pushes away) joins the Mngeni . . .' (1969: 12).

Stayt (1971) opts for the **-i** ending, but makes the common mistake of misspelling the river by using an **s** where there should be a **z**: '**UMSINDUSI RIVER**: "The River that Pushes Away", of which there are several and whose name appeared variously spelt. The best known river of this name runs

The **uMsunduzi** River, near Elandskop, about 15 kilometres west of Pietermaritzburg.

through Pietermaritzburg, and is a tributary of the Umgeni, joining the bigger river at the foot of Table Mountain.'

As Lugg says, the best-known of the seven **uMsunduzi** rivers is the one that flows through Pietermaritzburg and provides the course for the canoe race universally known as the 'Dusi Canoe Marathon', even though three-quarters of the race takes place on the uMngeni river.

The difference between the **-e** and the **-i** endings can be explained grammatically as outlined below.

If the verb **sunduza** becomes a noun, then it needs the class 3 noun prefix **um-**, commonly used for rivers, and the nominalising suffix **-i** to make the noun **umsunduzi** ('the forceful pusher').

If, on the other hand, the verb **sunduza** becomes an imperative with the object concord **-m-**, then the verb will end in **-e**: **msunduze** ('push him/her forcefully'). This would then require an extra **u-** to be prefixed to make the name **uMsunduze.** Both interpretations are perfectly acceptable, but I think that the first form (**uMsunduzi**) is the more likely, firstly, by analogy with similar forms such as **uMfolozi** and **uMlalazi** (which are never ***uMfoloze** and ***uMlalaze**), and secondly, because the object concord **-m-**, in the form **uMsunduze**, refers to a person and not to a river.

No writers have come up with the suggestion that **umsunduzi** is a compound consisting of **um-** (noun prefix) + **(i)sundu** (*Phoenix reclinata* palm) +

(ulu)zi ('fibre used for thread, cordage, etc.'), even though the Phoenix palm *is* found along river beds, and *is* used for cord and fibre.

Let us continue with our bus tour. We head south-east towards Durban along the N3 highway, and approximately 15 kilometres out of Pietermaritzburg, we can see on our left the flat top of Natal's own Table Mountain, known in Zulu as **eMkhambathini**.

9.2.2 eMkhambathini

All writers named above are agreed that **eMkhambathini** is the locative form of the noun **umkhambathi**, given by Doke and Vilakazi (1958: 377) as the 'camel-thorn tree, Acacia xanthophloea'. Other writers (Lugg, 1970; Stayt, 1971; Raper, 1987) refer to the 'camel-thorn tree' and Bulpin introduces a variation by using the Afrikaans name *kameeldoorn*: 'Dominating their lands and, indeed, the whole valley – a veritable castle of the giants – stood the massive 3,143-foot-high, flat-topped Table Mountain, known to the Debes as *emKhambathini* (the place of the kameeldoorn trees)' (1969: 12).

None of these writers, however, have thought to question either Doke and Vilakazi's English name or the Latin name for the tree which has given this mountain its Zulu name. Doke's 'Acacia xanthophloea', according to Pooley (1993: 140), Moll (1981: 511), and Coates-Palgrave (1977: 253), is in English the 'Fever Tree', for which Pooley gives the following four Zulu names: '**umhlosinga, umhlofunga, umdlovune, umkhanya-gude** [*sic*]' (1993: 140).

> The name **umkhanya-gude** is a misspelling of **umkhanyakude** ('that which shines from afar' – a reference to the bright yellow-green bark of this tree).

The Zulu word **umkhambathi** correctly refers to the tree with the English name 'Paperbark Acacia' and the Latin name *Acacia sieberiana*, the tree which is indeed the dominant acacia in the **eMkhambathini** area.

In fact, some years ago, the suburb of Lincolnmeade of Pietermaritzburg, a suburb which is characterised by these trees and also overlooks Natal Table Mountain, opened a community hiking trail which ran in the direction of Table Mountain. The trail was named the '**Siy' eMkhambathini** Hiking Trail', a name deliberately chosen which could either mean 'We are walking towards eMkhambathini Mountain' or 'We are walking under the Paperbark Acacias.'

But to return to the interpretation of the place name **eMkhambathini**: although all writers concur that this place name is based on the tree name **umkhambathi** in Zulu, there are two schools of thought as to why. Lugg believes that this is because there are many such trees in the area: '**e<u>n</u>Khambathini** [*sic*]. Amidst the camel-thorn trees. Table Mountain near Pietermaritzburg. These trees were once very plentiful at its bsea [*sic* = "base"?]' (1970: 40).

Raper prefers to follow Doke and Vilakazi's theory that the mountain was so-named because it has a flat top similar to the flat top of the **umkhambathi** tree: '**Khambathi:** Zulu name for Table Mountain 20 km east of Pietermaritzburg. Meaning "camel-thorn tree", it was bestowed because it has a flat top, just as this tree has [note that Raper has decided to dispense with the locative inflection of this word]' (1987: 175).

There is no reason why one should have to choose between these two explanations: the poetry of many Zulu place names is based on their deliberate ambiguity.

Our bus continues along the N3 highway on the way to Durban, and halfway between Pietermaritzburg and Durban, we encounter road signs pointing to 'Shongweni', a misspelling for the correct name **eNtshongweni**.

9.2.3 eNtshongweni

Lying midway between Pietermaritzburg and Durban is the 'Shongweni' Polo Club, taking its name from the nearby 'Shongweni' Dam, at one time an important feeder dam for Durban's water supply. The Shongweni Dam is itself on the **eNtshongweni** River, a small tributary of the **uMlaza** River which flows into the sea just south of Durban. Here again there are two schools of thought: the 'Misty Spray' school, and the 'Milky Shrub' school.

Lugg is the originator of the 'Misty Spray' theory, and we first find this interpretation in *Natal Family*: '**eNtshongweni (Shongeni)** [*sic*]. Name of a tributary of the Umlazi whose waters fall over a high precipice in a long misty spray to resemble a high column or *ntshongwe*' (1970: 43).

Bulpin tells us of 'the place called *Shongweni* (the place where the Xysmalobium shrubs grow) . . .' (1969: 42), a reference to two closely related plants of which Doke and Vilakazi say:

> i. **i(li)shongwe**: milk-shrub Xysmalobium lapathifolium, white flowers eaten as greens . . .
> ii. **intshongwe**: small sp. of xysmalobium shrub, not eaten (1958: 744).

According to Pooley's 1998 *Wild Flowers of KwaZulu-Natal*, the Zulu name **ishongwe** is used for the herb *Asclepias albens*, the herb *Xysmalobium undulatum* (this is D&V's *Xysmalobium lapathifolium* above), the herb *Schizoglossum atropurpureum*, and the herb *Pachycarpus concolor*. All occur in the Shongweni area. The species mentioned by Doke and Vilakazi is clearly a very useful plant, and Pooley gives the following details: 'Used in traditional medicine to treat headaches, dysentery, colic and as charms to divert storms, prevent poisoning and make dogs keen hunters. Widely used medicinally in Afr and elsewhere. Sold in Europe under the name *Uzura*. Young leaves used as a pot herb. "Parachute" hairs from seeds used to stuff pillows' (1998: 544).

Clearly this is not just some obscure or unknown plant, but a plant of some value in the area where it grows.

The basis of Lugg's interpretation can be found in Doke and Vilakazi's entry **isintshongo**, which they gloss as 'wreath of smoke or dust rising'. The same word is found in Bryant's *Dictionary*, the meaning given as 'perpendicular pillar of smoke, as from a fire on a windy day'.

Leaving behind the wreaths of smoke rising from the Shongweni Polo Club, our bus continues on the N3 highway until it gets to Durban. The Zulu name for Durban is **eThekwini** and, again for reasons of space, this name is discussed in Chapter 10. At Durban let us travel south along the coastal N2 highway as there are three coastal names in close proximity to Durban which we need to look at. The first, only some 15 kilometres south of Durban, is the beach and the residential area named after the river known in Zulu as the **iSiphingo**.

9.2.4 iSiphingo

The **iSiphingo** River enters the sea just south of Durban. Raper explains:

> Of Zulu origin, the name has been variously explained as a type of vine growing along the banks (*Scutia commersonii*); to its winding course, reminiscent of twigs intertwined to construct a hut [**iphingo**, 'wattle-work, interlacing', < **phinga**, 'intertwine wattles']; to the ebb and flow of the river with the tide . . . (1987: 159).

The interpretation of the thorny vine is supported by Doke and Vilakazi, although they give the shrub **isiphingo** as being the species *Sentia indica*. Pooley (1993: 300), incidentally, only gives **isiphingo** as a *Xhosa* name, and says it is for the Cat-thorn (*Scutia myrtina*). As Doke and Vilakazi's second meaning for the word **isiphingo** is '2. name of a river near Durban', it is clear that they see this as being the interpretation of the river name.

Lugg gives a different interpretation: '**isiPhingo (Isipingo).** a long, penetrating channel of water mindful of the *iphengelo* wattle, sharpened at both ends, and used for holding down the thatch of a hut. Cf. *umphingo*, a spear with a blade loosely fixed to its shaft, and once used for killing elephants' (1970: 47).

I am not quite sure what Lugg is getting at here: the words **iphengelo** and **isiphingo** seem morphologically quite distinct, while **umphingo** seems semantically irrelevant.

Botha (1977: 86) draws our attention to three possible interpretations of **iSiphingo**: *firstly*, the thorny shrub theory. *Secondly*, he relates the hydronym to the Zulu verb **phinga**, which includes the meaning 'intertwine wattles and branches (in making fences, screens, etc.)'. The idea here is that the river winds in and out like the wattle twigs woven into the wall of a hut. This seems a reasonable interpretation, even though Doke and Vilakazi do not give this meaning for the noun **isiphingo**. The *third* interpretation relates **iSiphingo** to another meaning of the verb **phinga**, namely 'copulate (of dogs)'. According to this theory, the tides which push water up the estuary and then withdraw are like the penetration and withdrawal of copulating dogs. Botha says of this interesting possibility:

> Hoewel die deiningsverskynsel kenmerkend is van dosyne ander riviere aan die Natalse kus, hoef dit 'n mens nie skepties te stem jeens hierdie verklaring nie. *Sipingo* is 'n doodgewone persoonsname onder die Zoeloes en spruit dikwels voort uit 'n oortreding van hulle sedewete (86).
>
> [Although the tidal-wash phenomenon is characteristic of dozens of other rivers on the Natal coast, one should not be sceptical about this interpretation. *Sipingo* is a dead common personal name among the Zulus and stems from a transgression of their moral laws.]

I find this particularly curious as in over 20 years of relatively intensive study of Zulu personal names I have not once come across the 'dead common' personal name **Sipingo**. Consequently, I leave the reader to make up his or her own mind about this interpretation as we get back in the bus and travel only three or four kilometres to the residential area called '**uMbogintwini**', named after the **eZimbokodweni** River.

9.2.5 eZimbokodweni ('uMbogintwini')

The name 'uMbogintwini', originally for the small river which enters the Indian Ocean approximately 20 kilometres south of Durban, and now for a residential suburb and post office, seems to raise the most ire among purists, especially mother-tongue Zulu speakers, as an example of how 'arrogant colonialists' have mistreated the Zulu language (see the letter quoted on page 110). There seems to be no argument about what the name means, although there is still some variation about the correct orthography, as we can see in the following:

- Bulpin: '. . . the valley of the *emBokodweni* (place of round stones), whose name has been corrupted by Europeans into Umbogintwini' (1969: 14).
- Raper: '**Umbogintwini:** . . . The name is an adaptation of Zulu **Mbokodweni**, "river of round grinding-stones" . . .'.
- Stayt: 'More properly emBokondwini [*sic*] or emBokodweni meaning "At the place of the Round Stones"' (1971).
- Bryant's *Dictionary* gives two spellings, and also introduces an extra nasal which no other writers recognise: '**emBhoko<u>n</u>dweni (izi-mBhoko<u>n</u>do):** river in Durban county' (1905: 752).
- Botha gives a remarkable number of variations in the spelling of this river name, collected from a variety of sources: '**imbokondwe, imbokondo, imbokodo, imbokonte, impokonte, bongondwe, pongondwe, pokoto,** and **pokote**' (1977: 122).

Zulu speakers are unanimous that the river name should be in the plural form **eziMbokodweni.**

From the **eZimbokodweni** River it is only a matter of a few kilometres before we cross the next river, the **aManzimtoti**.

9.2.6 aManzimtoti

The **aManzimtoti** River enters the ocean 25 kilometres south of Durban, and has given its name to the very popular seaside resort at the river's mouth. There is general agreement about the meaning of this river name – 'Sweet Waters' – and the supposed reason behind it. Bulpin explains it as follows:

> . . . the army reached a certain river. Shaka's personal attendant filled a calabash with water from this stream and carried it to his master. Shaka, resting in the shade of an umDoni tree, sipped it tentatively and was pleased. *'Kanti Amanz'a mtoti.'* ('So, the water is sweet'), he said, delicately using the *hlonipha* (respectful alternate) word for the taboo name of his mother, *Nandi* (the sweet one). The army, as usual, acclaimed his saying, and the pleasant little river was henceforth known as *Amanzamtoti* (the sweet waters) (1969: 68).

See Chapter 2, pages 18 to 20, for details about **hlonipha** avoidance of names.

It is curious that Bulpin uses the spelling 'Amanzamtoti' here when talking about the derivation of the name. Elsewhere in his book he uses the far more common spelling 'Amanzimtoti'. Either spelling is in fact acceptable in terms of the grammatical structure of the word.

Most renderings of this anecdote imply that the river was not yet named when Shaka sipped its sweet waters and then subsequently **hlonipha**'d his mother. Lugg, though, makes the suggestion that the river '. . . may have originally been named Amanzamnandi, but changed to its present form in deference to Shaka's mother, Nandi . . . under the **hlonipha** custom' (1975: 89).

Botha raises the interesting question which so often comes to mind when stories link Shaka to the naming of places, and that is:

> Het die rivier nie reeds sy naam gehad voordat Shaka sy gevleuelde opmerking gemaak het nie? Die gebied om die rivier was indertyd beslis nie 'n niemandsland nie (1977: 111).
>
> [Did the river not already have its name before Shaka made his winged statement? The area around the river was after all in those times not a no-man's-land.]

But as Botha points out in answer to his own question, it is not always possible to distinguish between reality and fiction when it comes to traditions in which Shaka figured. In answer to queries about whether it is likely that a river would be named for its taste, Botha gives the Zulu river names **uMnambithi** ('the tasty one', the Kliprivier running through Ladysmith) and **aManzaduma** ('sour waters', a small river in the Maphumulo district).

Now we need to travel approximately 100 kilometres southwards, passing *en route* such tantalising names as **iLovu** Beach, **uMgababa**, **uMkhomazi** River, **uMdoni** Park, **Sezela**, **iFafa** Beach and **uMthwalume**, before we get to Port Shepstone and the mouth of the **uMzimkhulu** River.

> Most of these names were mentioned in Chapter 8, but here are the meanings again: **iLovu** ('fruit of the *Cordia caffra* tree'); **uMgababa** (meaning obscure – possibly an abbreviation of **um[uzi] kababa** 'my father's homestead'); **uMkhomazi** ('female whales'), **uMdoni** ('*Syzygium cordatum* tree'), **Sezela** (meaning obscure), **iFafa** ('misty place'); and finally **uMthwalume** (literally, 'what it carries must stand upright' – a species of tree).

9.2.7 uMzimkhulu

The **uMzimkhulu** River, which enters the ocean at Port Shepstone on Natal's South Coast, is one of the province's major rivers, with a catchment area only exceeded by the Tugela River. Bulpin gives the size of the river as the underlying reason for its name: 'The *Mzimkhulu* (the great home of all the rivers), so named from its size and number of tributaries . . .' (1969: 14).

The word **umzimkhulu** is a compound of **umuzi** ('homestead, village') + **mkhulu** ('it is big'), so there is really no reason for Raper to use the word 'probably': '. . . derived from Zulu, the name probably means "large village"' (1987: 233).

With a morphological structure as clear as this, it seems unlikely that there could be any other interpretations, but in fact there are three others, all from Harry Lugg. His first analysis of the name is to be found in the 1968 booklet *Zulu Place Names*, where he says: 'emZimkhulu (Umzimkulu). A great kraal. A complimentary name, and probably a play on amanzimakhulu or great waters' (11).

Here we see both the 'standard' interpretation of 'great kraal' ('large village', etc.) as well as the 'probability' that the name is a contraction of **amanzimakhulu** ('great waters'). Stayt ('The Wayfarer') tells us that when he wrote in his newspaper column that the word 'Umzimkhulu' meant 'Great Waters', a correspondent wrote to the newspaper saying that such an interpretation was not at all true, and that the name meant 'Place of the Great Affairs'. Stayt then 'turned to my good friend Harry Lugg, former Chief Native

Commissioner and a man whose knowledge of the Zulu and the Zulu language is vast and understanding', and it would seem that what Lugg told him was that the name meant 'Great Kraal' but was probably a play on 'Great Waters'. Faced with this vacillation, Stayt (1971) took the easy way out, and his *Where on Earth?* informs the reader that the name means 'Place of Great Affairs' as well as 'Great Waters'.

But Lugg had not yet finished with this place name. Although almost all the toponymical material in the 1968 *Zulu Place Names* is repeated word for word in the appendix of *Natal Family* two years later, the entry for uMzimkhulu did change. In the 1970 version it reads: '**emZimkhulu.** Suggests that it was originally known as Mzilamkhulu or river with the great trail or water course' (48).

In this new interpretation, Lugg has decided that the first part of the compound noun, **uMzi**, is not a contraction of **umuzi**, or **amanzi** ('water'), but of **umzila** ('track', 'trail'). However, this new Luggian theory did not last long, for by 1975, when *Zulu Shield* appeared, Lugg had changed his mind again. In *Zulu Shield*, we find *this* statement: '[uMzimkhulu] The large picturesque river that forms the boundary between Alfred County and the rest of Natal derives its name from **zima**, weighty, dignified, impressive and **kulu** (khulu), big, large, great, and thus means the river of great impressiveness (umZima-khulu)' (108).

These various interpretations reveal a certain characteristic of Lugg's linguistic thinking: his belief that many place names must be contractions of some earlier and longer form. We see the same belief in his interpretation of 'uMfolozi' on page 151.

Now we need to turn our bus around and head northwards again, for if we continue another 30 or so kilometres we will meet the artificial linguistic boundary, the **uMtamvuna** River that marks the boundary between Zulu-speaking KwaZulu-Natal and the Xhosa-speaking Eastern Cape. I say 'artificial' because a river will never have only speakers of one language on the one bank and speakers of another on the other bank. In fact, some years ago while on holiday on the banks of the uMtamvuna River, I asked the local residents: '**Nina bantu enihlala lapha – niyakhuluma noma niyathetha?**' ('You residents of hereabouts – do you "khuluma" or do you "thetha"?' – using the Zulu and Xhosa verbs respectively for 'speak'). Back came the laconic answer: '**Asikhulumi, asithethi, siyamiksa**' ('We do not "khuluma", we do not "thetha", we mix').

Heading north from Durban along the same coastal N2 highway, almost immediately we find ourselves crossing the **uMngeni** River.

9.2.8 uMngeni

The entries for this river name are characterised by each writer being uncertain about the spelling, and so giving two, three or more variations, as in the following examples:

- Stayt: **UMGENI:** 'Variously mNgeni or emNgeni, "The River that Flows Through the Thorn Trees or Acacias". Tributaries include Lions, Karkloof, Impolweni, Umqeku and Umsindsi [*sic*]. The higher regions of the Umgeni were called Msanginyathi [*sic*] or "The Gatherer of the Buffaloes"' (1971).
- Raper has this river under **Mgeni**, but says 'also encountered as *uMgeni*, *Umgeni*, *Umngeni*, etc.' He favours the meaning 'River of the acacia trees' (1987: 220).
- Lugg: '**eMgeni (Umgeni**). Amidst the thorn trees at Durban' (1970: 46).
- Botha uses the spelling **Mngeni** for the tributary of the Buffalo at Msinga, but **Mgeni** for the river that runs through the Valley of a Thousand Hills, although he explains that this is a corruption of **em(u)ngeni** 'place of the *Acacia natalitia*' (now the *Acacia karoo*) (1977: 146, 129).
- Bulpin is one of the few authors courageous enough to commit himself to a single spelling: 'This river with its tortuous course so full of beautiful waterfalls and rapids, was given two names. In its upper reaches it was called the *Msonginyathi* (gatherer of the buffaloes) while lower down where it flowed into the mighty valley of a Thousand Hills, it was named the *Mngeni* (river of acacia trees)' (1969: 12).
- Doke and Vilakazi give the form **umNgeni**, say that it is derived from the verb **ngena** ('enter'), and then state 'Name of a river entering the sea in Durban.' This alternative derivation does not explain why, of all the rivers entering the sea along the KwaZulu-Natal coastline, this lone river should be named 'The Enterer'.

The interpretation given by all the sources except the last, that is, that this river takes its name from the locative form of **umunga** (*Acacia karoo*) makes far more sense in the light of the number of rivers named after the dominant vegetation in the area.

Continuing northwards along the N2, we see signs pointing to 'Tongaat', a small village which has taken its name from the **uThongathi** River.

9.2.9 uThongathi

The **uThongathi** River enters the Indian Ocean approximately 35 kilometres north of Durban. The various interpretations of this river name can be roughly divided into two: those that see the name as (**tho** + **ngathi**) and those that see the name as (**thonga** + **thi**).

a. tho + ngathi

This first interpretation sees the first syllable of the name as being the Zulu noun **u(lu)tho** ('something') and the second two syllables as **nga** ('according to') and **thi(na)** ('we', 'us'), that is, 'Something according to us'. Botha gives two popular anecdotes based on this interpretation (1977: 205):

- Shaka's army, being thirsty on their return from a long, hot campaign on the South Coast, stopped in the vicinity of this little stream and asked the locals where their river was. On being shown the little stream, Shaka's warriors sneeringly said, 'do you call this little nothing a river?', to which the locals replied, 'It may be nothing to you, but it is *something according to us.*'

- When Shaka and his army first arrived in the area where this little river was, it was the first time that he had appeared in this rather isolated spot. From his point of view, the very fact that he had visited this place had given it an importance which it had not had before, and he remarked to the local inhabitants, 'You have now become *something because of us.*'

A variation on this theme appeared in the pages of the *Natal Witness* (29 January 2000) in connection with Indian behaviour to African workers:

> . . . there is a story commonly known in KwaZulu-Natal that traces the origin of the place-name 'Tongaat'. Some Zulus were working on the sugar-cane plantations and a group of Indian indentured labourers joined them on a north coast plantation. The Indians soon acquired a reputation for carrying stories to the white bosses about the Zulus.
>
> The plantation became known as a place where Indians gained preferential treatment by exposing flaws in African labour – '*lezinto zizenza utho ngathi*', meaning 'these things are spit-polishing their stars at our expense.' Hence, *utho + ngathi* = Tongaat.

b. thonga + thi

This theory assumes that the word 'uthongathi' is structured in the same way as the two tree names 'umthombothi' and 'umsimbithi', that is, **umthombo** ('spring') + **(umu)thi** ('tree') and **(in)simbi** ('iron') + **(umu)thi** respectively. The noun stem **-thonga** is assumed to come from the noun **isithonga** ('*Strychnos mackenii* tree') to which **-thi** is suffixed.

This is the interpretation given by Bulpin: 'The Cele people . . . established themselves in the lands between the rivers known as the *Zinkwazi* (place of the white-headed fish eagle) and the *Thongathi* (place of *Strychnos mackenii* trees)' (1969: 11).

Stayt (1971) also favours this interpretation, but adds the alternative 'The Twisting River': 'Variously Thongathi, Umtongate and known originally as Victoria when it was founded for Byrne settlers in 1849 on the banks of the Tongaat River ("The Twisting River" [for which I can find no justification] or "The Place of the Thonga – Strychnos Mackenis [*sic*]").'

Pooley's 1993 *Trees of Natal* recognises neither *Strychnos mackenni* nor the noun stem **-thongathi**, but she does, tantalisingly, give the name **umthongothi** for the Spiny Gardenia (*Hypercanthus amoenus*).

Various different *Strychnos* species do indeed seem to have had some influence on the hydronyms of KwaZulu-Natal's north coast, for Bulpin, having opted for the *Strychnos mackenii* theory for 'Thongathi', then goes further and states that **uMhlali** takes its name 'from the number of monkey-orange trees (*Strychnos spinosa*) growing on its banks', while the **Nonoti** River is named 'from the mnono trees (*Strychnos henningsii*) growing there' (1969: 335).

Curiously enough, according to Doke and Vilakazi the Zulu name for the small town of Tongaat is not Tongaat/uThongathi at all, but **oHlawe**, meaning 'gravelly place'(1958: 323).

We continue to head northwards, and at **kwaDukuza**, until May 1999 known as KwaDukuza to all Zulu speakers, but 'Stanger' on all the maps, we briefly turn inland on the R74 to Kranskop and Greytown. The village Kranskop takes its name from the nearby mountain with the same name, a mountain famous in Zulu folklore as **iNtunjambili**.

9.2.10 iNtunjambili

iNtunjambili is the Zulu name for the striking hill which is otherwise known as Kranskop, approximately midway between Greytown and Dukuza/Stanger. Raper says: 'Of Zulu origin, the name means "two openings", referring to two apertures in the hill, one of which has crumbled away' (1987: 247).

Lugg gives both names in a confusing statement: '**Kranskop** or **Ntunjambili** (*The Two Apertures*). So named from a hole under the "bridge" connecting the kop with the main and and [*sic*] the gap above it, is one of Natal's outstanding landmarks' (1949: 89).

The noun **intunja** can mean either a small aperture, such as the eye of a needle, or a very large one, such as a tunnel through a hill. In the name **iNtunjambili**, the noun is linked to the adjective stem **-bili** ('two'), as originally this hill near Greytown had two openings, as Raper says. In the Natal Drakensberg, the hill named **iNtunja** has only one hole, albeit one big enough to drive a double-decker bus through. This hill also has the Afrikaans name *Gatberg* (literally, 'hole-mountain').

iNtunjambili is a name of special significance for children, for in **izinganekwane** (Zulu folktales) it is **iNtunjambili** that traditionally is regarded as a safe haven for little children who are running away from some danger, for example, angry parents, or **amazimu** ('wicked cannibals'). When the children arrive at the base of this mountain they sing in their high treble voices:

Litshe likaNtunjambili!
Rock of Two-Holes!
Litshe likaNtunjambili!
Rock of Two-Holes!
Ngivulele ngingene!
Open for me that I may enter!
Ngivulele ngingene!
Open for me that I may enter!

When the rock opens, the children enter and are safe from pursuit, even if the pursuing monster or cannibal sings the same song, for the Rock of Two-Holes is clever enough to recognise a child's voice, and will not open when the song is sung in deep, mature tones. Occasionally the pursuing cannibal is clever enough to go away and pierce his throat with a red-hot needle to make his voice high and child-like. When this happens and the rock subsequently opens, the story-teller has to exercise considerable ingenuity in getting the children to escape.

But it is time to leave behind the world of **izinganekwane** and return to our bus. We head back to the coastal road and continue to travel north, passing **iZinkwazi** Beach on our right and crossing the **uThukela** River a few moments later. At **Gingindlovu**, we ignore the R56 heading inland towards **eShowe**, and continue northwards to stop at **eMpangeni**.

> The meanings of these names are as follows: **iZinkwazi** ('fish eagles'); **uThukela** ('the angry one'); **Gingindlovu** ('entrap the elephant'); **eShowe** (popular theory has this name as onomatopoeic for the sound of the wind in the trees; more recent theories have this as a misspelling for **eKhowe**, 'mushroom'); **kwaMbonambi** ('the home of the Mbonambi clan')

9.2.11 eMpangeni

There seems little doubt that **eMpangeni** takes its name from Revd Grout's 1850s mission station, itself named for the **eMpangeni** stream which is a tributary of the **uMhlathuze**. The exact interpretation of the name **eMpangeni**, however, is a matter of much debate amongst linguists and historians. There are two main theories – the 'botanical' and the 'plunder' – which are both well summed up in Botha's *Watername in Natal* (1977: 73–76). The botanical theories debate the merits of the *Encephalartos* (cycad) species **umphanga**, and the hard-pear tree (*Olinia ventosa*, previously *cymosa*), in Zulu **impange**. Those in favour of the 'robbery, plunder' theory suggest that the name is based on the verb **phanga** ('rob, plunder, deprive'), and a variety of possible reasons are given: 'crocodiles in this stream used to grab the unwary', 'the fast-flowing stream plunders soil from the banks', 'Mpande once held court here and used to fine litigants', and so on. Cubbins, in an article which pays little if any heed to Zulu morphology, plumps for the 'plunder' theory and dismisses the botanical options with a splendidly sweeping 'so the possible botanical derivation is simply not tenable' (1992: 39). This opinion appears to be based entirely on *Lugg's* conviction that the name is not related to the word **umphanga** (cycad).

Botha also lists a number of the less popular theories: that the name is a corruption of the name of Cetshwayo's military establishment **eMmangweni** (< **ummango**, 'slope'); that it is an abbreviation of **eMpangeleni** (< **impangele**, 'guinea-fowl'); and that it is a corruption of **eMbangweni** (< **umbango**, 'dispute').

On we go, past **kwaMbonambi**, and some 20 kilometres north of this little village, we eventually cross the river that flows through the heart of old Zululand, the **uMfolozi**.

9.2.12 uMfolozi

The simplest interpretation of the name **uMfolozi** is to take it as a noun derived from the verb **foloza** ('to zig-zag') as indeed both branches of this river, the White uMfolozi and the Black uMfolozi have very zig-zag courses. This is the interpretation given by Doke and Vilakazi (1958: 212), where after defining the noun **imfolozi** as 'zig-zag or chevron pattern', they give it as the basis of the river name(s). Incidentally, they regard the spelling with an initial **u-** (**uMfolozi**) as incorrect, stressing instead that the river should be spelt **iMfolozi**.

Bulpin adopts the zig-zag interpretation, deftly avoiding the question of the initial vowel: 'The largest and most-storied of all the rivers of Zululand is the *Mfolozi* (the zig-zag) so named from its tortuous course and erratic nature' (1969: 10).

Lugg comes up with an alternative suggestion: 'The name is a contraction of **Umfula wozi** or River of the Ficus fibre fig which grows in profusion in places along their banks' (1975: 107).

Stayt (1971) gives both the standard 'zig-zag' interpretation as well as Lugg's 'Fibrous Fig' theory, and then adds a third possibility: 'Variously Mfolozi or emFolozi and variously described as "The River of the Ficus" from Umfulawozi, a species of figs [*sic*] growing on its banks; as "The Leading Span of Oxen in a Team" and "Zigzag", referring to the river's tortuous course'.

The second of Stayt's interpretations is clearly a confusion with the Zulu adoptive (loan-word) **ifolosi** ('leading ox in span'), an adaptation of Afrikaans *vooros* ('front ox'). The Zulu word **ifolosi** is today used for a front-line player in a team, especially a football team.

Like Stayt, Raper hedges his bets: 'Derived from Zulu, the name is said to mean "river of fibre", referring to wild fig-trees, the bark of which is used for

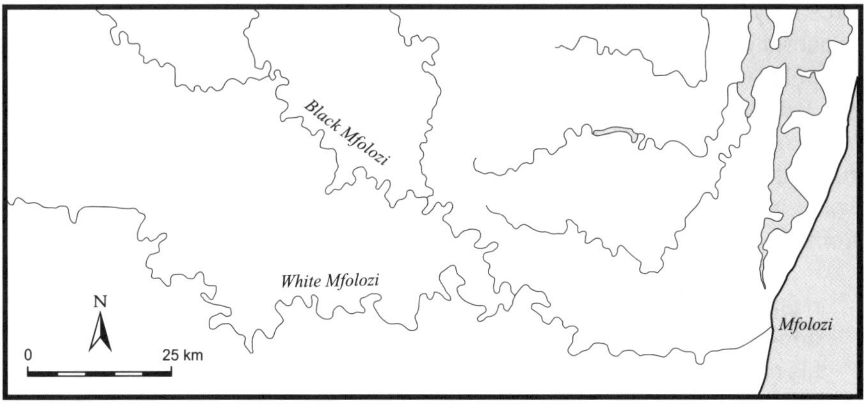

The zig-zag courses of the White **uMfolozi** and Black **uMfolozi** rivers.

sewing fibre, or to mean "the erratic one", after its meandering course' (1987: 219).

As regards the 'Fibrous Fig' theory, both Bryant and Doke and Vilakazi give the word **u(lu)zi** as meaning 'fibre' or 'cordage', but there is no mention of any kind of tree, let alone a species of fig tree, nor does Pooley (1993) give the word **u(lu)zi** in her very comprehensive list of Zulu tree names. In my opinion, Lugg's theory is an imaginative guess, which unfortunately has no solid linguistic basis. Nonetheless, it is interesting to see how such a theory is copied in other publications.

Another type of confusion raised by the name **uMfolozi** is that found in the early writings of Adolphe Delegorgue, traveller in Zululand in the 1840s. In the introduction to his *Vocabulaire de la Langue Zoulouse* ('Vocabulary of the Zulu Language') in the second volume of his *Travels in Southern Africa*, we find: 'I was given many different names for certain things; for example the word for "river" could be any one of the following: *om-phlène, om-fèlene, om-philos, um-filos, om-volos, folos* or *volos*, and *volosie* or *om-pholosie*' (translated) (1997: 286).

The first two in this list are variations of **emfuleni** ('in the river'), the locative form of **umfula** ('river'). The remaining seven forms are all variations of **uMfolozi**.

Our bus must now follow quite a complex route before the next stopping place: through the Umfolozi Game Reserve, out the back road heading directly westward until we come to **uLundi**, and then continuing directly west through a number of country roads, we come to the historically significant hill of **iSandlwana**.

9.2.13 iSandlwana

The hill of **iSandlwana**, about 75 kilometres west of Babanango in the heart of Zululand, is indelibly associated with the defeat of Lord Chelmsford's forces by Cetshwayo's army in the 1879 Anglo-Zulu War. Early writers apparently interpreted this name as a diminutive of **isandla** ('hand'), and we find references to 'The Battle of Little Hand'. The structure of this name is in fact **is(i)**, 'noun prefix', + **sa**, 'something like', + **(i)ndlu**, 'hut', + **ana**, 'little', giving 'something like a little hut'. But as many writers have pointed out, **sa** + **indlu** also gives the word **isandlu**, the name for the stomach of an animal, which in its diminutive form **isandlwana** specifically refers to the second stomach of a cow. Lugg gives more detail:

> In that part of the country miniature huts are used for the storage of grain, termed **isandlwana**, and the second stomach of a cow is also known by this name, presumably because it serves as a sort of storage bin. And the tribal story is that their Chief, Sihayo, or his father named this hill after the cow's second stomach because of its resemblance to that organ.

> Writers of the day wrongly confused the word with **sandlana**, a little hand (1975: 105).

Bulpin says much the same, without the detail: '*Sandlwana* was the name of this hill, a curious name for a curious hill, for it literally means "something like a small house", the name given to the second stomach of a cow, which it is said to resemble in appearance and shape' (1969: 264).

Bertram Mitford, in his 1883 *Through the Zulu Country* (Griggs & Co. reprint, 1975) follows the 'standard' interpretation of the cow's second stomach, somewhat disguised by the Victorian circumlocution 'bovine intestinal anatomy', and is particularly emphatic about a variation in spelling:

> The meaning of Isandhlwana, or more correctly Isandhlwane, is neither 'little hand', nor 'little house', nor any other of the hundred and one interpretations which were devised at the time of the disaster, but refers to a portion of bovine intestinal anatomy. The spelling of the word which I shall observe throughout these pages will be that which is now universally employed [that spelling is, 'Isandhlwana'], though 'Isandhlwan*e*' is the more correct (88).

Raper for some reason or another relates this name to the *third* stomach: ' . . . the name is said to refer to the "third stomach" or reticulum of an ox, which the hill resembles' (1987: 158).

Sir Henry Rider Haggard records a conversation he had with two eminent Zulu linguists – J.Y. Gibson and James Stuart – while travelling towards **iSandlwana**:

> By the way, Mr. Gibson declares that this name means 'like a little house'; Stuart, on the contrary, says that the true interpretation thereof is 'the second stomach of an ox'. When such learned doctors disagree, as they did with vigour, I may be pardoned if I cling to the old rendering 'the place of the little hand'. Certainly, it is not in the least like either a little house or an ox's stomach; whereas it has *some* similitude to an arm with a clenched fist at its end (2000: 200).

Two other Zulu place names, neither well-known at all, make interesting comparison with **iSandlwana**. The first comes from Lugg's *Historic Natal and Zululand*:

> **Sandlundlu.** A Native name, descriptive of a *conspicuous, hut-shaped*, bush-covered sand dune, about 200 feet in height, on the coast at Port Edward.
>
> Following the death of his mother Nandi in 1827, Shaka organised an *ihlambo* or ceremonial mourning-hunt to cleanse his spears against the amaMpondo under Chief Faku . . .

> During this campaign a large number of people took refuge in the Sandlundlu where they were surrounded and butchered . . .
> There is a small clump of scrub on this commonage traditionally known as *isiHlahla sikaShaka*, or *Shaka's Bush* (1949: 8).

The structure of **iSandlundlu** is **is(i)** + **sa** + **(i)ndlu** + **(i)ndlu**, using the same prefix **sa-** which indicates 'something like', and reduplicating the noun stem **-ndlu**. The reduplication of a noun stem normally indicates a number of things grouped together, so the name **iSandlundlu** would translate roughly as 'something like a collection of huts'.

The second name of comparative interest is the name of the range of hills which separates the Umfolozi Game Reserve from Ulundi to the west: the **iSangoyana** hills. This name has the structure **is(i)** + **sa** + **Ngoye** + **ana** and translates literally as 'something like a smaller version of the Ngoye hills', and indeed the iSangoyana hills are very similar in appearance, although they are somewhat lower in height, to the **Ngoye** Hills inland of uMthunzini.

For our last Zulu place name on this bus tour of KwaZulu-Natal, we need to make a wide westerly sweep before returning to our start at Pietermaritzburg. By travelling from **iSandlwana** Hill via the towns of Glencoe, Ladysmith, Bergville and Estcourt, we pass directly under the Drakensberg Mountains, known in Zulu as **uKhahlamba**.

9.2.14 uKhahlamba

Doyle Liebenberg, on the first page of his 1972 *The Drakensberg of Natal*, says: 'The Zulu name *Ukhahlamba* (a barrier as though made of up-pointed spears) aptly describes the formidable character of this rock face.'

This interpretation is taken from a combination of two of the four meanings which Doke and Vilakazi give for the word **u(lu)khahlamba**: 'row of upward-pointing spears' and 'broken mountain range' (1957: 374). The other two meanings also have some slight relevance: 'rough, bony object' and 'tall, thin person', but clearly it is the first two meanings mentioned that have made the phrase 'Barrier of Spears' a synonym for the Drakensberg of Natal. Indeed, this is the title of R.O. Pearse's comprehensive 1973 work on the Drakensberg, and Pearse says of his choice of title: 'The Zulu name is Quathlamba, meaning "A barrier of up-pointed spears"' (i).

The curious rendering 'Quathlamba' is 'explained' by Pearse in a discussion on the orthography of Zulu place names in the Drakensberg, where he curiously says: 'I have also retained the westernized form *Quathlamba*, instead of the more correct *uKhahlamba*.'

Raper also subscribes to the commonly held 'barrier of spears' theory, but introduces another theory of 'anything thrown in a heap' which I have not been able to trace: '**Khahlamba** . . . Zulu name of the Witteberge, spurs of the Drakensberg. Said to mean "anything thrown on a heap", "a barrier of pointed spears" etc. referring to the rugged appearance of these mountains' (1987: 175).

> It is unusual that Raper ascribes **Khahlamba** to the Witteberg as all other writers say that **uKhahlamba** is the name of the Drakensberg itself.

Lugg introduces another element when he says in *Zulu Shield*, 'Zulu name for the Drakensberg, meaning the "Jumble crash barrier"' (1975: 99); and in *Natal Family*, '**uKhahlamba** . . . the "crashing" mountain barrier' (1970: 39).

Stayt (1971) adds Lugg's suggestion to the generally recognised interpretation, although for reasons of his own he changes Lugg's 'crashing' to 'crushing': '**Khahlamba**: The name by which the Drakensberg was known to the Zizi tribe. It means simply "the Mountain Barrier" though Lugg suggests a "crushing" mountain barrier . . .'.

Lugg's 'crashing' theory probably lies in the onomatopoeia which Zulu speakers themselves attribute to the name **uKhahlamba**. In the 1980s, when I was conducting fieldwork into Zulu place names in the Natal Drakensberg (Koopman, 1983), I asked a number of the older residents for their interpretations of the word, and many of them said that the word came from the sounds made by rocks that fall from the high cliffs: **Khahla! Mba!** This may sound somewhat far-fetched, but Doke and Vilakazi do in fact give the Zulu ideophone **khahla!** with the meaning 'of crashing down' as well as the ideophone **mba!** 'of striking' (1958: 374, 489).

9.3 CONCLUSION

In this chapter I have discussed the various theories which have been put forward by a number of different writers to explain the Zulu names of ten rivers and four mountains in KwaZulu-Natal. That it has taken twenty-one pages to look at these theories shows if nothing else that there is, and always has been, among 'colonial' writers at least, a great deal of controversy over the interpretation of Zulu place names. Some of the theories put forward may seem fairly far-fetched, and others more likely, but in very few cases can one say definitely of a place name, 'This is the only possible interpretation'.

My intention in this chapter has also been to introduce some of the main contributors to the collecting of Zulu place names, and to show how much reliance some writers place on the interpretations of others. Lugg, particularly, despite some of his more curious guesses, has played a major role in bringing Zulu place names to the notice of the non-Zulu-speaking inhabitants of KwaZulu-Natal, and even among some academic writers on Zulu toponymy, Lugg's word is law. As mentioned previously, Cubbin, for example, writing on the history and meaning of **eMpangeni**, states: 'Harry Lugg . . . the eminent Zulu linguist and authority, is adamant: "The word is not related to umphanga, a variety of cycad". So the possible botanical derivation is simply not tenable' (1992: 39).

However, care needs to be taken with some of Lugg's statements. An example of this is a statement, which has nothing to do with place names, but which is uttered with the same definiteness as his statements on Zulu place names, namely that 'Cane rats are not rodents but members of the swine family' (1970: 91). Any Zoology reference work will confirm that cane rats (Zulu **ivondwe**) are indeed of the order *Rodentia*.

Chapter 10 looks at two Zulu place names – **eThekwini** and **uMgungundlovu** – the names of Durban and Pietermaritzburg respectively.

Chapter 10

eThekwini and uMgungundlovu: The Zulu names of Durban and Pietermaritzburg

10.1 INTRODUCTION

This chapter continues the approach of Chapter 9 by looking at various interpretations of place names: in this case, **eThekwini** (Durban) and **uMgungundlovu** (Pietermaritzburg). The section on **eThekwini** focuses on a lively debate in the press about two rival interpretations of the name, while the section on **uMgungundlovu** examines the remarkable number of variations in the spelling of this name, while simultaneously indulging in an elephant hunt.

10.2 ETHEKWINI: DURBAN

The Durban Metro Tourism web site that I consulted states: 'The harbour, once a natural lagoon, is the largest and busiest in South Africa today. The bay also gives Durban its Zulu name, eThekwini.'

This is a straightforward, no-nonsense statement. However, as soon as we let Stayt loose on this name, not only does doubt creep in, but there is also a suggestion that the name eThekwini might not even be Zulu. He explains 'Thekweni' [*sic*] as 'Name by which Durban is known to the Zulus . . . The actual meaning of the word is doubtful although Lugg suggests that it was probably Lala meaning a lagoon or estuary' (1971).

Doubt there may be here, but at least there is only one interpretation: the idea of the bay or lagoon that the Durban tourist web page gives. Once we look at Raper's *Dictionary of South African Place Names*, however, we find another potential interpretation: '**Thekwini** . . . Zulu name for **Durban**. Primarily applied to Durban bay, the name is said to mean either "lagoon" or "the one-testicled one", referring to the appearance of the bay' (1987: 316).

This brief suggestion of an alternative interpretation of 'Thekwini' gives no inkling of the heated correspondence on this issue which took place in the letter columns of the *Natal Mercury* from November 1978 to January 1979.

The debate was started by a correspondent who said that as a recent immigrant to Durban, he had heard that the Zulu name for the city was 'Thekwini' and could anyone tell him what this meant. Several 'armchair experts' immediately wrote in with the information that **ethekwini** was the locative form of the Zulu noun **itheku** ('bay', 'lagoon'), and that Durban was therefore the 'place of the lagoon' in Zulu.

There the matter would have rested had not an unidentified correspondent with access to a Zulu-English dictionary, pointed out that an alternative meaning for the word **itheku** is 'the one-testicled thing', suggesting that Shaka's warriors had so named Durban because of the shape of the bay when seen from the hills of the Berea.

Durban's residents were furious at this suggestion and a number of letters followed decrying this theory. Then came one from Louis Rencken of Eston, who stoked the flames by quoting the Revd A.T. Bryant:

> Sir – This is something for the worthy citizens of Durban to ponder: the origin of the Zulu name for Durban, 'Itheku', locative Ethekwini', as explained by the worthy Reverend A.T. Bryant in his work *Olden Times in Zululand and Natal* page 500:
>
> > Over the Tukela, Shadwa sped on his way, along the coast, till finally held up by a broad and calm lagoon flanked by beautiful wood-clad hills and connected by a narrow channel with the ocean. Looking down upon the oval lake from the adjacent hills, the tribal wag playfully dubbed it the 'iTeku' (or One-testicled thing'), a name the local natives have since affixed to Durban (eTekwini), built around the land-locked bay.

Note that 'Shadwa' is not a misprint for 'Shaka' as you might expect, but the name of the chief of the Luthuli clan.

This quote from Bryant prompted Commandant Sighurt Bourquin, a well-known authority on Zulu history and language, to write in defence of the 'place of the lagoon':

> Sir – With reference to the letter which appeared in your paper on November 29, under the heading 'Origin of Durban's Zulu Name'. I have no quarrel with the well-known linguistic knowledge of both your correspondent Mr. L.T. Rencken and his source of information, the Rev. A.T. Bryant, in regard to the words 'Itheku' and 'Ethekwini'.
>
> However, to reassure the residents of Durban who might have felt dismayed at the meaning of Durban's Zulu name [that is, the white, or

at least the non-Zulu-speaking residents], I believe that the Rev. A.T. Bryant must have given his version, as quoted by Mr. Rencken, with his tongue in his cheek because the same Rev. Bryant, in his Zulu dictionary (1905) gives two meanings for the word Itheku, viz, (a) a person or animal with only one testicle, and (b) a bay, or lagoon. The same two meanings are given in Doke and Vilakazi's Zulu Dictionary (1948). There are, of course, many Zulu words which have more than one meaning. The second meaning in this particular instance seems to have been of Lala origin, hence its application to the Bay of Natal.

In any case, the story about the tribal wag, although amusing, must appear tenuous because I very much doubt whether, having regard to the vastness of Durban bay, its then mangrove-fringed beaches, and the relative lowness of the surrounding hills, any observer could really have formed an idea of its shape and the particular 'one-sidedness' suggested by the first meaning of 'itheku'.

Bourquin probably gets the Lala idea from Lugg: '**eThekwini**. Loc. of *itheku*, an old, and probably Lala word for a lagoon or estuary' (1970: 48).

Clearly some readers of this debate found the issue more amusing than offensive, and the 'tongue-in-cheek' approach that Commandant Bourquin ascribes to Revd Bryant was itself adopted by David Dale, who wrote to the newspaper a week after Bourquin's letter, this time bringing in the authorities Harry Lugg and Bishop Colenso:

Sir – The letter from S. Bourquin (Dec 12) refers to Durban's Zulu name 'eThekwini'. Does it mean 'The place of the bay or lagoon' or 'A person or animal with one testicle'? Basing one's reply on such authorities as the late Harry Lugg one must side with Mr Bourquin on the 'lagoon' version.

In the first place the Zulu is most apt at giving clear and concise names to people and places. And in the second he does not, in dealing with personalities, resort to intimacies. Indeed, his conversation generally lacks those bawdy or coarse references found in other tongues [here Mr Dale is clearly unfamiliar with the oral 'praise'-poems of the Zulu people – particularly those created by women with men as the topic].

Mr. Bourquin remarks that 'itheku' has two meanings, like so many English or Zulu words, but to apply the testicular reference in this instance is surely not in keeping with Zulu custom or outlook. If, however, and for sake of argument, the pudenda observation was deliberate, why did the observation not go the whole hog and include the Bluff in the geographical picture? The Bluff, after all, lies in immediate juxtaposition to the lagoon, and with its Zulu name of 'Isibubulungu', meaning a 'long sausage-like or bulky thing', at once demands inclusion in the aforesaid name. And the Zulu, always acutely observant, would never have missed this point (or angle) had he intended to translate the layout into testicular topography.

Further credence that the testicle is the basis of Durban's Zulu name is postured by the intelligent and erudite Janie Malherbe. In her excellent history *Port Natal* she remarks that the authoritative J.T. Bryant [*sic*] gives 'iteku' this interpretation, but at the same time notes that Bishop Colenso, who wrote the very first Zulu dictionary, does not, by omission, support that meaning. Colenso's reading is 'an open mouth of a river or bay'.

Venturing what seems to be an explanation of the omission on the Bishop's part, Mrs. Malherbe offers – I interpret the ploy with every respect – a delightful piece of rationalisation.

'Could it not be,' she asks, 'that this was an improvisation by a prudent Bishop for propriety's sake?'

It's here that we look at the Bishop . . . with reverence. His Zulu name was 'Sobantu' – 'the father of the people', a v.i.p. standing that has inspired one wag to observe: 'a paternal promiscuity which, taken literally, proclaims a vigorous marital history.'

This is an aside, perhaps, though with a tongue-in-cheek relevance that could set the Bishop up as a knowledgeable and worldly, as well as a spiritual and practical, officer. And mark this, one obviously ready to include in his dictionary interpretations of a variety of Zulu words pertaining to the pudenda and the more intimate functions of the body.

The fact, I think, rather negates Janie Malherbe's suggestion that Colenso's omission of 'iteku' and its interpretation in the testicular sense, was an episcopal 'improvisation' based on 'prudence' and 'for the sake of propriety'. No man, not even a Bishop, can detrouser himself for one purpose, and at the same time keep his shirt on to deactivate the effect of such an exposure.

So, in conclusion, and with a gamesy lighthearted counterplay to cope with any misinterpretation of my gesture, I leave Janie and her fellow protestants for the testicular character of Durban's Zulu name, with the ball, as it were, in her court.

One may have thought that this closely-reasoned letter, however tongue-in-cheek, would have marked the end of the matter. But no, the readers of the *Natal Mercury* had not yet heard from Chief Mangosuthu Buthelezi, who, writing from Ulundi some two weeks later, contributed the following:

Mr Dale does not say so in his letter (pages 159 to 160), but he is probably thinking of Lugg's comments in his *Life Under a Zulu Shield*:

> [eThekwini] means a large sheet of water, and also – according to Bryant – a man or beast with one testicle . . . but **ithweka** or possibly **ntweka** are the only words I have ever heard for this, but never **theku**, nor have I met a Bantu who has done so.
>
> The story that it was so named by a chief driven out of Zululand in Shaka's time cannot be accepted. The name definitely refers to water and **thekwane** the name of our common hammerkop, or mud lark, a frequenter of muddy pools and lagoons, confirms it. (1975: 107).

The logic of this last comment about the **thekwane** escapes me.

> Sir – I have no intention of entering the controversy of the original meaning of the word 'Itheku', the Zulu name for Durban. I, however, wish to point out that in this part of the country where I grew up, the Zulu word for a person or animal with only one testicle is 'Ithweka', not 'Itheku'.
>
> But I would not dispute that it may well be that in some other parts of the country people use 'Itheku'. I just think that for the record I must point out that Zulus in this part of the world know the word as 'Ithweka'.
>
> I am sorry that my contribution will not throw more light on the controversy on Itheku.

It is not clear whether the editor had been waiting for an authoritative statement from Chief Buthelezi or not, but it was at this point that he declared the correspondence closed, leaving his readers to decide, on the evidence presented, whether they believed the lagoon theory or its testicular alternative. Suffice it to say, in the years since this correspondence took place, I have not seen the city of Durban produce tourist brochures describing their city as 'the city of the single testicle'.

David Dale, in his letter quoted above, says that: 'Mr. Bourquin remarks that "itheku" has two meanings, like so many English or Zulu words, but to apply the testicular reference in this instance is surely not in keeping with Zulu custom or outlook.'

However, Pooley, in her book on the trees of Natal gives as one of the Zulu names for the Tonga-kerrie (*Cladostemon kirkii*) the word **umthekwini**, a clear reference to the *single* small round fruit on the end of each stem (1993: 106). I would suggest that the English name (Tonga-kerrie) and the Afrikaans *Tongakierie* make similar reference, via the metaphorical reference

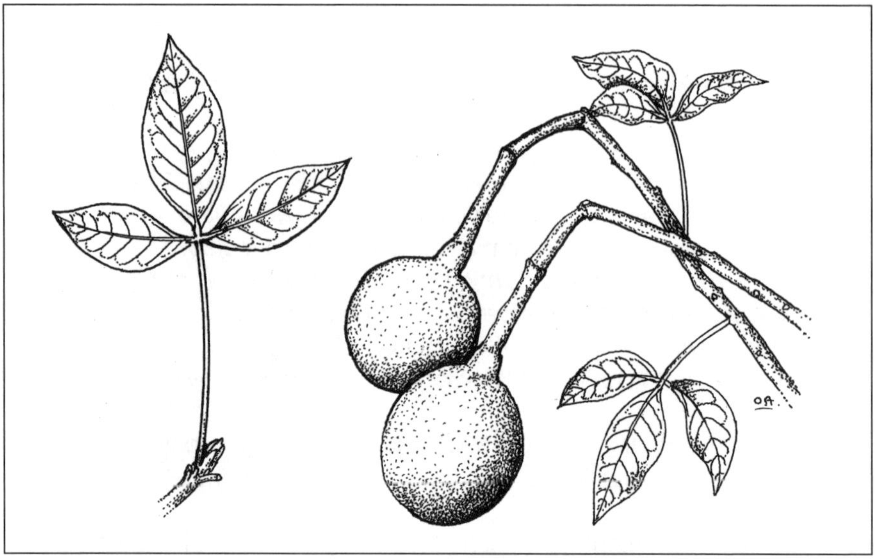

Cladostemon kirkii (**umthekwini**, Tonga-kerrie, *Tongakiere*).

to a knobkerrie, with its single round ball at the end of the stick (see the sketch above).

Umthekwini is not in Doke and Vilakazi's *Dictionary*, but it is clearly the locative form of **um-theku**, and I cannot imagine the relevance of the 'bay, lagoon' meaning here. This must be, to use Mr Dale's phrase, a 'testicular reference'.

'Testicular reference', again, is the only possible interpretation of the hill near Natal Table Mountain called 'Spitkop' or 'Spitz Kop' in Afrikaans, but according to Stayt (confirmed by Bryant, 1905: 761) referred to by the Zulus as **inTweka**, which as we will remember from Chief Buthelezi, is the word people in his area use if they wish to refer to a beast with one testicle. Stayt says: '**inTWEKA**: "inTWEKA, The Hill Resembling a Testicle" – Spitkop near Table Mountain opposite Camperdown.'

We could also perhaps consider another name mentioned by Bryant, the Zulu name for Mount Erskine in the 'Bushman's River Range' – an area that I am not familiar with – which he gives as **kwaMasende** ('the place of the testicles') (1905: 756).

Nor does the story end there. Many of the experts quoted above have referred to Doke and Vilakazi's *Dictionary* as an authority, but none of them have mentioned that the same D&V give an *alternative* Zulu name for Durban Bay, the name **umHlume**, derived from the noun **umhlume**, of which D&V say: 'large tree growing along rivers, *Adina Galpini,* resembling mangrove, having an astringent bark' (1958: 338), a clear reference to another feature of Durban's bay, the mangroves that were once so plentiful. It may seem that this presents a way out of the impasse, a way to escape references to the testicular – but alas – Doke and Vilakazi also give another meaning for **umhlume**: 'young castrated animal'. I dare not dabble into the possible implications of this interpretation.

Then, there is an interesting theory from Bryant, which seems to have escaped the notice of the various contributors to the 'Thekwini debate'. He notes in his *Dictionary*: '**eThekwini (i[li]Theku)** Durban (name prob. imported by Xosa-speaking pioneer Colonists, from Xo. **i[li]-Teko**, place of meeting)' (1905: 760).

And, finally, as we go to press, I discover yet another alternative name for Durban: the Zuluised form **eMdubane**. Zulu students and colleagues assure me that this is a commonly used alternative for **eThekwini**, and one that 'goes way back'.

10.3 UMGUNGUNDLOVU

uMgungundlovu is the name of the erstwhile capital of Natal, presently (as at December 2001) involved in an ongoing tussle with Ulundi for the status of capital of KwaZulu-Natal. Originally the name of the capital of Zulu King Dingane, the half-brother of Shaka, the name was transferred to the newly laid out *dorp* of Pietermaritzburg in 1838, after Piet Retief's defeat of Dingane's forces at Blood River, and the subsequent sack of Dingane's capital. Forsyth-Ingrams suggests that the transfer of the name from Dingane's capital to that of the Boers was a 'natural transition': '"Umgungunhlovu", the Kafir name for the city . . . was originally applied to Dingaan and his Kraal. By a natural transition it came to signify the seat of Government and Capital of the Colony' (1898: 52).

> Much of the material in this section on **uMgungundlovu** has already been published in my article, 'The Place of the Elephants?', in Haswell and Laband (1988).

A statement by a Zulu who was eight years old at the time, which is recorded in Volume IV of *The James Stuart Archives* is just as vague: 'The name Mgungundhlovu . . . was the name of Dingana's great kraal. This was burnt and destroyed by the Boers, so we natives call Pietermaritzburg Mgungundhlovu because the other had been destroyed . . . The name . . . was given only after Dingana's kraal had been destroyed' (Webb & Wright, 1986: 2).

10.3.1 Spellings of 'uMgungundlovu'

The name **uMgungundlovu** has been subject to a remarkable number of variant spellings in its lifetime. The following are variations that I have recorded. I have given the list in alphabetical order because establishing the date of first usage in order to draw up a chronological order was not easy to do in many cases.

1. **Goobinschlofe**: Nathaniel Isaacs, in *Travels and Adventures in Eastern Africa* (Struik, 1970), first published in 1836: 'we came in sight of our goal – Goobinschlofe, the king's residence' (219). Isaacs was responsible for a number of curious spellings of Zulu place names, such as 'Gibbeclack' for Shaka's military establishment **Gibixhegu** (149).
2. **Gungunhlovu**: From the *Journal of the Revd George Champion* (1835–1839) (ed. A.R. Booth), 'At Gungunhlovu, Dingaan's capital . . .' (30). The editor's endnote on page 139 glosses this as 'lair of the elephant'.
3. **Megoonloof**: From *Statements Respecting Dingaan*, by William Wood (interpreter to Dingane), published in Cape Town in 1849. In the same statement, we find 'Megoonloof', then 'Ngungunhlovu', then 'Megoonloof' again.
4. **Mgungundhlovu**: This is the 'modern' spelling (up to approximately 1949) from various writers. The initial **u-** is missing, and **-dhl-** is now **-dl-**, although it is still found in a number of Zulu clan names, such as 'Dhlomo' and 'Dhlamini'.
5. **Mgungundlovu**: The modern spelling of **uMgungundlovu**, without the initial **u-**. Widely accepted.
6. **Mgung u ndlovu**: From a newspaper advertisement (late 1980s) from the Pietermaritzburg Publicity Association, advertising 'The Latest Official PMBurg Tie'. Spelling as in (5) above, apart from the curious spacing.
7. **Mkunkundhlovu**: In Bertram Mitford's 1883 *Through the Zulu Country* (Griggs & Co., 1975 reprint: 57).
8. **Ngungunhlovu**: See under (3) *Megoonloof* above.
9. **Umghunglove**: '*Moord van P. Retief en de zijnen te* **Umghunglove** *den 4 Febr. 1838*' ['Murder of Piet Retief and his (men) at Mgungundlovu on 4 Feb. 1838']. Two-tone lithographic plate removed from H.J. Hofstede, *Geschiedenis van den Oranje-Vrijstaat* ('s-Gravenhage, 1876). (In the 1999 Catalogue of Christison Rare Books.)
10. **Umgingginghlovu**: From a letter to the *Natal Witness* from L.M. Johnson of Townbush Road, Chase Valley, dated 25 March 1988, complaining about the CBD: 'Umgingginghlovu – home of the elephant – is just what the CBD could end up – a large white elephant.'
11. **Umgingiloova**: '. . . Dingaan's kraal, Umgingiloova . . .' from evidence led by Dr Toohey to the Kafir Commission of 1852, in Bird, Vol. I: 218.
12. **Umgunghlovu**: From an undated Letter of the Missionaries in Bird, Vol. I: 218.
13. **Umgungundhlovu**: A surprisingly accurate spelling from Captain Gardiner's 1835 report (in Bird, Vol. I: 292). Earlier in the report he spelt the same name as 'Umkungunglovu'.
14. **uMgungundlovu**: The correct modern spelling.
15. **Umgungunhlovu**: Revd Owen in a letter dated October 1838 (Bird, Vol. I: 292). This is also the spelling recorded in Pietermaritzburg's civic coat of arms.

16. **Umkugings Sloave**: 'Date-line' of the original document of Cession of Port Natal to the Boers by Dingane, 4 February 1838 – in Bird, Vol. I: 366.
17. **Umkungunglovu**: From Capt. Gardiner's 1835 report (see [13] above).
18. **Umkunkinglove**: Revd Owen in a letter dated Aug 1837 (Bird, Vol. I: 292). In another letter 14 months later this had changed to *Ungungunhlovu.*
19. **Umkunkunglovu**: In a December 1839 letter from Captain Jervis to Sir George Napier in Bird, Vol. I: 602.
20. **Ungungunhlovu**: This is one of Champion's variations in his 1835–1839 Journal (see [2] above).
21. **UngunKuncklove**: One of Adulphe Delegorgue's variations, in Vol. I: 112. Note the capital 'K' in the middle of the word.
22. **Ungunklove**: Heading of a letter dated 8 November 1837, written on behalf of King Dingane by Revd J. Owen to Piet Retief. In Delegorgue, Vol. II: 60.
23. **Ungunkunklove**: One of Adulphe Delegorgue's variations, in Vol. I: 40.
24. **Unkunglove**: One of Adulphe Delegorgue's variations, in Vol. I: 40.
25. **Unkungunklovo**: To be strictly accurate, this example is *not* intended to be a rendering of the Zulu name for Pietermaritzburg, but rather the Zulu word for an elephant, in Rider Haggard's *King Solomon's Mines*: 'Hardly had we done so, when from the pool, about a hundred yards off, we heard the strident trumpeting of an elephant. "*Unkungunklovo! Indlovu!*" "Elephant! Elephant!" whispered the Kafirs, and a few minutes afterwards we saw a succession of vast shadowy forms moving slowly from the direction of the water towards the bush' (School edition, 1962 [originally 1885]: 34).
26. **Unkunkinglove**: Heading of letter from King Dingane to Piet Retief dated 4 February 1838, quoted in Delegorgue, Vol. II: 73.

The second-last example is very curious. Haggard gives the correct form of the word for elephant – **indlovu** – so why does he put 'Unkungunklovo' in front of 'Indlovu'? In the first edition (1885) this is given as 'Unkungunklovo! Unkungunklovo! Elephant! Elephant!'; in the revised (1905) edition as 'Unkungunklovo! Indlovu! Elephant! Elephant!'; and in the 1956 Cassell edition as 'Indlovu! Indlovu! Elephant! Elephant!'. It is curious that the 1962 school edition goes back to the 1905 version 'Unkungunklovo! Indlovu!'.

I am greatly obliged to Stephen Coan for the above Haggard information. Coan also points out that although Haggard was probably aware that **uMgungundlovu** was the Zulu name for Pietermaritzburg, he was not a Zulu speaker.

The various spellings of the name became standardised in the 1800s as 'Umgungunhlovu'; in the first half of the 1900s as 'Umgungundhlovu'; and in the second half of the twentieth century as 'Umgungundlovu', preferably with the capital on the second letter: 'uMgungundlovu'. However, the motto of the civic coat of arms, registered in the College of Arms, London, in 1961, still retains the nineteenth century spelling 'Umgungunhlovu'.

Just as this book goes to press, I must add two more spellings to my list of 26, both taken from an undated poster found in the Citrusdal (Western Cape) museum. The poster is headed 'De Moord van Piet Retief' ('The Murder of Piet Retief'), and the caption referring to the scene of Retief's death contains the words '. . . zyne hoofd-kraal te Gugundlovo (foutief gespeld Gugundekloof in het opschrift)' ['. . . his (that is, Dingane's) head-kraal at Gugundlovo (wrongly spelt as Gugundekloof in the inscription).'].

10.3.2 Meanings of 'uMgungundlovu'

The number of different spellings of 'uMgungundlovu' is almost matched by the number of interpretations of the name. The following are the various suggestions put forward by historians and linguists over the years:

- Enclosure of the Elephant;
- The Place of the Rumbling of the Elephant;
- The Secret Conclave of the King;
- The Secret Plot of the Elephant;
- Lair of the Elephant;
- What is Surrounded by Elephants;
- The Gathering Place of the Royal Elephant;
- The Conqueror of the Elephants.

Small wonder that Pietermaritzburg is popularly known as the 'Place of the Elephant'.

Mitford favours a combination of onomatopoeia and elephant to interpret his version 'Mkunkundhlovu', and states in a footnote: 'The name is given in Holden's *History of Natal* to mean "the rumbling noise of the elephant", which exactly conveys the idea. "Mkun-kun" and "indhlovu", elephant. One is apt to confuse it with "Gingindhlovu", but the latter is quite a different word' (1975: 57).

Attempts by Zulu linguists to analyse the name have been ingenious, such as the explanation put forward by James Stuart in his 1925 book *uKulumetule* ('he speaks while being silent'):

> The name Mgungundlovu seems to have derived from *isangungu* a bull with horns so bent that they almost meet. Also it is like the tusks of elephants which are curved (*kumbele*) in such a way that if you put them on the ground so that they face each other like those of a cow

they look like a circle of warriors (*umkhumbi wamabuto*) or a cattle kraal. That is the origin of the name.

Harry Lugg, the well-known Natal historian and Zulu linguist, was clearly impressed by this theory, for in his *Life under a Zulu Shield*, he writes: 'The kraal was designed by placing two curved elephant tusks on the ground to form an oval (*umgungu*) . . . It is therefore an abbreviation of *Umgungu-wendlovu* or enclosure of the elephant, i.e. the king. Pietermaritzburg, known also by this name, was named after it' (1975: 108).

It is clear that most of the proponents of the various interpretations above were aware of the Zulu verb **gunga** 'to surround, enclose, encircle', and the Zulu noun **indlovu** ('elephant'). It is correct that the Zulu name for Pieter-maritzburg is a compound noun consisting of the noun prefix **um-**, the verb **gunga** and the noun **indlovu**. There is, however, a problem here.

In the structure **gunga** + **indlovu**, the vowels **a** and **i** come together, and the Zulu language does not allow two vowels to come together. **Gunga** and **indlovu** may not, and do not form 'gungaindlovu' when added together. Occasionally, when two such vowels come together like this, they fuse together and form a new vowel, with **a** + **i** giving rise to **e**. This has not happened in *this* word, otherwise it would be 'Umgungendlovu'.

Normally, in a compound noun, the problem of two vowels coming together is solved by dropping one of the vowels. In personal names, this is always the first of the two vowels. So when **bonga** ('thank, praise') is added to **inkosi** ('Lord'), the name **uBonginkosi** is formed, with the **-a** at the end of **bonga** falling away. In compound nouns that are not personal names, the second of the two vowels is dropped. When **dlula** ('surpass') is added to **imithi** ('trees') to form **indlulamithi** ('giraffe', that is, 'that which surpasses the trees'), the first **i-** in **imithi** is dropped.

Compound place names go either way, and when **gunga** and **indlovu** are added together, we could expect either 'Umgungandlovu' or 'Umgungi-ndlovu'. But in fact we have neither: Pietermaritzburg is 'Umgungundlovu'.

Stuart and Lugg's theories of **isangungu** and **umgungu** (both words ending with **-u**) are clearly an attempt to explain the presence of the third **-u-** in 'Umgungundlovu'. Their theories are marred somewhat in that **umgungu** does not exist as a separate Zulu word, and **isangungu**, according to Doke and Vilakazi's *Dictionary* is a 'flat-topped basket or earthenware pot with small mouth used for beer' (1958: 12).

So what is the answer? Lugg put his finger on it when he wrote '. . . of the elephant, i.e. the king' (1975: 108). Since at least Shaka's day, the elephant has been used as a symbol of the king and his majesty. '**Wena wendlovu**!' ('You of the Elephant!') is still used as a royal salute today. **Indlovu** is a noun in noun class 9, a noun class commonly used for animals (cf. **inyathi**, 'buffalo', **inkunzi**, 'bull', **inja**, 'dog'). The Zulu language transfers these nouns to noun class 1a, a noun class with the prefix **u-**, used for the names of people, when it wishes to use these animal terms for people. Thus Shaka becomes **uNyathi**

('Mr Buffalo', 'Sir Buffalo') and **uNdlondlo** (< **indlondlo**, 'ferocious mamba'). In the same way, **indlovu** becomes **uNdlovu** ('Sir Elephant'), providing us with the mystery **-u-** in 'uMgungundlovu'.

Charles Pettman, in his *South African Place Names* has stated: 'Umgungundhlovu, the name of the "great place" built by the monster Dingaan, immediately after his murder of Chaka the terrible, means "the place of the rumbling of the elephant"' (1985: 38).

But despite such rumblings, the name of Dingane's capital, since transferred to Pietermaritzburg, is much more prosaic. It simply means 'Royal Capital': '[the place that] surrounds the king'. Samuelson comes to the same conclusion, but via a curious back route that sees 'gungu' as having to do with ineffectual nibbling:

> Umgungundlovu . . . This was the chief kraal of Dingana, and its name is composed of Gunguluza, 'to nibble ineffectually on the surface of', as the roots of grass which had been eaten down already, and Indhlovu, an elephant. The Zulu kings were called by the name of Lion, Elephant, Tiger, etc., when addressed, or spoken about, so the name Ungungundhlovu would mean the place where the king (here Dingana) lived and had his being (1929: 242).

Having said that, it must be acknowledged that whatever the interpretation of the name '**uMgungundlovu**', Pietermaritzburg has become *de facto* 'The Place of the Elephants'. The incorporation of the elephant into the civic coat of arms, the subsequent display of this on lamp posts and building fronts in the centre of the city, and the deliberate marketing of the elephant symbol by businesses and the Pietermaritzburg Publicity Association, has meant that elephants can be found in the city in great profusion. There remains one curious fact: Pietermaritzburg is an African city, and the Zulu language which has given the name uMgungundlovu is an African language. Despite this, all the elephants which decorate the inner city of Pietermaritzburg are *Indian* elephants.

The apparent link between Pietermaritzburg and elephants can be used in a number of ways. Here is an editorial about the Inkatha Freedom Party's (IFP) espousal of Ulundi as the capital of KwaZulu-Natal. The editorial, which is from the *Natal Witness* of 17 June 1998, is headed 'Jumbo logo':

> Students of animal behaviour, knowing the destructiveness of the beasts and the fact that they have to be culled to save the environment from degradation, will be surprised at the IFP's curious choice of a family of three elephants for its new logo. Students of history, knowing of the colonial name of Pietermaritzburg as Umgungundlovu, the place of the elephant, cannot but note the irony of the adoption of such a logo by a party which officially espouses the claim of Ulundi as the capital of the province.

These twin Indian elephants decorate a boot scraper outside the main entrance of the Pietermaritzburg City Hall.

This lone elephant, with five stars of the Colony of Natal, can be found on all the old lamp posts in the vicinity of the Pietermaritzburg City Hall. The city's Zulu name is given as 'Ungungunhlovo'.

This stylised elephant, to be found on all municipal litter bins, dates back to the 1980s.

This single elephant is part of the iron-work on a rear exit gate of the Pietermaritzburg City Hall.

A trio of modern, stylised elephants, found above the heads of the passers-by on the corner of Church and Commercial Streets in central Pietermaritzburg.

The Zulu name for Dingane's chief palace, later used for Pietermaritzburg, is occasionally confused with the unrelated **Gingindlovu**, a small town between the Tugela River and Eshowe in KwaZulu-Natal. Stayt, for example, writes: 'UMGUNGUNDHLOVU: The Zulu name for Pietermaritzburg, it is also the name of what was Dingane's chief kraal, now Gingindhlovu on the North Coast. The name is subject to a variety of interpretations both symbolic and literal, but fundamentally is derived from Isigungu, meaning a secret place and Indhlovu, meaning an elephant' (1971).

Gingindlovu was the site of a camp for British soldiers during the Anglo-Zulu War of 1879, and it is said that their popular name for this place was 'Gin, Gin, I love you'.

The name **uMgungundlovu** is the generally recognised Zulu name for the city of Pietermaritzburg, but there are also two other Zulu names that are not as well-known.

Bryant, in his *Dictionary* gives the name **eThawini** (an adoptive from the English word 'town') as being another of Pietermaritzburg's Zulu names (1905: 760). This word is still used today by some Zulu speakers. In the praises of Sir Theophilus Shepstone (**uSomtsewu kaSonzica**) we find both **eThawini** and **uMgungundlovu** side by side: 'UMhlophe wakithi waseThawin' eMgungundlovu'. This Cope translates as 'Our white man of the Town of Pietermaritzburg' (1968: 194), an incorrect translation in my view, as it implies that **eThawini** is not used as a proper name.

The use of the adopted form **eThawini** as a specific place name is similar to the Xhosa name **eBhayi** for Port Elizabeth. The word **eBhayi** is adopted from the English word 'bay', but **eBhayi** does not just refer to any bay, it is the name for Port Elizabeth, a city earlier known as Algoa Bay.

Pietermaritzburg is also known by the name **KwaNdongazibomvu** ('the place of the red walls'), which although apparently very suitable as a name for a city that prides itself on its Victorian red-brick buildings, was, it seems, a praise name for Dingane's **uMgungundlovu**, the reference being to walls red with blood. Like the name **uMgungundlovu**, the name **KwaNdongazibomvu** was transferred to Pietermaritzburg. This alternative name is well-known to Zulu speakers I have interviewed, but I can find no mention of it in the various published sources.

A final intriguing sideline to the Pietermaritzburg-elephant saga is found in Bryant's *Dictionary* where he gives **kwa'Khehlelifantini** as being the Zulu name for 'Town Hill, Maritzburg' (1905: 754). I cannot trace this name anywhere else, and my earlier thought was that it is a compound of **ikhehla** ('old man') and **elifantini** (an adoptive from 'elephant'). It seems more likely, however, that this is a Zuluised form of the name of the original farm in this area: 'Ketelfontein', a name which can still be seen on the gate of one of the properties on the Town Hill road.

Ketelfontein, the name of the original farm west of the Pietermaritzburg city centre, has been 'Zuluised' as **eKhehlelifantini**'.

Chapter 11

Names of schools

11.1 INTRODUCTION

This chapter and Chapters 12 and 13 deal with toponyms in that buildings, whether of schools, homes, or shops, are places, with a specific geographical location. They could be called 'minor toponyms', or 'local toponyms', but they are clearly names of places. On another level, these names are more than just the names of the buildings themselves, they are the names of the institutions, the organisations, and the inhabitants of the buildings.

To illustrate this, let us invent the name 'PMB Boys' High'. If I use this name in a sentence such as: 'PMB Boys' High is a splendid school occupying 15 hectares of land close to the uMsunduzi River', then clearly I am talking about it as a place. By contrast, if I use the same name in a sentence such as, 'PMB Boys' High is a splendid school which took top honours in local athletics this year', then clearly I am not referring to the place, but to the institution, which includes the learners.

The same sort of dichotomy between place and institution applies to other buildings such as factories, hotels and, as in Chapters 12 and 13, homes and shops.

What sets these 'minor toponyms' (the names of schools, homesteads, and shops) apart from the toponyms discussed in previous chapters (names of towns, rivers, mountains, etc.) is that the names of schools, homesteads and shops *characteristically carry a social message*. Besides the primary function to distinguish and differentiate (that is, the function of identifying), these names are also intended to communicate: to convey a message, or to make a statement. In this way, these names have similarities with the personal names discussed in Chapter 3, and they also have similarities with the names of domestic animals, discussed in Chapter 14.

11.1.1 Sources

Data for this chapter has come from two distinct sources: in the *first* place, a 40-page supplement to the *Natal Witness* (November 1998) put out by the KwaZulu-Natal Education Department, listing every single educational institute in the province, from pre-primary schools to colleges of education (but excluding universities) together with the names of the teaching staff at each institution. This data source was too large for the purposes of this book, and I have simply taken the first 250 school names of the several thousand listed. The *second* source is the contributions from a number of Honours students over the last 11 years. The most useful of these was the Honours dissertation of Phindi Msomi (1989), simply entitled *Analysis of School Names*. I have taken one or two examples from Mathunjwa's 1996 Honours dissertation, and some examples from various postgraduate seminar presentations.

The data from the KwaZulu-Natal Education Department was not subdivided according to different categories of meaning, but the various Honours students have tried to do this with their data. Rather than give their findings here, I will attempt to co-ordinate their categories with the categories I found after analysing the Education Department data. Zulu school names can roughly be divided into three groups:

1. Those based on other names (anthroponyms, toponyms, ethnonyms, etc.);
2. Descriptive names;
3. Those which have been coined by members of the community to convey a social message.

Those taken from other names include schools named after clans (including the use of clan praises), after individuals (including historical figures, the names of those instrumental in the development of the school, especially local chiefs), the place where the school is situated (that is, name of village, town or region), the local river or mountain, and a few schools are named after trees, animals, or birds.

Descriptive names describe the nature of the school itself or its locality, or may link the school to characteristic wildlife or plants in the area.

Schools whose names communicate a special social message usually draw attention to the value of education, and may be injunctions, moral maxims, inspirational messages, promises of various kinds, and so on.

11.2 SCHOOL NAMES BASED ON OTHER NAMES

The most common type of school name in this category is that which is based on the name of an individual. Frequently, the individual so honoured is the local chief of the area, who has either taken it upon himself to fight for a school, or has helped to pay for the building of a school, or has donated land for a school, or is simply honoured because he is the chief of the area where a new school is built.

Molefe (1992) gives the following school names in the Msinga district, all of which are taken from the first names of chiefs in the district: **Zwelinjani**, **Mawele**, **Khetheyakhe**, **Mpikayizekanye**, **Nyoniyezwe**, **Nomafu**, **Maweni**, **Velaphi**, **Phathizwe**, **Madudula**, **Somashi**, **Batshazwayo**, **Mqamathi**, **Dlabesuthe** and **Jajile**.

In the Sweetwaters Circuit near Pietermaritzburg, the **Shayabantu** School is named after the current Zondi chief, and the following schools in the area after past Zondi chiefs: **Etetelegu**, **Ebhekizizwe**, **KwaNobanda**, **Eladuma**, and **Ensika**.

Langalakhe ('his day') Secondary School near Elandskop takes its name from a local chief, Langalakhe Ngcobo.

Names of schools taken from the names of Zulu kings include **Mpande** High and **Zwelithini** High, while **Ngwenyama** Combined takes its name from the common praise term for Zulu royalty: **Ingwenyama** ('Black Leopard').

Schools may be named after individuals who have been instrumental in the establishment of the school, as in the **Ethel Mthiyane** School. There are many more examples of this in the Education Department data.

Schools may be named after historically famous regiments, as in **Ufasimba** and **Siphezi** (both named after regiments of Shaka), and **Ngobamakhosi** (a regiment of Cetshwayo).

Schools may take their names from clan names or clan praises: **AmaZizi**, **AmaNgwane**, **Wosiyane** (clan praise of Nzama), **Emconjwana** and **Elugaju** (clan praises of Zuma), and **Ebovaneni** (clan praise of the Ngubane clan).

Many schools, as might be expected, take their name from the village, town or district where they are situated: **Nokweja** in Ixopo, **Pholela** in Bulwer, **Dlangezwa** in Empangeni, **Hluhluwe**, **Mbongolwane** (Eshowe area), **Hlabisa**, and **Umhlali**. The name of the school may also come from a nearby river, as in the examples **Thukela**, **Umhlathuzana**, **Umlalazi**, **Mpanzakazi** (a stream near Greytown), and **Amatimofu**. Nearby hills may also give their names to schools, as in the examples **Ntabantuzuma**, **Ntumeni**, and **Ntaba-nkulu**.

11.3 DESCRIPTIVE NAMES

A number of names in the Education Department list are in the locative form, but cannot be linked to existing place names, so it would appear that they are names which are descriptive of the physical location or surroundings of the school. The following are examples:

- **Ethafeni** ('on the plateau');
- **Evutha** ('on the dry, stony ground');
- **Macotshaneni** ('among the little sandstone outcrops');
- **Ngebeza** (< **amangebeza**, 'pleasant woodland glade with rocks and trees');
- **Hlungwini** ('on the newly burnt veld');
- **Echwebeni** ('at the lagoon');
- **Ngudwini** ('in bare, uninhabited country').

Nyonithwele ('the bird is carrying') Secondary School in Edendale, Pietermaritzburg, is named after the mountain behind the school which, from a certain angle, is said to resemble a bird carrying something.

A brutally honest descriptive is seen in the school name **Edakeni** ('in the mud'). Two slightly different 'locational descriptives' are **Manqindi** ('where the chairs are cut short') and **Ezifundweni** ('among the lessons').

Some school names are derived from words for trees, shrubs, animals and birds. The *Phoenix reclinata* palm seems to be a favourite here, and in the first two pages of the Education Department list we find three examples:

- **Sundumbili** ('two Phoenix palms');
- **Ubuhlebesundumbili** ('the beauty of two Phoenix palms');
- **Emasundwini** ('among the Phoenix palms').

The **Mngampondo** school takes its name from the Zulu name of the Horned Thorn Tree (*Acacia grandicornuta*), a compound of **umunga** (acacia) and **(izi)mpondo** ('horns'). The full form of the class 3 noun prefix, **umu-** is only used when followed by a single syllable, thus **umu-nga** (acacia species). When this single syllable becomes disyllabic or polysyllabic, the second 'u' in **umu-** is deleted. Thus the combination **umunga** + **mpondo** gives **umngampondo**, and **umunga** + **eni** (the locative suffix) gives (the river) **uMngeni**.

Nkiwaneni uses the locative form of **umkhiwane** ('species of wild fig tree'). The three school names **Mhlakaza**, **Ndulinde**, and **Mvuzane**, refer to unidentified plants, and **Ncemaneni** is named for the economically important **incema** grass. Mushrooms (Zulu **amakhowe**) are referred to in **Makhowe**.

Snakes are represented in the school names **Inhlwathi** ('python'), **Mamba** ('mamba') and **Ndlondlo** (**indlondlo**, a term for a legendary horned or crested mamba, was a praise name for Shaka). The school name **Nkume** is derived from **inkume** ('centipede'), and **Nhlolini** is a name which means 'place of the hedgehog'. Bird references are seen in the school names **Nkonjane** ('swallow'), and **Gilonki** ([*sic*], 'heron').

11.4 SCHOOL NAMES WITH A MORAL MESSAGE

More than half of the school names in the various data sources are based on some kind of message which has to do with education in its various guises of knowledge acquisition, character-building, community spirit, and so on. Msomi (1989) divides her names into categories such as 'joy in education', 'ambition', 'gratitude for knowledge' and so on. However, there are so many semantic overlaps between these various categories that I do not wish to adopt her categories. Nonetheless, I will try to group the examples that follow according to some similarities in meaning.

11.4.1 Unity in education

Many names include the first person plural subject concord **si-** ('we'), thus linking the name of the school to pupils, staff and members of the community. In this way a name such as **Sibongulwazi** ('we are grateful for knowledge') includes among those expressing gratitude: those who are dispensing knowledge, those who are gaining knowledge, and the community who will benefit from the knowledge. The following are examples of such names expressing unity in education:

- **Masibumbane** ('let us come together');
- **Masithandane** ('let us love one another');
- **Asibemunye** ('let us be one');
- **Sobonakhona** ('we'll see over there');
- **Siyakhona** ('we are going over there');
- **Siphimfundo** ('give us education');
- **Siyaphambili** ('we are going forward');
- **Siyathuthuka** ('we are progressing');
- **Siyakhula** ('we are growing');
- **Masijabule** ('let us be happy');
- **Sakhisizwe** ('we build the nation');
- **Sikhulile** ('we have grown up');
- **Sinqobile** ('we have conquered');
- **Sokwetshatha** ('we will carry on the shoulders' – **So-** is a contraction of **sizo-** ['we will']);
- **Masizakhe** ('let us build ourselves');
- **Sibongimfundo** ('we are grateful for education');
- **Sesiyabonga** ('now we are grateful');
- **Sibongakonke** ('we are grateful for everything');
- **Siyazama** ('we are trying').

Mfundwenhle ('a good education') Junior Primary School can be found in the suburb Imbali in Pietermaritzburg.

11.4.2 Light as a symbol of education

School names may use a variety of different symbols for knowledge and education. One of the most pervading symbols in the names is that of light, which manifests as lamps, candles, stars and dawn with the rising sun. Light (education) chases away the darkness (ignorance). With the idea of the dawn and the rising sun comes the associated idea of waking from sleep. The following school names are examples:

- **Sekusile** ('it has dawned');
- **Khanyisa** ('enlighten');
- **Tholukukhanya** ('gain the light');
- **Muzokhanyayo** ('house of light');
- **KhanyiseluZulu** ('light up for the Zulu nation');
- **Isibani** ('lamp');
- **Khanyangodumo** ('shine through fame');
- **Nkwenkwezi** ('star');
- **Ekuvukeni** ('place of awakening').

One of the earliest mission schools was that of Bishop Colenso, near Pietermaritzburg, named **Ekukhanyeni** ('in the place of light').

Together with light comes the associated idea of seeing and vision, hence *eyes*, as seen in the following names:

- **MehlokaZulu** ('eyes of the Zulu nation');
- **Isolezwe** ('eye of the nation');
- **Mehlokadeli** ('eyes are not satisfied');
- **Gcotsheni** ('something pleasant to the eye');
- **Mehlwana** ('little eyes').

Msomi gives the interesting example of the school named **Chibelihle** ('good pond') and explains that this refers to the biblical story of the blind man who washed his eyes at the pond, and they were opened. Opening and shutting, of course, is another contrast associated with the contrast of light and dark. Shutting the mind keeps it in darkness, while opening the mind lets in the light of knowledge, hence the name **Vulingqondo** ('open the mind').

11.4.3 Other symbols of education

Education as a tool to develop future potential may also have associated symbols. For example, school names can use the symbolism of an inheritance, as in **Phangifa** ('snatch an inheritance') and **Mafa** ('inheritances'), or may refer to the future more simply, as in **Ikusasalethu** ('our tomorrow'). Or symbols of sowing and reaping may be used to express this idea, as in **Imbewehle** ('good seed'), **Bhamu** (**ibhamu**, 'abundance, large yield of crops') and **Siyavuna** ('we are reaping'). A more simple name, without any metaphorical or symbolic weight, but referring to the same thing is **Mbuyiselo** ('repayment', 'return of investment').

These are symbols of education which Zulu shares with Euro-Western cultures, and indeed, Zulu is likely to have borrowed these symbols from the American, British, German, Swedish and Norwegian missions which first brought education. There is one interesting symbol of education, however, found in a few school names, which is not shared with Euro-Western thinking, and yet it is based on a visual symbol of education which is specifically Euro-Western. This symbol is the willow tree. Msomi's example of the school name **Eminyezaneni** ('among the willow trees') first drew my attention to the use of the willow tree (1989: 81). She explains this (and it is confirmed by Nyembezi in his 1992 dictionary) that the drooping branches of the willow tree are likened to the drooping tassel of the academic cap, an easily recognisable symbol of education (see sketch below). I am told by Zulu speakers that the expression **'Ugqok' umnyezane'** ('s/he is wearing a willow') means that so-and-so is very bright, or is well-educated.

The drooping branches of the willow tree are similar to the drooping tassel of an academic cap.

11.4.4 Positive injunctions

The path to success (itself expressed in the two names **Indlelenhle**, 'the good path' and **Impumelelo**, 'success') often depends on hard work and discipline. School names that include reference to this are:

- **Gcininhliziyo** ('strengthen the heart');
- **Enembe** ('place of perseverance');
- **Thembamandla** ('trust in strength');
- **Julukandoda** ('sweat, man!').

Mathunjwa gives the example of the school named **Phezukomkhono** ('red-chested cuckoo'), explaining that the call of this bird at the beginning of spring calls people to put hoe to shoulder (**phezu komkhono**) and set to work in the fields (1996: 22). The bird's name may be used as a general exhortation to hard work.

A variety of different messages, of togetherness, of wealth in knowledge, of hope, trust and joy, of clarity of thought, are all expressed in names such as:

- **Gcwalamoya** ('fill with spirit');
- **Hlanganani** ('join together');
- **Bambanani** ('hold together');
- **Kanyekanye** ('all together');
- **Igugulabasha** ('treasure of the youth');
- **Gugulesizwe** ('treasure of the nation');
- **Khombindlela** ('show the way');
- **Fundokuhle** ('learn good things');
- **Fundukhaliphe** ('learn and become sharp');
- **Zuzulwazi** ('gain knowledge');
- **Vumulwazi** ('accept knowledge');
- **Ekucabangeni** ('place of thinking');
- **KwaHluzingqondo** ('clarify the mind').

The secondary function of a school, to instil responsible patterns of behaviour in the young, is not forgotten either, and we find names such as **Hloniphani** ('show respect') and **Ncwabakazi** ('clean, neat, tidy person').

And, finally, a wonderfully practical image in **Mshanelowesizwe** ('nation's broom'), which Msomi explains as 'education will sweep away their ignorance' (1989: 72).

Chapter 12

Names of homesteads

12.1 INTRODUCTION

The traditional Zulu **umuzi** ('homestead', or 'kraal' in earlier terminology), is not a single building. The typical homestead, still commonly found in rural areas today, consists of a number of huts (**indlu**, plural **izindlu**), the number depending on the number of the homestead head's wives, grouped around a central cattle byre (**isibaya**), the whole surrounded by a fence (**uthango**), made of branches. Some of the individual huts may have their own names, but the homestead itself always has a name (and occasionally more than one name). It is these names which are the subject of this chapter.

Homestead names are another neglected area of Zulu onomastic study. Ntuli pioneered the study of Zulu homestead names with his two 1992 articles in *Nomina Africana*, and Shabalala's 1999 Masters study is devoted to the study of homestead names in the Mabengela community in the Nkandla district of Zululand. As these are the only studies of homestead names which I have been able to find, I have relied on them extensively for this chapter. The four volumes of Webb and Wright's *James Stuart Archives* (*JSA*), while not being specific studies of homestead names, do nevertheless contain much material on the names of the homesteads of past kings and chiefs of the Zulu clans, and I have used these volumes to give Ntuli's and Shabalala's work a historical perspective.

12.2 THE NAMING OF THE HOMESTEAD

In Zulu society ownership or headship of a particular homestead may pass through a number of generations, with the eldest son inheriting the responsibility from his father. In such cases, the name given by the original builder of the **umuzi** normally remains unchanged. For example, Shaka's homestead **kwaNobamba**, which he inherited from his father Senzangakhona, apparently went back several generations, as one of James Stuart's informants stated: 'Nobamba is the very oldest kraal of Zululand. That is what I have usually heard. Ndaba, or even, Punga and Mageba, not Jama, may have first built it' (Webb & Wright, II: 252).

If this information is true, then this homestead, and its name, was five generations old before Shaka inherited it.

There are a number of reasons why a homestead may not pass on to another generation. The homestead may, for example, be completely destroyed in battle, or a series of unfortunate incidents may persuade the inhabitants that the site has permanent bad luck. Another reason is clearly explained by a Stuart informant: 'The reason why kraals are sometimes shifted to another site is when one's parents die and are buried within the kraal. It then becomes highly improper for a young son and heir to continue to live, tread on, cast his shadow on, and play about where his father is buried' (Webb & Wright, III: 141).

Frequently if the site of a homestead is changed, the name remains the same. Ntuli quotes Kathi's story (1975: 72) of Chief Phakathwayo of the Qwabe who built a homestead named **eMthandeni** ('love him'), that was destroyed by Shaka's forces. Phakathwayo was killed and his brother Nqetho, after fleeing to Pondoland, established another homestead, which he also named **eMthandeni**. After a clash with the Pondos, Nqetho moved to the Amanzimtoti area, where he built a third homestead, again named **eMthandeni**. A final move to the Maphumulo district saw the establishment of a fourth homestead, which was once again named **eMthandeni**. As Ntuli says: 'To the Qwabes, *EMthandeni* was not just an ordinary homestead. It was a symbol of the love and peace which Phakathwayo had cherished before his death' (1992a: 19).

In other situations, a homestead may remain on the same site but receive a new name for various reasons. Ntuli says: 'When I was young my homestead was known as *OSizini* (sorrow). Later on my father changed the name to *KwaBhekinhlanhla* (expect good luck)' (1992a: 19). Ntuli does not tell us the reason for this change, but the Stuart Archives give an example of such a name change, and the reason behind it:

> [After Zulu heroes Hlathi and Ndlela were severely wounded in battle, but had recovered] . . . A large present of cattle was given to them. The king [Shaka] said to Ndhlela, 'What is your elder brother's homestead called, then?'. He answered, 'It is called eManweleni ['place of excitement, of frenzy'].' Tshaka said, 'No, let that name be dropped. I now name the homestead eManxebeni, after the wounds (amanxebe) which the Ndwandwe gave you. Go and set up a homestead, and establish yourself with these cattle' (Webb & Wright, II: 209).

Two things are noteworthy here: *firstly*, Shaka's play on the original name **eManweleni** in giving the new name **eManxebeni**, and *secondly*, that the new name, given to commemorate the wounds that these heroes sustained, was given to their *brother's* homestead, whereas they were required to take the gift of cattle and go off and establish a new homestead of their own, which presumably would be called neither '**eManweleni**' nor '**eManxebeni**'.

Another case from the Stuart Archives which involves a gift of cattle, and a king giving a name to a homestead, concerns King Mpande of the

Zulus (Webb & Wright, IV: 86). It would appear that Mpande's brothers, kings Shaka and Dingane, had been in the habit of presenting the royal steward Noradu with gifts of cattle, which gifts had continually been 'swallowed up' by Noradu's elder brother Manqondo. When Mpande subsequently presented Noradu with a gift of cattle (after having had his name called out loudly for some time), he directed that these should specifically not be given to the elder brother, but that Noradu should use the cattle to establish his own homestead, to be called, by directive of the king, **eKwelamaneni** ('the place of the next one following in age'). As there were in fact sufficient cattle to set up two homesteads, Noradu named one **eKwelamaneni**, as directed, and a second one **oValweni** ('place of fear'), as he had been very frightened to hear his name called out so loudly for so long.

What is interesting in this story, besides the narratives about how the names came to be, is that it would appear that a homestead was built around cattle, rather than the other way around: a man without cattle, in this case, is unable to establish a homestead. Mpande gives him cattle for the express purpose of establishing a homestead, and there are sufficient cattle for him to be able to establish two.

It is normally the **umnumzane** (homestead head) who names a new homestead, although other members of the family often make suggestions. Ntuli has pointed out, however, that occasionally the name, or more often an extra additional name ('nickname') may be given by the community:

> The name given by the community may be more appropriate or popular than the original one so that the former [that is, the community name] becomes more widely used. Such a name may express sentiments which the members of the family may be too modest [or too embarassed] to express about themselves. On the other hand the name popularised by the community may justifiably be critical of the behaviour of some members of the family. This implies that when the community gets involved, name giving may serve as a form of social control (1992a: 18).

12.3 FUNCTION OF HOMESTEAD NAMES

Most Zulu homestead names serve two functions. The first, or primary, function is to identify the homestead, to single it out from other homesteads in the district. Ntuli states: 'The obvious reason for giving a name to each homestead is to distinguish it from the others. People of the same clan usually settle next to one another; therefore one cannot use the clan name to identify a homestead. According to the hlonipha (respect) custom one cannot freely use the homestead head's personal name' (1992a: 14).

This function of the homestead name has nothing to do with the underlying meaning of the name, and in this respect the name fulfils the same function as a street number in a westernised urban setting.

The second, or secondary, function of the homestead name has everything to do with the underlying meaning. The name may be used to describe the homestead as well as to single it out, as in **eKuphakameni** ('on a high place'); it may refer to the character of the inhabitants or homestead head, as in **eNkaneni** ('place of stubbornness'); it may refer to a particular incident, as in **kwaBonezinkulu** ('see great things'), a name which Ntuli tells us refers to the unexpected and chaotic visit of a baboon to the homestead; or it might convey a warning to the neighbours, as in **kwaMuntungifunani** ('what does the person want of me?'). The various categories of these underlying meanings, and the different types of social messages which they convey, form the bulk of this section on homestead names.

As we have already noted with some personal names, and as we will note again with some of the dogs' names in Chapter 14, the reasons for giving a particular name are not always directly inferable from the underlying meanings. In Chapter 3 I gave the example of thc personal name **uThulani**, which has the underlying meaning of 'be quiet', a name which usually refers to the bickering and squabbling of other family members, but may also be an instruction to the ancestral spirits to cease their child-producing activities. Ntuli gives a wonderful example of a reason for a homestead name that surely could not have been inferred from the underlying meaning.

The name of the homestead in question was **kwaMabonw' abulawe, imamban' eluhlaza** ('The place of killed on appearance like a little green mamba'). Ntuli tells us that his initial assumption was that the head of the homestead must have been a hated person whom people wanted to kill, but when he found the true explanation for the name, it was, as he says, 'a mundane anticlimax': 'my father likes green colours' (1992a: 19).

Shabalala's data provides accurate correlation between underlying meanings of homestead names and reasons for naming because she did intensive field research, visiting every homestead in the Mabengela district, and asking of each homestead head the background to the name of his **umuzi**.

By contrast, it is almost impossible to provide accurate links between underlying meaning and reason for naming for the approximately 116 homestead names contained in the Stuart Archives. On one or two occasions, Stuart's informants included a little anecdote to explain the origin of a particular homestead name, but by and large they simply listed the names of the homesteads of this or that chief, without any further explanation. This has the result that today, although we can translate the names, we can only guess at why they were given.

12.4 SEMANTIC CATEGORIES OF ZULU HOMESTEAD NAMES

Shabalala's preliminary categorisation of homestead names provided seventeen categories, which she later combined into seven broader categories, which, in order of frequency, are:

1. Friction (including gossip, allegations of witchcraft, etc.) 32,1%
2. Family unity (including peace, harmony, injunctions to children) 26,7%
3. Improvement and prosperity (including struggle & progress) 15,8%
4. The homestead itself (including location, description & incidents) 11,6%
5. Wishes and aspirations 5,5,%
6. Religious affiliations 2,1%
7. Other 6,2%

Ntuli gives six categories of underlying meanings of homestead names, these being:

1. Position of homestead
- **eNhlalamatsheni** ('sit on the stones');
- **eGqumeni** ('on the hill').

2. Commemorative names (based on story or anecdote)
- **kwaDeqheluka** ('keep on shifting');
- **kwaBonezinkulu** ('see great things').

3. Prevailing conditions
- **kwaMpondo** ('many horns'): prosperous cattle owner;
- **kwaZinjaziyamluma** ('dogs bite him'): vicious dogs around.

4. Personality attributes (inmates or homestead head)
- **kwaGonokwakhe** ('cling to his own') selfishness;
- **eNkanini** ('obstinacy');
- **kwaBhekezakhe** ('mind your own business').

5. Desire for peace and harmony
- **eKuthuleni** ('at peace');
- **eKuphumuleni** ('at rest');
- **eNtokozweni** ('in happiness') (all of these very popular, very common).

6. Foreign influences, for example, Christian faith
- **eMseniwenkosi** ('the Lord's mercy');
- **kwaNkosikhona** ('the Lord is here').

Their two classifications reveal that there are areas of overlap. Consequently, I have decided to combine Shabalala and Ntuli's semantic categories with those suggested by the historical names found in the Stuart Archives. In the examples that follow, 'MAS' marks one of Shabalala's examples; 'DBN' one of Ntuli's, and '*JSA*' one from the Stuart Archives (where the name of the chief will also be given).

It seems to me, going through the three sets of data, that a major distinction can be made between those names that refer to the homestead itself (a description of certain features of the homestead; its location, etc.) and those names that make a social statement (accusation of witchcraft, background to the naming, expression of hopes, etc.). Names that refer to the inhabitant(s) of the homestead fall between these two categories, with a name such as **eNdlwayini** ('place of the tall, lanky person': *JSA*: Senzangakhona) being more descriptive, while **eMdumezulu** ('where the heavens resound': *JSA*: Mpande) is more of a social message.

12.4.1 Names that refer to the homestead itself

Let us start with those names that refer to the homestead itself. Many of these refer to the physical environment of the homestead. Examples are:

- **eMahlabaneni** ('place of the little prickly aloes': *JSA*: Ngqengelele of the Buthelezis);
- **eLangeni** ('in the sun': *JSA*: Macingwane of the Mchunus);
- **eHlanzeni** ('in the bushveld': *JSA*: Mtsholoza of the Nxamalala);
- **eNkungwini** ('in the mist': *JSA*: Maphitha of the Mandlakazi Zulu);
- **eMungwini** ('place of fine dust': *JSA*: Ntombela clan chief);
- **eHlathini** ('in the bush': *JSA*: Magaye of the Celes);
- **uQekethe** ('hard spot, hard, unploughable land': *JSA*: Shaka);
- **oNdini** ('on the heights': *JSA*: Cetshwayo);
- **kwaVimbukhalo** ('blocking the ridge': MAS);
- **kwaHlumentabeni** ('growing on a mountain': DBN).

Vegetation that is characteristic of a particular environment may also be referred to in a homestead name, as in the following:

- **eNkomba** ('place of the Pondo Coconut *Jubaeopsis caffra*': *JSA*: Macingwane of the Mchunus);
- **eMbungeni** ('place of the *Greyia sutherlandia* tree': *JSA*: Mtsholoza of the Nxamalala);
- **eMpenqaneni** ('place of the small bushveld tree': *JSA*: Mpande);
- **eNsindeni** ('place of excellent grazing grass': *JSA*: Dinuzulu);
- **eZimfabeni** ('place of scrubby mimosa bushes': *JSA*: Cetshwayo).

Names that describe the homestead itself instead of its location include the following:

- **eNdulo** ('ancient times': MAS: the homestead had the beehive huts which were characteristic of days gone by);
- **kwaMasangomabili** ('the place of two gates': *JSA*: this is another name for Shaka's Dukuza homestead).

If we accept that a homestead consists not only of the location and the physical structure, but the inhabitants as well, then part of the description of the homestead will concern the type of person or persons who are living there. If such a name is a critical one given by members of the community rather than by the household head himself, then there are certainly elements of social message as well as description. Ntuli gives three examples:

- **eNkanini** ('obstinacy'), whose inhabitants 'were obviously notorious for their stubbornness';
- **kwaGonokwakhe** ('cling to your own'), which 'was given this name because of the selfishness of the people there';
- **kwaBhekezakhe** ('mind your own business'), of which name one of the inhabitants said that they did not like interfering in other people's affairs.

Names from the Stuart Archives which apparently refer to the character of the inhabitants generally or to the chief specifically, include the following:
- **uMahambehlala** ('he goes and stops', that is, an undirected person: Senzangakhona);
- **uBekenya** ('person with angry, scalding tongue': Shaka);
- **oDlambedlwini** ('place of the fierce, wild man': Dingane);
- **uMgungundlovu** ('what surrounds the king-elephant': Dingane);
- **kwaGqikazi** ('place of the great authority': Mpande);
- **eNgonyameni** ('place of the Royal Lion': Macingwane of the Mchunus).

12.4.2 Names that convey a social message

We can divide these names into three categories:
1. Those that tell a story, refer to some incident, or narrate the background to the family settling in this particular homestead;
2. Those that indicate the family's hopes and aspirations, especially towards positive goals such as peace and harmony in the community;
3. Those that refer to tensions and friction in the neighbourhood, identify witchcraft and give warnings to potential enemies.

a. Narrative, anecdotal names

Ntuli calls these 'commemorative names'. Among his examples are **kwa-Phumphele** ('get out completely') which 'echoes the words which were uttered when one of the members was told to leave the common homestead' (1992a: 16), and **kwaDeqheluka** ('keep on shifting') which refers to a family's continual removal from one area to another until they arrived at this destination.

Among Shabalala's 'incident names' we find **KwaMathunywa** ('the one sent'), a reference to an inheritance dispute, when an elder son of a junior wife *was sent* to live in the chief wife's hut so that he would inherit, and **KwaBhadazi** ('walk clumsily'), a reference to an unidentified footprint which had been left in the freshly-smeared floor of one of the huts. From the Stuart Archives comes the name of one of Mpande's homesteads – **eKuweleni** ('place of crossing over'). This is a reference to Mpande's decision to cross the Tugela River and seek an alliance with the Boers.

An alternative to the commonly believed theory that Shaka's main homestead **kwaDukuza** ('go astray, get lost') – which is on the site of the town now officially called Dukuza, but which was known until 1998 as

Stanger, some 50 kilometres north of Durban – was so called because it was such a big place that it was easy to get lost, comes a suggestion from a Stuart informant that the name is a reference to an incident in which Shaka was stabbed by one Ntintinti ka Nkobe, whose assegai struck Shaka in the arm and missed his vital organs, that is, his assegai 'went astray' (Webb & Wright, II: 161). A different informant suggests that another of Shaka's military kraals **kwaHlomendlini** ('being armed at home') was named after the same incident (Webb & Wright, III: 74). The common theory is that this was named for the **Hlomendlini** ('home guard') regiment, an older group of warriors with purely domestic defensive duties. The relationship between regimental names and names of military homesteads (**amakhanda**) is very close, and in many cases it is difficult to work out whether the regiment was named after the barracks, or whether the barracks took the name from the regiment stationed there.

Many other homestead names from Zulu history suggest incidents of one sort of another, but without the actual explanation we can only guess at the story behind the name. For example, are the cattle metaphorical in the name **eMqekwini** ('place of young cattle separated from the herd'), the name of the homestead of Shaka's great-grandfather Ndaba? What was the lucky find that made Shaka's father Senzangakhona name one of his homestead's **eNtoleni** ('place of the real find or lucky strike')? What caused Shaka to be so uncharacteristically hesitant or reluctant to act when he names one of his homesteads **Zindela** ('act reluctantly, be hesitant')? Why was the unidentified Mthethwa king so much in a hurry when he named a homestead **eMpangisweni** ('place of hastening')? And what led Cetshwayo to name a homestead **eNtonteleni** ('place of hopping about')?

Some of the names suggest ongoing activities rather than isolated incidents. Cetshwayo seemed to have some interest in wood-carving, for he named two homesteads in reference to this activity: **eKubazeni** ('place of carving'), and **Ceza** ('chip off pieces of wood or stone'). Shaka's father Senzangakhona, as we know from his **izibongo** (praises), was a great womaniser, and perhaps this is what led him to name a homestead **eSiklebeni** ('place of the inner female organ' [Webb & Wright, I: 20]). Other chiefs with similar interest in sexual activities variously named homesteads:

- **eSokeni** ('place of the courting youth': Magaye of the Celes);
- **uTshokovu** ('thin, sterile semen': Mkokeleli of the Celes);
- **eMaganukeni** ('place of the urethral discharge caused by sexual excitement': Phakathwayo of the Qwabes).

Whether the last name in this list above had anything to do with the Qwabe desire to perpetuate the homestead name **eMthandeni** ('love him/her'), as described above, we can only guess.

R.C.A. Samuelson says of Shaka's regiment **Isiklebe**: 'This regiment was named after the kraal of that name, whose derivation is unfathomable but may be from Klibhi klolo, jeer at one as much as to say "you fool, you cannot do it"' (1929: 240). Suspecting that this bizarre linguistic red herring could possibly have stemmed from a modest reluctance to give **esiKlebeni** its true translation, I turned to Samuelson's *King Cetywayo Zulu Dictionary*, to see what gloss he had given to the word **isiklebe**, only to find this word missing from his dictionary. Wondering if Doke and Vilakazi were in fact correct in interpreting this word as 'inner female organ', I then turned to Bryant's *Dictionary*, where I found the word **isiklebe** (spelt as **isi-Rrebe**) glossed as 'Partes rubentes pudendorum feminæ' (1905: 556).

All these names are suggestive and intriguing, but although we have the names, we do not have the stories. Like Mpande, who named a homestead **Zwangendaba** ('hear about the matter'), we have heard about these names, but we do not have the background information.

b. Names reflecting wishes and aspirations
Ntuli states that:

> A large number of homestead names reflect the inmate's desire for peace, good health and happiness. The most popular choice in this category is *eKuthuleni* (peace). A common explanation is that parents or grandparents always wish that cordiality would prevail in their homestead. In some cases gratifying peace already existed and a wish was expressed through the name that nothing should disturb it (1992a: 17).

In this quote Ntuli is noting two different functions of the name. In the first function, with the grandparents 'wish[ing] that cordiality would prevail in their homestead', the name serves as an injunction, something requiring others to 'follow the name' and behave in a certain way. In this way a name like **eKuthuleni** is similar to the boys' names **uBhekuyise** ('respect the father') and **uThembinkosi** ('put trust in the Lord'), discussed previously. By contrast, when Ntuli says that 'in some cases gratifying peace already existed' the name is less of an injunction and more of a statement acknowledging existing conditions. Ntuli notes that the following are all very popular names for homesteads expressing similar wishes:

- **eKuphumuleni** ('place of rest');
- **eNtokozweni** ('place of joy');
- **eKujabuleni** ('place of happiness');
- **eKuthabeni** ('place of joy').

That names in this semantic category are indeed popular can be seen by the number collected by Shabalala in the relatively small area of the Mabengela community:

- **eKuphumuleni**, **eNtokozweni**, and **eNjabulweni** ('place of happiness');
- **kwaJabula** ('place of Mr Happy');
- **eNkululekweni** ('place of freedom');
- **eThembeni** ('place of hope');
- **kwaBhekithemba** ('place of look for hope');
- **eMthandazweni** ('place of prayer');
- **kwaCelimpilo** ('place of ask for health').

We are reminded here of Ntuli's statement about the way in which the Qwabe people kept naming their main homestead **eMthandeni**, even after four resettlements (see discussion on page 184): 'To the Qwabes, *eMthandeni* was not just an ordinary homestead. It was a symbol of the love and peace which Phakathwayo had cherished before his death' (1992a: 19).

c. Tensions, friction, witchcraft, and jealousy

In an ideal society, all people would live in peace and harmony. That this is not so, and has never been so since homesteads were first named can be seen by the equally large number of homestead names that reflect social tensions: whether jealousy among co-wives; in-fighting among co-heirs of an inheritance; the eternal suspicions of the mother-in-law; the suspected witchcraft of neighbours; or, in the case of the historical names from the Stuart Archives, widespread fighting accompanied by mass slaughter and looting.

The following examples of homestead names come from Shabalala's data:

- **kwaMuntungifunani** ('what does a person want from me?');
- **eNdina** ('in anger');
- **kwaBhekomzondayo** ('look at the one you hate');
- **kwaSukasikhulume** ('get out of the way and let us talk', that is, let us see if we can resolve our differences);
- **eMpithini** ('in chaos');
- **kwaMuntungibukani** ('why is the person looking at me?');
- **kwaPhumuhambe** ('get out and go away' – the homestead built by a bitter younger son who had been chased out of his father's homestead);
- **kwaPhumangezwi** ('leave because of talk');
- **kwaPhumuzumlomo** ('give the mouth a rest' – a reference to gossiping neighbours);
- **eNsamlomo** ('take the mouth to', that is, stop gossiping behind my back and bring your complaints directly to me).

From the Stuart Archives come tales of scheming and intrigue, of strife and violence, and of death and destruction. Rather than trying to sort out the many examples, I will give them in the order in which I have culled them from the pages of the four volumes, and let the names create their own story of the disputes that marked the times of the kings and chiefs of Zululand:

- **uKudabuka** ('being sorry and grieved': Phakathwayo of the Qwabes);
- **eMngeneleni** ('place of attacking him unawares': Zihlandlo of the Mkhizes);
- **eSinyameni** ('place of foreboding, of drifting towards disaster');
- **eZintandaneni** ('place of orphans');
- **eMbangweni** ('place of strife and dispute': Macingwane of the Mchunus);
- **eNyenyezeni** ('place of whispering against': Dibandlela of the Celes);
- **eKuminzeni** ('place of swallowing voraciously': Dibandlela of the Celes): Remember that in this context the Zulu word **-dla-** ('to eat') is frequently used to mean 'conquer' or 'destroy';
- **eKubhubheni** ('place of perishing forevermore': Dibandlela of the Celes);
- **eKubuseni** ('place of ruling': Cetshwayo);
- **kwaBulawayo** ('place of the one who is killed': Shaka);
- **kwaGibixhegu** ('place of take out [that is, kill] the old man': Shaka);
- **iMpiyakhe** ('his fight', 'his army': Dingane);
- **eNhlulweni** ('place of harsh treatment': Dibandlela of the Celes);
- **eNdungunyeni** ('place of the serious charge or accusation': Dibandlela of the Celes);
- **Bangizwe** ('dispute the land': Cetshwayo);
- **kwaNengwa** ('place of being offended': Dinuzulu): Dinuzulu's name itself means 'offend the Zulu nation';
- **eMthetheni** ('scold him': Phakathwayo of the Qwabes);
- **eMangweni** ('place of the poisonous **amangwe** bushes used in witchcraft': Cetshwayo);
- **iMpisendlini** ('the fight is in the house': Dinuzulu).

One can only guess at the dark and terrible deed that led Phakathwayo, chief of the Qwabes, to name his homestead **oDwini** (which is from the obsolete word **uludu**, indicating that some thing is taboo, and only found in the phrase **Ngadla ulovu, inkomo** ***yasodwini***: 'I have taken poison, I have taken a taboo'd beast', that is, 'I have done a terrible wrong').

The military nature of much of Zululand's past can also be seen in such homestead names as:

- **eZembeni** ('place of the war-axe': Senzangakhona);
- **eZinhlendleni** ('place of the barbed assegais': Cetshwayo);
- **eMkhontweni** ('place of the assegai': Dinuzulu);
- **eSikwateni** ('place of the broad-bladed assegai': Cetshwayo);
- **eNgwazini** ('place of the expert spearsman, renowned warrior': Mkokeleli of the Celes);
- **eMdlela** ('place of the small shield': Magaye of the Celes).

d. Names of European establishments

When travelling around those suburbs of South African cities that were before 1990 reserved for whites, it is possible to find names of houses taken from the local African languages. In Pietermaritzburg we can find names such as **eMoyeni** ('in the breeze') as well as **eNtabeni** ('on the hill'). An old favourite in South Africa, which has given its name to an international race-track near Johannesburg is **Kyalami**, a corrupted version of **ikhaya lami** ('my home').

Kyalami, derived from **ikhaya lami** ('my home') is a popular suburban home name, in this case used for a block of flats in Pietermaritzburg.

This suburban home is named **UMUZI** ('homestead'). It was found near aManzimtoti.

This practice is by no means a recent one. The Stuart Archives record the Zulu names of the residences of many of the well-known earliest settlers of Port Natal, long before it became known as Durban. We find, for example, that Henry Francis Fynn had a homestead named **eMpendwini** ('at the turning') near the mouth of the eZimbokodwini River, that Ogle had three homesteads, named **kwaToyana**, **Bekane** and **Zembeni** ('place of the axe'). Captain King's homestead was clearly at a river crossing for it was named **eSihlengeni** ('place of the float or raft for crossing rivers'). Captain Gardiner's homestead was called **Vimbindhlela** ('block the path'). One of Stuart's sources has an interesting note about these very early colonial establishments: 'All these Europeans built on this plan: they all had a number of wives and ordinary natives kraals, but also a differently constructed house not far off, where they actually lived and at which they received European visitors' (Webb & Wright, I: 11).

Chapter 13

Shop names

13.1 INTRODUCTION

This chapter contains the names of supermarkets and 'superettes', wholesalers and general dealers, butcheries, pharmacies, hair salons and funeral parlours. It covers restaurants, 'eating houses', tuckshops, cafés, and bars. The establishments discussed range from large wholesale merchants in buildings covering hundreds of square metres to the simple 'spaza'.

> A spaza is a 'mini-shop', often housed in a shipping container. It is frequently placed on a road verge, and sells basics such as cooldrinks, snacks, cigarettes, sweets, etc. Spazas are usually situated to supply workers from factory complexes, bus and taxi ranks, or other places where the passing traffic provides a steady flow of customers. The origin of the word 'spaza' is unknown.

I have not been able to locate any research on the names of shops and was consequently required to conduct my own field research to gather the data contained in this chapter. The names discussed below come from urban forays in the streets of Pietermaritzburg and Durban, as well as further afield: Eshowe, Empangeni, Mtubatuba, Dukuza-Stanger, Tongaat, and the roads that link these KwaZulu-Natal towns. Most of the material was collected in May 2000.

The shop names discussed here all consist of two parts: a specific and a generic, as in the toponyms Mooi River, Table Mountain and Indian Ocean, where 'Mooi', 'Table', and 'Indian' are the specifics, and 'River', 'Mountain' and 'Ocean' the generics. The first part of each shop name discussed here is the specific and is in Zulu: '**Simunye** Supermarket', '**Sizabantu** Butchery', '**Kushibile** Furnishers', '**KwaMahleka** Restaurant', etc. The second part – the generic – is, with the exception of one type of shop, in English: 'Isizwe *Butchery*', 'Kwa Thandanani *Superette*', 'Sokhela *Café & Take-Away*', and 'Umgungundlovu *Tavern*'. The exception to these is the name of shops selling traditional herbal medicines, where the generic part of the name is expressed as '**indlu yemithi yabantu**' ('house of the people's medicines'), or variations of this, as in the following examples: **KwaDabulamanzi Wemithi Yomdabu** ('Dabulamanzi's place of traditional medicines'), and **Kwa Inkanyezi iNdhlu yeMithi yaBantu** ('Place of the Star House of People's Medicines').

Clearly this chapter is dealing with the Zulu specifics, and not trying to analyse the patterns of 'butchery' versus 'meat market', or 'supermarket' versus 'wholesalers', and so on. Despite this focus, in the discussion that follows, in each case the whole name will be given (with both specific and generic).

13.2 FUNCTIONS OF SHOP NAMES

As with the school and homestead names discussed in Chapters 11 and 12, most shop names have a dual function. The primary function of the name is to identify:

> 'Where did you get those beautiful chairs?'
> 'At **Kushibhile** Furnishers.'
> 'Oh yes, they're at the bottom end of Church Street, aren't they?'

The secondary function of shop names varies depending on the name. They may serve simply to identify the owner of the shop as well as the shop itself, as in '**Hlophe's** Butchery'. They may serve as an enticement, an exhortation to the passer-by to choose this particular shop from amongst the others, as in '**Zamanawe** Tavern' ('you try too!'). They may make some kind of promise to the customer, as in '**Kalula** Finances' ('Easy Finances'). The remainder of this chapter is devoted to an examination of the different categories of secondary functions. The following categories have been identified, in order of their frequency:

1. Positive images and values 22,3%;
2. Eponyms 18,6%;
3. Promises 16,7%;
4. Community spirit 11,2%;
5. Exhortations 8,7%.

Finally, there is the 'Miscellaneous and queries' category which accounts for 22,3 per cent of the data collected.

13.2.1 Positive images and values

Shop names under this heading are those which attract customers by using words with positive values. These are words such as **jabula** ('be happy'), **mamatheka** ('smile'), **hleka** ('laugh'), **khululeka** ('be free') and **amandla** ('strength'). Certain symbols may also be used, such as stars and light, and dawns and diamonds. Names may be associated with success in the sporting field, and South Africa's national football team **Bafana Bafana** can be found linked to many commercial enterprises. Let us look at some examples of shop names associated with positive values.

The following are all *happy* names, and the most common word used is **jabula** ('be happy'):

- **Jabula** Wholesalers, **Jabula** Cash & Carry, **Jabula** Game Centre & Restaurant;
- **Jabulani** (plural form) Furnishers, **Jabulani** Take Aways;
- **Masijabule** ('let us be happy') Take Away;
- **Mamatheka** Store, **ekuMamathekeni** ('place of smiling') General Store: These two were recorded within a kilometre of each other on the Eston–Umbumbulu Road;
- **eKuthandeni** Shop ('place of liking, loving'), and **Khululeka** Shoe Repairs.

Cabangubuhle ('think about beauty') Store: an uplifting moral message from a store on the Elandskop road west of Pietermaritzburg.

Names associated with light include:

- **Khazimula** ('shine, sparkle, gleam') Butchery and Bottle-Store;
- **Inkanyezi** ('star') Cash & Carry (a chain store found in most KwaZulu-Natal towns);
- **Ikhwezi** ('morning star') Wholesalers, **Kwezi** Cash & Carry;
- **Kwa Inkanyezi Indhlu Yemithi Yabantu** ('Place of the Star House of People's Medicines' – a herbalists' shop);
- **Sekusile** ('now it has dawned') Dressmaking.

A variety of positive images are conveyed in:

- **Amandla** ('strength') Meat;
- **Phumelela** ('succeed') Fresh Produce;
- **iGugulethu** ('our treasure') Tearoom;
- **Dayimani** ('diamond') Restaurant;
- **Kwa Nonhlanhla** ('place of luck') **Indlu Yemithi**;
- **Yebo** ('yes!') Cash & Carry.

Social mobility through association with the 'upper classes' has long been an advertising gimmick in the Euro-Western world. In shop names this is done by using the word **amakhosi** ('chiefs, kings'): **Amakhosi** Supermarket, **Amakhosi** Restaurant, **Kwa Amakhosi** Supermarket, and Salon **Makhosi**. This word for 'chiefs' should not be confused with **iNkosi** ('lord God') in the opening lines **'Nkosi sikelel'iAfrika'** of the South African national anthem, from whence comes the (misspelt) shop name **Nkhosi Sikhelele** Supermarket.

Amakhosi may also be a reference to the Kaiser *Chiefs* football team, because it is clear from other shop names that positive associations with names of football teams may well prove desirable. The national football team **Bafana Bafana** ('boys boys') has lent its name to the **Bafana Bafana** Factory Shop, **Bafana** Pies, and **Bafana Bafana** Furniture, while **Laduma** Sports Bar, **Laduma** Supermarket, and **Kwa Sundowns** Supermarket are all inextricably linked with football.

> **Laduma**, which literally means 'it thundered', has become a popular 'buzzword' associated with football, and Sundowns is a well-known football team.

An iconic name of note is '**Madiba**' the praise name of ex-president Nelson Mandela, and I am surprised that I only found one example: **Madiba's** Meat Market.

13.2.2 Eponyms

An eponym, according to the *Collins English Dictionary* is (1) a name, esp. a place name, derived from the name of a person; (2) the name of the person from which such a name is derived. The example given is the place name **Constantinople**, derived from the personal name **Constantine**. Both Constantinople and Constantine can be considered to be eponyms.

Eponymous shop names normally link the shop to its owner, and very often this relationship is shown by a possessive apostrophe, as in **Chili's** Tearoom, **Thema's** Fashion Designs, **Hlophe's** Butchery, and **Mtungwa's** Funeral Parlour. The names may be first names, as in the examples **Thabo's** Superette, **Thoko** Salon, **KwaDumisani** Supermarket, and **KwaMandlendoda**

Livestock. They may be clan names, as in **Maphoboza** Takeaway, **Khoza's** Mini Market, **Sokhela** Café & Take Away, and **Mnguni** Funeral Services. They may include clan praises (**izithakazelo**), as in **KwaKhumalo: Mtungwa's** Store, where 'Khumalo' is the clan name, and 'Mtungwa' the clan praise. Sometimes the owner of the shop gives both first name and clan name, as in **Siyabonga Hlophe's** Butchery.

Some of the eponyms appear to be nicknames, as in **Kwa Mani** Take Away, and **KwaNtshebe** Supermarket ('Place of Mr Beard'), which is echoed in **Isilaha sikaNtshebe** ('Mr Beard's Butchery').

'Mzala's Supermarket' may be using a nickname, for **umzala** ('cousin') can be used as a nickname or as a general form of address, or it may refer to the use of a kinship term in place of a personal name. This is clearly the case with the number of shops using **umkhulu** ('grandfather') in place of the personal name: **Mkhulu** Supermarket, **KwaMkhul**u Store, and **Mkhulu's** Spaza, just to give three examples. It seems to me that in these examples – as in '**Gogo**'s Bake and Take' (where **ugogo** is 'grandmother') – there is more than just an identity: there is almost a promise of some kind, perhaps a promise of old-fashioned values.

13.2.3 Promises

The shop names under this heading are those that promise the customer some kind of reward if he or she comes into the shop and makes a purchase. The reward might be in the quality of the merchandise, as in **Mnandi** ('good to the taste') Butchery. Perhaps the name promises good service, as in **Siyasiza** ('we help') Cash Loans, or a pleasant ambience, as in **Kuhlekwethu** ('it is good at our place') Wedding Centre.

Value for money is always an important consideration, so it is no surprise to see shop names which emphasise that their goods are inexpensive, as in the following, based on the verb **-shibile** (< *cheap*): **Kushibile** Furnishers (two examples) and **Shibile** Phones. Similar in intent is **Siyonga** ('we are saving/ economising') Furnishers, with its promise 'You will save money if you shop here'. Value for money is expressed indirectly in **Mahawukela** ('envy') Furnishers, with the promise 'Your friends will *envy* you your furniture bought here', and also in **Zamokuhle** ('try the best') Store, with its promise 'You've shopped at other places, where there was second-best; now try shopping here'. The **Siyazama** ('we are trying') Tuckshop and the **Siyazama** Restaurant & Butchery both promise the customer that 'We are trying our best to give you a good deal'.

Promise of product quality is evident in **Siphamandla** ('we give strength') Restaurant ('If you eat our food, you will become strong'); **Vela** ('appear') Salon ('You will appear to your best advantage when we have finished with your hair'); and **Shisa** ('hot') Nice Take Away.

A pleasant experience is promised in both **KwaMahleka** ('the place of Mr Laughter') Restaurant, Bar & Eating House and **Hlekisa** ('make you laugh') Tuck Shop & Tavern. Places like this make you want to come back, as with the promise contained in **Sibuyile** ('we have come back') Trading Store.

Miscellaneous promises are contained in **Cimukoma** ('quench the thirst') Bottle Store, **Msizi** ('helper') Trading Store, and **Kwa Jabula Izimbuzi**. The last is a rather ungrammatical construction based on the verb **jabula** ('be happy') and the noun **izimbuzi** ('goats'), with its promise 'You will be happy if you buy a goat from us'.

The name **Kwa Mdaphuna** (with its variant **Kwa Mtapuna**) is often found, applied to stores, wholesalers, sellers of livestock, and other commercial ventures. The name is based on the verb **daphuna** which means 'to grab with the hand a soft mass, such as pumpkin-mash, porridge' or 'to bite out a mouthful of something'. The name suggests helping oneself to a mouthful of something delicious, a sense of self-indulgence.

A name which contains a rather unclear promise is **Siyabonga** ('we are grateful') Furnishers: are the shop owners grateful because you, the shopper,

Thib' Indlala ('ward off hunger') is a splendid name for a roadside hotdog stall, found in central Pietermaritzburg (see discussion on page 203).

have chosen to shop here? or (more likely) is this an *indirect promise*, putting the words into the mouths of the customers: 'We are really grateful that we shopped here'? **Siyaduma** ('we are famous') Supermarket is similarly ambiguous, but whatever it is they are famous for, whether good quality, good services, or good prices, the name promises that you will not be disappointed in them.

I save to last under this heading the name **Thib' Indlala** ('ward off famine') Take Away (see page 202), not only for its combination of promise, hyperbole and wit, but because this particular combination has been applied to perhaps the smallest trading venue of all those I encountered: a pavement barrow selling hot dogs. On a subsequent journey, I have come across the **Qedindlala** ('bring famine to an end') Supermarket. The picture below was taken in Paulpietersburg.

The **Qedindlala** ('bring an end to hunger') Supermarket was photographed in Paulpietersburg in northern KwaZulu-Natal.

13.2.4 Community spirit

Some shop owners attract customers by choosing a name that expresses a feeling of community spirit, a feeling of togetherness: 'This is a community shop: we are yours; we belong together'. Such names are intended to invoke feelings of loyalty. This feeling of community togetherness, of 'belonging', can be expressed in a name as simple as **Eyethu** Butchery, where **eyethu** means 'ours'. Equally simple is **Simunye** ('we are one'), which in addition to expressing community unity has the advantage of being a 'buzzword' or popular 'catch-phrase', being the slogan of the predominantly African-languages South African Broadcasting Corporation Television Channel One. This combination of community message and buzzword has made **Simunye** the most popular shop name in all my data and I have recorded several examples: a **Simunye** Store, a **Simunye** Supermarket, a **Simunye** Bar & Restaurant, **Simunye** Fashions, a **Simunye** Funeral Parlour, a **Simunye** Driving School, and a **Simunye** Eating House and Take-Away.

A sense of responsibility to the community is expressed in **Sizabantu** ('help the people') Butchery, another popular name, seen also in **Sizabantu** Furnishers and **KwaSizabantu** Sand & Stone. A similar meaning is found in **Sizumphakathi** ('help the community') Tuckshop.

Other community messages are expressed in **Sizanani** ('help one another') Supermarket & Wholesalers, **Bambanani** ('pull together') Furnishers, **Thandanani** ('love one another') Supermarket, and **Kwa Thandanani** Superette. Similar in meaning to the last two is **Thanda Bantu** ('love the people') Butchery.

Reaching out to the widest possible community is **Isizwe** ('the nation') Butchery.

13.2.5 Exhortations

These are names which urge the customer to do something, as in the examples **Woza Nawe** ('You come too') Superette and **Thenga Duze** ('buy nearby') Café & Phones. **Jwayelani** ('get accustomed to . . .') Butchery & Supermarket urges the customer to get used to buying at this particular establishment. This is a popular exhortation, and I have found it with two other butcheries in different towns. The name may simply ask a potential customer to *try* this shop, as in **Zama** ('try') Furnishers, **Zama** Hardware, and **Zamanawe** ('you try, too') Tavern.

The word **siza** ('help') is used in the sense of 'do yourself a favour' in both **Siza** Cash & Carry and **Siza** Furniture & Hardware. The **Phuza** Restaurant & Bar simply exhorts its customer to drink (**phuza**), while the **Sukasambe** Record Bar says to its customers 'Come, let's away!'.

Promise and exhortation are combined in the **Phuzimpilo** ('drink health') Restaurant & Beerhall, and perhaps the same could be said of the **Buka** ('look') Clothing Factory Shop, which is either *promising* its customers 'You will *look* really good in our clothes' or *exhorting* them '*Look* at our clothes'.

13.2.6 Miscellaneous

There are a few shop names that can be regarded as 'descriptives' in that they simply tell the customer what is for sale, without making any promises, exhorting any action, or doing anything else. For example, **Samakhekheni**

The **Vukuzakhe** ('arise and build for yourself') Supermarket can be found along the Elandskop Road west of Pietermaritzburg.

('something like cakes') Bakery and Cakes and **OSakazane** ('sugar pocket') Bulk Food Supermarket. Two other examples are **KwaNyanga Yezizwe** ('herbalist of the nation' – although there is certainly a bit of boast in this name), and **Tsheleka** ('borrow') Cash Loans.

Indawo Yokudla Take Away presents us with a puzzling contradiction: **indawo yokudla** literally means 'place of eating' (that is, right there on the premises) while 'Take Away' says 'take this food away from this place of eating'.

Euro-Western shop names are frequently toponymical in nature in that they use the name of the city or town in which they are situated. The Pietermaritzburg Telephone Directory is full of 'PMB this', and 'Maritzburg that', but this is not apparently a popular way of forming shop names in Zulu. The data produced three: **Umgungundlovu** Tavern and **Msunduzi** Liquors, both predictably in Pietermaritzburg, while **Mamelodi** Supermarket, which refers to a Pretoria Township, is curiously enough also found in Pietermaritzburg.

The name **Vuka Phansi** Tuck Shop refers to the owner's having started out all on his own with absolutely nothing (**vuka phansi** literally means 'awake [from the] bottom').

And finally, **Siyekhaya** ('we are going home') Funeral Services presents us with the only metaphorical shop name in all the data.

13.2.7 Queries

Names under this heading are either untranslatable, or when translated seem to make no sense. That is to say, there is no clear reason why anyone would want to name a store in such a fashion. For example, in '**Abathakathi** herbalist', **abathakathi** refers to the hated and evil witches in Zulu society. No one in their right mind would publicly claim association with **abathakathi,** and yet here is such an association in a shop name. The word **shalaza** means 'avoid, flit from place to place to avoid meeting, shun, dodge', surely a totally unsuitable word for a convivial meeting place. And yet I found the **Kwa-Shalaza** Tavern and Restaurant. A wholesale meat business has the name **Kwa Magwegwe**, with the drawing of an ox with down-pointed horns. The word **igwegwe** means (1) 'crooked or bowed thing, like an ox with twisted horns', but also (2) 'moral crookedness' – not exactly the ideal image for one's business.

Not necessarily unsuitable, yet still not clear, are the following names: **Shonalanga** Bar and **Shona Langa** Butchery and Restaurant (an ingenious and sensible combination). The words **shona** ('to disappear, sink from sight')

Kwa Mbuzi Zikhal Ewen Supermarket, in East Street, Pietermaritzburg (see discussion on page 207).

and **ilanga** ('sun') usually combine in **intshonalanga** ('sunset', 'the West'), but just how they are linked to a butchery and a restaurant is not clear. I have also come across the **Pumalanga** Wholesalers (< **phuma**, 'to go or come out', + **ilanga**, 'sun' [**impumalanga**, 'sunrise', 'the East']).

Siyakhula ('we are growing') Tuckshop may well be so named because it is situated next to a school, but this is not the case for **Khulani** ('grow up') Store. Proximity may also be the reason for the **Epulangweni** ('place of planks') Restaurant & Bar, which, judging by the number of heavily-laden timber trucks on the road near this establishment, must be in the vicinity of a sawmill.

It is possible that the name **Siyathunga** ('we are sewing') Hair Salon refers to the intricate ways of braiding hair, but what does one make of **Gonondo** Herb Specialist, where **igonondo** refers to the lower portion of the human back?

And a final puzzle, spelt just as recorded from the shop front (see page 206): '**Kwa Mbuzi Zikhal Ewen** Supermarket'. When puzzled out this is '**Kwa (izi)mbuzi zikhal(a) ewen(i)**' ('The Place of the Goats Crying on the Cliff Face') Supermarket. There just has to be a story behind that one.

Part 4

Miscellaneous names

Chapter 14

Names of domestic animals

14.1 INTRODUCTION

The naming of domestic animals is one of the most neglected areas of Zulu onomastics, and very little has been published in this field. Much of the material in this chapter is based on Koopman 1992, an article which itself was based almost entirely on material collected in the field from Zulu speakers. To this material some examples have been added from Molefe's (1992) research on the praises of domestic animals, as well as a few examples from postgraduate students in onomastics research seminars.

The two groups of animals which are consistently named are cattle and dogs. Although it has been possible over the years to collect a few examples of names for animals such as horses and donkeys, and to an even lesser extent, cats, it is the cattle names and dog names which are usually given when examples of the names of domestic animals are asked for.

The importance of cattle in Zulu society is well known. Cattle are important economically, their by-products (milk, hides, etc.) are of great importance in daily life and, of course, their cultural importance should not be underestimated, with the custom of **ilobolo** (discussed in some detail in Chapter 3, pages 35 to 36 and 48) as well as the need for offerings of cattle to maintain communication with the ancestral spirits. It is not surprising, then, that the naming of individual cattle is considered to be important. However, it *is* surprising, given the importance of cattle, that so many cattle names are derived from European culture, as we will see below. This chapter will focus mainly on the names of oxen, *firstly* because the bulk of my cattle names' data is on oxen, and *secondly* because for various linguistic, historical and cultural reasons, they are the most interesting of cattle names. There will be brief mention of the naming of cows, and reference to bulls will be left to the last section, when the praising of domestic animals is discussed.

Dogs have a less obvious cultural role to play in Zulu society, their main functions being those of guarding and hunting. Nonetheless, dogs are regularly named, and the naming patterns involved are very similar to the naming patterns of oxen.

The names of domestic animals can be categorised according to their origin and according to their function. When we look at the origin of the names, we can distinguish between those of Euro-Western origin and those of 'pure' Zulu origin. If function is the criterion, then it should be noted that *identification* is the primary function, as is the case with the vast majority of names of any sort. But as with so many different kinds of names, there are secondary functions as well. In the case of the naming of domestic animals, we can distinguish between those names which refer to the *particular characteristics* of the animal named, whether behavioural or physical, and those names which can be used as *social comments*. Names which describe the animal are predominantly Zulu in origin, and 'social message names' are entirely Zulu.

The way in which these different categories will be handled in this chapter is as follows:

1. Firstly, names which are taken from Euro-Western naming traditions, and thus are almost entirely adoptives;
2. Secondly, names which refer to the particular characteristics of the animal named, whether physical or behavioural;
3. Thirdly, names which are used as social comments.

14.2 NAMES FROM THE EURO-WESTERN NAMING TRADITION

The animals will be discussed in the following order: cattle (with oxen preceding cows), then donkeys, followed by dogs, and ending with cats.

14.2.1 Oxen

By far the majority of the names of oxen are derived from Dutch/Afrikaans. This phenomenon became clear when I first started collecting ox names in the mid-1970s, when nine out of ten of my examples were names like **uBhulobehe** (< *Blaauwberg*, 'Blue Mountain') and **uVitikopu** (< *wit kop*, 'white head'). It is only recently, however, that I have managed to find material on the naming of oxen in the early days of the Voortrekkers and, later, transport riding. It is worth quoting in full the extracts from Gibson and Burman below, because much of the Zulu system of ox nomenclature has been adopted *as a whole* from the Dutch/Afrikaans system.

> The major use of oxen in the nineteenth century was for 'transport riding': the conveying of goods from the ports to the interior of the country by ox wagon.

Gibson's 1918 article 'The Kap-tent Wagon' explains in detail the underlying strategy of Dutch/Afrikaans ox naming:

> The names of oxen became somewhat stereotyped, and were not of very great variety. Although some of them would appear to suggest an earlier association with particular places, such as *Tafelberg, Blaauwberg* or *Witzenberg*, it is remarkable that they were generally associated in application with the colour of the animal named; thus the second was invariably given to a grey animal, a colour which the Boers described as *blue*, and the third to one mostly or entirely white. They were chosen chiefly with the view to ease and distinctness in enunciation. Common names were *Bontman*, for a parti-coloured animal, *Bandom* for one with a belt across it, *Donker* for a dark brown, *Jan Bloed* for one of a peculiar shade of redness (the meaning being 'John Blood'), *Rodeland* for an ordinary red, *Kruisman* for one with a white back suggesting a cross, *Vaaltyn* (or possibly *Vaaltuijn*, 'Fallow garden') for a *vaal* or dun-coloured beast, and *Geelbek* for one with a yellow muzzle. And then there were such neutral names as *Akkerman* (Ploughman); *Opperman* (Hodman or Labourer); *Bloem* (Flower); *Boekhouder* (Book-keeper); *Dwengeland* (Tyrant), *England; Fransman; Jonkman* (Youth); *Koopman* (Merchant); *Landman* (Rustic); and *Makman* (Tameman) (4–5).

Clear from this description is the relationship between the name and the appearance of the ox, especially with regard to colour and marking. In the following extract, Burman makes much the same points, and in place of a list of examples, gives us the names of a complete ox team:

> Every ox received its own name, with which it became familiar and to which it reacted. Ox names were traditional and were usually intended to give an indication of the particular ox either as to colour, origin or strength, and most of their names ended with 'berg' (strength), 'man' (nature), 'veld' (place) or 'land' (place).
>
> An authentic team which has come down to us from 1852 is: Colesberg, Human, Wildman, Platberg, Vryman, Sausman, Oortman, Kleinveld, Engeland and Koopman. Engeland and Engelsman were usually the most refractory or worst pullers in the team (1988: 60).

Burman's point that the ending *-berg* ('mountain') is an indication of strength is an interesting one, and suggests that names such as *Blaauwberg* and *Witteberg* (or *Witzenberg*) have a double reference, that is, to the coloration as well as the strength of the animal. I note with amusement that *Engeland* and *Engelsman* were names reserved for the 'most refractory or worst pullers in the team'. This suggests that in certain circumstances, Afrikaans/Dutch ox names, like Zulu ox names, could be used for social comment.

The name *Jan Bloed* has been adopted into Zulu as **uJamludi**. As this has become one of the most popular Zulu ox names, which has in turn spawned imitations such as **uJalidube** and **uJanidube**, there is a separate subsection devoted to the name **uJamludi** below.

Zulu ox names with the element *-berg*, phonologised into **-behe**, include the following:

- **uBhulobehe** (< *Blaauwberg* or *Blouberg*) which is used as a name for a blue-grey coloured ox, in the same way as the noun **ubhulomo** (< Afrikaans *blou*) is used as a general descriptive term (that is, not as a name) for any beast so coloured;
- **uVitibehe** (< *Witteberg*);
- **uTafulibehe** (< *Tafelberg*);
- and with the first element untraceable: **uKolibehe, uSkolibehe, uTilibehe,** and **uDilibehe;**
- **uBondbehe** combines *berg* with the element *bont* ('mottled', 'speckled').

The suffix -bisi, from Afrikaans *bees* ('beast') is found in **uVelebisi** (< *vuil bees*, 'dirty beast', that is, a muddy-coloured animal) and **uVitibisi** (< *wit bees*, 'white beast').

The suffix **-futhi**, which is from Afrikaans *voet* ('foot', 'hoof') is common to **uVelefuthi** (< *vuil voet*, 'dirty hoof'– and **Velefuthi** is also the Zuluised form of 'Verwoerd', the name of the architect of apartheid) and **uLevuthi** (< *lui voet*, 'lazy foot', suggesting a behavioural pattern rather than coloration).

The Afrikaans word *bles* refers to a white blaze on the face, and it is the first part of Zulu **uBlesiboku** (< *blesbok*, literally, 'blaze buck') as well as **uBlesimani** (< *bles* + *man*, 'man').

The suffix **-mani** (< *man*) is used in a number of Zulu ox names, such as the following:

- **uLasimani** (< *last man*);
- **uDayimani** (< *daai man*, 'that man'): Although, the alternative interpretation – from 'diamond' – has occurred to me;
- **uGwayimani** (< *kwaai man*, 'angry man');
- **uVelemani** (< *vuil man*, 'dirty man');
- **uGopumani** (< *Koopman*);
- **uAkelmani** (< *Akkerman*, 'ploughman');
- **uSayimani** (< *saaiman*, 'seed man');
- **uSoyisimani** (?< *Sausman*, as given in Burman's 1852 ox team above.)

uPhaphamani looks as if it belongs to this group, but it is in fact a 'social comment' name, described below.

Burman mentions the suffix *land* ('land'), giving only the example *Engeland*. Zulu examples with this suffix are **uKhafalande** (< *Kaffir lande*) and **uSikhohlande** (< *Scotland*), a name which commonly appears as **uSohlande, uSohlanti**, and **uKholande**.

Miscellaneous adoptive ox names include:

- **uFethiboyi** (< *fat boy*);

- **uBokvele** (< *bokvel*, 'buckskin');
- **uLentusi** (< *lente oes*, 'spring harvest');
- **uLenkhasi** (< *rinkhals*, literally, 'ring halter [around neck]', but more specifically a reference to the spitting cobra which is so marked, *Haemachatus haemachatus*).

The influence of Afrikaans/Dutch in the naming of oxen in other indigenous South African languages can also be seen. For example, Mzamane, writing about Xhosa, states: '. . . [the influence of Afrikaans] . . . has extended into cattle and horses. It is no exaggeration to say that more than seventy percent of the cattle . . . bear names derived from Afrikaans stems' (1962: 227). Mzamane gives a list of 17 cattle names, including:

- **Falimeyisi** (< *vaal muis*, 'tawny mouse');
- **Lenkalisi** (< *rinkhals*, indicating, as he says, a white ring around the neck);
- **Lomani** (< *rooi man*, 'red man', always used for a red beast).

Mzamane's inclusion of **Kaflani** (< *kaffir lande*) in a list of colour terms suggests that this name is used for black or dark-coloured beasts.

uJamludi

This is one of the most common and popular ox names, and I have also found it used for cows, dogs, and even as a nickname for a person. Recipients of the name **uJamludi** always have red hair, leading me originally to speculate (in my 1992 article) that this word was derived from *Jan Roodt* ('Jack-the-Red'), along the lines of *Janbruin* (the fish also known in South Africa as 'John Brown'), and *JanGroentjie* ('little green Jack' – the name of the little green Malachite Kingfisher). I have since discovered (see quote from Gibson above) the existence of the Afrikaans/Dutch metaphorical name *Jan Bloed* ('John Blood') for a red ox, and it is quite clear that this is the origin of the Zulu name **uJamludi**.

> For extensive discussion on the use of Afrikaans 'Jan' and English 'Jack' as a basis for the naming of animals, birds, fish, etc., see Koopman (1998).

The status of **Jamludi** as a sort of 'all-encompassing' Zulu ox name can be seen in the photographs on pages 229 to 230. The top picture on page 229 was taken at a cattle feedlot catering specifically for the Zulu trade. This is located alongside the N3 national highway at Umlaas Road, about 20 kilometres east of Pietermaritzburg. The sign simply has one word – **JAMLUDI** – underneath a striking red silhouette of an ox. The bottom picture on page 229 was taken in Kranskop, a small village east of Greytown. It is used to advertise a local butchery. The pictures on page 230 were taken in Victoria Road, Pietermaritzburg, to advertise one of the outlets of the distributer **Jamludi** Fresh Meats.

The name **uJamludi** is often extended into the three word praise **uJamludi obomvu njengentolwane** ('Jamludi who is red like the shrub *Elephantorrhiza elephantina*', a shrub with reddish roots used to tan and colour hides [Pooley, 1998: 150]).

The name **uJamludi** has close linguistic and onomastic cousins in the ox names **uJanidube** (also found as **uJalidube**) and **uJantoni**, both of which have Afrikaans *Jan* as a base, but in fact refer to historical figures whose first name was John. John Langalibalele Dube, the renowned political leader, newspaper editor, and educator of the first half of the twentieth century, is surely commemorated in **uJanidube**, while **uJantoni** was the name give to the 'White Chief' John Dunn, the confidant of Zulu king Cetshwayo kaMpande in the late nineteenth century. I suggest that these two famous 'Johns' have been transmogrified into ox names, on analogy with, and following the pattern of, the original *Jan Bloed*.

14.2.2 Cows

Cows can be named with adoptives referring to musical instruments:

- **uMfiliji** (< Afrikaans *fluitjie*, 'mouth organ');
- **uVawulini** (< *violin*);
- **uHogani** (< *organ*);
- **uNkositini** (< *concertina*);
- **uStolotolo** from the Zulu word *isitolotolo* ('Jew's harp') is not an adoptive, but is a musical instrument, so it is included here.

Cows may be named from the place where the owner of the cow was working when he bought the cow:

- **uKhimbali** (< *Kimberley*);
- **uTheku** (Durban);
- **uMkhumbane** (Cato Manor, Durban).

Or, they could be named from the place where the cow was bought:

- **uBekivili** (< *Bergville*);
- **uMkhomazi**, **uMandaplisi** (< *Mondi Place*);
- **uNyuvela** (< *Yeoville*).

Cows can be named after European foodstuffs or kitchen utensils or even, in one case that I encountered, after an item of clothing, using adoptives:

- **uSosishi** (< *sausage*; this name is usually for red cows);
- **uThisipuni** (< *teaspoon*);
- **uSosipani** (< *saucepan*);
- **uBhasikidi** (< *basket*);
- **uKlabishi** (< *cabbage*);

- **uShukela** (< *sugar*);
- **uNkomishi** (< Afrikaans *kommetjie*, 'cup');
- **uTafula** (< Afrikaans *tafel*, 'table');
- **uTawula** (< *towel*);
- **uSokisi** (< *socks*).

14.2.3 Donkeys

I only have four names here:

- **uS'pele Misipele** (the meaning of which is given as 'reader', probably a reference to a school reader with the title 'Spell and Misspell');
- **uS-noboli** (< *snowball*);
- **uVetifuthi** (< *wit voet*, 'white foot');
- **uJamludi**.

14.2.4 Dogs

Adopted dog names in Zulu all seem to be adopted from English. Sometimes there is no attempt to phonologise the name into a Zulu phonological pattern, and the only difference between the English original and the Zulu dog name is the prefix **u-**: **uSheba**, **uRex**, **uSmash**, **uDanger**, **uSpecial**, and **uBrown**.

Others have been phonologised into Zulu:

- **uThayikeni** (< *tiger*);
- **uSayitsheni** (< *sergeant*);
- **uSipoti** (< *spot* or < *sport*);
- **uPhilinsi** (< *prince*);
- **uDenja** (< *danger*);
- **uS'pesheli** (< *special*).

The first three names in the list above I have found to be particularly common. It is interesting to note how many of these are used as dogs' names in English. In such cases, is it the onomastic or the lexical item which has been taken over? In the case of the 'royal' names *Rex* and *Prince*, both common dogs' names in English, clearly it is the *name* which has been adopted into Zulu. However, in the cases of **uDanger** and **uSpecial**, which I personally do not recognise as dog names in English, it is presumably the English *noun* 'danger' and the English *adjective* 'special', which have been adopted into Zulu, there to achieve onomastic status as dog names.

14.2.5 Cats

Cats are very seldom given names in Zulu society. When I was researching Zulu personal names, and collecting the names of domestic animals 'on the side', as it were, I found 72 names for dogs, but only 3 names for cats, even though the proportion of cats to dogs was about the same in the households I visited. Of the three named cats, one was called **uJinja** (< *Ginger*), and two were called **uPhusi** (< *Pussy*). It is not clear, however, whether **uPhusi** is really a proper name, and not just another word for cat. I have often wondered why Zulu uses the adoptive **ikati** (< Afrikaans *kat*, 'cat'), when the Zulu language has the expressive word **umangobe** ('cat', literally, 'the one that arches the back'). See also Chapter 4, page 65, where the general nickname for a cat – **idlalesula** ('what eats and wipes away') – is given. I recall some years ago asking an elderly Zulu man whether the Zulu language had an original word for 'cat' instead of the word **ikati**. After much pondering he finally produced the word **uphusi**.

I have asked why it should be that cats hardly ever get names, and the following are reasons which have been put forward.

a. Cats are recent acquisitions

While the dog has been associated with Bantu-speaking pastoralists for millenia, the cat is a comparatively recent acquisition, having only been associated with the Zulu people for 200 years or so. Even the word for cat – **ikati** – is an adoptive, the Zulu language never having had its own word. For this reason, cats have never been part of the Zulu naming system. I find this reason difficult to accept since there *is* an 'indigenous' word for cat, the word **umangobe** mentioned above, and 200 years is ample time for a cat-naming tradition to start.

b. Cats are not properly domesticated

Dogs relate to and identify with human 'owners'. Cats are far more aloof and 'keep to themselves'. Dogs are always given food in the Zulu society, cats are always expected to fend for themselves. Cats are seen in the same light as certain snakes which choose to live in the environment of the homestead: wild creatures which physically locate themselves within a homestead, but are not treated as part of the domestic group. Wild creatures are not named, therefore cats are not named. I can understand this reason. Cats have always been seen as creatures that hold themselves aloof, wandering off by themselves into the wild at night. And wild creatures are not given names unless as single individuals they become famous – as did Huberta the Hippo who, in 1928, travelled from Lake St Lucia in northern KwaZulu-Natal right down to the Keiskamma River in the Western Cape (Reynierse, 1988: 178, 253).

c. Cats are creatures of the night, with potential links to witchcraft

Cats tend to wander around at night, which is the time when witches (**abathakathi**) are working. There is always the possibility that a witch will be able to capture the cat and put it to work as a familiar, as they are known to do with other night creatures such as hyenas. If the cat was given a name by members of the homestead, the witches would find it easier to establish a link between their evil intentions and the homestead. It is well known that witches can work their magic through names. This link between cats and witchcraft is seen in the number of Zulu people who are petrified of cats and who will not enter a room or a homestead if there is a cat present. Seeing that witches can use names to establish such links, it is sensible not to name the night-wandering cats. This reason fits in very well with belief patterns about witchcraft and anthroponyms.

14.3 NAMES REFERRING TO THE CHARACTERISTICS OF THE ANIMAL

Names referring to the characteristics of a particular animal may refer to physical characteristics or behavioural characteristics. Take, for example, the following names of donkeys, of which the first five refer to physical characteristics, and the last two to behavioural characteristics:

- **uSinqundu** ('tail-less');
- **uGobandlebe** ('Droopy-Ears');
- **uS'bhense** ('heavy body');
- **uZ'phumpu** ('No-Ears');
- **uSinundu** ('Tatty');
- **uNodlula** ('passes [the others]');
- **uMbhekaphansi** ('[always] looks down').

The following eight dog names refer to a particular characteristic feature of the dog:

- **uDeda** ('get out of the way'): A reference to a fast-running hunting dog, which always raced ahead ('got out of the way') of other dogs in the chase.
- **uShiyabekhala** ('leave them crying'): A notorious sheep-killer, after whose depredations sheep-owners were left crying.
- **uNdlayivalwa** ('the house is not closed up'): The house does not need to be closed up when this vicious dog is around.
- **uVimba** ('lock up', 'shut up'): This dog was so vicious that even the inhabitants of the house used to shout '**Vimba uVimba**' ('close up Vimba') whenever the dog got out.
- **uQobo** ('the real thing'): When the father of the household heard this dog bark for the first time, he said, 'Now that is what I call a genuine dog'.
- **uBahlangene** ('they are gathered together'): This was the Zulu name given to my dalmatian when she was still a puppy. Named by a Zulu employee of the Pietermaritzburg University Club in 1983 when this was one of the very few places in Pietermaritzburg where whites and blacks were allowed to drink together under one roof, he explained his reason for naming the dog: 'As this is a private university club, both black people and white people can gather together in harmony to talk and drink, just as the black spots on your white dog are gathered together in harmony.'

- **uThandendlini** ('likes it in the house'): Said quite simply of a dog that liked home comforts.
- **uPhumaphela** ('now then, get out!'): The owner of this dog explained that when the dog was young, it used to roll in the dirt and dung, and so when it came into the house dirty and stinking, the whole family used to shout 'Phuma phela!'. This phrase had subsequently become the dog's name, and indeed the dog answered to this name. When I asked what phrase was *now* used to get the dog out of the house, seeing that 'phuma phela' brought the dog in, the answer was simple: 'When we want the dog to get out, we say "Heyyyi! Voetsek wena!".'

> The quintessentially South African expression 'Voetsek!' ('Go away!', 'Be off with you!') is originally from the Dutch *Voort seg ik!* ('Away, I say!'). The expression can now be found in all of South Africa's languages. In Zulu it is **futhiseke!**

I have no record at all of any cattle names which refer to their physical or behavioural characteristics, apart from the adoptives mentioned above, where terms such as **uVitibisi** ('white beast') and **uBulobehe** (< *Blaauwberg*, 'blue mountain') describe colour and strength.

14.4 ANIMAL NAMES USED AS SOCIAL COMMENT

Molefe (1992: 78ff.) reveals an interesting 'extra' function of the praises of a working ox team. The driver of an ox team pulling a wagon usually shouts out the names of individual animals in order to control the general movement and behaviour of his team. But a Zulu team driver, controlling the oxen he is using for pulling his plough, can go further. Certainly he calls out the individual names of his oxen, interspersing his cries with the crack of the whip, to exhort his oxen to greater effort. But the underlying meanings of certain of the names may be used for what Molefe calls 'disciplinary messages'. He gives as an example the following words from the driver of an ox team:

> **Iyaphi ngale Thakathani**
> *Where is it heading to, Thakathani*
> **Iyaphi Nquluzomjendevu!** (77, 78)
> *Where is it going Nquluzomjendevu!*

The name **uThakathani** ('keep on bewitching'), says Molefe, is directed to those people whom the driver suspects are bewitching him. By using the name of the ox loudly, or by simply having named the ox **'Thakathani'** and allowing the neighbours to find this out at their leisure, he is in effect saying to his neighbours 'I know you are bewitching me, but it doesn't bother me at all'. The other name, **uNquluzomjendevu** ('hips of the old maid') is a barbed comment to neighbours that they should have married off their daughters a long time ago.

Names from my own collection of ox names have similar messages:

- **uZwabesho** ('listen while they speak'): The owner suspects others of talking behind his back, and is letting them know that he is aware of this.
- **uBayangizonda** ('they hate me'): The owner of the ox lets his neighbours know that he is aware of their feelings about him.
- **uQedumona** ('end your envy'): An obvious message.
- **uSunduzisono** ('push away your sin'): A direct comment referring no doubt to a specific incident.
- **uDudulamakhansela** ('chase away the councillors'): Again, I imagine a specific incident is being referred to.
- **uSiyempini** ('we are going to war'): This is certainly a very direct warning to the neighbours.
- **uPhaphamani** ('wake up now, all of you'): A warning to the neighbours to wake up to the consequences of their actions.

Turner writes:

> In Zulu society, the use of names . . . is an extremely useful channel of expressing discontent or passing criticism at those in close proximity, and is a vital way of making others aware of the problem, or for the ultimate purpose of restraining or correcting an undesirable situation/ behaviour trait as direct confrontation or criticism is not an acceptable or preferred form of behaviour (1992: 45).

There is no question that this is one of the major functions of dogs' names, and a large proportion of my data shows that for many people a dog's name is specifically chosen in order to make a barbed comment about one's neighbours or in-laws. Before I look at the examples in my collection, I would like to put this onomastic practice into its African context by looking at some other African societies which use dogs' names in the same way. Hunt, writing about the naming of dogs in Karanga (a language of Zimbabwe), states: 'When any person conceives that he or she has a grievance against another, it is apparently the practice to bestow a name on a dog which will act as a perpetual reminder to the guilty party of his fault' (1952: 67).

Of interest in his article are his three separate subcategories:

1. those dog names coined and used exclusively by men, and these are almost entirely complaints about wives (she nags, she is lazy, she is impertinent, etc.);
2. those coined and used exclusively by women, some of which are complaints about husbands, but most of which refer negatively to co-wives;

3. those which may be coined and used by either sex, most of which refer to witchcraft by neighbours or distant family members.

Samarin refers to social comment in dog names in the opening paragraph of his article on Gbeya dog names:

> The dogs of the Gbeya . . . can be looked upon as screens upon which the Gbeya project their attitudes towards many different aspects of their life. Such projection is accomplished by giving to the dogs names that verbalize complaints, ridicule, humour, etc. They are short, even telegraphic, 'texts' about life in general or about one's particular place in it (1965: 57).

The 'extra meaning' which I referred to earlier when talking about the calling out of ox names when ploughing, is clearly revealed in Samarin's concept of the function of Gbeya dog names: 'It seems clear that dogs have names, not to facilitate communication between the master and dog, but for the sake of the human community. Except for those few instances where a name describes some characteristic of the dog itself, the names are used to remind the community of a particular incident or situation' (1965: 58).

This statement may well be said of the Zulu situation. There are names which we have seen are 'copies' of Euro-Western names such as **uRex** and **uSayitsheni**; there are names which tell us of some characteristic of the dog; but the majority are names 'for the sake of the community'. The only way in which Zulu seems to differ from Karanga and Gbeya societies, is that Zulu people in general are much happier with their husbands and wives, but far more suspicious of their neighbours!

The following are examples of Zulu dog names used as social comment:

- **uBayangizonda** ('they hate me'): We have already met this name in the discussion of ox names used as social comment, and it is the only example in my data where ox name and dog name coincide.
- **uZondabathakathi** ('hate the wizards'): Whether this is an injunction to the dog itself, or the owner is stating publicly that he hates wizards, either way the message is clear to the neighbours.
- **uBathini** ('what do they say [about me]?'): The owner indicates that he knows people are talking behind his back.
- **uBafazi** ('women [have been talking about me]'): The ellipsis in this name is an excellent example of what Samarin called 'telegraphic texts'.
- **uBathabangiboni** ('they think "no one can see me"'): Wizards always operate under the delusion that their deeds are unknown. This name tells them that this is not the case.
- **uBathangiboni** ('they think I do not see'): Similar to the name above in form and in meaning.
- **uBangihlebani** ('what are they whispering about me?'): This name is similar to **uBathini** above.

- **uBangithintile** ('they have touched/provoked me'): The owner states that he knows about all the activities of those who are against him.
- **uBayakhuluma** ('they are talking [about me]'): Similar to **uBathini** above.
- **uBashokonke** ('they say everything [about me]'): A variation of the sentiment expressed above.
- **uBamzwani** ('what do they feel about him?'): 'They' are the neighbours' while 'him' refers to the dog's owner.
- **uBamnukile** ('they have smelt him'): In other words, they suspect him to be a witch.

Perhaps the most common name in this category is the name **uBahlangene** ('they are gathered together'), which we already saw above with a positive reference to a spotted dalmatian. This name normally indicates that the owner is aware that the neighbours are gathered together against him, but the name may carry other social messages as well. Let us look at the reasons given by four different dog owners to explain their choice of their name **uBahlangene**:

- Relationships within the house had been strained and the husband and wife had split up. They had, however, recently come together again, and the name of their new dog reflected this.
- The name **uBahlangene** is a summary of the statement '**Inja mayihlanganise abathakathi ibabulale**' ('let the dog gather together the wizards and kill them').
- The neighbours are all gathered together against us.
- This dog is a reminder of how well we used to get on with our neighbours before we moved.

It is noteworthy that in the majority of the examples given above, the third person plural subject concord **-ba-** starts the name. This suggests that these names are emphasising the division that has taken place between the owner of the dog and the neighbours: 'us' (represented by the dog) versus 'them' – the jealous neighbours.

It should also be noted that if the social system should change, for example, if a man should make peace with his neighbours, or if the neighbours should move away, the name of the dog remains unchanged until its death.

14.5 NAMES, NICKNAMES, PRAISE NAMES AND PRAISES

As we saw in Chapter 4, there is often an overlap between names, nicknames and praise names. We also saw how easily praise names can be extended and developed into praise poems, providing a linking continuum between the onomastic function of single names, and the epic and laudatory function of oral praise poetry.

This kind of overlap and onomastic-literary continuum is also true of the names and praises of domestic animals in Zulu society.

One of the major contributors to the study of the praising of domestic animals in Zulu has been Lawrence Molefe, whose 1992 research was based on extensive field research in the area between Pietermaritzburg and the Drakensberg Mountains. Molefe's research concentrates on the more extensive oral praise poems for animals such as cattle, dogs, horses, pigs and goats, rather than on single names, but his work is nonetheless illuminating for students of Zulu onomastics. The attitudes of the owners of oxen and dogs, to pick out just two of the variety of animals whose praises Molefe gives, are shown to reflect much the same picture as we have seen already. There are praises that make social comment, critical or otherwise, praises with a large element of adoptives from English and Afrikaans, and praises that reflect on the characteristics of the animal being praised.

On the links between the names of domestic animals and their praises, Molefe says that a number of the names of domestic animals derive directly from their praises, and conversely, praises may be an expansion or extension of a name which is given first. When it comes to horses, for example:

> The owner of a horse never gives the beast a name unless it is fully broken in riding. He will never give the name before he composes praises that disclose that it has been broken in. The name Jet-Pilot derives from the praises that the owner gave to the horse when he (the owner) had finished breaking it in (1992: 74).

In the same way, the owner of a donkey gave his animal the name **uGqakaza** after it showed remarkable strength in fighting rival donkeys during mating, but this name derived from praises which preceded the name, praises which started with the word **'Gqakaza'**:

> **UGqakaza-petu,**
> *The rough-grinder who opens his mouth,*
> **Impolompolo engadle ngamasondo**
> *The train without wheels,*
> **Ushewula bedudlana**
> *He who bit his opponent during a fight* (1992: 28).

On praises that develop from names, Molefe has this to say:

> Popular animals like cattle are given names soon after birth. The name uJamludi, for example, is given to a calf and it grows up knowing it. When Jamludi is given praises the name is included now and again. We have a phrase: UJamludi obomvu onjengentolwane!' (Jamludi who is red like an *ntolwane* shrub) in the praises of this bull. Certainly the name came first, then its praises.

> . . . The dog is another animal that is given a name when it is still a young puppy. When the poet composes praises for this dog at a later stage he uses its name within the praises. My general observation concludes that, if the animal is given the name before it is given praises, the praises develop around the name, and vice versa (1992: 74).

To illustrate the links between names and praises, let us look at Molefe's example of the praises of a whole span of oxen, and then analyse the names of the individual oxen that constitute part of the praises:

Iyaphi laphaya
Where is it going there
Velfudi, Bhentrogi, Khalisamadoda!
Witvoet, Bentrog, Khalisamadoda!
Iyaphi ngale Thakathani,
Where are you going, Thakathani,
Iyaphi uNquluzomjendevu,
Where are you going, Nquluzomjendevu!
Jibh' omasondosondo!
Jeep with super wheels!
Nkalankala ziyawugudl' uMngeni,
Crabs that are migrating along uMngeni River,
Yinde lenyoni kayiboni kwaZulu!
This bird is tall but cannot see Zululand,
Ndlala kaMadlantule,
Madlantule's hunger,
Siswana sophuthu,
Tiny stomach who only eats stiff-pap,
Mbokodo kaMagayisa!
Magayisa's grindstone!
Kukud' eKholenso!
Colenso is far!
Bergville!
Bergville!
Iyaphi emazolweni?
Why is it going into the dew? (1992: 162).

The second line of these praises clearly contains three names: **uVelfudi, uBhentrogi** and **uKhalisamadoda**: **uVelfudi** is adopted from Afrikaans *vuil voet* ('dirty hoof'), while **uKhalisamadoda** ('makes men cry') could either refer to the frustrating behaviour of the ox itself but, more likely, to the behaviour of neighbours. **uBhentrogi** is a puzzler: it looks as if it is an adoptive from an Afrikaans ox name, but I do not recognise the base unless, perhaps, it is from Dutch 'ik ben terug' ('I have come back').

uThakathani and **uNquluzomjendevu** have already been discussed above.

The fifth praise line **uJibh' omasondosondo** reminds us of the well known praise of a successful courter, mentioned on page 55 in Chapter 4 above: **uGandaganda omasondosondo** ('tractor with powerful wheels').

In the line 'Crabs that are migrating along the uMngeni River', I suspect that **uMngeni** is the name of one of the oxen, for later in these praises we have the two place names Colenso and Bergville, and these are certainly the names of members of the team.

The line **Yinde lenyoni kayiboni kwaZulu** is a favourite and common praise for young men, and we have met it before, on page 58 in Chapter 4.

uMadlantule ('what eats and still wants') is the name given to the great famine which occurred in the times of Dingiswayo (Doke & Vilakazi, 1958: 474), and presumably refers to an ox which is very thin, or one which is a great eater.

I am not sure whether the phrase **siswana sophuthu** refers to an ox or not.

Mbokodo kaMagayisa, as we saw on page 65 in Chapter 4, is a praise name for the Royal Air Force. What it is doing in the praises for a team of oxen is anyone's guess. It could, of course, be a praise name for a powerful and fast-moving ox.

What is particularly interesting in these praises is the linking between the praises of oxen and various other categories of names and praises: at least two well-known praises of young men, three place names, the praise name for the Royal Air Force – all these are mixed together with names such as **uVelfudi** and **uThakathani**, ox names which fit squarely into the naming patterns which have been described above.

14.5.1 Praises of a bull

The praises of a bull which follow are taken from Makhambeni (*Ihluzo*, 1989[3]) as quoted by Molefe:

UJamludi obomvu onjengentolwane!
Jamludi who is red like the **ntolwane** *shrub!*
Uklevuklevu wezihlabathi;
Breaker of sands;
Umali wendima kanti uyazalela;
Measurer of a plot to be eradicated in the mealiefield
who measures it all by himself;
UNomalevulevu kaNomalekethe.
Nomalevulevu son of Nomalekethe.

Umpondo zicije zinjengenalithi,
You whose horns are as sharp as a needle,
Umahlabazihlangana onjengemfologo.
You stabbed like a fork when you met others.

Usihhonahhona sephalishi.
You who are like a thick porridge.
Awudli nengane ngob' uzoyiphangela.
You don't eat together with children because you are a glutton.

Ushishiliza kwelimaholo,
You slide on rough surfaces,
Limshaye limbhedule.
It hit you and caused an open wound,
Ubhukuda kwesinezingwenya,
He swims in the deep pool full of crocodiles,
Ingwenya imkhiyazelele.
Each of them fears him,
Iphume idl' amagwebu!
It only emerges to eat foam (1992: 156).

There are only two recognisable *names* here, as opposed to the number of 'praise phrases' which refer to the bull. One name is **uJamludi**, taking pride of place in the first line of the praises, and with its characteristic extension 'red like the **intolwane** shrub'. The other is **uNomalevulevu**, coupled with the patronym **kaNomalekethe** ('son of Nomalekethe'). This combination of name and patronym suggests a noisy chatter, for the first name is based on the ideophone **levu** ('of chattering incessantly') and the patronym on the verb **leketha** ('talk or scold incessantly'). Also of interest is the age of these names. We already know that **uJamludi** goes back to *Jan Bloed*, an ox name from Voortrekker times. The linked names **uNomalevulevu kaNomalekethe** go back as far, if not further, for according to James Stuart, in his 1926 book *uVusezakithi*, they appear in the praises of **uSicocosendoda** ('head-ring of a man'), which was a bull from the eMantungweni homestead of the Buthelezi chief uMnyamana kaNgqengelele. UMnyamana was a contemporary of King Shaka, so these names go back to the earliest years of the nineteenth century.

14.6 CONCLUSION

Evans-Pritchard, writing about the Nilotic Nuer people, states: 'Names of all kinds are social documents, which fix a person's position in the social structure and define his relations to other members of society' (1939: 237).

Although Evans-Pritchard is in all probability talking specifically of *human* names, this statement is certainly true of a large number of the names of domestic animals, especially dogs and oxen. It is particularly striking that the majority of the social comments expressed in such ox and dog names are of the type that draw attention to friction, particularly to the belief that one's neighbours are engaged in aggressive behaviour such as gossip and witchcraft. This social function of the names of domestic animals appears to be a characteristic of Zulu society and, as far as I am aware, this is not one of the functions of the names of domestic animals in Euro-Western society.

Another striking feature of the names of domestic animals is the large number adopted from words from colonial languages, with English providing a large proportion of the names of dogs, cows and other animals, while Afrikaans and Dutch are responsible for an extremely large proportion of Zulu ox names. As I have tried to show above, it is not just a large number of individual ox names which have been adopted directly from Dutch, but an entire system of nomenclature.

This red bull, named **Jamludi**, can be seen from the N3 highway near Umlaas Road, about 15 kilometres east of Pietermaritzburg. (Refer to discussion on page 215.)

Jamludi: This red bull was photographed in Kranskop. (Refer to discussion on page 215.)

This butchery can be found in Victoria Road in Pietermaritzburg. (Refer to discussion on page 216.)

The male and female Wattled Starling. (Refer to discussion on page 240.)

The Cape White-eye. (Refer to discussion on page 241.)

The Capped Wheatear and Yellowthroated Longclaw. Note their similar black neck collars. (Refer to discussion on page 242.)

A Red Bishop and an insinsi seed. (Refer to discussion on page 242.)

Chapter 15

Generic names of birds

15.1 INTRODUCTION

In Chapter 14 we talked of individual ox and dog names given to individual oxen and dogs by their individual owners. Linguists and onomasticians the world over would agree that these dog and ox names are 'true names', that is, 'proper nouns' functioning as given names. The 'bird names' in this chapter, however, are not the same linguistically speaking as I am talking here about *species names*: Zulu words for particular species of birds, for example, **intengu** for the Forktailed Drongo (*Dicrurus adsimilis*) and **ubantwanyana** for the Emerald Cuckoo (*Chrysococcyx cupreus*).

The issue of species names, whether in Latin for scientists, or in English, Afrikaans, Zulu or any other language for the lay person, is a debatable one. There is a sliding scale between 'names' and 'non-names' when it comes to the naming of species, and where to draw the line between the two is a matter for the individual. For the purposes of this book, I have decided to treat Zulu words for birds as 'names', believing that they have characteristics which are in many ways similar to Zulu personal names.

15.2 BIRD NAMES AND BIRD SPECIES IN ZULU

Let us examine the relationship between Zulu name and bird species by looking at the names of doves and pigeons. Restricted as such a brief sketch undoubtedly is, I hope it will give some idea of the relationship between name and species and also provide some warning about trying to fit the Zulu system of avian nomenclature into a Euro-Western framework.

In Maclean's 1985 edition of *Roberts' Birds of Southern Africa* – abbreviated to *Roberts' Birds* in the rest of the chapter – we find 13 different species of doves and pigeons. In their order of appearance in the book, and with their reference numbers, these are as follows (note that their scientific name is given later):

> 348 Feral Pigeon; 349 Rock Pigeon; 350 Rameron Pigeon; 352 Redeyed Dove; 353 Mourning Dove; 354 Cape Turtle Dove; 355 Laughing Dove; 356 Namaqua Dove; 357 Bluespotted Dove; 358

Greenspotted Dove; 359 Tambourine Dove; 360 Cinnamon Dove; 361 Green Pigeon.

For these 13 different species of birds, there are 13 different Zulu names:

1. **ijuba**
2. **ivukuthu**
3. **ivukuthu-lehlathi**
4. **ihophe**
5. **usamdokwe**
6. **ukhonzane**
7. **unkombose**
8. **isikhombazane-senkangala**
9. **isikhombazane-sehlanze**
10. **isikhombazane-sehlathi**
11. **isibhelu**
12. **isagqukwe**
13. **ijubantondo**

One might optimistically hope that as there are 13 species of bird here and 13 Zulu names for the 13 birds, that Zulu, like scientific nomenclature, operates on a 'one bird, one name system'. That this is not so is clear from the following table:

No.	English name	Latin name	Zulu name(s)
348	Feral Pigeon	*Columba livia*	no 'African' names
349	Rock Pigeon	*Columba guinea*	**ijuba, ivukuthu**
350	Rameron Pigeon	*Columba arquatrix*	**ivukuthu-lehlathi**
352	Redeyed Dove	*Streptopelia semitorquata*	**ihophe**
353	Mourning Dove	*Streptopelia decipiens*	not found in Zulu-speaking area
354	Cape Turtle Dove	*Streptopelia capicola*	**ihophe, usamdokwe**
355	Laughing Dove	*Streptopelia senegalensis*	**ukhonzane**
356	Namaqua Dove	*Oena capensis*	**unkombose, isikhombazane-senkangala**
357	Bluespotted Dove	*Turtur afer*	not found in Zulu-speaking area
358	Greenspotted Dove (Emeraldspotted Dove)	*Turtur chalcospilos*	**isikhombazane-sehlanze**
359	Tambourine Dove	*Turtur tympanistria*	**isikhombazane-sehlathi, isibhelu**
360	Cinnamon Dove	*Aplopelia larvata*	**isagqukwe**
361	Green Pigeon	*Treron calva*	**ijubantondo**

Various conclusions can be drawn from this table. *Firstly*, three of the bird species above have no Zulu name. The Mourning Dove and the Bluespotted Dove do not have Zulu names because they do not occur in areas where Zulu is spoken; the Feral Pigeon has no Zulu name because it is a relative newcomer to KwaZulu-Natal.

Secondly, some names are used for more than one species. The name **ihophe** is used for both the Redeyed and the Cape Turtle Dove, while **isikhombazane**, although differentiated by locational epithets (see below) is used for the Namaqua, Greenspotted and Tambourine Doves.

Thirdly, a number of birds have more than one Zulu name, as is clear from the list above.

Fourthly, the distinction between 'same name' and 'different name' is blurred in the case of **ivukuthu** and **ivukuthu-lehlathi** ('forest vukuthu'), and between **isikhombazane-senkangala** ('isikhombazane of the open-plains'), **isikhombazane-sehlanze** ('bushveld khombazane') as well as **isikhombazane-sehlathi** ('forest khombazane').

The scientific names indicate strict ornithological grouping by means of the genus name and the species name. Although there are 13 different species of birds given above, there are only six genuses: *Columba, Streptopelia, Oena, Turtur, Aplopelia*, and *Treron*. The Zulu names also suggest groups of birds, with the Rock Pigeon and the Rameron Pigeon linked with the word **ivukuthu**, the Redeyed and the Cape Turtle Doves (but not the Laughing Dove) linked with the word **ihophe**, and the two *Turtur* doves (the Greenspotted and Tambourine) linked to the Namaqua Dove (not of the *Turtur* genus), with the word **isikhombazane**. The list of names given above shows that the scientific grouping and the grouping suggested by the Zulu names overlap, but do not coincide exactly.

There is an important difference between the scientific system of nomenclature and the Zulu system. In the scientific system of 'one species, one name', there is no room for extra names, and the whole point of the name is the identification of a species. In the Zulu system, there *is* room for more than one name, and names are used for more than simple identification. They can, for example, be used for praise. They can refer to different aspects of the bird: such as different names depending on whether the bird is calling or not; or whether it is perched or in flight.

Let us look at each of the dove and pigeon names given above in the light of these introductory remarks.

1. **ijuba**: Although *Roberts' Birds* only shows this name used for the Rock Pigeon, in fact **ijuba** is a general term for all doves and pigeons. Doke and Vilakazi say 'dove, pigeon, of various kinds' (1958: 364), and certainly the term will be used for all the 13 species given above, especially by a Zulu speaker not familiar with the more specific names such as **isibhelu** and **isaqukwe**.
2. **ivukuthu**: This is an onomatopoeic name for the Rock Pigeon, with its call of 'VU-ku-thu-VUU'. Zulu speakers are more likely to use this term when the bird is actually heard calling.

3. **ivukuthu-lehlathi**: Although the Rameron pigeon does not have the same call as the Rock Pigeon, its physical similarity to the Rock Pigeon leads to the use of the term **ivukuthu**, although differentiated with the locational -**lehlathi** ('of the forest') as an indication of this bird's preferred habitat.
4. **ihophe**: Doke and Vilakazi state that this word is only used for the Spurwinged Goose (1958: 345). I have found it a general term of reference to the three neck-ringed doves: the Redeyed Dove, the Cape Turtle Dove, and the Laughing Dove.
5. **usamdokwe**: This word, which refers only to the Cape Turtle Dove, is another reference to birdsong. The Cape Turtle Dove is a notorious thief of sorghum, which is used to make the porridge known as **idokwe** or **umdokwe**. When the bird calls with its characteristic 'kuk-KOORR-ku' it is popularly believed to be saying **umdokwe uvuthiwe** ('the sorghum is ripe'). The name **usamdokwe** uses the rare formative prefix **-sa-**. This name would commonly be used of the bird when it is heard calling.
6. **ukhonzane**: This word for the Laughing Dove is derived from the verb **khonza** ('pay respects to'), in reference to the head-bobbing behavioural characteristic of this bird.
7. **unkombose**: This word for the Namaqua Dove is derived from the verb **khomba** ('to point out') with the name-forming suffix **-se**. This name is reference to the belief that the straight flight of this bird to and from water points out the location of water to travellers in arid areas. It is likely that the word **isikhombazane**, used for this bird as well as the next two species, is derived from the same source. As the next two species do not 'point out' water through their direct flight (as far as I know), it must be assumed that the name **isikhombazane** is used because of the physical resemblance of the Greenspotted and Tambourine Doves to the Namaqua Dove.
8. **isikhombazane-senkangala**: The Namaqua Dove – **isikhombazane** is further qualified with the habitat reference -**senkangala** ('of the open plains').
9. **isikhombazane-sehlanze**: The Greenspotted Dove – **isikhombazane** is qualified with -**sehlanze** ('of the bushveld').
10. **isikhombazane-sehlathi**: The Tambourine Dove – **isikhombazane** is qualified with -**sehlathi** ('of the forest').
11. **isibhelu**: Another name for the Tambourine Dove – the word is possibly derived from the ideophone **bhelu** ('of flicking up quickly exposing an inner portion'). Cf. another meaning of the word: 'tail of a buck or goat'.
12. **isagqukwe**: This word for the Cinnamon Dove has no clear derivation.
13. **ijubantondo**: This word for the Green Pigeon compounds the general term for dove or pigeon with the word **intondo** ('immense quantity'). I can only guess that in earlier times the Green Pigeon was found in immense flocks.

> **-azane** (as in the name **isikhombazane-senkangala**) is strictly speaking a combination of the augmentative and feminine suffix **-azi** and the diminutive **-ana**. It is found both as **-azana** and **-azane**, and with neither augmentative or diminutive meaning, suggesting that this combination has lost its full semantic value, and has simply become a meaningless suffix used in the formation of new nouns, many of which refer to zoological and botanical species.

It can be seen that in addition to general terms such as **ijuba** and **ihophe**, the Zulu bird names also make references to song, to habitat, and to behaviour. This aspect of bird-naming forms a major part of this chapter.

15.3 STRUCTURE OF BIRD NAMES

Bird names may be divided into three groups according to their structure: simple-stemmed nouns, complex-stemmed nouns, and nouns with compound stems.

15.3.1 Simple-stemmed names

All Zulu nouns can be divided into prefix and stem. Simple-stemmed nouns are those with a stem which cannot be further subdivided into meaningful parts. Let us take the two nouns **intengu** ('Forktailed Drongo') and **iqola** ('Fiscal Shrike'). Once the class 9 prefix **in-** is divided from the stem **-tengu** and the class 5 prefix **i-** is taken from the stem **-qola**, we are left with two units which cannot be further broken into anything meaningful. Certainly, we can divide **-qola** into the two syllables 'qo' and 'la' but neither of these have meaning on their own. Similarly, we can divide **-tengu** into the five phonemes /t/, /e/, /n/, /g/ and /u/, but none of these have any separate meaning.

We should note, however, that a number of bird names with simple stems are derived from ideophones. As a result, they do have an underlying meaning. For those not familiar with Zulu word classes, the ideophone perhaps needs a brief explanation. The English language has onomatopoeic words such as 'bang!', 'splash!' and 'whizzz!' which dramatise statements by imitating sounds. Zulu has similar onomatopoeic words, such as **phoqo!** ('snap!') and **nqo! nqo!** ('knock knock!'), but also words which refer to qualities such as texture, temperature, colour, smell, and movement. These words are known as ideophones. There are ideophones for different ways of walking, of striking, and of sitting down. There are ideophones for fullness and emptiness, for beginning and ending, and for eating and drinking (the ideophone **klamu** dramatises the eating of crisp fruit or vegetables, while **gimbilikiqi** suggests the gulping down of something oily). There is even an ideophone for silence – **du!** – which is used in the following way: **abantwana bathulile bathi du!** ('the children are quiet and go "du"', that is, 'they are dead-quiet').

Many of the bird names given under 'Song' and 'Habits' below are derived from ideophones of sound and movement.

15.3.2 Complex-stemmed names

Names with complex stems are those that can be broken down into smaller parts. Of the various parts into which a complex stem can be broken, only one has a lexical or dictionary meaning. For example, once we have taken the class 3a prefix **u-** from **ubantwanyana** ('Emerald Cuckoo'), we are left with the stem **-bantwanyana** which can be subdivided into **-(a)ba-** (class 2 noun prefix) + **-ntu-** (noun stem: 'person', 'people') + **-ana-** (diminutive) + **-ana** (diminutive). (When **-ana-** is duplicated to form a double diminutive, **-ana-** + **-ana-** becomes **-anyana**.) Of these four parts, **-ba-**, **-ana-**, and **-ana** are grammatical morphemes, while **-ntu-** is a lexical morpheme, that is to say, it carries the 'dictionary meaning' of 'person' (literally, the whole name means 'very little children bird'). In the noun **umehlwana** ('Cape White-eye'), there is a similar breakdown: **u-** (class 1a prefix) + **-(a)me-** (class 6 prefix) + **-hlo-** (noun stem: 'eye') + **-ana** (diminutive). Of these parts, only **-hlo-** has a lexical or dictionary meaning, and the whole word means 'little bird with (distinctive) eyes'.

> The class 6 prefix is normally **ama-**, as in **amadoda** ('men'), and **amandla** ('strength'). Only in the two words **amehlo** ('eyes') and **ameva** ('thorns') does this prefix become **ame-**.

15.3.3 Compound-stemmed names

Names with compound stems are those in which the stem can be broken down into a number of parts, at least two of which have dictionary, or lexical, meaning. Let us look at the word **isithandamanzi** ('Woollynecked Stork'). If we remove the class 7 prefix **isi-**, we are left with the stem **-thandamanzi** which can be divided into the verb **thanda** ('to like') and the noun **amanzi** ('water'), telling us that this is a bird which likes water. Both **thanda** and **amanzi** are complete and meaningful words that can be found in a Zulu dictionary.

The word **ukhozilwentshebe** ('Lammergeier', 'Bearded Vulture') consists of the two halves **ukhozi** ('eagle') and **lwentshebe** (**lwa**, 'of', + **intshebe**, 'beard'), telling us that this is a large raptor with a characteristic beard-tuft. Both **ukhozi** and **intshebe** are dictionary words.

15.4 RELATIONSHIP BETWEEN STRUCTURE AND MEANING

Most nouns with a simple stem have only a single meaning, and that is the living or 'real-world' entity to which they refer. A noun such as **iqola** ('Fiscal Shrike') has only one meaning, and that is 'Fiscal Shrike'. Let us put it another way: the meaning of the Zulu word **iqola** is 'any member of the bird species known as **iqola** in Zulu, Fiscal Shrike in English, and *Lannius collaris* in Latin'. There is no 'extra' or 'underlying meaning'. By contrast, names with a complex or a compound stem *do* have extra or underlying meaning. The dictionary meaning of the word **umehlwana** is 'any member of the bird species known as **umehlwana** in Zulu, Cape White-eye in English and *Zosterops pallidus* in Latin'. There is also, as we have seen, an underlying or extra meaning which is 'little bird with dramatic eyes'. The dictionary meaning of the noun **isithandamanzi** is 'any member of the bird species known as **isithandamanzi** in Zulu, Woollynecked Stork in English and *Ciconia episcopus* in Latin'. There is also, as we saw above, the extra or underlying meaning 'bird that likes water'.

Linguists and onomasticians sometimes use the terms 'denotative meaning' and 'connotative meaning'. The 'denotative meaning' identifies, points outs, singles out one thing from another. The denotative meaning of the word **isithandamanzi** identifies this bird as the species *Ciconia episcopus* and singles it out from all the other species of birds in the world.

The 'connotative meaning' implies or suggests associated ideas or information relating to that species, for example, that it likes water (in the case of **isithandamanzi**), or that it is small with dramatic eyes (in the case of **umehlwana**).

We saw examples of these underlying meanings in the list of names for doves and pigeons given above. The dictionary meaning of the word **ivukuthu** is 'Rock Pigeon', but the underlying meaning is 'bird that makes a sound like VU-KU-THU'; the dictionary meaning of **isibhelu** is 'Cinnamon Dove', but the underlying meaning is 'bird that flicks up its tail or feathers'.

Some examples of single-stemmed bird names with no underlying meaning are:

intengu	Forktailed Drongo	*Dicrurus adsimilis*
ifuba	White Pelican	*Pelecanus onocrotalus*
	Pinkbacked Pelican	*Pelecanus rufescens*
ibhoyi	Croaking Cisticola	*Cisticola natalensis*
indlazi	Speckled Mousebird	*Colius striatus*
ihoye	Spurwinged Goose	*Plectropterus gambensis*
uqaqashe	Flappet Lark	*Mirafra rufocinnamomea*
umntoli	Redcapped Lark (Short-toed Lark)	*Calandrella cinerea*
isichegu	Stonechat	*Saxicola torquata*
ufukwe	Burchell's Coucal	*Centropus superciliosus*

Some single-stemmed names have no underlying meanings which refer specifically to the birds, but have associated meanings which are of interest. For example, the single-stemmed word **iphothwe** ('Blackeyed Bulbul', *Pyconotus barbatus*) has the associated meaning 'chatterbox', a nickname for a person clearly based on the chattering habits of this bulbul. Note that 'chatterbox' is not an *underlying* meaning of the word **iphothwe**; it is an associated meaning derived from the primary meaning 'Blackeyed Bulbul'.

The bird name **iqola** ('Fiscal Shrike') has two associated meanings:

- 'black beast with white markings across the back and the side', that is, the same markings as the Fiscal Shrike has; and
- '(mod) ruffian, burglar, pickpocket', a reference to the aggressively predatory habits of this bird.

> For an exhaustive and erudite analysis of how several cattle colour terms are derived from features of the natural world such as shadows on water, the mottling of a bird's egg or, as in the above case, the markings of a bird's plumage, see Marguerite Oosthuizen (née Poland) (1995).

In similar fashion, the word **ukhozi**, with its primary meaning of Black Eagle (*Aquila verreauxii*), gives rise to the associated meanings 'black beast with white marks on belly and speckling on forehead' and 'violent passionate man'.

Sometimes these associated meanings seem rather to cast aspersions on avian character. For example, the word **uklebe** (sometimes **iklebe**) which is used for a variety of medium-sized raptors such as the Lizard Buzzard, has the associated meaning 'immoral person, person of no character', and **isihuhwa**, with the primary meanings 'Martial Eagle' and 'Crowned Eagle', has the secondary meaning 'rapacious person'.

Sometimes the other meanings of bird names appear to have no relationship to the bird itself. Why, for example, should **ilongwe** ('Egyptian Goose') also mean 'dry cake of cattle-dung (as used for fuel)'? And what does **umvemve** ('any of various species of Wagtail') have to do with 'young, feeble calf'? And, most intriguing of all, why should the word **isikhova**, which is a generic term for 'owl', also be used to refer to a banknote, especially a £1 note? (Doke & Vilakazi, 1958: 406). And **isikhova esiluhlaza** ('green/blue owl') refers to a five-pound note.

15.5 UNDERLYING MEANINGS OF COMPLEX- AND COMPOUND-STEMMED NAMES

The word **impofazana** ('Wattled Starling') is a complex-stemmed word based on the relative stem **-mpofu** ('tawny-coloured') to which **-azana** (see page 237 above) has been suffixed. The meaning 'somewhat tawny-coloured' must refer to the female, for the male Wattled Starling is a striking black-and-white, with a bright yellow head (see the illustrations on page 231). The underlying meaning here refers to *appearance*.

Ihlalankomo is a compound noun, consisting of the verb **hlala** ('sit', 'be seated') and the noun **inkomo** ('beast', 'head of cattle'). The word refers to both the Yellowbilled and the Redbilled Oxpeckers, and the name refers to the birds' *habit* of sitting on the back of cattle and other large mammals to feed on ticks.

The Bleating Warbler has two Zulu names: **imbuzana** (**imbuzi**, 'goat', + **-ana**, 'little') and **imbuzi-yehlathi** (**imbuzi** + **yehlathi**, 'of the forest'). *Roberts' Birds* says 'alarm note like small bleating lamb'. Zulu, English and Afrikaans names coincide in their reference to this call, with Zulu using a goat metaphor in both names, English describing the call as 'bleating', and Afrikaans using onomatopoeia in *Kwê-kwê-voël*. The underlying meanings of Zulu **imbuzana** and **imbuzi-yehlathi** refer to *birdsong*.

For a discussion on the use of description, metaphor and onomatopoeia in English, Afrikaans and Zulu bird names, see Koopman (1990).

Ikhwelematsheni is a compound noun consisting of the verb **khwela** ('climb up on') and **ematsheni** ('on the rocks'). This Zulu name for the Cape Rock Thrush is a reference to its preferred *habitat*, and the same reference is found in the alternative name **isihlalamatsheni** ('that which lives amongst rocks') as well as in the scientific name *Monticola* ('inhabitant of rocks').

The African Spoonbill has the Zulu name **isixulamasele**, a compound based on the verb **xula** ('seize up', 'grab at', 'take unawares') and the noun **amasele** ('frogs'). This name is a perfect description of the *habits and diet* of this stork-like bird.

These five birds have been chosen because their Zulu names reflect the range of underlying meanings that we find in Zulu bird names: appearance, birdsong, habits, and habitat. The following sections will enlarge on each of these subcategories of underlying meanings.

15.5.1 Appearance: Size, shape, colour, plumage, etc.

a. Specific features

Some bird names with an underlying meaning which refers to appearance draw attention to a particular detail, such as ear-tufts or specific markings. The Bearded Vulture, for example, with its characteristic chin-tuft, has the name **ukhozilwentshebe** ('eagle of the beard'), while the Cape Eagle Owl is named **isikhovampondo** ('owl with horns') in reference to the large tufts on the ears.

The two species of White-eye in South Africa (the Cape White-eye and the Yellow White-eye) share the name **umehlwane**, which, as we saw above, means 'little bird with striking eyes'. These two birds share another name which draws attention to the eyes, the name **umbhicini**, derived from the locative form of **izimbici** ('oozings from the eyes') (see the illustration on page 231).

The entry **unokilonki** which can be found in *Roberts' Birds*, for the Grey Heron and the Blackheaded Heron, is a puzzling one. This word is surely a corruption of **ugilonci**, a name which Doke and Vilakazi give for the 'Blue

Heron'. The word **ugilonci** appears to be a compound of **igilo** ('throat', 'pelican's pouch') + **nci** ('small'), in other words, a reference to the extreme narrowness of the heron's neck in comparison to its length.

The word **isangwili**, a name for the Capped Wheatear, is derived from the prefix **sa-** ('something like') and the noun **igwili** (Yellowthroated Longclaw). The underlying meaning of **isangwili** is thus 'something like a Yellowthroated Longclaw', and indeed both birds have big black neck collars, as can be seen in the illustrations on page 232.

b. Colour

Other bird names make reference to the colour of the bird. The Orange-breasted and the Greyheaded Bushshrikes, both of which have solid green backs, share the name **uhlaza** ('green'). To the same stem (**-hlaza**), **-azane** is suffixed (see discussion on page 237), to make the name **uhlazazane** ('green and small'), a reference to both the colour and the size of the Malachite Sunbird.

One of the names of the Fiscal Shrike is **ilunga**, derived from the adjective stem -**lunga** ('black or brown with white stripes').

The Red Bishop has two names, both of which make reference to its striking red plumage. The name **ibomvana** is simply a combination of the adjective -**bomvu** ('red') and the diminutive **-ana**, the whole name meaning that this is a small, red bird. The other term, **intakansinsi**, employs a clever metaphor: **intaka**, the word for any small finch-like bird, is compounded with **insinsi**, the black-and-red seed of the **umsinsi** tree (*Erythrina sp*). The image is a striking one, as can be seen from the illustrations on page 232.

The diminutive suffix **-ana** can also be used for colours where its meaning corresponds to English 'slightly' or '-ish', as in 'slightly red' or 'reddish'. Context must dictate whether the **-ana** in a bird's name is being used for this purpose, or to indicate size of the bird. **Ibomvana** could be a small red bird, or a bird which is reddish/pinkish in colour. In the particular case above – seeing that the Red Bishop is both a very small bird and a bright red – the diminutive suffix refers to the size of the bird.

c. Size

The words **incuncu** and **incwincwi** are both derived from the adjective stem **-ncu** ('tiny, very small'), and these names are used for the Malachite Sunbird, the Lesser Doublecollared Sunbird and the Greater Doublecollared Sunbird, all very small birds.

The word **indibilitshe**, a name for the Longbilled Crombec, another very small bird, is a puzzling one. It appears to be a metaphor based on the word **indibilishi** ('small coin'). The problem with this is that the word **indibilishi** is an adoptive (or 'loan word') from the Dutch *dubbeltje*. This means that if my interpretation is correct, the bird can only have got its name after Dutch-speaking settlers had arrived in KwaZulu-Natal, unless the word **indibilitshe** *replaced* an earlier word, as the word **ikati** ('cat' < Dutch *kat*) has replaced the earlier indigenous word **umangobe**.

15.5.2 Song

Bird names with an underlying meaning which refers to the bird's song or call are numerous. Two common techniques of song-reference are onomatopoeia and metaphor. In onomatopoeic names, the word is an imitation of the bird's call, as we have already seen with the Rock Pigeon, where the name **ivukuthu** imitates the call 'VU-KU-TU . . . VUUUU'. In metaphorical names, a comparison is made between the call of the bird and some other, well-known sound, as in the example **imbuzana** ('little goat') for the Bleating Warbler's goat-like 'mehhhh . . . mehhhh' call.

Metaphor, onomatopoeia, and other song-reference techniques are mixed up in the following examples.

The Croaking Cisticola (Zulu **ibhoyi**) and the Yellowthroated Longclaw (Zulu **igwili**) both have names derived from ideophones. Doke and Vilakazi give the ideophone **bhoyi** as 'of the sound of the bush-warbler' and the ideophone **gwili** as 'of undulating sounds'. Under the entry of the ideophone **gwili**, Doke and Vilikazi give a sentence which brings both birds and both sounds together: '**ibhoyi litshiloza izwi lithi gwiligwili**' ('the bush-warbler sings with sweeping notes undulating its voice').

The ideophone **gwa** ('of cawing') is the basis of **igwababa** (Pied Crow), and the ideophone **hloko** ('of noise') underlies the name **ihlokohloko**, a name used for the noisy Spottedback, Masked, and Golden Weavers. (In a personal communication to me, Anthony Davey makes the interesting suggestion that as these various weavers all have distinctively marked heads, the name **ihlokohloko** could be derived from the noun **inhloko** ['head']). Another ideophone referring to great noise is **gede** ('of loud speaking', 'of incessant noise') and this has given rise to the name **ingede**, used both for the Honeyguide and the Redbilled Woodhoopoe. The Honeyguide is also known as **inhlava** and **inhlavebizelayo** ('the **inhlava** that calls').

The Redbilled Woodhoopoe, though, is more well known by the name **inhlekabafazi** ('the laughter of women'), a metaphorical name for the cackling laughter that goes with the characteristic bobbing and swaying of these birds as they descend on a tree to probe for insects. Another laughing bird is the Arrowmarked Babbler, which has the Zulu name **ihlekehle**, a compound of the verbs **hleka** ('laugh') and **ehla** ('descend'). The name literally means 'it laughs as it alights'.

From laughing to crying. The Trumpeter Hornbill has an eerie wailing call which can easily be interpreted as the sulky cry of a demanding child, expressed in the name **ikhunatha**, which is from the verb **khunatha** ('be moody, sulky').

The following five birds have onomatopoeic names. Those who are familiar with the birds will probably recognise their call in the names. The Gorgeous Bushshrike has the Zulu name **ingongoni**, as well as the Afrikaans name *Konkoit*, which is also onomatopoeic. The Grey Lourie has its call echoed in the English folk-name 'Go-Awaaay Bird', in the Afrikaans name *Kwêvoël*, as well as in the Zulu **umklewu**, with variants **ikluwe** and **umkliwu**. The booming call of the Ground Hornbill is reflected in **ingududu**, and the harsh, strident, nasal call of the Hadedah Ibis in **inkankane** (and perhaps more so in Xhosa **ihahane**). Zulu **iwili**, a name for the Sombre Bulbul, has its counterpart in the Afrikaans *Gewone* ('common') *Willie*. In *Roberts' Birds* this call is 'verbalised' as 'Willy, come and have a fight, sca-a-a-ared' (1985: 501).

Many Zulu bird calls have been turned into Zulu phrases, and the call of the Emerald Cuckoo is popularly verbalised as '**Bantwanyana ningendi**' ('children don't get married'), leading to the bird name **uBantwanyana.**

Metaphor is the basis of the Zulu name of Burchell's Coucal, perhaps better known as the 'rain-bird' (and also well-known in KwaZulu-Natal by its other Zulu name **ufukwe**). The liquid gurgling of this bird's song, of which Maclean says 'song likened to water burbling out of narrow-necked bottle' is reflected in **umgugwane**, a diminutive form of **umgugu** ('strong rush of water, torrent').

Back to ideophones again, and we have **umhlohlolongwane**, the name for the Natal Nightjar, a word derived from the ideophone **hlo** ('of sound dying away into the distance'). A similar underlying meaning can be found in **umndweza**. This is a name used for both the Goldenbreasted and the Cape Buntings, derived from the verb **ndweza** ('sound faintly in the distance'). The Jacobin Cuckoo (**inkanku**) takes its name from the ideophone **khanku** ('of scolding'), and the Kurrichane Thrush, Olive Thrush, and Spotted Thrush all get the name **umunswi** from the ideophone **nswi**, an extremely versatile word which refers to squeaking, squealing, shrill-voiced, sizzling, moaning and whining noises.

The monotonous, non-stop clinking noise of the Tinker Barbet is referred to in **unogandilanga** ('what pounds away the whole day long').

Song reference may be used as an addition to a general term in order to indicate a particular species. The word **ihhoye** simply means 'plover', without any indication of which species of plover. When this is prefixed with **-titi-** to give **ititihoye**, then this refers specifically to the Blackwinged Plover, with its call *titi-reee* or *titi-tireee* (Maclean, 1985: 230).

15.5.3 Habits

Many bird names in this section refer to characteristic and habitual movements, and are derived from ideophones of movement. The following are examples.

The male Longtailed Widow (**ibhaku**), with its 'slow display flight' with 'wings flapping slowly and erratically' (Maclean, 1985: 742) takes its name from the ideophone **bhaku** ('of flapping, fluttering'). The name for the Yellow-throated Longclaw (**igwili**) comes from the ideophone **gwili**, which in addition to meaning 'of undulating sounds', as mentioned above, also means 'of bobbing up and down, as when hiding in grass'.

On page 236 above, we saw the name **isibhelu** for the Tambourine Dove, from the ideophone **bhelu** ('of flicking up and exposing underside'), while the ideophone **gaga** ('of moving backwards and forwards') forms the base of the name **ugaga** (Cape Robin); although Anthony Davey (pers. comm.) suggests a derivation from the noun **isigaga** ('person with well-developed chest').

The name **isizinzi**, used for both Baillon's Crake and the African Rail, may well come from the ideophone **zinzi** ('of settling down', 'squatting down') in reference to the habit of these birds of hiding in long marsh grass. A clear derivation from an ideophone is seen in **uheshe**, used for both the Peregrine and the Lanner Falcon, from the ideophone **heshe** ('of swooping onto, of snatching in flight'). The upright tail of the three wagtails that occur in the Zulu-speaking area (African Pied, Longtailed and Cape Wagtails) gives rise to the name **umvemve**, from the ideophone **vemvene** ('of standing straight up'). Also derived from an ideophone is **unomtsheketshe** (Honeyguide), from **tsheke** ('of quivering, moving from side to side').

Three pipits (Richard's Pipit, the Longbilled Pipit, and the Plainbacked Pipit) share the three variations **umngcelekeshu/umcelekeshu/umngcelu**, all of which are derived from the verb **ngcelekeshela** ('dart across', 'dart out into the open'), while three quail species (the Common Quail, Harlequin Quail, and the Blackrumped Buttonquail), far from darting out into the open, characteristically lie low in hiding when threatened, hence their shared name **isigwaca**, from the verb **gwaca** ('lie flat, lie low in hiding').

From its habit of following cattle to feed on disturbed insects, the Cattle Egret gets the name **umlindankomo** ('what waits for the cattle'), as well as the name **ilanda** (from the verb **landa**, 'to follow'). This latter name is shared by the Great White Egret. The Brownhooded Kingfisher has a habit of sitting motionlessly on a perch for a long time, and has the name **indwazela**, from the verb **ndwaza** ('loiter, dilly-dally').

The African Jacana's long strides over floating plants have earned it the Zulu name of **unondwayiza**, a name which is derived from the verb **dwayiza** ('walk with long strides'). Another water-bird is the Goliath Heron, which characteristically stalks its food in the shallow waters of pans, often in the company of young basking crocodiles, a habit which has given rise to the name **unozalizingwenyana** ('that which gives birth to little crocodiles').

The Rufousnaped Lark, which according to *Roberts' Birds* 'runs mouselike in crouched posture between grass tufts' (434), has the Zulu name **ungqangendlela** ('what goes straight along the path').

The Redbilled Woodhoopoe, in addition to the name which refers to the 'laughter of women' (see above), also has the name **unukani** ('what do you smell of?'). In the 1978 edition of *Roberts' Birds*, McLachlan and Liversidge remark, 'specimens held in the hand smell most disagreeable' (299).

Uthimbakazane is a name for the White Helmetshrike, and it is derived from the noun **uthimba** ('bridal party'), to which **-kazane**, a variant of **-azane** (see discussion on page 237), has been added. This name refers to the fact that these birds are always gregarious in laughing chattering groups.

Woodpeckers in general are known in Zulu as **isiqhophamuthi**, a compound of **qhopha** ('to tap') and **umuthi** ('tree'). The Goldentailed Woodpecker is also known as **usibagwebe** (literally, 'we prod them'), in reference to the same habit of tapping and prodding at trees to find food.

A more direct reference to food, and the naming of food species, is found in the names of the African Spoonbill (**isixulamasele**) and the White Stork (**unogolantethe**). **Isixulamasele**, as already noted above, is a compound derived from the verb **xula** ('seize up', 'snatch up') and the noun **amasele** ('frogs'). The verb on its own is found in the name **isixula** (Pied Kingfisher and Halfcollared Kingfisher).

The name **unogolantethe** (White Stork) compounds the verb **gola** ('catch by quickly covering with paw or hand, swoop over using beak or talons') with **intethe** ('locust, grasshopper').

15.5.4 Habitat

This subcategory of bird names can be divided between those that refer to rocky, mountainous habitats, and those that refer to water habitats: marshes, rivers, lagoons and pans.

Inkolotsheni is the Zulu name of the Buffstreaked Chat, and it is derived from the noun **inkolo** ('hollow place in tree or stone') + **etsheni** ('on, in the stone'). According to *Roberts' Birds*, it is found on rocky slopes of hills, and nests under rock, or in a hole in a rock or a wall. A similar underlying meaning is found in **intunjana** (White-eared Barbet), a diminutive form of **intunja** ('hole', 'tunnel'). Maclean tells us that this bird 'roosts communally in nest holes at night' (1985: 406).

The Cape Rock Thrush has two Zulu names: **isihlalamatsheni** ('that which lives among rocks') and **isikhweletsheni** ('that which climbs on rocks'). This name could be seen as a combination of habit and habitat.

The Woollynecked Stork, with a habitat described as 'rivers, pans, swamps, flood-plains, dams, lagoons [and] tidal mudflats' (*Roberts' Birds*, 65) understandably has the name **isithandamanzi** ('that which likes water').

One of the names for both the White Pelican and the Pinkbacked Pelican is the word **ivubu**. There is a strong possibility that this word is derived from

imvubu ('hippopotamus') on the same lines as the tree name **umvubu** (*Ficus trichopoda*, Swamp Fig/Hippo Fig) of which Pooley says: 'First described by the Rev. J. Gerstner, missionary/botanist from Zululand, who named it after the hippo whose distribution more or less followed that of the tree. Both animal and tree have the same Zulu name' (1993: 72).

It is not quite clear from Pooley whether Gerstner gave the tree its English name 'Hippo Fig' or its Zulu name **'umvubu'**, but we should assume that the Zulu name was already in existence, and that Gerstner gave the name 'Hippo Fig'. If the class 9 noun **imvubu** ('hippopotamus') has already been copied to another noun class (class 3 **umvubu**) to refer to a *tree* that occurs in the same habitat as a hippopotamus, then there is no reason why the same noun should not be copied to yet another noun class (class 5 **ivubu**) in order to refer to a *bird* that occurs in the same habitat.

15.5.5 Miscellaneous

The underlying meanings of a few bird names show a link between bird, weather and season. The calls of many birds are believed to predict rain, and this belief is shown in the underlying meanings of names such as **ihlolamvula** (used for both the European Swift as well as the Rock Martin), derived from **hlola** ('predict', 'warn of') + **imvula** ('rain'). In the case of the Spotted Dikkop, this bird does not *predict* weather, but rather *causes it*, according to the name **umbangaqhwa** ('causer of frost').

It is not just in Zulu society but all over the world that different birds are believed to predict rain. See the chapters 'The Rain-Goose' and 'The Bird of Doom and Deluge' and 'The Thunderbird' in Armstrong (1958).

The Redchested Cuckoo, with the onomatopoeic Afrikaans name *Piet-my-vrou*, is **uphezukomkhono** in Zulu, literally 'on top of the arm'. The call of this bird in spring marks the beginning of the ploughing seasons, when it is time for the field workers to put their hoes on top of their arms (shoulder?) and go to the fields. Slightly later in the year, an expression is used which refers to another species of cuckoo – the Jacobin Cuckoo (**inkanku**): **'inkanku isiwathathe amacimbi'** ('the Cuckoo has already taken the caterpillars'), in other words 'It is now early October'.

Some bird names have a perfectly clear underlying meaning, but how to relate that meaning to the bird is a puzzle. For example, the Jacobin Cuckoo has the name **undodosibona** (literally, 'the man who sees us'). What does this refer to? Perhaps it means the Jacobin Cuckoo is a bird which hides in leafy foliage looking out at possible threats, but keeping itself hidden. And what about **inhlunuyamanzi**? This name, shared by the Malachite Kingfisher and the Pygmy Kingfisher, literally means 'vagina of the water'. Why?

The name of the male Wood Owl is **umabhengwane**, a word that has no clear derivation or underlying meaning. But the name of the female of the species – **unobathekeli** – is perfectly clear: it is derived from **abathekeli**, which means 'those who solicit food from friends in times of trouble'. What is it about the female of the Wood Owl that leads to it being given this name?

And finally, a delightful image using the name **igwalagwala** (shared by the Purplecrested Lourie and the Knysna Lourie). The expression **ukumthwesa igwalagwala** (literally, 'to make him carry a lourie feather') can be used to describe striking someone a serious blow on the head, so as to draw blood. The victim's head will then look as if it is decorated with the red feather of a lourie, which is commonly worn as a hair ornament.

Chapter 16

Names of months and days

> **uTyelabani/uTyenabani** (who-do-you-tell?) *The Moon of Plenty, When People Get Drunk and the Food Over the Fires is Neglected and Gets Burnt, and No One Cares* (derived from 'Whom-do-you-tell [that the food is burning]?') – one of the 'Mkhuze Variations' of Zulu month names, from Faye (1923: 54–56).

16.1 INTRODUCTION

This chapter is about naming *time* and mostly deals with the Zulu names of lunar months. We go on to the names of the days of the week, and then names and praise names for various times of day. To complete the circle, the chapter returns to the lunar aspects of the months (or moons) and looks briefly at the Zulu names of other heavenly bodies.

Before going any further, here are some thoughts from one of the sources consulted, Carl Faye:

> The picturesque old Zulu way of referring to Lunar months by their Zulu names is in imminent danger of dying out. These names describe to a nicety the most noticeable manifestations in Nature during the reign of the particular moon named, but nowadays, through the white man's influence, Natives are getting out of the way of using these names, particularly the school-going generation, and use instead, in more or less Zuluised forms, the current English names. In this way the use of the names of our **calendar** months is in the ascendancy, and Zulu names of **lunar** months are falling into disuse.
>
> . . .
>
> It is not advisable, when interpreting, to give the name of an English calendar month as the equivalent of a Zulu lunar month; the two do not begin together, nor do they end together, and besides the Zulu name is expressive in a way peculiar all to itself (1923: 52).

There are two points worth commenting on here. *Firstly*, close on 80 years after Faye wrote the above, stating that the Zulu lunar months were falling into disuse, there is an apparent attempt to revive the use of these names. The Zulu newspaper *iLanga laseNatali* (literally, 'the Natal Sun') is now using Zulu lunar month names together with Euro-Western calendar month names. In doing so, it both reduces the variety of names for each month (see Section 16.2) to one name per month, and also links a specific Zulu lunar month to each month in the Western calendar (M.A. Hlengwa, pers. comm.).

Secondly, Faye's point about not linking Zulu lunar months to Western calendar months is worth noting. The Zulu lunar month begins with a new moon, no matter what time of the Western calendar month this starts. Zulu months are therefore all exactly 28 days long, and consequently there are 13 such months in the year, with one day left over (13 x 28 = 364 days). Faye has not tried to link his lunar months to any part of the Western calendar; other writers use phrases such as 'starts with the new moon in July', 'starts roughly towards the end of August', or 'between September and October'. I am led to believe that the *iLanga laseNatali* has 'overcome' this problem, not only by linking each Zulu lunar month exactly to a month from the Western calendar, but by arbitrarily 'scrapping' the thirteenth month of the Zulu year (M.A. Hlengwa, pers. comm.).

> Samuelson tells us that a 30-day month was known as **inyanga ka Hulumende** ('a Government month'), and a 31-day month as **inyanga yombhanso** ('a bonus month') (1923: 576).

16.2 THE NAMES OF THE ZULU LUNAR MONTHS

Let us take the Zulu lunar months one by one. The Zulu year begins in late July, for reasons explained by one of James Stuart's sources:

> There always existed something of a dispute in regard to when exactly the old year had come to an end and the new begun. According to Mkando, the deciding point was the appearance of the *isilimela* [that is, a constellation which I see Colenso calls the Pleiades].
>
> . . .
>
> The appearance on the horizon of the very first star of the group that make up the Pleiades (the star being called *uCwazibe*) would be taken to be the actual beginning of the new year, but there would always be dispute as to whether the star some pointed out as one of the Pleiades was in fact such, and this dispute would go on until the greater part of the group had come into view and so made all further disagreement impossible (Webb & Wright, III: 167).

The following sources have been consulted for the Zulu names of lunar months: Bryant (1967); Doke and Vilakazi (1958); Faye (1923); Samuelson (1923, 1929); and Webb and Wright (I, II, III, IV).

16.2.1 The first month: uNcwaba

UNcwaba, the first month of the Zulu year, begins with the new moon in July. The name is derived from the stem **-ncwaba** ('glossy, fresh, clean, attractive'). Samuelson says 'so called because it is then when vegetation begins to shoot out and become **ncwaba**, green' (1923: 576), but I find this a misleading statement, as it suggests natural spring growth, for a month which is still mid-winter. Doke and Vilakazi provide the more likely explanation of 'when the first grass appears after veld-burning' (1958: 535), echoed in Bryant's 'the new-grass moon' (1967: 254). The dry veld grass is indeed burnt in mid-winter to bring on new grazing. Faye tells us that this is the 'Moon When the Land's Taken on a Rich, Dark Green Hue' (1923: 53).

Doke and Vilakazi offer the alternative form **uNcwabakazi** (< **ncwaba** with the intensifying suffix **-kazi**, that is, 'the very new & green month'), as well as the alternative name **uNhloyile** ('Yellow-billed Kite'), as this much-loved bird, which is a seasonal migrator, returns to KwaZulu-Natal in July (1958: 535). Faye also recognises this name: '**uNtloyile**. *Lapo kusuk' untloyile es'ehwit' udumbha.* (The Moon) When the uNtloyile (Yellow Billed Kite) Snatches the Udumba, a small black bean' (1923: 54).

16.2.2 The second month: uMandulo

There is general agreement that this month, which begins with the new moon in August, was originally called **uMpandu** (< **phanda**, 'dig up', a reference to the preparation of gardens for planting), but that this was changed out of *hlonipha* avoidance of the name of King **Mpande**. The name was changed to the semantically similar **uMandulo** (< **andula**, 'to commence cultivation'). Bryant calls this the 'First-Fields Moon' (1967: 254), and Faye says it is the 'Moon of the Stinging Hot Sun, When Hoeing is Begun in the Fields' (1923: 53).

Doke and Vilakazi are again the only source to offer an alternative name in '**iSokanqangi** (literally, "the first lover": second month of the Zulu lunar calendar [cf. **uMandulo**])' (1958: 763). The relevance of this alternative name is not explained, and no other source mentions it.

16.2.3 The third month: uMfumfu

The lunar month **uMfumfu** begins with the new moon in September. There is general agreement on this name, and its derivation from the ideophone **-mfumfu** ('of coming out, of emerging'). Samuelson comments that **uMfumfu** 'refers to the hidden flower of the grasses, which were preparing to peep out of their sheaths' (1929: 305). Bryant calls this the 'Sprouting Moon' (1967: 254), and Faye 'A Summer Moon, When the Growing Mealies and Mabele are Beginning to Rise' (1923: 53).

Doke and Vilakazi are the only ones to offer an alternative, and this – **uNkanku** – is derived from **inkanku**, the migrant Jacobin Cuckoo which arrives in KwaZulu-Natal between September and October and departs in April. Doke and Vilakazi also give us the expression '**Inkanku isiwathathe amacimbi**' ('the Jacobin Cuckoo has already taken the caterpillars', that is, 'it is now early October') (1958: 381).

16.2.4 The fourth month: uLwezi

The month of **uLwezi** starts with the new moon in October. The name is derived from the noun **ulwezi**, which refers to a species of insect which clusters on tree branches and exudes a frothy liquid which drips down onto passers-by. Doke and Vilakazi call these 'spitting bugs', while Bryant refers to this month as the 'Frog-hopper Moon'. Skaife states:

> Small, spittle-like masses of white foam, or 'cucko-spit', may often be seen on the twigs and leaves of different plants. These shelter the immature plant bugs known as froghoppers, thus named because the adult is shaped rather like a tiny frog and can leap well. Sometimes called spittle bugs, these insects belong to the family Cercopidae.
> . . .
> The frog hopper feeds on the sap of the plant. This is a weak solution of sugars and salts and the insect has to imbibe a great deal in order to obtain sufficient nourishment; its watery excretion, therefore, is copious (1979: 87).

Faye does not recognise the name **uLwezi**, and Bryant says that **uLwezi** is an alternative name for **uZibandlela** (see Section 16.2.5).

16.2.5 The fifth month: uZibandlela

This month begins with the new moon in November, and the name is a compound of the verb **ziba** ('pretend, feign, deceive, mislead') and the noun **indlela** ('path, pathway'). Doke and Vilakazi translate the name as 'what pretends there's no road' (1958: 891), Samuelson says 'Zibandhlela refers to the covering over, at this time of year, of roads by grasses and weeds, and comes from Ziba, "to pretend", Indhlela, "a road"' (1929: 305). Faye has, '**uZibandlela.** *Yila' ihlobo selitwese, selizib' indlela.* When Summer has Come and She Hides the Paths, i.e. when the grass is in its luxurious summer growth and overhangs and obscures from view the narrow Native footpaths' (1923: 54).

Once again, it is Doke and Vilakazi who provide an otherwise unknown alternative name: **uDlolo**, which they say is a 'lunar month commencing early in November' (1958: 159). There is no indication as to whether this name is linked to the noun **udlolo**, which could either mean 'sterile person or beast' or 'evil-tempered person'.

16.2.6 The sixth month: uMasingana

This is the lunar month which starts with the new moon in December, and there seems to be general agreement that the name is a derivation from the verb **singa** ('to search for'). Exactly what is being searched for is not quite as clear, and we have a number of different suggestions. Doke and Vilakazi suggest the 'month for peering about, to see if crops are starting to ripen, as the feast of the first-fruits is held in the following months' (1958: 487); and Samuelson comes up with 'to search about for, as, at this time of year, native women look about to see how advanced their pumpkin tendrils are, so that they may nip their ends to get them to bear better' (1929: 305). By contrast, in Samuelson's *Dictionary* and according to Bryant, the women are simply searching for their pumpkin plants *per se*.

Faye tells us that **uMasingana** is 'The Moon When People Look Searchingly Below the Bearing Pumpkin Vines (to see what may be picked off for making spinach)' (1923: 53).

Doke and Vilakazi see **uNgcela** (see Section 16.2.8) as an alternative name for **uMasingana**, and give the alternative form **uNgcelamkhwekazi**, which they translate curiously as 'the mother-in-law of the Ungcela moon' (1958: 550).

16.2.7 The seventh month: uNhlolanja

This month begins with the new moon in January. All sources agree that this name is derived from the verb **hlola** ('inspect, examine') and the noun **inja** ('dog'). Translations include 'what governs a dog', 'investigate a dog', and 'the dog-copulating moon'. Samuelson says in *Long, Long Ago* that 'at this time the dogs copulate and their owners investigate as to what dogs they copulated with' (1929: 305); and in *The King Cetywayo Zulu Dictionary* he states 'owners go out to inspect [the dogs] so that they may not make wrong copulations' (1923: 576). One may well wonder what the owners then do if they find that their dog has made 'a wrong copulation'. Faye comes up with a novel idea here, but it is not clear whether he is being squeamish about copulating dogs, or whether he has confused this month with the previous one, which, as we noted, was interpreted by Doke and Vilakazi as women peering round their gardens before the First-Fruits Ceremony:

> **uNtlolanja.** *Kusuke sekuyohlowa (ukudla) emasimini. Ngu***Ntlolanja** *nje, kungati kuqala kwaku-ngu'***Ntlolanje.** (The Moon) When the Fields are Visited in Search of Food. This is **Ntlolanja** (lit. Examine-Dog) now,

but apparently originally was **Ntlolanje** (Examine Merely) – suggesting that this latter (Hlola nje, Examine Merely), had come to be used as an excuse for visiting the gardens when it was forbidden, according to national custom, to reap anything from them before the ceremony of the Feast of First Fruits (1923: 54).

16.2.8 The eighth month: uNdasa

The 'Well-fed' or 'Satiated' month begins with the new moon in February. Doke and Vilakazi derive the name from the verb **ndasa** ('be well fed'), while Samuelson has found what appears to be an ideophone in his exemplifying expression **se bethe dasa**, 'they are now full up, satiated' (1923: 576). Bryant refers to this as 'the Food-Abundance moon' (1967: 254), and Faye has a delightful picture of people being not so much 'full up', as 'fed-up', in his version: '**uNdasa.** *Sebekatazwe ngumbila (abantu), sekungen' ihlobo, sebeshayana ngawo.* (The Moon) When Folks are Weary of Green Mealies, in (the Height of) Summer, and they Shy Mealies at One Another' (1923: 53).

Doke and Vilakazi, as we noted above, saw **uNgcela** as an alternative name for **uMasingana**. By contrast, Samuelson and Faye are clear that this is an alternative name for **uNdasa**. Samuelson says that this alternative is from the verb **cela** ('to request, ask for') because at this time of year there is so much food that 'one has only to ask for it to get it' (1929: 306). Faye has a different, and not so clear interpretation of 'The Moon When the People "Beg of the Crops", Before the Feast of First Fruits (partaking of the crops before the ceremony of the Feast of First Fruits, which was forbidden)' (1923: 53).

16.2.9 The ninth month: uMbasa (uMbaso)

Doke and Vilakazi have this month commencing towards the end of February; Bryant says 'February – March' (1967: 255), and Samuelson says 'beginning with the new moon in March' (1929: 306). All agree that this name is derived from the verb **basa** ('to kindle a fire'), and the general impression is that this is because of the approaching chills of winter: 'when the fires are first lit during the chill of the rains' (Doke & Vilakazi, 1958: 68); 'because now the nippiness of winter begins' (Samuelson, 1929: 306); 'because at this time of year the sharp air of approaching winter begins to make itself felt, and fires are then made to keep the huts warm' (Samuelson, 1923: 576); 'The fire-kindling moon signifying the approach of the winter-season' (Bryant, 1967: 255) and 'The Moon That Prompts People to Make Fires, to Warm Themselves (i.e. beginning of winter)' (Faye, 1923: 53).

Those of us resident in KwaZulu-Natal, who know February–March to be the hottest time of the whole year, may well view this interpretation with some scepticism. I certainly prefer the interpretation of my colleague Msawakhe Hlengwa who sees the fires being lit to roast the first mealies, especially the fires lit by the herdboys who have stolen mealies to roast from the gardens and fields.

16.2.10 The tenth month: uNgulazibuya

Doke and Vilakazi have this month beginning towards the end of March; Bryant says 'March – April' (1967: 255). This is a compound noun, with the second part from the plural noun **izibuya** (< **isibuya**, 'threshing ground' or 'enclosed yard').There is no agreement about the first part of this compound name, and Doke and Vilakazi, Bryant, and Faye have different theories.

Doke and Vilakazi say that **uNgulazibuya** is an abbreviated form of **uNgululazibuya**, where the first half is the verb **gulula** ('sweep off', 'skim off', 'scrape off'), thus 'what sweeps the yards' (1958: 564). Bryant prefers to think that '**ngula**' is from the verb **ukwengula** ('to remove the surface scum') + **isibuya** ('threshing-ground') (1967: 255), but he does not explain the resultant compound, nor does he try to find out why the month should be so called. Faye has a different idea, namely that the first part of this compound is based on the verb gula ('to be sick'): '**uNgulazibuya.** *Lap' inkomo sezisuta, sekuti kazilale zibuyiswa.* (The Moon) When the Cattle Become Satiated, and Want to Lie Down when Being Driven Home for the Night (thus appearing to be sick, as the name uNgulazibuya suggests – "sick going homeward")' (1923: 53).

16.2.11 The eleventh month: uNhlaba

All sources are in agreement that this month takes its name from the noun **inhlaba** ('aloe'). Doke and Vilakazi have the month starting late in April; Samuelson (LLA) beginning with the new moon in April, while Bryant places this month between April and May. All of these options seem two months too early to me, and Pooley's *Field Guide to Wild Flowers of KwaZulu-Natal and the Eastern Region* records the Zulu name **inhlaba** for the following species of aloe: *Aloe chabaudii*: 'flowers . . . June–July' and *Aloe spicata*: 'flowers . . . July–Aug' (1998: 32, 228). It is possible that global warming or some other kind of climatic change has affected the flowering period of aloe plants. That **uMbaso**, occurring in early March, is said to refer to the onset of cold winter winds, suggests that winter now occurs a month or two later than it did in earlier years.

16.2.12 The twelfth month: uNhlangula or uNhlangulana

This month starts from the new moon in May and runs into June. Derived from the verb **hlangula** ('to drive off, brush off, scatter'), the name refers to the winds driving off the leaves from the trees. Samuelson says 'from Hlangula, to dust or drive off, as the wind the leaves of the trees' (1929: 306), and also 'because the trees are at this time shedding their leaves – **hlangula**' (1923: 576). Faye gives us 'The Moon When the Trees are Bare, Having Shed their Leaves' (1923: 54); Doke and Vilakazi translate the name as 'the windy, dusty month' (1958: 568); and Bryant comes up with the curious interpretation 'the little-rubbish-sweeping moon' (1967: 255).

Both Bryant and Faye give the alternative name **uLuthudlana** for this month, a name which is based on the diminutive form of **uthuli** ('dust'). Bryant translates this as 'the little-dust-moon' (1967: 255), and Faye as 'The Moon that Starts Dust' (1923: 52). Faye also says that this month is known as **uMaqub' omncane**, which he renders as 'The Lesser Dust Driving Moon' (53).

16.2.13 The thirteenth month: uNtulikazi

This month, starting with the new moon in June and going through into July, has a number of names. I choose the name **uNtulikazi** because all sources use this name. The name consists of the abbreviated plural form **(izi)ntuli** of **uthuli** ('dust'), with the augmentative suffix **-kazi**, combining to mean 'the great dusts'. The following variant forms are found in the sources: **uNtulini** ('among the dusts'), **uLuthuli** ('the dust'), and **uLuthuyana** ('small dust'). Together with the verb **qhuba** ('to drive'), we find **uMaqhubintuli** ('the driver of dust'). **UMaqhuba** ('the [dust] driver') also occurs on its own, or as **uMaqhub' omncane** ('the small [dust] driver') and **uMaqhub' omkhulu** ('the great [dust] driver').

An alternative name that has nothing to do with the wind driving the dust is **uNdida**, derived from the verb **dida** ('to puzzle'). Samuelson says 'Ndida, "the puzzler", from Dida, to puzzle, because there is a conflict of opinions now as to which moon is commencing, whether Ncwaba or Ntulikazi' (1929: 306). Faye also has this alternative name, explaining it as 'The Confusing Moon, When People Dispute Which it is' (1923: 53). Doke and Vilakazi give **uNdida** as an alternative name for the month which runs from June to July, but Bryant adds his own confusing touch by giving this name as a nickname for the month **uNgulazibuya** (March/April):

> Naturally, we cannot make twelve moons fill a solar year (which has thirteen). Nor could the Zulu. Hence regularly once a year he became 'perplexed' (*ukuDida*); and this somehow usually occurred about April time; so that the moon thereabouts (**uNgula-ziBuya**) became a source of constant contention amongst the older men, who accordingly nick-named that month the **uNdid'-amaDoda** (1967: 255).

16.2.14 Other months

Faye gives the names of two months, which, because he does not try to link these to the western calendar, we cannot approximate to any of the other months:

> **uZibhebhu**: *Izibhengu-bhengu zomoya, otata zonk' izinto, nomlil' esikoteni. 'Ano-bhek' umlilo. seketwas' uZibhebhu!'*. The Windy-Windy (Moon), Which Carries Away Everything, Including Fire Through the Grass. Watch (ye) the fire, for Zibhebhu's beginning, a seasonable warning when Zibhebhu begins her reign.

uNtlukanisa: *Inyang' eyahlukanis' unyaka, ihlobo nobusika, sekupel' ubusika, kwetwas' ihlobo.* The Moon that Divides the Year, Summer and Winter, When Winter's O'er and Summer's Come (1923: 54).

16.2.15 Mkhuze variations

Faye notes that a 'difference occurs between the usage in Zululand proper and the usage in the northern part of Zululand, where Tonga and Swazi influences are felt' (1923: 52). He calls this the 'Mkuze Area'. Faye is the only source of these 'Mkuze variations' – which can be found on pages 54 to 56 of his book – and as he again declines to give an approximate equivalent for the calendar equivalents, I am unable to assign many of the following names to a particular time of the year. The statement in italics after each name is Faye's translation of the explanation of the name as received from his Zulu sources.

uKolo (**uKholo**) Yellow-billed Kite (= **uNhloyile**) *The Moon when the Yellow-billed Kite lays its eggs.*

uMabasa/uMabas'endlini/uMbasa/uMbaso: This is the same as the KwaZulu-Natal month.

uMgan'omkulu/uMganu ('[Big] marula tree') *The moon when the large uMganu trees bud.*

uMganywana ('small marula tree') *The moon when the small uMganu trees bud.*

uMhlaba (rare) = **uNtlaba**

iMpala ('impala') *The Moon when the impala calves.*

iNdlovu ('elephant') *The Moon when the elephant calves.*

iNganga (species of termite) *Same as iNqumati. Inganga is the Stinking Ant, the 'Stinkman' of the bushveld.*

iNgulube ('wild pig') *The Moon when the wild pig litters down.*

iNkonkoni ('wildebeest') *The Moon when the wildebeest calves.*

iNqumati (not traceable – although Doke and Vilikazi give **ingqumathi** as a **hlonipha** form for **umlotha** 'ash' [1958: 563]) *The Moon when the Flying Ants come out of the ant heaps.*

iNkwekwezi/iNkwenkwezi ('morning star') *The Moon of the Morning Star.*

uNtlaba ('aloe') *The Moon when the aloe flowers* (as for KwaZulu-Natal).

uNtloyile/uNtloyiya/uNtloyiye: The last two here are '**thefuya**' forms, where standard /l/ is replaced by /y/ – same as **uKholo**, and same as KwaZulu-Natal month.

iNyati ('buffalo') *The Moon when the buffalo calves.*

iSiduli/iSidulu ('ant-heap') = **iNqumati**

iSilimela ('the Pleiades') *The Moon when the Pleiades appear.*

uTyelabani/uTyenabani ('who-do-you-tell?') *The Moon of Plenty, When People Get Drunk and the Food Over the Fires is Neglected and Gets Burnt, and No One Cares* (< Whom-do-you-tell [that the food is burning].)

iZe ('nothing') *The Moon of the End of the Year, When Everything is Utterly Bare.*

We can make an attempt to fit these names into the year, starting with those that have equivalents in the 'standard' set of moon names.

Clearly **uMabasa**, **uNtlaba** (with its variant **uMhlaba**), and **uNtloyile** (with its two **thefuya'd** variants **uNtloyiya** and **uNtloyiye**) are the same as the 'standard' ninth, eleventh and first months described above.

There is a small problem with 'uKolo': **ukholo** is one of a number of names for the Yellow-billed Kite, and at first sight it seems that this must refer to the same month as **uNhloyile**, that is, the first month of the Zulu lunar year (July–August), when the Yellow-billed Kites return from their migration to the north. The problem, however, lies in the words 'The Moon When the Yellow-billed Kite lays its eggs'. According to *Roberts' Birds* the breeding season of the Yellow-billed Kite is from September to November (1985: 113).

Clearly the Yellow-billed Kite plays an important role in the establishing of seasons. In the following quote from a Stuart source, the bird's first appearance coincides with 'the Great uluTuli' (that is, **uNtulikazi** – late June), it then goes off to moult, and then its return in late July – **uNcwaba** – marks the beginning of a new year:

> As regards the *ukolo* hawk which appeared when the Great uluTuli was drawing to a close, this bird, after appearing, would vanish again, go to the trees, live on food previously accumulated, and moult its feathers, and come out once more when the grassfields were being burnt, ready to catch the grasshoppers which flew up off the ground in the smoke, and this would be in the month of Ncwaba. As soon as the *ukolo* hawk had actually been seen there would no longer be any dispute (Webb & Wright, III: 167).

Another Stuart source also uses this bird as a sign for the start of cultivation, and mixes in a bit of reed symbolism:

> They say the Great uLutuli carries a reed from one place to another. A reed is taken up in a whirlwind (*a whirlwind of uKolo*); it ascends right

> up and is carried to another part. *Kolo or nhloyile* is a hawk. . . . People will begin to cultivate as soon as the *kolo* is reported as having been seen . . .
>
> During the beginning of Ncwaba the remaining grass is burnt off and the *ukolo hawk swoops at grasshoppers* (Webb & Wright, IV: 363).

There are two interesting points to note in this quote, both of which suggest that Stuart's informant had become a little muddled. One is the reed which is tossed about by the great dusty winds. The reed – **umhlanga** – plays a strong symbolical role in Zulu thought, standing for creation or original life forms. When one talks of ancestors beyond all memory, one says **idlozi lomhlanga** ('ancestor of the reed'), while it is common belief that 'mankind originated in a reed-bed'. Is this reed blown about by the wind somehow representing the new life which will come with the new year?

And the other curious point is the phrase 'a whirlwind of uKolo'. Doke and Vilakazi give **uNhloyile kaGelegele** ('kite of the whirlwind or dust-devil') as a praise name for the Yellow-billed Kite (1958: 241). In other words, they say that 'kite, son of wind' is a praise name for the kite, while Stuart's source says that 'wind, son of kite' is a praise name for wind.

Whatever is happening here it seems clear that the Yellow-billed Kite functions as a seasonal harbinger, and somehow manages to link the dusty winds of winter to the freshness of the green grass that follows.

Faye's 'Mkuze Variations' provide us with five calving mammals: the impala, the elephant, the bush pig, the wildebeest, and the buffalo. Smithers's *The Mammals of the Southern African Sub-Region* gives the following information about calving seasons: '*impala*: from November to January; *elephant*: any time of year, with a peak in October/November; *bush pig*: November to February; *wildebeest*: November to December; and *buffalo*: any time, but peaking in January/February' (1983).

All we can deduce from this is that a mammal-moon is a summer-moon, but more detailed or specific than that we cannot go.

From mammals to insects: the two references to termites, in the months named **iNganga** and **iSiduli**, presumably refer to the highly seasonal 'flying ant' phenomenon, which most KwaZulu-Natal residents would place at October/November.

As regards the month **uMgan' omkhulu** ('the moon when the marula trees bud'), Pooley says that the Marula Tree buds between September and November (1993: 240). I have not been able to trace the '**umganywana**' or 'small marula'.

The moon of the Pleiades (**isiLimela**) is more easily identifiable, and as we saw at the beginning of this chapter, the appearance of the Pleiades marked the beginning of the lunar year.

The Month of Nothing (**iZe**) when 'everything is utterly bare' (Faye, 1923: 56) surely coincides with the dry dusty **uNtulikazi** month of the standard lunar set.

And that brings us to **uTyelabani**, the Who-do-you-tell Month quoted at the beginning of this chapter. That this is referred to as the 'Moon of Plenty' suggests that this is another name for **uNdasa** (February). This is borne out by a statement from a Stuart source where **uNdasa** is described as the month 'when people have plenty to eat *and children leave maize cobs to burn on the hearth*; when maize is plentiful' (Webb & Wright, III: 148). Here we see another reference to 'the Food Over the Fires is Neglected and Gets Burnt, and No One Cares'.

16.3 DAYS OF THE WEEK

From the *James Stuart Archives* comes reference to the testimony of one Ndukwana, recorded in 1900:

> Names of days of the week came into use after Ndondakusuka [that is, the civil war of 1856], and long after missionaries had entered the country. In the earlier part of Mpande's reign no names of days were in vogue, i.e. about the time Ndukwana was *buta'd*. There had previously been no division of time into weeks, no such thing even as a week (*isonto*). N. knew nothing of words like *msombuluko* or *mgqibelo*. Time was divided into days and months, the moon being the basis of calculation. Men reckoned so many days after the moon's first appearance, so many days before full moon and so many after. There was no division of time into seven-day periods. Nor, as all days were alike, was there any day of rest or Sunday – *it was unknown* (Webb & Wright, IV: 334).

Bryant gives us: '**isonto** Sunday; church or religious meeting-house, religious service' (1905: 598). (Dutch *Sondag,* Sunday).

Doke and Vilakazi show how this meaning has become extended in several ways: (i) Sunday; (ii) week; (iii) church building; (iv) religious service, church meeting; (v) denomination (1958: 766).

From the noun **isonto** the verb **sonta** has been derived. This has the meanings:

- go to church; attend a religious service; observe a Sunday;
- belong to a specific denomination, as in the question: **usontaphi**? ('where do you "sonta"?'); and the answer: **ngisonta eLoma** ('I "sonta" at Rome', that is, 'I am a Roman Catholic');
- spend a weekend.

Before this verb was derived from the noun **isonto**, there was already a verb **sonta** in the Zulu lexicon, with the meaning 'twist', 'misstate', 'distort', and Samuelson confuses these two similar verbs when he says: '**Isonto** Sunday comes from the word **sonta** to twist and implies that, that day is twisted out of the course of the other week days and specialised' (1923: 581).

Notwithstanding Samuelson's speculation, it seems reasonably clear that **isonto** is an adopted word, if not from the Dutch, then very likely from the Norwegian, as there was a very strong Norwegian presence in KwaZulu-Natal in the nineteenth century (for more on this see the section 'Christianity and the missionaries' in Koopman, 1999c).

The Zulu name for Monday is **uMsombuluko**. According to Doke and Vilakazi, this noun is derived from the verb **sombuluka** ('become unrolled, unravelled') (1958: 764). In addition to the meaning 'Monday' for **umsombuluko**, they also give the meaning 'day of dispersal after an important ceremony' (1958: 764), that is, after the holy day of Sunday. Monday is thus seen as the start of the week.

The next four days are based on the various Zulu words for 'second', 'third', 'fourth' and 'fifth'. Tuesday is **usuku lwesibili** (**lwa-**, 'of', + **isibili**, 'the second'), abbreviated to **uLwesibili**. Wednesday is **usuku lwesithathu** (**lwa-** + **isithathu**, 'the third'), abbreviated to **uLwesithathu**. Thursday is **usuku lwesine** (**lwa-** + **isine**, 'the fourth'), abbreviated to **uLwesine**. Friday is **usuku lwesihlanu** (**lwa-** + **isihlanu**, 'the fifth'), abbreviated to **uLwesihlanu**. The name for Saturday is **uMgqibelo**, a noun derived from the verb **gqibela** ('finish off, complete'), as this is the day which completes the week.

It can be seen that the names of the weekdays emphasise the isolation of Sunday as a day of rest, a day apart from the working weekdays: Monday starts the week, Saturday completes the week, and Sunday is a day semantically and etymologically associated with the church.

16.4 TIMES OF DAY

The following phrases, referring to various parts of the day, can in no way be regarded as names. I have included them here because after dealing with the division of the year into months, and the division of the week into days, it seems appropriate to give some of the divisions of the day as well. The following are some of the more prosaic terms for time of day, ranging from midnight, through the day to night again:

- **phakathi kwamabili** (literally, 'between the two'): midnight;
- **ngovivi**: 'first light in sky', very early dawn;
- **ekuseni** (< **ukusa**, 'to become light'): morning;
- **emini**: midday;
- **ntambama**: late afternoon to early evening;
- **ngoku swelela**: at dusk;
- **kusihlwa** (< verb **hlwa**, 'become dark'): evening;
- **ebusuku**: at night.

What follows are the less well known and the more poetic words and phrases which refer to different times of day. There are also one or two expressions relating to the moon.

The time of first light, very early in the morning before the sun is risen, is known as **mpondozankomo** ('horns of the cattle'). One explanation of this phrase is that the horns of the cattle are more easily seen than their bodies; another is that often at this time there is a light mist hugging the ground, above which only the horns of the cattle can be seen. When this morning mist lies over the rivers it is known as **umlalamvubu** ('what lies on the hippopotamus'). A less explainable variant of **mpondozankomo** is **mpondozamthini** ('horns of the otter').

Midday is sometimes known as **eminibebade** ('at noon they being tall'), and it has been suggested as an explanation that at this time of day people are tall in comparison to their shadows. The normal word for midday is **emini**, and this is the base of **iminana** (< dim, **imini**): the early afternoon.

As the afternoon progresses, the word **mathunzi** ('shadows') may be used, and then later still **mtshwanduna** (**umutsha**, 'loin-covering', + possessive **-wa-** + **induna**, 'headman'), or alternatively **mtshwendoda** (**umutsha** + possessive **indoda**, 'man'). Doke and Vilakazi do not explain these expressions but it would be reasonable to suggest that at this time of the late afternoon the shadows are as long as the **ibheshu** ('back loin-covering') of a man, as opposed to the very short **ibheshu** worn by boys.

Late afternoon is also known as **malangashona** (literally, 'sun's setting'): towards sunset, late afternoon, and the very last ten minutes or so of sunlight is known as **bantubahle** ('the people are beautiful') a reference to the very flattering light of those last few minutes.

Doke and Vilakazi tell us that when the sun is actually setting, one may say **Hamba, ndondo!** ('Goodbye, big brass ball!'), as a farewell salute (1958: 167).

Expressions relating to the moon are **isihlekwa inyoni** ('it is now laughed at by the birds'): said of the moon just as it sets before sunrise (Faye, 1923: 57), and **isiyaselwa** ('it is now being overtaken by dawn'): said of the moon when it sets during daylight, after full moon (Faye, 1923: 57).

From Samuelson (1923: 576) comes these three expressions referring to seasons rather than times of day:

- **Nxa kukhahlel' umbila** 'when the mealies are about to get into flower': on the coast, about end of October or beginning of November; up-country, beginning of January to beginning of February/March;
- **Nxa kukhahlela amabele** 'when the sorghum starts flowering': up-country: around March; on the coast: around February;
- **Nxa amabele esebomvu**: 'when the sorghum is red ripe': up-country: end of April, beginning of May; on the coast: about March.

16.5 STARS AND PLANETS

Having started this chapter with the names of lunar moons, it seems fitting to end with the names of stars and planets.

Starting with the biggest star of all, from a human point of view, here is a comment from Samuelson about the sun: 'It is supposed that there is a large luminous body in the East, from which a spark scintillates every morning to grow into the glorious eye of day, and to be devoured every evening in the West by a race of pygmies called the Iziicwe, a name [which is] also given to Bushmen . . .' (1929: 304).

The planet Jupiter has a number of Zulu names, all of which are found in Doke and Vilakazi: **iNdonsa** (< **donsa**, 'tug', 'pull'): 'the planet Jupiter (so-called because of its slow movement, as though straining)'. This name is 'also applied to the planet Mars, as it rises in the evening'. The name **iNdonsa** also occurs in the variant form **iNdosa**. **iNdonsa** is also the first part of the following two compound names: **iNdonsakusa** ('what draws the dawn') and **iNdonsamasuku** ('what draws on the days'). Jupiter is also known by the name **iNqonqoyi**.

The planet Venus is named differently according to whether it is seen as the morning star or the evening star. In its role as the morning star, it has the two names **iKhwezi** and **iNkangakusa** (**khanga** + **ukusa**, 'attract the dawn'). However, when it is first seen in the evening, it is called **iSicelankobe**, a name which literally means 'the one who begs for boiled mealies'. Incidentally, both **iKhwezi** and **iSicelankobe** are also used as bird names: Doke and Vilakazi tell us that **iSicelankobe** also refers to a 'species of bird' (which I have not been able to identify), and **iKhwezi** is one of the names of the Glossy Starling.

Samuelson has clearly mixed up the identities of Venus and Jupiter when he states: '**Undonsamasuku** also called **iSicelankobe** is the name of Venus' and '**iKhwezi** is the name of Jupiter' (1929: 306).

The most obvious grouping of stars in the sky is the Milky Way, and this has the Zulu name **uMthala**. There are two constellations which have been identified by name in Zulu: Orion and the Pleiades.

Orion is known as **iMpambano**, a word derived from the verb **phambana** ('lie across one another'). Doke and Vilakazi give the following two names as if they are separate names referring to separate entities, but it seems clear to me that both are variant forms of the noun **udwendwe** ('file or row of people, animals, trees, etc.'), with the first name in the locative form, and the second name in the diminutive: **oNdwendweni** (plural only): 'a small string of stars near Orion' (1958: 542); and **oNdwenjana** (plural only): 'small string of stars faintly visible on the right of the belt of Orion' (542). When Orion is first seen in the summer sky, his sword lies to the top right of his belt, and this is the 'small string of stars' referred to. The plural and diminutive form of **udwendwe** is **izindwenjana**, and Samuelson gives **Izindwenjana** as the name of 'the Pons Asinorum constellation' (1929: 306). Whether this is the same 'small string of stars near Orion', I cannot say.

The Zulu name of the Pleiades is **iSilimela**, derived from the verb **lima** ('plough, cultivate'). Here we have a name which does not describe the constellation (as does, for example, the name **iMpambano**), but instead describes the human significance of the time of this constellation's appearance. As we saw above, the first appearance of the Pleiades marks the commencement of the new year, and also marks the time for the start of ploughing. Doke and Vilakazi state: '**isilimela:** 1. ploughing time, early spring; 2. the constellation Pleiades, whose appearance marks the season for the commencement of ploughing' (1958: 457).

The name **iNkwenkwezi**, according to Doke and Vilakazi, refers to a 'certain conspicuous star (the "a" of the constellation *Argo*) appearing in the south-east in the early mornings of July and preceding the appearance of the Pleiades' (1958: 581). According to my colleague Rogan Roth, a member of the South African Astronomical Society, this is the star Canopus, the second brightest star in the sky after Sirius. Canopus marks the month of May in the Xhosa lunar calendar: **ekaCanzibe** ('Moon when Canopus is visible'). Another very bright star is Aldebaran of the constellation Taurus, which has the Zulu name **uCwazibe** (< **cwazi**, 'of shining brightly'). Given that these two bright stars have their own Zulu names, it is surprising that the brightest star in the sky – Sirius in the constellation Canis Major – has no apparent Zulu name. Perhaps this is the identity of the Zulu **iNtsantsa**, of which Samuelson says, 'the star that is especially bright and scintillates numerous rays, but whose scientific name I am not acquainted with' (1929: 306).

The final three star names which we have may well all refer to the same star. **iNtshola**, according to Doke and Vilakazi is 'a star which precedes the morning star about September, possibly one of the Spica constellation' (1958: 607). This is, in fact, the star Spica, which is the brightest star in the constellation of Virgo. This could be the same star as **iNqonqoli**, which Samuelson says is 'the star that rises about 3 a.m. preceding the morning star' (1929: 306). And finally, another 'star seen about September in the early morning' is **iQhubankomo** (< **qhuba**, 'drive', + **inkomo**, 'head of cattle'), and this time it is Bryant, in his *Dictionary*, who can give us the story behind the name: '**i(li)-Qubankomo** . . . Name sometimes applied to a cattle-thief . . . certain star (perhaps *Spica* of the constellation *Virgo*) which precedes the morning-star about September time, and indicates the time when stolen cattle are carried off' (1905: 545).

Part 5

Linguistics

Chapter 17

Linguistic structures

17.1 INTRODUCTION

All names are nouns. This is true for all languages, and Zulu is no exception. Therefore in order to understand something about the structure of names one needs to know something about the structure of nouns, and the way in which they fit into the noun class system.

All Zulu nouns consist of a prefix and a stem. The noun **umuntu** ('person'), for example, consists of the prefix **umu**- and the stem **-ntu**. The plural form of this noun – **abantu** ('people') – consists of the prefix **aba**- and the same stem **-ntu**. The word **ubuntu** ('humanity'), has the same stem, but with the prefix **ubu**-. The word for a Zulu person is **umZulu**, with the prefix **um**- and the stem **-Zulu**. Related nouns with the same stem, but different prefixes, are **amaZulu** ('Zulu people'), **ubuZulu** ('Zulu-ness', 'Zulu culture') as well as **isiZulu** ('Zulu language'). In every noun it is the stem which carries the 'real' meaning of the noun (the lexical meaning), while the prefix tells one whether the noun is a singular or a plural, or whether the noun is an abstract noun. The prefix has another function in Zulu: it also tells one what set of concordial agreement should be used so that the noun agrees with the adjectives, pronouns, verbs and other parts of speech in a sentence. Consider the following three statements, all exactly the same except for the subject noun:

Lo muntu omhlophe omkhulu usebalekile ('that big white person has run away').
Laba bantu abamhlophe abakhulu sebebalekile ('those big white people have run away').
Lezo zinkomo ezimhlophe ezinkulu sezibalekile ('those big white cattle have run away').

The following is the full set of Zulu noun classes, showing singular and plural relationships:

Please note:
- Zulu no longer has classes 12 and 13, both of which are regularly found in Bantu languages north of the Limpopo River.
- Class 10 serves as a plural class for both classes 9 and 11.

Singular classes			Plural classes		
cl 1	**u-mu-ntu**	'person'	cl 2	**a-ba-ntu**	people
cl 1a	**u-baba**	'my father'	cl 2a	**o-baba**	'my fathers'
	u-Sibongile	personal name		**o-Sibongile**	'Sibongile and her friends'
cl 3	**u-m-fula**	'river'	cl 4	**i-mi-fula**	'rivers'
cl 5	**i-hhashi**	'horse'	cl 6	**a-ma-hhashi**	'horses'
cl 7	**i-si-kelemu**	'rogue'	cl 8	**i-zi-kelemu**	'rogues'
cl 9	**i-n-kabi**	'ox'	cl 10	**i-zin-kabi**	'oxen'
cl 11	**u-phondo**	'horn'	cl 10	**i-zimpondo**	'horns'
cl 14	**u-bu-hle**	'beauty'	no plural form		
cl 15	**u-ku-dla**	'food', 'eating'	no plural form		

17.2 ANTHROPONYMS AND NON-ANTHROPONYMIC ZULU NAMES

17.2.1 Anthroponyms

No matter what part of speech they are derived from, all human names (anthroponyms) belong without exception to class 1a, and therefore all have the prefix **u-**. When these names are used in English or other European languages, it is normal to drop this class prefix, and talk of Sibongile and Jabulani (**amagama asekhaya**: Zulu first names), Ephraim and Mirriam (Euro-origin first names), Bhengu and Dlamini (clan names/surnames), Mabaso and Madlokovu (clan praises or **izithakazelo**), as well as Mehlomane ('four-eyes') and 'Baby-Jake' (nicknames).

In Zulu these names *will all have the prefix* **u-**:
- **uSibongile** and **uJabulani**;
- **uEphraim** and **uMirriam**;
- **uBhengu** and **uDlamini**;
- **uMabaso** and **uMadlokovu**;
- **uMehlomane** and **uBaby-Jake**.

The prefix **u-** falls away when the name is used in direct address, thus:
i. Direct address: **Sawubona Jabulani**! ('Greetings, Jabulani!').
ii. Subject of sentence: **uJabulani uhambile** ('Jabulani has gone').
iii. Object of sentence: **Umbonile uJabulani**? ('Have you seen Jabulani?').
i. Direct address: **Woza Lapha Aaron**! ('Come here, Aaron!').
ii. Subject of sentence: **uAaron usebenza eGoli** ('Aaron works in Johannesburg').
iii. object of sentence: **Ngimbonile uAaron** ('I saw Aaron').

As a noun in class 1a, any anthroponym will have a plural form in class 2a. Thus **uSipho** has a plural form **oSipho**, which could mean 'Sipho and friends', 'Sipho and his usual crowd', or simply 'more than one person named Sipho'. A clan name such as **uDlamini** can be found in the plural form **oDlamini**, which, again, could mean 'Dlamini and his gang' or 'a group of people all named Dlamini'.

17.2.2 Non-anthroponymic Zulu names

Zulu names that are not anthroponyms, that is, place names, the names of schools and shops, of regiments and months, and of plants and birds, may belong to any noun class, including class 1a. So we find place names such as **uMgungundlovu** (class 3), and river names such as **aManzimtoti** (class 6), regimental names such as **iNtshamathe** (class 9) and **iZimpohlo** (class 10), school names such as **uBuhlebesundumbili** (class 14), homestead names such as **eKuphakameni** (class 15) and **eSinyameni** (class 7), school names such as **iGugulethu** (class 5), month names such as **uLwezi** (class 11), and star names such as **iNdonsa** (class 9).

17.2.3 Simple, complex and compound stems; phrasal names

Names may have simple stems, where the stem cannot be broken down into any smaller meaningful units. There are not many of these, and this will only be the case if the name has been derived from a single-stemmed noun. For example, the personal name **uQhawe**, derived from the noun **iqhawe** ('hero'), the stem **-qhawe** cannot be broken into smaller units with meaning. The same can be said of the regimental names **iSangqu** ('Orange River') and **uVe** ('Paradise Flycatcher'): the stems **-angqu** and **-ve** cannot be further analysed into smaller units.

Complex stems are those names which *can* be broken down into smaller units, but only one of these units has a dictionary meaning. The personal name **uSibongile** has a stem which consists of three parts: the verb concord **si-** ('we'), the verb root **-bong-** ('be grateful') and the past tense suffix **-ile**. The month name **uNtulikazi** ('very dusty') also has a stem with three parts: the class 10 prefix **izin-**, abbreviated to **-N-**, the noun stem **-t(h)uli-** and the augmentative suffix **-kazi**. Likewise, the clan name **uMaphumulo** has a tripartite stem: the class 6 class prefix **(a)ma-**, the verb root **-phumul-** ('rest') and the noun-forming suffix **-o**.

Compound stems are those with two parts or more (usually more), two of which can stand on their own as single words. For example, the personal name **uVusumuzi** consists of the verb **vusa** ('rouse') and the noun **umuzi** ('homestead'), each of which are separate words in Zulu. The river name **aManzamnyama** consists of the noun **amanzi** ('water') and the adjective **-mnyama** ('black'); the hill name **iNtabankulu** can be broken into **intaba** ('hill') and **enkulu** ('big'); and the month name **uZibandlela** can be divided into the verb **ziba** ('deceive, hide') and the noun **indlela** ('road, path'). In each case the two 'halves' of these names can stand on their own in a Zulu sentence.

Phrasal names consist of more than one word. Examples can be found of nicknames which have more than one word: **uNogwaja ozikhundla-khundla** ('Rabbit-with-many-holes') and **uGandaganda eMasondosondo abanye** ('Tractor-who-is-wheel-wheels-the-others'); school names such as **Ethel Mthiyane High**; homestead names such as **Kwa Mabonw' abulawe, imamban' eluhlaza** ('The Place of It-is-killed-as-soon-as-it-is-seen, the-little-green-mamba'); and shop names such as **Simunye** ('we are one') **Supermarket**, **KwaDabulamanzi Wemithi Yabantu** (Dabulamanzi's Place of People's Medicines), and **Bafana Bafana Factory Shop**.

The material in Section 17.3 below is covered in greater detail in Koopman (1976, 1979).

17.3 THE STRUCTURE OF ZULU PERSONAL NAMES (*AMAGAMA ASEKHAYA*)

As we have said above, all names are nouns. But names may be derived from various other parts of speech, as well as be derived from other nouns. In this section we shall look at names derived from other nouns, names derived from verbs, names derived from various other parts of speech, and names derived from combinations of various parts of speech, such as noun + adjective, verb + noun, etc.

17.3.1 Names derived from other nouns

One of the more common Zulu names for a boy is **uSipho** ('gift'). This name is derived from the noun **isipho** ('gift'), which in turn is derived from the verb **pha** ('to give'). The common noun **isipho** can be divided into four parts:

1. the initial vowel of the noun class prefix;
2. **si-** the basic prefix of noun class 7;
3. **-ph-** the verb root for 'give';
4. **-o** a derivational suffix that turns a verb into a noun.

When this noun **isipho** becomes the personal name **uSipho**, the initial vowel **i-** is replaced by the **u-** which is the class prefix of class 1a, to which all anthroponyms belong. Because **uSipho** is a personal name, and is therefore a 'proper noun', Zulu follows the convention used by most languages, and gives the name a capital letter, capitalising the first letter of the noun stem.

We can see exactly the same process of replacing the initial vowel of a common noun with the **u-** of class 1a to make a personal name in the following examples:

	Boys' names			Girls' names	
uMandla	< **amandla**	'strength'	**uNtombi**	< **intombi**	'girl'
uKhehla	< **ikhehla**	'old man'	**uMakhosazane**	< **amakhosazane**	'girls'
uSibusiso	< **isibusiso**	'blessing'	**uSalukazi**	< **isalukazi**	'old woman'
uMuntu	< **umuntu**	'person'	**uGugu**	< **igugu**	'treasure'
uBantu	< **abantu**	'people'	**uMbali**	< **imbali**	'flower'

> Two well-known **oBantu** in South Africa are the late activist Steven Bantu Biko, and the politician General Bantu Holomisa.

In the example **uMuntu** above, there seems to be no difference between the name and the noun **umuntu** from which it is derived, apart from the capital letter. But, in fact, these are now different nouns from different noun classes, as a few grammatical tests will show:

Plural formations:

uMuntu	> **oMuntu**	'Muntu & Co.', 'Muntu and his friends'
umuntu	> **abantu**	'people'

Possessive formations:

izinkomo zikaMuntu	'Muntu's cattle'
izinkomo zomuntu	'a person's cattle'

When we come to names derived from class 1a nouns, however, there is absolutely no difference between the name and the noun except for the capital letter:

uBaba	< **ubaba**	'my father'
uGogo	< **ugogo**	'grandmother'

This feature of Zulu names, the combining in one word of more than one class concord, sets Zulu names apart from other common nouns. In many other Bantu languages north of the Limpopo River, it is common to find nouns with more than one prefix (when they are normally referred to as the primary and the secondary prefix). The only common nouns that I can think of in Zulu that do this are **usihlalo** ('chairman', < **isihlalo**, 'chair') and **usikhwama** ('treasurer', < **isikhwama**, 'purse'). Many people treat these as proper nouns and spell them **uSihlalo** and **uSikhwama**.

17.3.2 The use of -so-, -no-, -ma- and -se

In a name such as **uSipho**, we effectively have two noun class prefixes: the **u-** of the new noun class 1a, and the **-si-** of the original class 7 noun **isipho**. In Zulu personal names we often find that these two noun class prefixes are separated by **-so-**, **-no-** or **-ma-**. For example, the name **uBantu** given above may also occur as **uSobantu**, the name given to the well-known cleric and Zulu scholar of the nineteenth century, Bishop Colenso. The name **uNtombi** ('girl') often occurs in the form **uNontombi**. One may also find **uMantombi.**

-So-, supposedly a historical abbreviation of **uyihlo** ('your father') – as proposed by Doke in his *Textbook of Zulu Grammar* – is used to form male names, while **-no-** and **-ma-**, supposedly historical abbreviations of **unyoko** ('your mother') and **umntaka-** ('child of') respectively, are used to form female names. **-So-** is not used as much as it used to be 100 years ago. A look through the index of historical works such as Bryant's *Olden Times* and the *James Stuart Archives* will show a number of examples of male names with **-so-**. Volume III of the *James Stuart Archives*, for example, gives **uSomangqephu, uSomaphunga, uSomfula, uSomhashi, uSomhlolo, uSomkhele, uSondoda, uSoshenge**, and many more. Today it is rare to find boys whose names include **-so-**. One well-known public figure who was given a **-so-** based name was the Native Affairs Administrator of the nineteenth century, Sir Theophilus Shepstone, known to the Zulu people as 'Somtsewu', an unusual name indeed, because the **-so-** has been prefixed to the Sotho adjective **-tsewu**, meaning 'white'. 'Somtsewu' thus means something like 'father of Whiteness' or perhaps 'Great White Father'.

> For a discussion of the relevance of Doke's theories today, see Koopman (1992b).

Unlike **-so-**, **-no-** is still used extensively in the formation of names for girl children, and is responsible for the formation of 10,5 per cent of girls' names (Koopman, 1979b: 166). The most common is **uNomusa** (< **umusa**, 'mercy', 'grace'), but other common ones are:

- **uNomvula** (< **imvula**, 'rain');
- **uNozipho** (< **izipho**, 'gifts');
- **uNobantu** (< **abantu**, 'people');
- **uNomazulu** (< **amaZulu**, 'Zulu people');
- **uNonhlanhla** (< **inhlanhla**, 'luck').

-Ma- is used very rarely for forming **amagama asekhaya** (first names) but is regularly used for prefixing to a married woman's maiden clan name. While occasionally one may come across a personal name such as **uMantombi** (< **intombi**, 'girl'), all married women are regularly referred to as **uMaCele, uMaDlamini, uMaNgcobo**, etc. (assuming, of course, that they were born to the Cele, Dlamini and Ngcobo clans).

The suffix **-se** was once used regularly to form personal names, but now it is rare to find a name such as **uNtombise** (< **intombi**). As noted in Chapter 4, the clan names of today are the personal names of yesterday, and evidence of how often **-se** was used for forming personal names can be seen in today's clan names, such as **uMpungose**, **uMdlalose**, **uNyawose**, and **uShangase**.

When used in personal names, **-so-** is strictly used for male names, and **-no-** for female names. When used for forming common nouns, however, the male and female references fall away, and we find words such as **usomabhizinisi** ('entrepreneur', < *business*), and **usomashibhi** ('*shebeen* owner') as well as **unompempe** ('referee', < **impempe**, 'whistle') and **unozinti** ('goalkeeper', < **izinti**, '[goal]posts'). Business-persons, shebeen owners, referees and goalkeepers can of course all be of either sex.

Masojabulase Liquor Store, in the area known as 'eShowe' about 12 kilometres west of Pietermaritzburg on the Elandskop Road. The name is based on the verb **jabula** ('be happy') and uses the name formatives **-ma-**, **-so-**, and **-se**. A very loose translation of the name would be 'Father characteristically happy'.

17.3.3 Names derived from verbs

The Zulu language regularly derives common nouns from verbs according to the following patterns:

a. Personal nouns

The personal noun class 1 prefix **um-** + verb root + personal suffix **-i**:

um-enz-i	'doer', 'maker'	< **enz-a**	'do, make'	all
um-fund-i	'learner'	< **fund-a**	'learn'	noun
um-cul-i	'singer'	< **cul-a**	'sing'	class
um-hamb-i	'traveller'	< **hamb-a**	'go, walk, travel'	1

b. Impersonal nouns

Any noun class prefix + verb root + impersonal suffix **-o**:

is-enz-o	'deed'	< **enz-a**	'do'	class 7
isi-fund-o	'lesson'	< **fund-a**	'learn'	class 7
i-cul-o	'song'	< **cul-a**	'sing'	class 5
u-hamb-o	'journey'	< **hamb-a**	'go, travel'	class 11

c. Personal names

Personal nouns derived from verbs may also become names:

- **uMduduzi** ('The Comforter') < **umduduzi** ('someone who comforts') < **duduza** ('to comfort').
- **uMsizi** ('The Helper') < **umsizi** ('a helper') < **siza** ('to help').

The two methods shown above of deriving personal and impersonal nouns from verbs are the only ways in which common nouns may be made out of verbs. In each such noun it is only the verb root which is used. When making names out of verbs, however, there is no such limitation, and verb roots are used together with subject and object concords, present and past tense markers, positive and negative forms, verbal extensions, and a wide variety of other verb forms. The simplest way of forming a name from a verb is to prefix the class 1a **u-** to the dictionary form of the verb, thus:

uBonga	< **bonga**	'be grateful, give thanks';
uThemba	< **themba**	'trust';
uLinda	< **linda**	'wait';
uThokoza	< **thokoza**	'be happy'.

This form of the verb can suffix the plural imperative **-ni**:

- **uBongani** ('be grateful');
- **uThembani** ('be trustful');
- **uThokozani** ('be happy');
- **uJabulani** ('be happy').

The plural imperative can have the object concord **-m-** ('him'), which becomes part of the stem:

- **uMlindeni** ('await him');
- **uMthembeni** ('trust him');

- **uMkhonzeni** ('worship Him');
- **uMbongeni** ('praise Him').

Various tense morphemes can be used, in which case a subject concord may be used. The present tense **-ya-** is seen in **uSiyabonga** ('we are grateful') and **uSiyamtusa** ('we praise Him'). The perfect tense suffix **-ile** is extremely common in girls' names:
- **uSibongile** ('we are grateful');
- **uDuduzile** ('having comforted');
- **uThembisile** ('having promised');
- **uFikile** ('having arrived').

> In my own collected data I have found **uSibongile** to be the most common girl's name.

The perfect tense may occur in the passive as well:
- **uLindiwe** ('the awaited one');
- **uThandiwe** ('the loved one');
- **uBusisiwe** ('the blessed one');
- **uKhethiwe** ('the chosen one').

The present tense passive is a feature of boys' names:
- **uMcashelwa** ('the one hidden from');
- **uMbalelwa** ('the one counted for');
- **uMbhekwa** ('the guarded one');
- **uMfuniselwa** ('the awaited one').

The verb may occur with an interrogative suffix:
- **uBafanini** ('when did they die?');
- **uSilwayiphi** ('which [battle] are we fighting?');
- **uCashephi** ('where is she hidden?');
- **uQondeni** ('what do you understand?');
- **uSweleni** ('what are you lacking?');
- **uThembeni** ('what did you hope for?').

As can be seen from many of the examples above, the verb may include one or more verbal extensions when it is the base of a name. Among the examples already given, we find the Applied extension **-el-** in **uMcashelwa** and **uMbalelwa**, where it is combined with the Passive extension; we find the Causative **-is-** in **uThembisile**, and both Applied **-el-** and Causative **-is-** in **uMfuniselwa.** The neuter extension is found in names such as **uBonakele** ('being visible'), and **uSizakele** ('being helpful').

The verb combines readily with nouns and other parts of speech to form compound personal names and examples will be given when compounds are discussed in detail in a later section of this chapter.

17.3.4 Names derived from other parts of speech

Names may be derived from adjective stems, as in:

- **uMuhle** ('he/she is nice, good-looking');
- **uZintathu** ('they are three');
- **uZiningi** ('they are many').

Names such as **uZintathu** ('they are three') and **uZiningi** ('they are many') may be given as complete names but usually these are abbreviations of the fuller forms **uNtombizintathu** ('the girls are three in number') and **uNtombiziningi** ('the girls are many').

The same may be said for names with a pronoun as a base. Names such as **uZodwa** ('they alone') and **uZonke** ('all of them') may be given as names in their own right, but they are usually abbreviations of **uNtombizodwa** ('only girls') and **uNtombizonke** ('all girls').

In my Honours Dissertation I stated that names may be derived from ideophones, giving as examples the two names **uNdo** and **uVu** (1976: 82). Looking back at this after 25 years it is easy to see that these are abbreviated forms of **uNdoda** ('man') and **uVusumuzi** ('awake the family'), both very common male names. On going back through my original data and looking at many other data sets of personal names, I see that there are in fact no names which could possibly be ideophone-based that are not obvious abbreviations of common personal names.

> For more detail on the material in Section 17.4 below, see Koopman (1979b).

17.4 DIFFERENCE BETWEEN MALE AND FEMALE NAMES

In talking about the difference between male and female names in Zulu. I would like to use the concept of 'marking for sex'. Let us start by looking at some common nouns in English in the next three sentences:

a) That is a beautiful dog! Is it a spaniel or a setter?
b) That is a beautiful bitch! Is it a spaniel or a setter?
c) That is a beautiful spaniel! Is it a dog or a bitch?

In (a) the word 'dog' could mean either a male or a female dog. In other words, in this context the word 'dog' is unmarked for sex. In (b) the word 'bitch' can only mean female, and it only ever does mean 'female dog'. In other words, the word 'bitch' is marked for sex, not just in this context, but always. In (c) the word 'dog' is marked 'male', but only in the context of being contrasted with 'bitch'.

We can see exactly the same happening with 'man' and 'woman' in the following set:

a) Man discovered fire approximately 100 000 years ago.
b) Woman discovered fire approximately 100 000 years ago.
c) Look at that person with the long hair over there! From the back it's impossible to tell whether it's a man or a woman.

In sentence (a) 'man' is unmarked and includes both 'male' and 'female'. We can read this word as the equivalent of 'human beings'. Sentence (b) bothers us, because the word 'woman' is specifically marked 'female', and therefore excludes all men from any role in the discovery of fire. Sentence (c) marks the word 'man' as 'male' because it is in specific contrast with the marked word 'woman'.

Some pairs of words have both the male and the female permanently marked, such as 'king' and 'queen', 'boar' and 'sow', 'ram' and 'ewe', etc. In other pairs, the female is marked by the addition of a feminising suffix:

- prince/princess;
- actor/actress;
- author/authoress;
- usher/usherette;
- drum major/drum majorette.

This is very often the case with personal names in English, where we find suffixes such as **-ina/-ine**, **-etta/-ette**, and others, giving us pairs such as:

- **Paul** and **Pauline**;
- **George** and **Georgina**;
- **Joseph** and **Josephine**;
- **Henry** and **Henrietta**;
- **Adrian** and **Adriana**;
- **Stephen** and **Stephanie**, and so on.

In each of these pairs, the male name is the 'basic' or 'shorter' form which has been feminised by the addition of a feminising suffix. I know of no examples where the female name is the basic form, which has been or can be added to prefixally or suffixally to create a male name.

Marking for sex in Zulu names is very similar. While there are nouns which are already marked for sex before they become names, such as **indoda** ('man') which then becomes the name **uNdoda**, and **intombi** ('girl'), which then becomes the name **uNtombi**, there are many neutral nouns such as **inhlanhla** ('luck') and **umusa** ('grace, mercy') which need the extra feminising morpheme, in this case the prefix **-no-**, before they can become the female names **uNonhlanhla** and **uNomusa**.

In looking at the difference between male and female names in Zulu, we should consider the following: semantic marking, morphological marking, double marking, contradictory marking, and unmarked names.

17.4.1 Semantic marking

Names that are semantically marked are those which are derived from nouns which themselves have a definite male or female meaning. When a noun such as **intombi** ('girl') becomes the name **uNtombi**, clearly this name can only be for a girl. Equally clearly, if the name **uBaba** is derived from the noun **ubaba** ('father'), then **uBaba** must be a boy's name.

Boys' names that are semantically marked 'male' include the following:

uBanfanyana	< **abafanyana**	'small boys'
uMalusi	< **umalusi**	'herd-boy'
uNdoda	< **indoda**	'man'
uKhehla	< **ikhehla**	'old man'
uMalume	< **umalume**	'uncle'
uMakhosi	< **amakhosi**	'chiefs'

Less obvious are names based on **umuzi** ('homestead', but also 'family line') and **inkosi** ('chief', and 'Lord God'). These nouns are associated with males, and are only found as bases in male names.

Names that are semantically marked 'female' include:

uNtombi	< **intombi**	'girl'
uNtombazana	< **intombazana**	'young girl'
uNtombazanyana	< **intombazanyana**	'small young girl' or 'very young girl'
uMakhosazane	< **amakhosazane**	'girls'
uQhikiza	< **iqhikiza**	'mature girl'
uSalukazi	< **isalukazi**	'old woman'

Less obvious are:

- **uMbali** (< **imbali**, 'flower');
- **uGugu** (< **igugu**, 'treasure');
- **uNana** (< **unana**, 'child, baby').

Nouns that as nouns are semantically neutral in terms of sex marking became male names:

uNhlanhla	< **inhlanhla**	'luck'
uJubane	< **ijubane**	'speed'
uMatshe	< **amatshe**	'stones'
uLizwe	< **ilizwe**	'country'
uLizwi	< **ilizwi**	'voice'
uMbokodo	< **imbokodo**	'grinding stone'

17.4.2 Morphological marking

Certain morphemes (prefixes, suffixes) have become specifically associated with either the male of the female sex when used in personal names.

We have already mentioned the prefixes **-so-** and **-no-**, and these without doubt mark male names and female names respectively. Whenever **-no-** is prefixed to a neutral common noun such as **imvula** ('rain') or **izipho** ('gifts'), the resultant **uNomvula** and **uNozipho** are strongly marked as female.

The reason why **-so-** is far less commonly used is that neutral nouns without the **-no-** marker are, by contrast with the nouns which do have the **-no-** marker, marked as male when they become names. Let me try to put this more clearly: the English word 'dog', as we saw on page 276 is *un*marked for sex, until it is contrasted with the word 'bitch' in 'Is that a dog or a bitch?' The word **imvula** ('rain') is neutral or unmarked in the Zulu language. By contrast, the *name* **uMvula** is marked male, because the name **uNomvula**, the female name, is in common and contrastive existence. There is no necessity to give it extra marking and make the name **uSomvula** (although there is absolutely no bar to any parent who wishes to do this). Again, because the girls' name **uNomusa** is so common, the name **uMusa** takes on male meaning in contrast. There is no need to create **uSomusa**.

For reasons that have continued to evade me for over 25 years, the Zulu perfect suffix **-ile** is used as a female marker. This is true of the passive form **-iwe** as well. This, as far as I know, has never been the case with Xhosa, and in that language a name ending with **-ile** could be either male or female.

Having said that **-ile** is a female marker, I have to add that I have noticed a growing trend over the last 15 years or so in Zulu personal naming to give boys certain names ending with **-ile** or **-iwe**, especially names like **uSimphiwe** ('we have been given him'), that is to say, names based on the verb **pha** ('to give'). It is possible that this has been influenced by the enormous popularity of the boy's name **uSipho** ('gift'). Certain boys' names ending with **-ile** have always been acceptable, such as **uMfanufikile** ('a boy has arrived') which obviously refers to a boy. The simple name **uFikile** ('[a child] has arrived'), however, is marked as female, as are the names:

- **uBongekile** ('being grateful');
- **uSibongile** ('we are grateful');
- **uDuduzile** ('having comforted');
- **uKhanyisile** ('she has lit [us] up');
- **uPhumuzile** ('having given rest');
- **uThembile** ('having hoped');
- **uThokozile** ('having been happy').

Also marked as female are those with the passive perfect suffix **-iwe**, as in:

- **uBoniwe** ('having been seen');
- **uBusisiwe** ('having been blessed');
- **uKhethiwe** ('having been chosen');

- **uLindiwe** ('having been awaited');
- **uThandiwe** ('being loved');
- **uNelisiwe** ('having been satisfied');
- **uTholiwe** ('having been obtained').

Also marking female names is the neuter perfect suffix, only common in the three names:
- **uBonakele** ('being visible');
- **uSizakele** ('being helpful');
- **uTholakele** ('being available').

The perfect suffix **-ile** is abbreviated to **-e** when **-phi?** ('where?') and **-ni?** ('what?') are added to the verb. Such names still are marked female:
- **uDumeleni** ('thunder at what?');
- **uGcinephi** ('finished off where?');
- **uThembeni** ('hoped for what?');
- **uMilephi** ('grown where?').

Certain verbal structures are restricted to male names, and as a result they become male markers. One such structure is 'Plural Imperative with Object Concord', as in 'We Madoda, *mbambeni* lowo mfana!' ('Hey men! Catch-him that boy'): **uMbambeni** ('catch-ye-him') is a male name. So are the following:
- **uMbangeni** ('dispute him');
- **uMbongeni** ('praise Him');
- **uMbongeleni** ('be grateful for him');
- **uMbukeni** ('look at him');
- **uMcabangeleni** ('think of him');
- **uMgcineni** ('take care of him');
- **uMtuseni** ('praise Him');
- **uMthandeni** ('love him' or, perhaps, 'love Him').

Another verbal structure which is restricted to male names and thus becomes a morphological marker is the structure **M** + verb root + passive **-wa** (often with the Applied Extension so it becomes **M** + verb root + **el** + **wa**). Here are a number of male names with this structure:
- **uMbhekisiswa** ('the carefully watched one');
- **uMbinelwa** (the sworn-at one');
- **uMfulathelwa** ('one against whom backs are turned');
- **uMhawukelwa** ('the pitied one');
- **uMkhethwa** ('the chosen one');
- **uMkhishwa** ('the cast-out one');
- **uMnikelwa** ('the one who is given things');
- **uMzingelwa** ('the hunted-for one').

The compound structure (verb + object) is exceptionally productive when it comes to male names. Some of the more common ones are:

- **uBhekinkosi** ('have regard for the Lord');
- **uBhekumuzi** ('look after the family');
- **uBhekuyise** ('look up to the father');
- **uBonginkosi** ('thank the Lord');
- **uThembinkosi** ('trust the Lord');
- **uThandukwazi** ('love knowledge');
- **uVusumuzi** ('revive the family').

Some of the less common names using the same structure are:

- **uBangifa** ('fight over the inheritance');
- **uBhekumthetho** ('have regard for the law');
- **uBhekizitha** ('look out for enemies');
- **uChithumuzi** ('disperse the family');
- **uHluphuyise** ('irritate his father');
- **uHolimali** ('earn money');
- **uGodlumthakathi** ('hold back the wizard');
- **uQedukwenza** ('stop doing that');
- **uThengumuzi** ('buy a house');
- **uVusindaba** ('revive the matter').

This structure is never used for female names, and so these are all marked as male.

Male names using a variety of compound structures are common. Without giving exhaustive lists here, I can provide one example of each of a number of different structures:

VERB + POSSESSIVE PRONOUN: **uSengezakhe** ('milk his [cows]') [**senga** + **ezakhe**]

VERB + PRONOUN: **uThathazonke** ('take everything') [**thatha** + **zonke**]

VERB + ADVERBIAL ADJUNCT: **uGcinangokubusa** ('end up by ruling') [**gcina** + **ngokubusa**]

VERB + DEPENDENT VERB: **uPhumasilwe** ('come out and let us fight') [**phuma** + **silwe**]

MA + VERB + DEPENDENT VERB: **uMavelajahe** ('one who continually appears and hurries off') [**vela** + **ajahe**]

NOUN + POSITIVE VERB: **uMfanufikile** ('a boy has arrived') [**umfana** + **ufikile**]

NOUN + NEGATIVE VERB: **uMandlakapheli** ('strength never ends') [**amandla** + **akapheli**]

NOUN + INTERROGATIVE VERB: **uMzuthini** ('what does the family say?') [**umuzi** + **uthini**]

NOUN + POSITIVE NON-VERBAL PREDICATE: **uNkosinathi** ('the Lord is with us') [**inkosi** + **inathi**]

NOUN + NEGATIVE NON-VERBAL PREDICATE: **uMuzikawukho** ('the family is not present') [**umuzi** + **kawukho**]

NOUN + POSSESSIVE NOUN: **uMandlenkosi** ('strength of the Lord') [**amandla** + **enkosi**]

NOUN + POSSESSIVE PRONOUN: **uBukhosibakhe** ('his chieftancy') [**ubukhosi** + **bakhe**]

NOUN + POSSESSIVE LOCATIVE: **uMuntuwasembo** ('a person from eMboland') [**umuntu** + **waseMbo**]

NOUN + ADVERB: **uMfanafuthi** ('another boy') [**umfana** + **futhi**]

NOUN + ADJECTIVE: **uMfanomkhulu** ('big boy') [**umfana** + **omkhulu**]

NOUN + RELATIVE: **uNkunzebomvu** ('red bull') [**inkunzi** + **ebomvu**]

NOUN + PRONOUN: **uMakhosonke** ('all chiefs') [**amakhosi** + **onke**]

For a far greater number of examples, see Koopman (1976: 74–78).

Very few of these structures are found with females names, and even for those structures, there are far fewer examples, so few that I will give all my examples:

NOUN + POSITIVE VERB: **uNtombifikile** ('a girl has arrived'), **uNtombifile** ('a girl and has died'), and **uNtombizibuyile** ('the girls have come back')

NOUN + POSSESSIVE: **uNtombizabantu** ('girls of the people'), **uNtombikanina** ('her mother's girl'), and **uNtombikayise** ('her father's girl')

NOUN + ADJECTIVE: **uNtombenhle** ('pretty girl'), **uNtombenkulu** ('big girl'), and **uThembelihle** ('nice hope')

NOUN + RELATIVE: **uNtombebomvu** ('red girl')

NOUN + DEMONSTRATIVE PRONOUN: **uNtombilezi** ('these girls' – using the demonstrative pronoun **lezi** ['these']).

It will be seen from the above that with the single exception of the name **uThembelihle**, every compound noun is based on the word **intombi** ('girl'). From the limited structures available, the extremely limited number of examples for each structure, and the fact that each compound (with the single exception) is marked with 'intombi', one must conclude that compound names are marked as male.

17.4.3 Double marking

Some Zulu personal names are doubly marked for sex. Take, for example, the name **uNontombi**, which includes both the morphological marker **-no-** and the semantic marker **intombi**. The name **uNtombifikile** has both **intombi** and the perfect tense suffix **-ile**.

Compound names being much the provenance of male names, any compound with a lexical marker will be doubly marked, such as **uMfano-mhlophe** ('light-skinned boy') and **uNdodenzima** ('hard man'). So too would be a name such as **uSokhehla**, with the morphological marker **-so-,** and the lexical marker **ikhehla** ('old man').

17.4.4 Contradictory marking

Some personal names have markers which conflict, as in **uMfanufikile** ('a boy has arrived'), where the lexical marker **umfana** contradicts the female marker **-ile**. In such a case, it is clear that the lexical marker overrides the morphological marker, as there is no way this name could be regarded as female. The power of such a lexical marker over morphological markers is seen in compound names such as **uNtombikayise** ('girl of her father') and **uNtombenhle** ('pretty girl'). Compound structures, as we have pointed out above, are exclusively male, unless the lexical marker **intombi** is included.

Some names with conflicting markers are just not possible. For example, the hypothetical name ***uSontombi**, with the conflicting **-so-** and **intombi**, would arouse ridicule. I have to say, though, that I once collected the name **uNondoda**, with the conflicting markers **-no-** and **indoda**, from the records of inhabitants of a house in KwaMashu Township near Durban. Students I have shown this name to have either been totally open in their disbelief, or have expressed amazement and scepticism.

17.4.5 Unmarked names

There are a few personal names in the Zulu naming system that are not marked for sex, and so can be used for either males or females. These are the names based on the simple dictionary form of the verb, names such as:

- **uBonga** ('thank');
- **uLinda** ('wait');
- **uDuduza** ('comfort');
- **uThandaza** ('pray');
- **uThemba** ('hope, trust').

Even with forms such as these, certain verbs are more favoured for boys' names and others for girls' names. For example, happiness and joy are often expressed at the birth of a child, but the parents of a girl are more likely to choose the verb **thokoza** ('be happy') while the parents of a boy are more likely to choose the verb **jabula** ('be happy'). Having said this, such unisex names are not common, and for every parent choosing a name such as **uJabula** to show their happiness at getting a son, there are 20 others choosing a name such as **uJabulani**, the plural imperative form of the verb which is marked as male. And for every parent choosing **Thokoza** to indicate happiness at getting a daughter, there are another 20 choosing the female-marked name **uThokozile**.

For more detail on the material in Section 17.5 below, see Koopman (1991).

17.5 CLAN NAMES (*IZIBONGO)*

Unlike most Euro-Western surnames, whose only potential for morphological change is the plural ('keeping up with the *Joneses*'), Zulu clan names can undergo a number of morphological changes, with accompanying meaning change. Take, for example, the clan name **uMthembu** which can occur in the following forms:

- **umThembu**: a Thembu, a member of the Thembu clan;
- **abaThembu**: Thembu people, clan members of the Thembu clan;
- **abakwaThembu**: those of the house of Thembu, referring to the chiefly line;
- **ebaThenjini**: of the Thembu area, literally 'among the Thembus';
- **isiThembu**: Thembu language and customs.

The clan name can take a number of different locative inflections, each subtly changing the meaning of the name. Look at the following variations of the clan name **uMbatha**:

- **uMbatha**: an Mbatha clan member;
- **amaMbatha**: members of the Mbatha clan;
- **emaMbatheni**: in the Mbatha clan area
- **kumaMbatha**: with the Mbatha clan (generally speaking);
- **koMbatha**: with a specific group of people all called Mbatha;
- **kwabakwaMbatha**: among those of the house of Mbatha (the chiefly lineage).

These variations are often used in Zulu speech, and have led to clan names being recorded in different fashions, sometimes causing confusion for historians, particularly those without a grasp of Zulu phonology and morphology. As a prime example of the kind of problem caused by variations in the form of the Zulu clan name, I can cite the example of **Mzolo**. The form '**Mzolo**' is the modern form, used in English, to refer to people of the **uMzolo** clan. Those trying to find where the **Mzolo** clan had originally settled, on Bryant's map entitled 'The Location of the Zulu Clans in pre-Shakan Times' (insert in *Olden Times in Zululand and Natal*) will not find '**Mzolo**' on this map. They will, however, find the word '**Tolweni**' on the map, and if they know something about Zulu morphology, Zulu phonology, and some of the characteristics of the historical dialects in KwaZulu-Natal, they will be able to link '**Mzolo**' and '**Tolweni**'. For those without this specialised knowledge, the link is as follows.

The full form of modern '**Mzolo**' is **umZolo**, a class 1 noun. Most Zulu nouns in class 1 have their plural in class 2, the **aba-** class, but names of clans usually find their plural in class 6, the **ama-** class. This gives us the plural form **amaZolo**. If we look back in history, the original **umZolo** clan belonged to the *tekela*-speaking Nguni, whose speech was characterised by a **/t/** where today's Zulu has **/z/,** as in **amaSwati** where Zulu people today say **amaSwazi**. The *tekela*-speaking Mzolos pronounced their own name **amaTolo**, not **amaZolo**. The locative form of this word is **emaTolweni** ('among the Mzolos'), and Bryant leaves off the prefix **ema-**, and simply writes the clan name as **Tolweni**.

Clan names today are all in class 1a, thus we have: **uNxumalo**, **uMkhize**, **uDlamini**, **uCele**, **uSibiya**, **uKunene**, and so on. As nouns of class 1a, these all take their plurals in class 2a: **oNxumalo**, **oMkhize**, **oDlamini**, etc.

As we have seen above, such a plural means 'a small group of Nxumalo clan members', 'a small group of Mkhize clan members', etc.

Zulu clan names are like Zulu personal names in that, although all nouns of noun class 1a, they may be derived from various noun classes. (But note that as we saw in Chapter 5, not all of these may be traced back to an identifiable Zulu word.) The following are examples from the various noun classes.

As class 1 (**umu-**) is a class for humans generally, it is not surprising to find many **izibongo** derived from this class, such as **uMbatha**, **uMbonambi**, **uMchunu**, **uMdlalose**, **uMdluli**, **uMhlongo**, **uMkhize**, **uMngadi**, **uMsomi**, **uMthembu** and **uMthethwa**.

No modern forms of **izibongo** are derived from class 2. Bryant's forms such as **ebaThenjini** (loc of **abaThembu**) are today simply **uMthembu**. We could note that the class 2 form **abakwa-** ('those of the house of . . .') can be used with any clan name when reference is made to the chiefly lineage of that clan. So **abakwaMkhize** means the chiefly line of the Mkhizes, and **abakwa-Zondi**, the ruling house of the Zondi clan. Zulu also uses **aba-** and its variant **abe-** for groups larger than clans: **abaNguni**, **abeSuthu**, **abeTswana**.

Classes 3 (**umu-**) and 4 (**imi-**) contain only impersonal nouns, and they are not used as bases for Zulu **izibongo**.

Examples of class 5 origin clan names are **uDube** (< **idube**, 'zebra') and **uGwala** (< **igwala**, 'coward').

Class 6 (**ama-**) gives rise to a very large number of modern **izibongo**, such as **uMabaso**, **uMadondo**, **uMagwaza**, **uMajola**, **uMakhathini**, **uMaphu-mulo**, **uMasondo**, and **uMazibuko**.

Today's clan names **uSibiya**, **uSikhakhane**, **uSibisi** and **uSithole** are all derived from class 7 (**isi-**) nouns. From class 8 (**izi-**), we find **uZikalala**, **uZikhali** and **uZiqubu**.

Class 9 (**in-**) gives us the following clans' names:

- **uNdlazi** (< **indlazi**, 'mousebird');
- **uNdlela** (< **indlela**, 'path');
- **uNdlovu** (< **indlovu**, 'elephant');
- **uNgobese** (< **ingobese**, 'bogwood');

- **uNgwane** (< **ingwane**, 'cuttlefish');
- **uNgwenya** (< **ingwenya**, 'crocodile');
- **uNkomo** (< **inkomo**, 'head of cattle');
- **uNkosi** (< **inkosi**, 'chief, 'lord').

Nouns from class 11 (**ulu-**) are the root nouns for the following clan names:

- **uLukhozi** (< **ukhozi**, 'black eagle');
- **uLushaba** (< **ushaba**, 'ferocious temper');
- **uLuthuli** (< **uthuli**, 'dust').

Class 14 (**ubu-**) gives rise to very few clan names, and only **uBulose** and **uButhelezi** are well-known.

uKubheka ('to watch') is the only example of class 15 that I can find, and **uKunene** the only example of a clan name from a class 17 noun.

Of particular interest in the morphology of clan names is the use of the class 7 prefix **isi-**. We have seen above that nouns from this class can form clan names, where the basic prefix **-si-** of class 7 is retained in the **isibongo**: **uSikhakhane**, **uSibiya** and **uSibisi**. The class 7 prefix can also be used with Zulu nouns which refer to a particular nation or grouping to mean the language and customs of that group. Consider the following:

- **um-Xhosa** (cl 1: a Xhosa person) > **ama-Xhosa** (cl 6: Xhosa people) > **isi-Xhosa** (class 7: the Xhosa language);
- **um-Zulu** (cl 1: a Zulu person) > **ama-Zulu** (cl 6: Zulu people) > **isi-Zulu** (class 7: the Zulu language);
- **i-Ngisi** (cl 5: an English person) > **ama-Ngisi** (English people) > **isi-Ngisi** (English language).

Doke and Vilakazi give **isiMelika** (< *America*) as 'American accent, manners, etc' (1958: 498).

When a clan name is placed into class 7 in this way, it refers to the speech habits, the dress, the practices, or the customs of that clan. Thus one can say **Laba bantu basina isiMbatha** ('These people dance in the style of the Mbatha clan'), **IsiNgubane ukunquma umunwe** ('It is the Ngubanes' practice to cut off the little finger'), or **Ukhuluma isiMkhize** ('He speaks in the way the Mkhize clan do').

There is also another use of class 7 **isi**- when prefixed to clan names, and that is to refer to the direct line of patrilineal descent in that clan. For example, **isiNtuli** and **isiHlengwa** do not only refer to the customs and practices of the **Ntuli** and **Hlengwa** clans, but to their genealogies as well.

17.6 COMPOUNDS

At first glance, the grammatical process of compounding looks to be a relatively simple task: one merely takes two parts of speech, a verb and a noun, say, and joins them together to make a new noun. When compound nouns are subjected to linguistic scrutiny, however, a number of complex issues arise, such as the syntactic relationship between the compounded elements, rules of deletion, and others. It is not my intention in this book to examine these complexities in detail, and the interested reader is directed to Koopman 1984 and 1998. However, we do need to look at the process of compounding itself.

Although almost any two parts of speech can be joined together to form a Zulu compound noun, verbs and nouns are the most commonly compounded elements, and we find compounds with *noun + noun*, as in the personal boys' name **uMandlenkosi** ('strength of the Lord'), *noun + verb*, as in the nickname **uMbamboziyabalwa** ('ribs are counted'), *verb + noun*, as in the name of the seventh month **uNhlolanja** ('inspect the dog'), and *verb + verb*, as in the dog's name **uShiyabekhala** ('leave them crying').

When the second element of the compound begins with a consonant, there are no problems in the joining together of the two elements. If we look at the examples above we see that the nickname **uMbamboziyabalwa** has the two elements **(izi)mbambo** ('ribs') and **ziyabalwa** ('they are counted), with **ziyabalwa** beginning with a consonant. In the dog's name **uShiyabekhala** the first element is the verb **shiya** ('leave'), and the second is the verb **bekhala** ('they crying'), which also begins with a consonant.

The first element of the compound will always end with a vowel for the simple reason that Zulu words end in vowels. A problem arises if the second element *begins* with a vowel for then when the two halves of the compound are joined together, two vowels will come together, that is, the final vowel of the first half, and the initial vowel of the second half, *and the Zulu language does not permit two vowels to come together*. Let us look at the two examples **uMandlenkosi** and **uNhlolanja** above. The two halves of **uMandlenkosi** are the noun **amandla** ('strength') and the possessively-prefixed noun **enkosi** ('of the Lord'). If we simply joined these together, we would have '**uMandla-enkosi**', and this is not permissible in Zulu. The two halves of **uNhlolanja** are the verb **hlola** ('examine') and the noun **inja** ('dog'), and if these were merely joined, the result would be the impermissible '**uNhlolainja**'.

When the workings of the language produce a situation where two vowels find themselves next to one another, one of three things may happen. *Firstly*, the two vowels may 'fuse' together and produce a 'combined vowel'. This is what happens when, for example, **na-** ('and') and **nga-** ('by means of') are prefixed to a noun. When **na-** is prefixed to **izinja** ('dogs') the */a/* of **na-** and the initial */i/* of **izinja** fuse together ('coalesce' is the technical term') to make an */e/*, and we get **nezinja** ('and the dogs'). When **na-** is added to **ubaba**, the */a/* and the */u/* fuse together and make */o/*, and we get **nobaba** ('and father'). This process of coalescence is not found in compound nouns.

Secondly, two vowels that find themselves uncomfortably next to one another may be separated by a consonant (technical description: an 'intervocalic consonant'). In the negative present tense of the verb, for example the negative **a-** may be prefixed to the subject concords **-i-** or **-u-**. In such a case /y/ will be placed between **a** and **i,** and /w/ between **a** and **u**, as in the following examples:

- positive: *intombi ihamba manje* ('the girl is going now');
- negative: *intombi* **ayi***hambi manje* ('the girl is not going now');
- positive: *umuthi ukhula kahle* ('the tree is growing well');
- negative: *umuthi* **awu***khuli kahle* ('the tree is not growing well').

Intervocalic consonants are not used in Zulu compound nouns. *Thirdly,* one of the two consonants may be 'elided', or 'deleted'. This is what happens when a subject concord such as **li-** or **ba-** is prefixed to a verb beginning with a vowel such as **enza** ('do') and **osa** ('roast'); **li** + **enza** simply gives **lenza** and **ba** + **osa** simply becomes **bosa.** The same thing happens to the final vowels of words in fast speech. When one writes down or pronounces slowly the phrase **bonke abantu abahle** ('all the nice people'), all the final vowels are in place. But when this phrase is spoken in normal fast speech, the final vowels disappear (are 'elided', are 'deleted') and we hear **bonk'abant'abahle.**

Vowel deletion (or 'vowel elision') *is* what takes place in Zulu compound nouns.

17.6.1 Vowel deletion

Having decided that vowel deletion is how compound nouns avoid the problem of two vowels coming together, the next question is '*Which* of the two vowels should go?' When **hlola** is added to **inja**, should we delete the final **a** of **hlola** and so end up with **uNhlolinja**, or should it be the initial **i** of **inja** and so get **uNhlolanja**? When the verb **vusa** is added to the noun **umuzi**, do we end up with **uVusamuzi** or **uVusumuzi**?

There is a set of rules that we can follow here and these are discussed below.

a. Rule 1

If the compound noun is a personal name (that is, an **igama lasekhaya**, the Zulu name given to a young child), *it is always the final vowel of the first element which is dropped.* Look at the following examples of personal names:

bonga + **inkosi**	> **bong' inkosi**	> **uBonginkosi** ('praise the Lord')
bheka + **uyise**	> **bhek' uyise**	> **uBhekuyise** ('look to the Father')
amakhosi + **onke**	> **amakhos' onke**	> **uMakhosonke** ('all chiefs')
intombi + **enhle**	> **intomb' enhle**	> **uNtombenhle** ('beautiful girl')
umfana + **ufikile**	> **umfan' ufikile**	> **uMfanufikile** ('a boy has arrived')
thanda + **ukwazi**	> **thand' ukwazi**	> **uThandukwazi** ('love knowledge')

There are no exceptions to this rule: *all* personal names delete the final vowel of the first element if the second element begins with a vowel. Clearly, if the second element does not begin with a vowel, there is no need for this deletion. For example, in **uMfanafuthi** ('another boy'), there is no need to delete the last **a** of **umfana** because the second half of the compound – **futhi** – begins with a consonant.

b. Rule 2

If the compound is a common noun, and not a personal name, *it is always the first vowel of the second element which is dropped.* Consider the following examples of compound nouns referring to birds and plants:

hlala + inyoni	> hlala + nyoni	> **umhlalanyoni** ('where the birds sit'), the Natal Mistletoe
lala + inyathi	> lala + nyathi	> **ilalanyathi** ('where the buffalo lies') Septee Tree
khwela + imfene	> khwela + mfene	> **isikhwelamfene** ('where the baboon climbs') Water Ironplum
inkolo + etsheni	> inkolo + tsheni	> **Inkolotsheni** ('hollow place in tree, in stone') Buffstreaked Chat
hlola + imvula	> hlola + mvula	> **ihlolamvula** ('what predicts rain') European Swift
qhopha + umuthi	> qhopha + muthi	> **isiqhophamuthi** ('what taps the tree') Woodpecker

c. Rule 3

If a common compound noun (that is, not a personal name) is prefixed with the formative **-ma-**, then the compound noun will behave as if it is a proper name. That is, it will delete the final vowel of the first element. Look at the following examples:

ma + hleka + ehlathini	> ma + hlek' ehlathini	> **umahlekehlathini** ('he who laughs in the bush'): a heavily-bearded man
ma + hlaba + ekufeni	> ma + hlab' ekufeni	> **umahlabekufeni** ('what strikes at death'): The Lavender Fever-berry
ma + gana + inyoni	> ma + gan' inyoni	> **umaganinyoni** ('what marries a bird'): woman who marries a poor man
ma + qunda + uswazi	> ma + qund'uswazi	> **umaqunduswazi** ('what blunts the whip'): sp. of herb (*Chironia krebsii*) whose roots are used to harden the skin against corporal punishment
ma + hlamba + ehlale	> ma + hlamb'ehlale	> **umahlambehlale** ('what washes and sits down'): sp. of Thorn-Pear (*Scolopia zeyheri*)
ma + hlanza + inyoka + endala	> ma + hlanz'inyok'endala	> **umahlanzinyokendala** ('what vomits up an old snake'): exceptionally villainous witch

d. Rule 4

The above rules do not apply to names such as school names, regimental names, place names, names of the months, etc. because these names are neither personal names nor common nouns. With toponyms, for example, one finds almost exactly a half-and-half distribution between those behaving like personal names and those behaving like common nouns. Take, for example, the two river names **aManzimtoti** ('sweet waters') and **aManzamnyama** ('black waters'): **aManzimtoti** behaves like a common noun does, deleting the initial vowel of the second element (**amanzi + (a)mtoti**), while **aManzamnyama** behaves like a personal name does, deleting the final vowel of the first element (**amanz[i] + amnyama**).

The following is a list of examples of compounds from a variety of different Zulu name categories, showing in each case whether the compound behaves like a personal name (PERSNAME) or a common noun (COMNOUN). In cases where the second element begins with a consonant or the same vowel, of course, there is no difference (NODIFF) between the two types. In each case I will also identify the parts of speech, for example 'NOUN + NOUN'.

Schools

Ubuhlebesundumbili ('the beauty of two Phoenix palms') (NOUN + NOUN + ADJECTIVE: NODIFF)
Sibongulwazi ('we are grateful for knowledge') (VERB + NOUN: PERSNAME)
Sobonakhona ('we'll see over there') (VERB + ADVERB: NODIFF)
Sibongimfundo ('we are grateful for education') (VERB + NOUN: PERSNAME)
Tholukukhanya ('gain the light') (VERB + NOUN: PERSNAME)
Muzokhanyayo ('house of light') (NOUN + VERB: PERSNAME)
KhanyiseluZulu ('light up for the Zulu nation') (VERB + NOUN: PERSNAME)

Homesteads

KwaBonezinkulu ('see great things') (VERB + ADJECTIVE: PERSNAME)
KwaMuntungifunani ('what does the person want of me?') (NOUN + VERB: NODIFF)
eNhlalamatsheni ('sit on the stones') (VERB + LOCATIVE NOUN: COMNOUN)
KwaZinjaziyamluma ('dogs bite him') (NOUN + VERB: NODIFF)
KwaBhekezakhe ('mind your own business') (VERB + PRONOUN: PERSNAME)
KwaVimbukhalo ('blocking the ridge') (VERB + NOUN: PERSNAME)
KwaHlumentabeni ('growing on a mountain') (VERB + LOCATIVE NOUN: PERSNAME)

Shops

Sizabantu Butchery (VERB + NOUN: NODIFF)
Kuhlekwethu ('it is good at our place') Wedding Centre (ADJECTIVE + PRONOUN: NODIFF)
Zamokuhle ('try the best') Store (VERB + ADJECTIVE: PERSNAME)

Names of the months, stars

uZibandlela ('conceal the paths') (VERB + NOUN: COMNOUN)
uNhlolanja ('inspect the dog') (VERB + NOUN: COMNOUN)
iNdonsakusa ('what draws the dawn') (VERB + NOUN: COMNOUN)
iNdonsamasuku ('what draws on the days') (VERB + NOUN: NODIFF)
iNkangakusa ('attract the dawn') (VERB + NOUN: COMNOUN)
iSicelankobe ('the one who begs for boiled mealies') (VERB + NOUN: COMNOUN)
iQhubankomo ('drive the cattle') (VERB + NOUN: COMNOUN)

Names of birds

isithandamanzi ('what likes the water') (VERB + NOUN: NODIFF)
ukhozilwentshebe ('eagle of the beard') (NOUN + POSSESSIVE NOUN: NODIFF)
ihlalankomo ('what sits on a cow') (VERB + NOUN: COMNOUN)
ikhwelematsheni ('what climbs on rocks') (VERB + LOCATIVE NOUN: PERSNAME)
isixulamasele ('what catches frogs') (VERB + NOUN: NODIFF)
isikhovampondo ('owl with horns') (NOUN + NOUN: COMNOUN)
intakansinsi ('finch of the *Erythrina* seed') (NOUN + NOUN: COMNOUN)
inhlekabafazi ('the laughter of women') (NOUN + NOUN: NODIFF)
ihlekehle ('it laughs as it alights') (VERB + VERB: PERSNAME)

Regiments

inDluyengwe ('dwelling of leopard') (NOUN + POSSESSIVE NOUN: NODIFF)
amaKhabaludaka ('Kickers of Mud') (NOUN + VERB: COMNOUN)
uCijimpi ('press on with the battle') (VERB + NOUN: PERSNAME)
amaBuzangenduku ('ask by means of a stick') (VERB + ADVERBIAL: NODIFF)
uDlambedlu ('swallowing impatience') (VERB + NOUN: COMNOUN)
inTshamathe ('spurt out saliva') (VERB + NOUN: NODIFF)
uGibabanye ('take out the others') (VERB + NOUN: NODIFF)
inGobamakhosi ('bend the chiefs') (VERB + NOUN: NODIFF)
imPumangingene ('go out while I come in') (VERB + VERB: NODIFF)
amaShayizindlu ('strikers of huts') (VERB + NOUN: PERSNAME)
uShisizwe ('burn the country') (VERB + NOUN: PERSNAME)
umThulisazwe ('what quietens the country') (VERB + NOUN: COMNOUN)

Nicknames

uMbamboziyabalwa ('ribs are counted') (NOUN + VERB: NODIFF)
uSiswanasophuthu ('little putu-stomach') (NOUN + POSSESSIVE NOUN: NODIFF)
uBhavelimboqo ('bent washbasin') (NOUN + ADJECTIVE: PERSNAME)
uSinqekasikho ('has no buttocks') (NOUN + NON-VERBAL PREDICATE: NODIFF)
uFishonamasondo ('fish with wheels') (NOUN + RELATIVE: NODIFF – because the adopted word **ufish** has no final vowel)
iSwelandlebe ('Mr Lack-Ears') (VERB + NOUN: COMNOUN)
uZikhalozembuzi ('nostrils of a goat') (NOUN + POSSESSIVENOUN: NODIFF)
uMacoshamaphepha ('picker-up of paper') (VERB + NOUN: NODIFF)

Plant names
umhlalampunzi ('where the duiker lives') (VERB + NOUN: COMNOUN)
ilalanyathi ('where the buffalo lies') (VERB + NOUN: COMNOUN)
umdlankawu ('what the monkey eats') (VERB + NOUN: COMNOUN)
ugobandlovu ('what the elephant bends') (VERB + NOUN: COMNOUN)
inzwabuhlungu ('feel the pain') (VERB + NOUN: COMNOUN)
ubuhlungubemamba ('pain of the mamba [bite]') (NOUN + POSSESSIVE NOUN: NODIFF)
umvusankunzi ('what rouses the bull') (VERB + NOUN: COMNOUN)
icishamlilo ('put out the fire') (VERB + NOUN: COMNOUN)

Toponyms
The main point of treating toponyms separately from other names is to discuss the issue of the locative form of the name. If we take a name such as **uMzinto** on the Natal South Coast: should it not really be **eMzinto**? Or are both correct? And if so, which one should go on the map? Both of them? When does one use the locative form and when not? Are there different kinds of locative formations? Why do we say **KwaZulu** and not **eZulwini**, but we say **eThekwini** and not **KwaTheku**?

The question of whether to use the non-locative form or the locative form of a place name has already been discussed in Chapter 7. To answer the other questions, we need to know something about the structure of Zulu locative forms.

The Bantu languages of Africa have three noun classes which play a similar role to the English prepositional phrase in a sentence. These noun classes are classes 16, 17 and 18, and in Zulu (and all the Bantu languages south of the Limpopo River), these noun classes have become fossilised as locative adverbs. So, for example, the class 16 prefix **pa-** is no longer added to any noun in the language, but is only found as the first syllable of **phandle** ('outside'), **phakathi** ('inside'), **phansi** ('down, below') and **phambili** ('in front', before'). In the word **phezulu** ('above'), the **pha-** has coalesced with the initial **i-** of **izulu** ('sky').

Zulu has replaced the use of these locative noun classes with a system of 'locative inflection' which in its most common form means substituting **e-** for the first vowel of the noun, and suffixing **-ini** to the noun where it adapts to the final vowel of the noun. The following table shows nouns ending with the five different vowels, and shows the adaptation of the suffixal **-ini**:

ilanga ('sun')	> **elangeni** ('in the sun')
umsenge ('*Cussonia* tree')	> **emsengeni** ('on the *Cussonia* tree')
amanzi ('water')	> **emanzini** ('in the water')
umsindo ('noise')	> **emsindweni** ('amidst the noise')
izulu ('sky')	> **ezulwini** ('in the sky')

These rules account for a number of place names, such as:

- **eMthunzini** (< **umthunzi**, 'shade');
- **eThekwini** (< **itheku**, 'bay' – although see Chapter 10);
- **eMthonjaneni** (< **umthonjana**, 'small fountain, spring').

There are, however, a number of exceptions to the above, which must also be considered.

Nouns of class 11 and 14 usually prefix **o-** instead of **e-**, so the locative of **ugu** ('coast') is **ogwini** ('on the coast').

Nouns of class 1, 1a and 2 prefix **ku-**, instead of using **e . . . ini**, so we find **kubantu** ('among the people') and **kumfundi** ('to the student') instead of **ebantwini** and **emfundini**.

Some nouns only prefix **e-**, without the **-ini** suffix, like **ekhaya** ('at home') and **emhlane** ('on the back'), not **ekhayeni** and **emhlaneni**.

Not an exception to the **e . . . ini** rule, but often causing problems for the non-Zulu speaker are the changes that take place if the last consonant of the noun is a bilabial or a combination of bilabials (**m, mb, ph, mp, b, bh**) and this is followed by **u** or **o**. Look at the following nouns:

ingubo	'blanket'	> **engutsheni**	'on the blanket'
umlomo	'mouth'	> **emlonyeni**	'in the mouth'
impuphu	'maize meal'	> **empushini**	'in the maize meal'
imbobo	'hole'	> **embotsheni**	'in the hole'

eMpushini is the name of an area on the eastern outskirts of Pietermaritzburg where there was a very large maize-meal rail depot in the earlier years of the twentieth century.

Another locative prefix found usually with class 1 and 1a is **kwa-**, with the particular meaning of 'at the home of', or 'at the establishment of'. **Kwado-kotela** means 'at the doctor's surgery', as opposed to **kudokotela**, which means 'at, in the vicinity of the doctor', wherever his physical person might be. **KuSipho** means 'in Sipho's vicinity', or 'on Sipho', whereas **kwaSipho** means 'at Sipho's house' (whether or not he himself is actually present). The prefix **kwa-** features in a lot of place names, such as **kwaMashu**, **kwa-Mbonambi** and **kwaZulu**.

The locative form of a place name is always used in a locative context:

ngihlala eThekwini	'I live <u>in</u> Durban'
basebenza eMlazi	'they work in uMlazi'
siya eMzinto	'we are going to uMzinto'

The 'nominative' (non-locative) form of the place name is used when the name is not in a locative context, such as when the place name is the subject or the object of a sentence:

ngiyalithanda kakhulu iTheku	'I like Durban very much'
uMlazi yindawo esiwaziyo	'uMlazi is place which we know'
uMzinto kuseNatali	'uMzinto is in Natal'

Both the locative and the nominative forms can be found on the signboards and the maps of KwaZulu-Natal, with names such as **iSiphingo** and **uMlazi** representing non-locative forms and **Empangeni** and **eShowe** representing locative forms. Names such as **eMpangeni** have raised an interesting debate over the last few years, on what exactly the nominative or non-locative form is.

Clearly the name as found on maps and signboards – **eMpangeni** – is in the locative and is therefore correct for locative contexts such as **Ngiya eMpangeni** ('I am going to Empangeni'). But what is the correct form for 'Empangeni is a lovely town'? Do we say '**eMpangeni yidolobha elihle**'? or '**iMpangeni yidolobha elihle**'? or '**iMpange yidolobha elihle**'? In fact, most Zulu speakers would use '**iMpangeni**' thus violating a rule which I once stated as a fact in 'Zulu Place-Names in the Drakensberg', when I said:

> If the place name has a locative suffix, there must be a locative prefix. **eThekwini** can never be '**iThekwini**'; **eShongweni** can never be '**iShongweni**' . . .
>
> This is a simple fact of Zulu grammar : a locative prefix does not necessarily require a locative suffix, e.g. **esitolo**, **ekhaya**, **ekhanda**, but a locative suffix does require a locative prefix (1983: 299).

Linda van Huysteen has recently argued very convincingly against my 'rule' in an article entitled 'The Zulu Place Name as a Morphological Exception' (1994), where she makes it clear that although *common nouns* ending in an **-ini** form must have an **e-** or **o-** prefix, this is not necessarily the case for place names, and in non-locative contexts it is perfectly common to find **uMngeni** River, **iMpangeni**, **iThekwini**, **iMadadeni**, and so on.

The prefix **kwa-**, which as we saw above, means 'the home of' or 'the establishment of' when linked to a personal noun, is also used for making place names. Although it occurs most often with personal names, as in **KwaMashu** – the home of Sir *Marshall* Campbell, sugar farmer and philanthropist – and with clan names, as in **KwaMbonambi**, it is also found with descriptive compounds, such as **kwaThwalilitshe** ('the home of carrying a rock'), a hill characterised by a balancing rock, in the Drakensberg, and **kwaDedangendlale** ('the home of Move-out-of-my-way-and-let-me-unrollmy-blankets'), the Zulu name for the Valley of 1000 Hills between Durban and Pietermaritzburg.

Not surprisingly, very many of the homestead names discussed in Chapter 11, from Ntuli's data, Shabalala's data, and the historical data, form a locative with **kwa-**, and this is not combined with the homestead owner's name, but with the social message that is in the name:

- **KwaBonezinkulu** ('see great things');
- **KwaMuntungifunani** ('what does the person want of me?');
- **KwaDeqheluka** ('keep on shifting');
- **KwaMpondo** ('many horns': a prosperous cattle owner);
- **KwaZinjaziyamluma** ('dogs bite him': vicious dogs around).

Shop names also use the **kwa-** locative: **KwaMahleka** Restaurant, **Kwa Amakhosi** Supermarket, **Kwa Inkanyezi Indhlu Yemithi Yabantu** (a herbalist's shop), **Kwa Mdaphuna**, and **Kwa Thandanani** Superette. The spaced or unspaced nature of the **kwa-** in these examples reflects the preference of the signwriter reponsible for a particular sign.

It is perhaps surprising that school names do not reflect the view of the community that a school is a 'home of knowledge' and give names like **KwaThandulwazi**. In fact, in all the data that I used on school names, only one used the **kwa-** locative: the school **kwaHluzingqondo** ('clarify the mind').

Chapter 18

Onomastic shift

18.1 INTRODUCTION

'Onomastic shift' takes place when there is a change in the onomastic status of a name. These changes are of three basic types which are described below.

18.1.1 A name may become another type of name

In this case, a name moves into a different subcategory of names. An anthroponym may become a toponym, as in various KwaZulu-Natal towns such as Harrismith, Colenso and Durban. In these three examples, the well-known Natal historical personalities Sir Harry Smith, Bishop John Colenso, and Sir Benjamin D'Urban have been commemorated. Conversely, a toponym may become an anthroponym, as when the River *Merwede* (in Holland) becomes the well-known South African surname *Van der Merwe*. Similar examples are the surnames – taken from the Pietermaritzburg telephone directory – *Van Rensburg* ('castle on the Rhine'), *Van Amsterdam*, and *Van Breda* (a town in North Brabant, Holland).

18.1.2 A name may become a 'non-name'

In this case, a proper noun may lose its proper noun status and become a common noun, as has happened when the Duke of Wellington, the Earl of Sandwich, and the Earl of Cardigan gave their respective names to *wellingtons*, *sandwiches*, and *cardigans*.

There are a number of examples of this phenomenon in Zulu. An early example is that of Mr Buckley, who sold beads at his store at the lower Tugela Drift during the late 1800s. The light blue bead still known today as **ubhokli** is derived from his name. The names of the Checkers supermarket chain has gone into Zulu as **ushekazi** ('plastic shopping bag' – such a bag is still known as an **ushekazi** even if it has the name of another supermarket or shop written on it), and into Xhosa as **itshekazi** and Northern Sotho as **tšhêkase**. A T-shirt is known as an **isikibha**, from the Skipper Shirt Factory in Durban, and a knife with a folding blade is an **i-okapi**, from Okapi Knife manufacturers. At the time of writing, Zulu students no longer know that in the early 1990s a Kombi taxi was known as **izolabudd**, a reference to the South African long-distance runner, but today's students still talk about a two rand coin as an **i-deklerk**, referring to then President F.W. de Klerk, head of the South African government at the time of the introduction of this coin.

18.1.3 A 'non-name' (common noun) may become a name

The common nouns *hunter*, *cook*, *smith*, *mason*, *baker* and *miller* are all well-known English surnames. Place names such as Oxford, Cape Town, Table Mountain, Fish River, and Kloof are all based on common nouns.

In Koopman (1994a) I gave two examples of onomastic shifts where a noun has become a name and then become another type of name:

> *ford* (common noun: river crossing) > *Ford* (common English surname)
> > Henry Ford (manufacturer) > Ford (famous make of car)
> and
> *urban* (English adjective) > *D'Urban* (surname) > *Durban* (toponym)
> > *Gobius <u>durban</u>ensis* (species name: type of fish)

In this book on Zulu names we have mainly seen two types of onomastic shift taking place: names becoming other names, and 'non-names' becoming names. The third type of onomastic shift, where a name becomes a 'non-name', as in the examples **ushekazi** and **izolabudd** above, are not as common.

> Consult Koopman (1994a) for a full discussion of the term 'onomastic shift', and see Koopman (1999c: 42–43) for examples of Zulu adoptives ('loan words') which exhibit onomastic shift.

18.2 NAMES BECOMING OTHER NAMES

Let us look at four such onomastic shifts.

18.2.1 Anthroponyms become eponymous shop names

We have seen in Chapter 13 that shop names may be taken from the name of the owner (or possibly to honour a third person or persons – as in **Bafana Bafana** Factory Shop, which honours the national football team, or as in **Madiba** Butchery, which honours former President Nelson Mandela). Personal names (**amagama asekhaya**), nicknames, clan names and clan praises can all become eponymous shop names.

Examples of first names are **Thabo's** Superette and **Thoko** Salon; clan names are seen in **Maphoboza** Takeaway and **Khoza's** Mini Market. A clan praise (**isithakazelo**) is added to the clan name in **KwaKhumalo: Mtungwa's** Store, where 'Khumalo' is the clan name, and 'Mtungwa' the clan praise. Sometimes the owner of the shop gives both first name and clan name, as in

Siyabonga Hlophe's Butchery. Some of the eponyms appear to be nicknames, as in **Kwa Mani** Take Away, and **KwaNtshebe** Supermarket ('Place of Mr Beard').

In these examples, a name has become another name. In other words, there is neither loss nor gain of onomastic status, but rather a movement from one onomastic subcategory to another.

18.2.2 Toponyms become school names

We noted in Chapter 11 that a number of schools were named for the locality in which they were situated. **Hluhluwe** Combined gets its name from both the village and the district of Hluhluwe, **Umhlali** Higher Primary from the village of Umhlali, and **Hlabisa** Lower Primary from the district of Hlabisa. **Mbongolwane** Combined takes its name from an area near Eshowe, and **Pholela** High is named for the district which in turn takes its name from the Pholela River.

Other schools named after rivers include the examples: **Thukela** High, **Umhlathuzana** High, **Umlalazi** Lower Primary, **Mpanzakazi** Combined (a stream near Greytown), and **Amatimofu** Lower Primary. Nearby hills may also give their names to schools: **Ntabantuzuma** Junior Secondary, **Ntumeni** High, and **Ntabankulu** Lower Primary.

Again, in these examples there is no gain and no loss in onomastic status, but a shift in subcategories.

18.2.3 River names become regimental names

In Chapter 6 we saw that: 'The names of a number of rivers coincide with the names of regiments. Whether the regiment was named after the river, or the river after the regiment, or both river and regiment were independently named the same way, is not clear.'

Rivers have of course been on the Earth longer than humans, and it is likely that the rivers were named prior to the establishment of the regimental system (although we have to admit that a number of scholars write that such-and-such a river received its name when Shaka's armies passed by on their way to such-and-such a place). However, whether the river name is derived from the regimental name or vice versa, there is no change in onomastic status, just a shifting of subcategories.

The **umKhuze** River and regiment were mentioned in Chapter 6, as well as the **isAngqu** regiment (< Zulu name for Orange River). Several other river–regiment combinations are the **imFolozi**, the **umLambongwenya**, and the **umZinyathi**. Near Nhlazatshe, we find the **oHlwayi** stream, eponymous with the Zulu regiment **uHlwayi**, also known as the **uMxhapho**.

18.2.4 Clan names become place names

Naming places after people is by no means as common in the Zulu naming system as it is in the English system. KwaZulu-Natal abounds with place names in honour of this or that colonial personality (Raper, 1987):

- *Port Shepstone* (< Sir Theophilus Shepstone);
- *Port Edward* (named after the then Prince of Wales, who later became King Edward VII);
- *Estcourt* (British MP Thomas Estcourt);
- *Pinetown* (colonial administrator Sir Benjamin Pine);
- *Melmoth* (Resident Commissioner Sir Melmoth Osborne);
- *Harding* (Chief Justice Sir Walter Harding).

Zulu toponyms derived from anthroponyms tend to come from clan names rather than the names of individuals. They occur in a number of forms:
- **Kwa MaMshube** north of Kranskop uses the **kwa-** ('abode of') prefix together with the **ma-** prefix which refers to the maiden name of a married woman. The clan name is **Mshube**.
- **MaBomvu** on the edge of the Ithala Game Reserve could also be using the married woman's prefix **ma-**, or this could be a class 6 noun class prefix.
- **KwaNgwenya**, the name of a settlement some thirty kilometres east of Vryheid, simply prefixes the locative **kwa-** directly onto the clan name **Ngwenya**.
- **Nondlovu**, the name of a small village near Mahlabathini, uses the name-forming prefix **no-** with the clan name **Ndlovu**.
- **eMaMbatheni**, five kilometres west of Mahlabathini, uses the locative form of the plural form **amaMbatha** ('the Mbatha clan collectively').
- **Simelane**, a village east of the Ngome forest, is the simple form of the clan name **Simelane**.

18.3 'NON-NAMES' BECOME NAMES

So many Zulu names are derived from nouns ('common' nouns) that one could fill a book with examples. Indeed, this book on Zulu names *is* filled with examples of names that are derived from nouns. Zulu personal names (**amagama asekhaya**) may be derived from all sorts of common nouns, as in:
- **uSipho** (< **isipho**, 'gift');
- **uSibusiso** (< **isibusiso**, 'blessing');
- **uMandla** (< **amandla**, 'strength');
- **uBuhle** (< **ubuhle**, 'beauty');
- **uNtombi** (< **intombi**, 'girl').

The same may be said for all sorts of anthroponyms and toponyms, as well as the names of animals, regiments, buses and anything else that is named. In this section on 'non-names' (common nouns) becoming names, I would like to concentrate on the strong influence that birds and plants have on the Zulu onomastic tradition.

18.3.1 The influence of bird 'names'

In Chapter 8 we saw a number of examples of place names derived from the names of birds. These included:

- **iZinkwazi** River (< **inkwazi**, 'Fish Eagle');
- **iNgqungqulu** River (< **ingqungqulu**, 'Bateleur Eagle');
- **aMajuba** Mountain (< **amajuba**, 'doves');
- **iNtendele** Camp (< **intendele**, 'partridge');
- **aMankankazane** River (< **amankankane**, 'Hadedah Ibises');
- **eNkwalini** Valley (< **inkwali**, 'quail');
- **iKholwane** Hill (< **ikholwane**, 'hornbill').

Bird references are seen in the school names **Nkonjane** ('swallow'), and **Gilonki** ('heron'), and we may remember the strong moral message of the **iphezukomkhono** (Redchested Cuckoo) in the field of education.

The nickname **uJuba** (< **ijuba**, 'dove') was given to a youth because of his mild manners, while **uMpangele ekhal' igijima** ('guinea-fowl that cries as it runs') is the praise of a man who habitually sings to himself when travelling.

In Chapter 6 we found examples of regimental names referring to birds. These included:

- **izinKonjane** ('swallows');
- **inSewane** ('small bird resembling **intiyane** [the waxbill]');
- **izinTaka** ('finches');
- **uluVe** ('Paradise Flycatcher');
- **izinYoni** ('The Birds').

We also noted the powerful symbolism of the regimental name **oNobhongoza** ('Egyptian Vultures') combining as it does the image of large raptors circling above scenes of death and destruction, as well as the image of paired birds reflecting the 'phalane' status of the uNobhongoza regiment, that is, always in partnership with another regiment.

18.3.2 The influence of plant 'names'

Plants have an even stronger influence on the Zulu onomastic system than birds do.

The following are examples of **izibongo** (clan names) which are derived from plant names:

- **uDuma** (< **iduma**, Winged Mistletoe, *Viscum anceps*);
- **uKhumalo** (< **ikhumalo**, Lemon Thorn, *Cassinopsis ilicifolia*);
- **uNgobese** (< **ingobese**, species of bogwood plant);
- **uSikhakane** (< **ikhakhane**, species of thistle);
- **uNgcobo** (< **ingcobo**, Broadleaved Hypoxis, *Hypoxis colchicifolia*);
- **uNgcolosi** (< **ungcolosi**, Wild Pentas, *Conostomium natalense*).

A number of schools have taken their names from plant life. The *Phoenix reclinata* palm gives us three examples:

- **Sundumbili** ('two Phoenix palms');
- **Ubuhlebesundumbili** ('the beauty of two Phoenix palms');
- **Emasundwini** ('among the Phoenix palms').

Nkiwaneni uses the locative form of **umkhiwane** ('species of wild fig tree'), and the **Mngampondo** school takes its name from the Zulu name of the Horned Thorn Tree (*Acacia grandicornuta*). **Ncemaneni** School is named for the economically important **incema** grass, used for making sleeping mats of the highest standard.

There are numerous river names referring to the characteristic plants that grow along their banks. Some have already been mentioned in Chapter 8:

- the **uMkhuze** River, named after a particular aromatic tree (*Heteropyxis natalensis*);
- the **uMhluhluwe** River a reference to the Thorny Monkey-rope (*Dalbergia armata*);
- the **oQalweni** River, named after the **uqalo** bamboo (*Arundinaria tessellata*);
- the **eMhlwazini** River, named after the Bushman's Tea (*Catha edulis*, Zulu **umhlwazi**).

The following are examples of minor rivers, tributaries and streams all over KwaZulu-Natal. The **uMbubu** stream near Cato Ridge refers to the soft, long **imbubu** grass. Near Gluckstadt is the **Hlonyane** stream which is named for the African Wormwood (*Artemisia afra*, Zulu **umhlonyane**). This is also the origin of the **Hlonyana** stream near Nhlazatshe. The Mbabane stream near Vryheid is either a diminutive of **imbaba** ('sunburnt pumpkin') or of **umbaba** (Wild Chestnut, *Calodendron capense*).

Many rivers and streams take their name from the thick reed beds (Zulu **umhlanga**) that grow in the slow-moving waters. The **uMhlanga** river is found only a few kilometres north of Durban; the **uMhlanganeni** ('place of the small reed bed') near Nhlazatshe; and the **uMhlangana** stream is near Vryheid.

Also near Vryheid are the following examples: the **Ngcaza** stream, a reference to **ingcaza** (a species of wild vegetable, *Amaranthus thunbergii*), the **Mfule** (from **imfule**, the creeper species *Adenia gummifera*), and the **Msuzwane**, the name being from the shrub *Lippia asperifolia* (Zulu **umsuzwane**).

In Chapter 6 we found a few regiments with names based on plants, including:

- **iMbabazane** ('stinging nettle');
- **iHlaba** ('species of aloe');
- **uDonqabathwa** (literally, 'the Bushmen's oilplant': a field weed).

The regimental name **uMkhuze** could refer to the uMkhuze River or to the species of aromatic tree known as an **umkhuze**.

18.4 NAMES BECOME 'NON-NAMES'

Mention was made above of how the Checkers supermarket brand has now become **ushekazi** ('plastic carry bag') and how then-President de Klerk gave his name to the two rand coin. As stated above, examples of this type of onomastic shift are not common, and have to be carefully searched for.

uPhathe is the name of a ravine in Northern Zululand into which the Zulu warrior Bongoza cleverly led the Boers into a trap (1830s). Ever since then an ambush has become known as an **uphathe**.

Zungu's 1995 Ph.D. thesis on 'contemporary codes and registers' (that is, 'slang') has a number of examples. From the football field (117) come the words **khabazela**, an interjection from the spectators instructing the player who is in possession of the ball to pass it to another player, and **ulanga**, a slang term for a goalkeeper. The word **khabazela** comes from the Mkhize clan praise **Khabazela**, inspired by the verb **khaba** ('to kick'), while **ulanga** is derived from the clan name **uLanga** (< **ilanga**, 'sun') 'because [the goal-keeper] wears jersey No.1 and stands alone like the sun in the sky'.

University slang (124) provides us with two opposites: **i-arabhu** and **i-romani**. An **i-arabhu** is a male student without any girlfriends; an **i-romani** has many girlfriends. The term **i-arabhu** 'emerged at a time when the Arabs imposed oil sanctions on South Africa. Because such boys have nobody to make love to, they are mocked by other students saying that they are saving their sperm like the Arabs saving their oil'. The contrasting term **i-romani** is derived from Shakespeare's play ***Romeo and Juliet***.

Slang found in hospitals (129) includes the word **umtopia** for a kwashi-orkor victim, as such patients are thin like the starving multitudes of *Ethiopia*.

From township slang (135) comes the word **uphawulina**, referring to a person who likes to make comments (to **phawula**) at social gatherings. Here the verb **phawula** is merged with the English girl's name *Pauline* to create the hybrid **uphawulina**.

Other miscellaneous examples include:

- **ubrenda**: a stolen car, derived from an incident in the song 'Ayashisa amalahle' by well-known singer *Brenda* Fassie (144);
- **iladeshi**: bankruptcy, a reference to the perceived state of Bangladesh, 'a country infected with bankruptcy in the early 1990s' (183);
- **ukuba nguCarl Meinhof** (the renowned German philologist who laid the groundwork for comparative Bantu studies in the late 1800s): to be a lecturer in the Zulu discipline at the University of Durban-Westville (234).

Nicknames for certain car-marques are derived from the initials of the marque:

- **iFirst-in-all-trouble** < *Fiat*;
- **iBe-my-wife** < *BMW*.

And finally, a loan-translation, sometimes known as a calque, in the word **ibhubesi** (Zulu 'lion'), not when used in reference to the large cat *Panthera leo*, but to the beer *Lion* Lager.

Chapter 19

The onomastic–oral literature continuum

One thing that has become clear in this book is how *few* entities in Zulu society only have *one* name. Sometimes, as in the case of certain birds, the entity is known by several different names, and the name actually used on a given occasion depends on the region and on what the bird is doing at a particular time. Sometimes, as is the case with humans, the individual has a 'real' name, that is hardly ever used, and one or more less formal names (nicknames, praise names) that are in daily use. Clan names, as we have seen, have corresponding clan praises, and sometimes these are completely interchangeable, so that a person with Ngema as her surname in one document and Mngadi as her surname in another document, can validly say that these two names are one and the same.

Occasionally the 'extra names', the alternative forms, the nicknames and the praise names, can be joined together, embellished with metaphor, expanded with narrative, and the result is a praise poem, which, while still fulfilling the function of identifying the entity referred to, has gone beyond the onomastic concept of a name. In effect, through the naming system of the Zulu language, there is a continuum which runs from the single unembellished name through the simple nicknames and one-word praises, through simple praise phrases, to the fully developed praise poem of several lines.

At one end of the scale are places with few, if any, alternative forms, nicknames or praise names. Most place names are the sole name for a particular place, and it is only rarely that we find a nickname such as **eJozi** for **eGoli** (Johannesburg), or a praise name such as **KwaNdongazibomvu** for **eMgungundlovu** (Pietermaritzburg), or an alternative form such as **uMhlume** for **eThekwini** (Durban). Interestingly, this last example – **uMhlume** – is not known to those Zulu speakers of today whom I have approached. Homesteads, too, occasionally have an alternative name, a 'nickname' only used perhaps by members of the family rather than the wider community in a particular area.

Birds too may have a number of names. Sometimes the variety in names is caused by regional differences. For example, the Glossy Starling is known as **ikhwezi** north of the Tugela River, and **ikhwinsi** south of the Tugela. Other variations will depend on whether one is talking about the bird generally, or as a stealer of crops, or whether the bird is flying or singing when seen. For example, the Ground Hornbill is generally known as **insingizi**, and this is certainly the name used when the bird is being discussed as a bringer of rain. But when the bird's deep 'Du, Du, Du' booming call is heard rolling over the plains, then the onomatopoeic name **ingududu** is used instead.

Some birds, though, do have praise names, as when the Yellow-billed Kite (**unhloyile, unohheshe, isikhokwane, ukholwe**) is praised by herdboys as **Nhloyile kaGelegele** ('Kite, son of the Whirlwind'). Many bird songs are also verbalised in Zulu, the result often being described as 'folk poetry', suggesting that the Zuluised bird songs are seen as the birds' praises. The Fiery-necked Nightjar (*Caprimulgus pectoralis*), for example, is believed to say '**Zavolo, zavolo, sengel'abantabakho**' ('nightjar, nightjar, go and find milk for your children'), while the Hamerkop (*Scopus umbretta*) is believed to say '**Ngangimuhle, ngangimuhle, kodwa ngoniwe yilokhu, nalokhu, nalokhu,** . . .' ('I used to be beautiful, but I have been spoilt by this, and that . . .'). These renderings of the birds' calls into Zulu are part of the birds' identities, so there is a naming process of sorts going on here.

Samuelson (1929: 413ff.) gives a number of examples of the verbalisation of Zulu bird calls, as does Bulpin (1969: 26–27). The most exhaustive collection is in Dunning (1946), and for a more academic and analytic approach see Gcumisa (1992).

Some of the months of the year have alternative names, and in Chapter 16 Faye (1923) has given us a complete list of alternative regional forms, as used in Northern Zululand, the forms he calls the 'Mkuze' variations. It is doubtful that these alternative forms are praise names, or even nicknames, but more likely simply alternative names, some of which are used more commonly than others.

Military regiments, as we saw in Chapter 6, can have nicknames or praise names. We saw that Shaka's regiment the **uDubinhlangu** had the alternative name **inTontela** but became popularly known as the **uJubingqwanga**. Bryant tells us that when the **umGumanqa** regiment 'was sent down to the flats near Port Natal to keep an eye on the newly arrived whites, they became known by the nickname **uKhangela-amaNkengane** ("keep an eye on the vagabonds")' (1929: 644). These nicknames and praise names are single names or, at the most, short praise phrases.

Domestic animals have praises rather than nicknames, and Molefe has given us a number of examples of the praises of dogs, horses, bulls, and other animals (see Chapter 14). It is interesting to note that wild animals do not have names in the same way as domestic animals (that is, an individual [proper] name for an individual animal, given by the owner). Some wild animals, as a species rather than as individuals, do, however, have praises. Some years ago I was fortunate enough to have been able to record some of these praises from the late Maqubu Ntombela, the well-known scout, tracker, and wild-life *savant*. These praises, according to Ntombela, were recited early in the morning by a group of hunters going out to hunt that particular species, and were recited again in the evening if they returned from the hunt successfully. The following praises of a leopard are an example:

USothwala odla amadoda,
Carrier who eats men,
Umnqabula-khanda lamadoda
One who cracks men's heads
Izinwele zimboze amehlo,
So that hair covers eyes,
Umnqibula-nhloko wendoda ihlomile,
Head-stamper of armed men,
Kuchitheke izikhali zayo.
Until weapons fall aside.

Certain groups of people have official group names and popular nicknames. Sports teams, for example, have official names such as 'The Protea Cricket Team' or 'The National Soccer Team', but nicknames such as **amabhobhoko** (Springbok Rugby Team), **Ama-glug-glug**, **Ama-kroko-kroko**, etc.

The human groups with the most extensive system of praise names and praises are clans, and the relationship between clan name and clan praise has already been given in some detail in Chapter 4. On the one hand, sometimes the clan praises consist of nothing but a list of names, usually in a fairly rough genealogical order, as in the clan praises of the Hlongwa clan recorded by Sithole (1982: 31):

1. **Shozi!**
2. **Hlophe!**
3. **Khayisa!**
4. **Ngangaz'izulu!**
5. **Nyathela kobhoka**
6. **Fihlela!**
7. **Hlela!**
8. **Majozi!**

Here we see simply a collection of names, no more and no less. None of the names has been expanded into praise phrases, and there are no narrative elements. On the other hand, consider the **izithakazelo** of the Hadebe clan, also from Sithole's collection (1982: 29), with my translation under each line:

1. **Mthimkhulu!**
   Mthimkhulu! ['Big Tree']
2. **Bhungane!**
   Bhungane! ['Beetle']
3. **UNdlubu zamil' ebubini**
   Ndlubu-beans that grew in an evil place
4. **Ngoba zesab'ukwehlela**
   Because they feared to descend
5. **Ingab'emhlabeni zesabani?**
   What could they possibly fear on earth?
6. **Mafuz' afulele njengefu lemvula**
   Thatcher who thatched like a cloud of rain
7. **Lapho kungavalwa ngesivalo**
   There where it is not closed by means of a door
8. **Kuvalwa ngenhloko yendoda**
   It is closed with the head of a man
9. **Mashwabada!**
   Mashwabada! ['Voracious eater']
10. **Owashwabadel'inkomo**
    Who ate voraciously of a beast
11. **Kanye nezimpondo zayo**
    Together with its horns
12. **Gob' izembe**
    Bend the axe
13. **Ndleb'enhle zombili**
    Beautiful ears, both of them
14. **Zulu! Bhungane!**
    Zulu! Bhungane!
15. **NoNkulunkulu mkhulu**
    Even God is great
16. **Kodwa akangangaBhungane**
    But not as great as Bhungane
17. **Iziyengan'eziyeng'umuntu**
    The tempters who tempt a person
18. **Zimyenga ngendaba**
    Beguiling him with stories
19. **Abanzipho zimnyama ngokuqhwandana**
    Those of the toenails black from scratching one another
20. **Makhulukhulu!**
    Great-great One!
21. **Mehlomakhulu!**
    Great-Eyes!

22. **Nin' enalala nomunwe**
    You who slept with your finger [up your anus]
23. **Navuka nakhwif'ilanga**
    And on awakening spat it at the sun
24. **Sigoloz'esimehl'abomvu**
    Starer with red eyes
25. **Mashiy'amahle**
    Beautiful eyebrows
26. **Nina bakaLangalibalele**
    You born of Langalibalele
27. **Bhungane wamakhulukhulu**
    Bhungane of the great-great ones
28. **Nina basemaHlutshini**
    You born of the Hlubi clan
29. **Ngelengele**
    Ngelengele! ['The One of the Steep Descent']

This is far more than simply a collection of names: there are narrative stanzas and descriptive stanzas. And yet a solid proportion of these Hadebe clan praises *are* simply names, or are simple expansions from names. Lines 1, 2, 9, 14, 20, 21, 25 and 29 are names or nicknames of chiefs of the Hadebe lineage. Line 26 refers to the people of the Hadebe clan as 'the children of Langalibalele', a famous Hadebe chief of the late nineteenth century. Line 28 refers to them as 'children of the Hlubi nation', a wider grouping of people under whom the Hadebe clan fell.

One could argue that the example given above and other clan praises constitute the fullest possible statement of the identity of a particular individual. Given the close association between naming and identity, it could also follow that such praises, taken *in toto*, are a form of 'super name' or 'ultra name'.

Although clearly such extended praises are too lengthy to be used in casual address, they are nevertheless often recited in full, such as when the 'owner' of the praises is competing in some event, and when that person is being thanked, or congratulated on some achievement. And finally, when the 'owner' eventually becomes an **idlozi** ('ancestral spirit'), his or her praises will not die but will continue to be used whenever his or her children **thetha amadlozi** ('speak with the spirits').

Bibliography

Armstrong, E.A. 1958. *The Folklore of Birds*. London: Collins.

Beattie, J.H.M. 1957. Nyoro Personal Names. *Uganda Journal*, Vol. 21.

Berglund, A-I. 1976. *Zulu Thought-Patterns and Symbolism*. Cape Town: David Philip.

Bird, J. 1965. *Annals of Natal 1495 to 1845. Vol. I*. Cape Town: C. Struik.

———. 1965. *Annals of Natal 1495 to 1845. Vol. II*. Cape Town: C. Struik.

Booth, A.R., ed. 1967. *Journal of the Rev. George Champion (1835–39)*. Cape Town: C. Struik.

Botha, T.J.R. 1977. *Watername in Natal*. Pretoria: R.G.N.

Bryant, A.T. 1905. *A Zulu-English Dictionary*. Pinetown: Marianhill Mission Press.

———. 1929. *Olden Times in Zululand and Natal*. London: Longmans.

———. 1967 [1949]. *The Zulu People*. Pietermaritzburg: Shooter & Shuter.

Bulpin, T.V. 1969. *Natal and the Zulu Country*. Cape Town: Books of Africa.

———. n.d. *To the Shores of Natal*. Cape Town: Howard Timmins.

Burman, J. 1988. *Towards the Far Horizon: The Story of the Ox-Wagon in South Africa*. Cape Town: Human & Rousseau.

Chuks-Orji, O. 1972. *Names from Africa*. Chicago: Johnsons.

Coates-Palgrave, K. 1977. *Trees of Southern Africa*. Cape Town: C. Struik.

Cope, A.T. 1968. *Izibongo: Zulu Praise Poems*. Oxford: Oxford University Press.

Copley, G.J. 1971. *English Place Names and their Origins*. Newton Abbot: David and Charles.

Cubbin, A.E. 1992. Origin and Meaning of the Place Name Empangeni. *Nomina Africana*, 6(2).

Delegorgue, A. 1990. *Travels in Southern Africa Vol. I*. Pietermaritzburg: University of Natal Press.

———. 1997. *Travels in Southern Africa Vol. II*. Pietermaritzburg: University of Natal Press.

Doke, C.M. 1986.*Textbook of Zulu Grammar*. Cape Town: Maskew Miller Longman.

Doke, C.M. and Vilakazi, B.W. 1958. *Zulu-English Dictionary*. Johannesburg: Witswatersrand University Press.

Dunning, R.G. 1946. *Two Hundred and Sixty-Four Zulu Proverbs, Idioms, etc., and the Cries of Thirty-Seven Birds*. Durban: Knox.

Ennis, E.L. 1945. Women's names among the Ovimbundu of Angola. *African Studies*, 4(1).

Evans-Pritchard, E.E. 1939. Customs and Beliefs Relating to Twins among the Nilotic Nuer. *Uganda Journal*, Vol. 3.
———. 1948. Nuer Modes of Address. *Uganda Journal*, Vol. 12.
Faye, C. 1923. *Zulu references*. Pietermaritzburg: City Printing Works.
Finnegan, R. 1970. *Oral Literature in Africa*. Oxford: Oxford University Press.
Frazer, J.G. 1949. *The Golden Bough*. London: MacMillan & Co.
Gcumisa, S.M. 1992. *Bird Song Reference and Verbalisation of Bird Songs in Zulu*. Unpublished Honours Dissertation. Pietermaritzburg: University of Natal.
Gibson, J.Y. 1918. The Kap-tent Wagon. *South African Journal of Science*, July 1918.
Grieshaber, N. 1990. A Rolls by any other name: would it sell as sweet? *Nomina Africana*, 4(2).
Gulliver, P.H. 1948. Bell-Oxen and Ox-names among the Jie. *Uganda Journal*, Vol. 12.
Gunner, L. and Gwala, M. 1994. *Musho! Zulu Popular Praises*. Johannesburg: Witswatersrand University Press.
Haggard, R.H. 1962. *King Solomon's Mines*. London: Cassell.
———. 2000. *Diary of an African Journey*. Ed. Stephen Coan. Pietermaritzburg: University of Natal Press.
Haswell, R. and Laband, J., eds. 1988. *Pietermaritzburg 1838–1988: A new portrait of an African city*. Pietermaritzburg: University of Natal Press.
Herbert, R.K. and Bogatsu, S. 1990. Changes in Northern Sotho and Tswana Personal Naming Patterns. *Nomina Africana*, 2(1).
Heyerdahl, T. 1954. *The Kon-Tiki Expedition*. London: George Allen & Unwin.
Hunt, N.A. 1952. Some notes on the naming of dogs in Chikaranga. *NADA*, Vol. 29.
Hutchings, A. 1996. *Zulu Medicinal Plants*. Pietermaritzburg: University of Natal Press.
Ingram, J.F. 1898. *The Story of an African City*. Pietermaritzburg: Coester.
Janes, M., ed. 1995. *Harraps French Pocket Dictionary*. Edinburgh: Chambers Harrap Publishers Ltd.
Junod, H.A. 1927. *The Life of a South African Tribe*. London: MacMillan.
Kamera, W. 1999. *Tinanatelo: Swazi Family Praises*. Durban: Centre for Oral Studies, UND.
Khathi, N.P. 1975. *'n Historiese-Taalkundige ondersoek na Zoeloeplekname in die distrikte Mapumulo*. Ongepubliseerde Meesters Skripsie. KwaDlangezwa: Universiteit van Zululand.
Khumalo, E. 2000. *Factors affecting changes in Zulu Western and Zulu African personal naming patterns*. Unpublished Honours essay. Pietermaritzburg: University of Natal.
Kidd, D. 1904. *The Essential Kaffir*. London: Adam & Charles.
Koopman, A. 1976. *A Study of Zulu Names*. Unpublished Honours Dissertation. Durban: University of Natal.

———. 1979a. The Linguistic Difference between Nouns and Names in Zulu. *African Studies*, 38(1).
———. 1979b. Male and Female Names in Zulu. *African Studies*, 38(2).
———. 1983. Zulu Place Names in the Drakensberg. In G.S. Nienaber, *'n Huldeblyk*, edited by A.J.L. Sinclair. Cape Town: University of the Western Cape.
———. 1984. Zulu Compound Nouns: Towards a Preliminary Analysis. *South African Journal of African Languages*, 4(1).
———. 1986. *The Social and Literary Aspects of Zulu Personal Names.* Unpublished Masters Dissertation. Pietermaritzburg: University of Natal.
———. 1987a. Zulu names and other modes of address. *Nomina Africana*, 3(2).
———. 1987b. The Praises of Young Zulu Men. *Theoria*, Vol. 70.
———. 1988. Place of the Elephant? In *Pietermaritzburg 1838–1988*, edited by J. Laband and R. Haswell. Pietermaritzburg: University of Natal Press.
———. 1989. The Aetiology of Zulu Personal Names. *Nomina Africana*, 3(2).
———. 1990. Ornimatopoeia: Song-reference in English, Afrikaans and Zulu Bird Names. *Nomina Africana*, 4(1).
———. 1991. Some Notes on the Morphology of Zulu Clan Names. *South African Journal of African Languages*, 10(4).
———. 1992a. The Socio-cultural aspects of Zulu ox and dog names. *Nomina Africana*, 6(1).
———. 1992b. -So- and -no-: Aged Parents in New Guise. *South African Journal of African Languages*, 12(3).
———. 1994a. Onomastic Shift: From Sir Benjamin to *Gobius durbanensis*. *Nomina Africana*, 8(1).
———. 1994b. Semantic Levels in Zulu bird and tree names. Unpublished paper read at the 1st World Congress of African Linguistics. July 1994. eKuluseni, Swaziland.
———. 1998. Another Look at Zulu Compound Nouns. In J.B. Hlongwane, ed. *Some Issues in African Linguistics: A Festschrift for Professor A. Nkabinde*. Pretoria: Van Schaik.
———. 1999a. Names within Names: the case of Jack and Jan. *Nomina Africana,* 12(1).
———. 1999b. Bongesihle sabaNguni. In W. Kamera, *Tinanatelo: Swazi Family Praises*. Durban: Centre for Oral Studies, UND.
———. 1999c. *Zulu Language Change*. Howick: Brevitas.
Krige, E.J. 1950. *The Social System of the Zulus*. Pietermaritzburg: Shuter & Shooter.
Laband, J. 1995. *Rope of Sand*. Johannesburg: Jonathan Ball.
Liebenberg, D. 1972. *The Drakensberg of Natal*. Cape Town: T.V. Bulpin.
Lugg, H.C. 1949. *Historic Natal and Zululand*. Pietermaritzburg: Shuter & Shooter.
———. 1968. *Zulu Place Names in Natal*. Durban: The Daily News.
———. 1970. *A Natal Family Looks Back*. Durban: T.W. Griggs & Co.

———. 1975. *Life Under a Zulu Shield.* Pietermaritzburg: Shuter & Shooter.
Maclean, G.L. 1985. *Roberts' Birds of Southern Africa.* Cape Town: The John Voelcker Bird Book Fund.
Maclean, C. 1990. *The Clan Almanac.* Kent: Eric Dobby Publishing.
Madubuike, I. 1976. *A Handbook of African Names.* Three Continents Press.
Mathunjwa, T.I. 1996. *Naming of Schools in Zulu in some KwaZulu Circuits,* Honours research essay. Dept. of African Languages, University of Zululand.
Mbatha, L.L. 1992. *Zulu Place Names in Ithala: a Morphological Analysis.* Unpublished Honours Dissertation. Pietermaritzburg: University of Natal.
McLachlan, G.R. and Liversidge, R. 1978. *Roberts' Birds of South Africa.* Cape Town: The John Voelcker Bird Book Fund.
Mdunyelwa, M.C.L. 1999. *A Comparative Study of Zulu, Xhosa and S.Sotho Clan Names and Clan Praises.* Unpublished Masters Dissertation. Pietermaritzburg: University of Natal.
Middleton, J. 1961. The Social Significance of Lugbara Personal Names. *Uganda Journal,* Vol. 25.
Mitford, B. 1975 [1883]. *Through the Zulu Country.* Durban: Griggs & Co.
Molefe, L. 1992. *The Praises of Domestic Animals.* Unpublished Masters Dissertation. Pietermaritzburg: University of Natal.
———. 2000. *Onomastic Aspects of Zulu Nicknames with Special Reference to Source and Functionality.* Unpublished Ph.D. Thesis. Pretoria: University of South Africa.
Molema, S.S. 1963 [1920]. *The Bantu: Past and Present.* Edinburgh: Cape Town: Struik.
Moll, E. 1981. *Trees of Natal.* Cape Town: University of Cape Town Eco-lab Trust Fund.
Mönnig, H.O. 1967. *The Pedi.* Pretoria: Van Schaik.
Msomi, P. 1989. *Analysis of School Names.* Unpublished Honours Dissertation. Pietermaritzburg: University of Natal.
Mzamane, G.I.M. 1962. *A Comparative Phonetic and Morphological Study of the Dialects of Southern Nguni Including the Lexical Influence of Non-Bantu Languages.* Unpublished Ph.D. Thesis. Pretoria: University of South Africa.
Mzolo, D.M. 1978. Zulu Clan Praises. In *Social System & Tradition in Southern Africa,* edited by J. Argyle and E. Preston-Whyte. Cape Town: Oxford University Press.
Neethling, S.J. 1996. January to December: Traditional Xhosa Nomenclature. *Nomina Africana,* 10(1&2).
———. 2000. An onomastic renaissance: African names to the fore. *South African Journal of African Languages,* 20(3).
Ngubane, K. 1972. *Uvalo Lwezinhlonzi.* Johannesburg: Educum.
Nsimbi, N.B. 1950. Baganda Traditional Personal Names. *Uganda Journal,* Vol. 14.

Ntuli, D.B.Z. 1992a. The Significance of Zulu Homestead Names. *Nomina Africana*, 6(1).

———. 1992b. House Naming among some South African Communities. *Nomina Africana*, 6(2).

———. 1999. The Names of Swazi Buses and Taxis. In *Language Mosaic*, edited by R. Finlayson. Pretoria: University of South Africa Press.

Nyembezi, C.L.S. 1992. *Isichazimazwi Sanamuhla Nangomuso*. Pietermaritzburg: Reach Out Publishers.

Oosthuizen, M. 1995. *UCibidolo: The Abundant Herds*. Unpublished Ph.D. Thesis. Pietermaritzburg: University of Natal.

Opland, J. 1990. Xhosa izibongo: improved line. *South African Journal of African Languages*, 10(4).

Parrinder, G. 1951. *West African Psychology*. London: Lutterworth Press.

Pearse, R.O. 1973. *Barrier of Spears*. Cape Town: Howard Timmins.

Pettman, C. 1985. *South African Place Names*. Johannesburg: Lowry Publishers.

Pooley, E. 1993. *The Complete Field Guide to Trees of Natal, Zululand & Transkei*. Durban: Natal Flora Publications Trust.

———. 1998. *A Field Guide to Wild Flowers of KwaZulu-Natal and the Eastern Region*. Durban: Natal Flora Publications Trust.

Raper, P.E. 1987. *A Dictionary of Southern African Place Names*. Johannesburg: Lowry Publishers.

Reynierse, C., ed. 1988. *The Illustrated Guide to the South African Coast*. Cape Town: AA The Motorist Publications.

Saarelma-Maunumaa, M. 1996. The Influence of Westernization on Ovambo Personal Names in Namibia. *Nomina Africana*, 10(1&2).

———. 1997. Finnish Personal Names in Ovamboland, Namibia. In *You Name It: Perspectives on onomastic research*, edited by R-L Pitkänen and Kaija Mallat. Helsinki: Finnish Literature Society.

Samarin, W.J. 1965. The Attitudinal and Autobiographic in Gbeya Dog Names. *Journal of African Languages*, Vol. 4.

Samuelson, R.C.A. 1923. *The King Cetywayo Zulu Dictionary*. Durban: The Commercial Printing Co.

———. 1929. *Long, Long Ago*. Durban: Knox Printing and Publishing Co.

Schapera, I. 1926. Customs Relating to Twins in South Africa. *Journal of the African Society*, Vol. XXVI.

Shabalala, M.A. 1999. *Homestead Names as a Reflection of Social Dynamics in Mabengela, Nkandla* [homestead names] Unpublished Masters Dissertation. Pietermaritzburg: University of Natal.

Sithole, E.T. 1982. *Izithakazelo Nezibongo ZakwaZulu*. Pinetown: Marianhill Mission Press.

Skaife, S.H. 1979. *African Insect Life*. Cape Town: C. Struik.

Smithers, R.H.N. 1983. *The Mammals of the Southern African Subregion*. Pretoria: University of Pretoria.

Soga, J.H. 1931. *The Ama-Xosa: Life and Customs.* Alice: Lovedale Press.
Stayt, D. 1971. *Where on Earth? Place-Names of Natal and Zululand.* Durban: The Daily News.
Stuart, J. 1925. *uKulumetule.* London: Longmans, Green and Co.
———. 1926. *uVusezakithi.* London: Longmans, Green and Co.
Suzman, S. 1994. Names as Pointers: Zulu Personal Naming Practices. *Language in Society*, 23.
Turner, N.S. 1992. Zulu Names as Echoes of Censure, Discontent, and Disapproval within the Domestic Environment. *Nomina Africana*, 6(2).
———. 1997. Onomastic caricatures: Names given to Employers and Co-workers by Black Employees. *Nomina Africana*, 11(1).
Van Huyssteen, L. 1994. The Zulu Place Name as a Morphological Exception. *Nomina Africana*, 8(1).
Voss, A.E. 1992. Alligator to Zulu Dawn: a Taxonomy of Durban Buses. *Nomina Africana*, 6(1).
Webb, C. de B. and Wright, J., eds. 1976, 1979, 1982, 1986. *The James Stuart archive of recorded oral evidence relating to the history of the Zulu and neighbouring peoples.* Vols I to IV. Pietermaritzburg: University of Natal Press.
Wood, W. 1849. *Statements Respecting Dingane.* Cape Town: Collard & Co.
Xaba, S.L. 1993. *The Changes in Zulu Personal Names in Rural and Urban Areas.* Unpublished Honours Dissertation. Pietermaritzburg: University of Natal.
Zungu, P.J. 1998. Toponymic lapses in Zulu place names. *Natalia*, 28.

Selected Index

It is not possible to index all of the names contained in a book such as this one. If you do not find what you are looking for in the index, please refer to the Contents for a detailed breakdown of the various chapters.